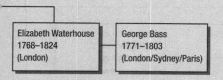

Elizabeth Waterhouse
1768–1824
(London)

George Bass
1771–1803
(London/Sydney/Paris)

The Waterhouse Family Tree

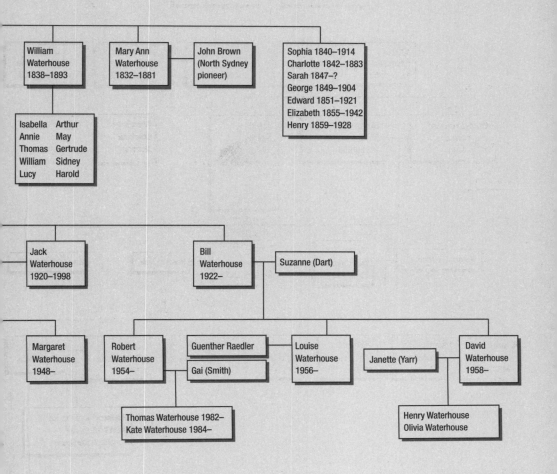

William
Waterhouse
1838–1893

Mary Ann
Waterhouse
1832–1881

John Brown
(North Sydney
pioneer)

Sophia 1840–1914
Charlotte 1842–1883
Sarah 1847–?
George 1849–1904
Edward 1851–1921
Elizabeth 1855–1942
Henry 1859–1928

Isabella   Arthur
Annie   May
Thomas   Gertrude
William   Sidney
Lucy   Harold

Jack
Waterhouse
1920–1998

Bill
Waterhouse
1922–

Suzanne (Dart)

Margaret
Waterhouse
1948–

Robert
Waterhouse
1954–

Guenther Raedler

Gai (Smith)

Louise
Waterhouse
1956–

Janette (Yarr)

David
Waterhouse
1958–

Thomas Waterhouse 1982–
Kate Waterhouse 1984–

Henry Waterhouse
Olivia Waterhouse

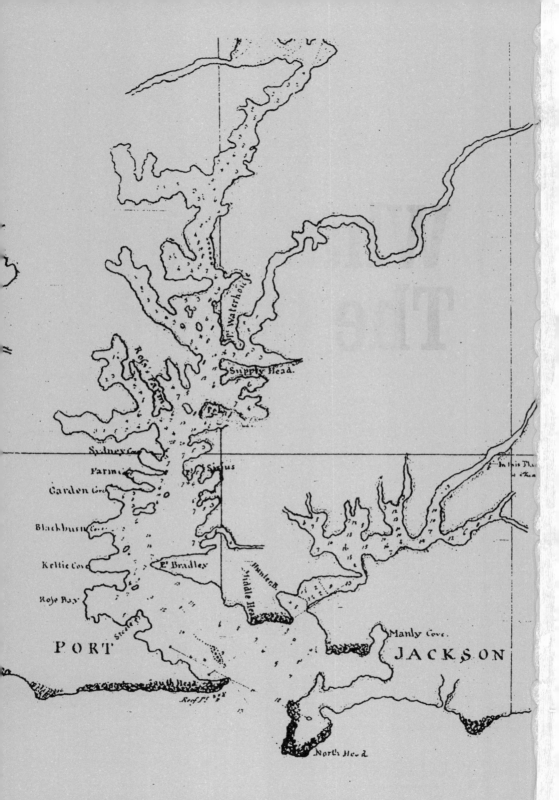

The first map of Port Jackson, chartered by Midshipman Henry Waterhouse and Lieutenant William Bradley in 1788. The headland marked as Point Waterhouse is now the Sydney suburb of Woolwich.

What Are The Odds?

To Roy,
Enjoy the read

Jan '10

What Are The Odds?

The Bill Waterhouse Story

Bill Waterhouse

BILL WATERHOUSE

KNOPF

A Knopf book
Published by Random House Australia Pty Ltd
Level 3, 100 Pacific Highway, North Sydney NSW 2060
www.randomhouse.com.au

First published by Knopf in 2009

Addresses for companies within the Random House Group can be found at
www.randomhouse.com.au/offices.

National Library of Australia
Cataloguing-in-Publication Entry

Waterhouse, Bill.
What are the odds?: the Bill Waterhouse story.

ISBN: 978 1 74166 630 4 (hbk.)

Waterhouse, Bill.
Bookmakers (Gambling) – Australia – Biography.
Bookmaking (Betting) – Australia.
Horse racing – Australia.

798.401092

Every effort has been made to identify individual photographers and copyright holders
where appropriate, but for some photographs this has not been possible. The publishers
would be pleased to hear from any copyright holders who have not been acknowledged;
omissions will be rectified in subsequent editions.

Jacket photograph by acpsyndication.com
Rear cover photograph by Peter Halmagyi
Jacket design by Louise Davis/Mathematics
Painting of Bill Waterhouse by Ralph Heimans
Family tree design by Ice Cold Publishing
Internal design by Midland Typesetters, Australia
Typeset in Sabon by Midland Typesetters, Australia
Printed and bound by Griffin Press, South Australia

Random House Australia uses papers that are natural, renewable and recyclable
products and made from wood grown in sustainable forests. The logging and
manufacturing processes are expected to conform to the environmental regulations
of the country of origin.

10 9 8 7 6 5 4 3 2 1

To my daughter, Louise

Contents

1

The Gamble of Life

I HAVE ALWAYS felt I was born at a lucky time in history. For any gambler, Lady Luck always has a role to play, but I also knew how to make my own luck. This was the case in 1950, when I was left for dead after a car crash on an icy English road, which eventually led to my falling in love for the first time. Already I had turned the luck around earlier, when my father died suddenly and tragically – I was just nineteen and, although the youngest, I took on the responsibility of the family and we prospered. Then a decade later, when I was devastated to lose my oldest brother, Charlie, I abruptly traded the respected profession of barrister-at-law for that of a bag-slinging bookie – and I became the world's biggest gambler.

The odds have never been far from my mind since I was a little boy. My mathematical leaning gave me an understanding of risk-assessment, and when making decisions I have always thought in terms of odds – on and off the track. This has been a great advantage right throughout my life. Some might call it a gambler's instinct, but really it is about hard work and weighing up a situation before making choices.

My philosophy – to try to make everything happen for the best – has meant I have thrived on a positive outlook on life. I love that feeling of being 'on top of the world'.

I know I have been fortunate in my surroundings and upbringing. Family has been the most important underlying theme of my life. I believe that 'united we stand and divided we fall'. Growing up, my family was everything. I have been totally blessed with my children Robbie and Louise, but bitterly disappointed when my younger son, David, left the family. I always said to my children, 'Everything I do is for you.' Furthermore, after losing my beloved brother, Charlie, my other brother Jack and I took on the responsibility of an extended family and supported Charlie's widow and four children.

Jack and I built up a property empire of hotels, offices and apartment buildings, driven not so much by the desire to live lavishly – I have never been a spender on life's luxuries – but for the challenge and exhilaration of making money and enjoying success. This motivation has been embedded in me ever since the hard days of the Depression. I have always been a 'big picture' thinker but I still hesitate before spending a dollar. I have loved my work and have travelled the world many times on business escapades – I never wanted the indulgence of holidays. I relied on my sense of humour for light relief.

I don't pretend to be a Simon Pure. I have sometimes cut corners to get what I needed, but I am certainly no crook. I have a deep-seated sense of what is right and wrong and believe in the principle of fairness. Laws and rules are essential for society, otherwise we'd have anarchy. However, there are times when the laws unnaturally try to curb normal human behaviour – such as Prohibition in the United States and, back home in Australia, the unreasonable trading hours for pubs that were imposed in Sydney until the mid-1950s. People are ingenious, and when they have to survive they will find ways to get around unfair laws. I certainly did what I had to do in those difficult times.

I have been lucky to mix with many of the world's elite, but I'm just as comfortable with the average man in the street or the punter at the races. As the father of the English turf, Lord

George Bentinck, said, there are only two places where people are equal: on the turf and under it! I learnt early on that a man's word is his honour, and that a gambler who doesn't stick to his word is not worth a grain of salt. Once a man has 'taken the knock', to me he is finished. Nevertheless, I could line my office walls with worthless cheques, sometimes from people considered bastions of society.

My numerous trials and tribulations with racing officials and court cases were all part of life's tapestry. The Fine Cotton betting scandal cruelly and unfairly took away my livelihood and almost made me an outcast, but it drew my family even closer. My son Rob showed incredible character and strength, holding everything together and keeping the whole family afloat. He changed my long-held belief that, in the end, the bookmaker would always beat the punter. Unable to go to the track, Rob used his cutting-edge form analysis and showed how even the TAB can be beaten. Rob is, in my view, a form and breeding genius; he has also helped his extraordinary wife, Gai, to find future champions and become Australia's leading trainer. His forward-thinking opinion on racing issues is now sought by the industry's administrators.

I endured an epic family court case where my late brother Charlie's children were to bite the hands that fed them. The court case threatened to take away everything I had worked so hard for all my life. Unfounded allegations were made publicly and, with all our assets frozen, it took a decade for the truth to come out and cost millions of dollars in legal fees. My daughter, Louise, ran the whole matter. She spent countless days and nights going through our old files, which dated back 40 years, to prove our case. With incredible tenacity she turned the runaway train around and saved us from the brink of ruin by adeptly dealing with the cards we had been dealt.

Business opportunities came along when the door to racing was closed. For several years I was the chairman of a public company, Network Entertainment, where Rob and I gambled on the corporate stage, bringing this failed company back to life and relaunching it into the betting world.

My father's teaching to continually adapt to life's changes meant I was always looking to the future and trying to think ahead of my time. I came up with crazy ideas and spouted them to anyone who'd listen – such as my idea to bring Japanese tourists to Australia in the early 1960s, or to start a Volkswagen plant in Fiji, both a decade ahead of their time. Other ideas were roaring successes, like when we plugged in to an untapped market for Fabergé Brut aftershave at a time when the Aussie bloke still thought fragrances were for sissies, or when we set up a chain of betting shops to entertain Fijians who had never even seen a racehorse. I am still thinking of ideas, and would like to take Australian-style racing to the United States, which I know would work.

Another one out of left field was when I agreed to represent the Kingdom of Tonga, a tiny Pacific island nation, as its honorary consul-general in Australia. For many years now I've done my best to help and promote Tonga on the world stage. In the 1970s, no one really knew about an honorary consul's role, whereas today there are more honorary than career consuls in Australia.

My grandchildren Kate and Tom have become lights in my life. Kate is a star and a beautiful soul. She has created a niche for herself as a fashion ambassador and a feature columnist for the Sunday papers. I came back as a bookmaker in 2002 after seventeen years in the racing wilderness so I could teach the classic art of bookmaking to Tom. I knew it was now or never. Tom was twenty and I was 80. When we started off he was timid; on the first day, when I opened my shoulders to take on the punters, he went to his father, Robbie, who was working on the Rails, to tell him I was reckless. I suspect Tom thought I had lost my marbles and was headed for disaster. Tom worked as my clerk for five years, and I found myself giving intense lectures in the car going home from the track about the gambler's philosophy. After a year or so, one day he quietly said, 'I used to think you were wrong, but I've come to realise how right you are.'

Tom took to the races like a duck to water, and together we fought our way back up on the interstate Rails. Tom and I then took out a licence in partnership and I could stand back and let him take the running, no longer knocking punters back but taking on bets from all and sundry. Within a year we were the number one holders and the Waterhouse name was back at the top. When in 2008 Tom rang to tell me that he'd lost a million dollars in the last race at Rosehill just after I had left the track, it showed me he'd come of age as a gambler – especially as he was still ahead on the day! Following in my footsteps, Tom moved to the Melbourne ring.

Operating on the Rails at Derby Day in Melbourne in 2008, this time as a licensed clerk for Tom, seemed to me the fulfilment of the circle of life. Tom, my grandson and 60 years my junior, was standing up at his first Victorian Spring Carnival, where half a century earlier I had stood for the first time and on the same stand. Tom, despite being the youngest on-course bookmaker in Australia, was already the largest. When I arrived in Melbourne, I was amazed to be greeted by a huge photo of Tom on a billboard that read: 'Bet with me'!

Tom had promoted his business well and was in full action. Handwritten ledgers and tickets had long ago been replaced by computer operators, and electronic betting boards had replaced the old manual ones with knobs to turn the prices. Several computer screens now gave access to online betting. The mobile phones never stopped ringing, with twelve people handling phones and six operating computers. But the bagmen were still toting the iconic Waterhouse betting bag and I could feel the familiar atmosphere, with the thronging crowd demanding attention to get their bets on.

Derby Day was eventful. Tom lost $2 million but took it in his stride. Incredibly, he was still able to claw his way back over the carnival and had turnover of $20 million. And Waterhouse Bookmaking was again benefiting Victorian racing in a big way, with $200,000 in turnover tax going into the race club's coffers. I stood tall all Derby Day, not sitting down, and the memories came flooding back of my times four decades earlier, when I had set the Melbourne ring on fire with my betting duels with Frank Duval, the Hong Kong Tiger, who had me spellbound when he placed bets to win a million dollars – an astronomical amount – on Oaks Day in 1966. That changed the face of gambling in Australia forever. Or Felipe Ysmael, the Filipino Fireball, who placed a million-dollar bet on an obscure race in 1967 – when I had planned to spend a quiet afternoon at the movies.

My love for gambling is still as strong as ever. Even though I am now a senior octogenarian, I am just as keen to take on the odds, plying my trade every week at the track. I know two things for sure: firstly, men are the same all over the world – they all like to have a drink, take out a girl and have a gamble. And, being a history buff, I know that history repeats itself and will forever more. The Waterhouse racing dynasty will continue.

Pondering the circle of life, with Tom now standing in my shoes, draws me back to how I became the biggest gambler in the world . . . with help from the luck I made myself.

2

A Slice of History

I WAS BORN IN 1922 in the northern Sydney suburb of Naremburn, on the four-hectare family property in West Street that sat on one side of a valley and faced the beautiful Northbridge Suspension Bridge. I was the youngest; Charlie had been born in 1914, Betty in 1916 and Jack in 1920.

The main home was an old three-storey building with no inside bathroom – I can still vividly recall being bathed in a portable tub by my nanny every weekend. There was another house on the property where my Uncle Tuck lived, as well as a smaller cottage for the handyman. There were several large paddocks and a stable complex for the horses and carriage. This may sound quite grand but we always considered ourselves battlers and certainly not toffs.

My father, Charles Hercules Waterhouse, came from a big family of three brothers and five sisters. I saw a lot of Tuck, his younger brother, whose real name was Albert. He was called Tuck because even though he was very skinny, just like Little Tommy Tucker of the nursery rhyme, he liked his tucker. I hardly saw Ossie, the youngest; their eldest brother, Alfie, had died when I was young.

My grandfather was also called Charles. He had separated from his wife, Matilda. Divorce in those days was considered a disgrace and was complicated – there had to be serious grounds, such as habitual cruelty, frequent drunkenness or repeated adultery. The marriage break-up bitterly divided the family. The girls all went with Matilda and the boys all stayed with Charles – except Ossie, who had been disowned by his father years before; he could not forgive Ossie for getting into opium smuggling. When my grandfather was dying, Ossie asked to see him but was refused.

Uncle Tuck never married. He was the caretaker on the farm but had run a dancehall at North Sydney when he was younger. Both he and Alfie had been bookmakers at one time or another, but they had never made a success of it.

The Naremburn property was paradise for me. It consisted of a series of small orchards containing nearly every kind of fruit: oranges, apples, emperor mandarins, plums, apricots, pears, nectarines, figs and persimmons. Even years after we moved away, I would go back and spend hours feasting on the fresh, tree-ripened fruit.

—

My father was always very proud of our ancestor, Henry Waterhouse, who came to Australia as a midshipman on the First Fleet in 1788. Dad would often tell us stories that he had been told by his own grandfather, Thomas, who was Henry's grandson. Henry, a protégé of Governor Arthur Phillip, distinguished himself in the first weeks of the colony by surveying Sydney Harbour with Captain John Hunter and Lieutenant William Bradley. The chart they produced shows Bradley's Head and Hunter Bay (Balmoral Beach). It also showed Waterhouse Point (at Woolwich), but Henry's name has not survived.

Henry was well connected: his father, William Waterhouse, was the page of honour to the Duke of Cumberland, younger brother of 'mad' King George III. The Duke was Henry's godfather and namesake. Henry had joined the navy when he was just eleven, and at sixteen he was chosen to serve on the *Sirius* in the historic First Fleet. He had excelled, and Governor Phillip promoted him in 1789 to second lieutenant.

Henry's reputation as a ladies' man was the talk around the colony's camp, and the trusted young Lieutenant Waterhouse accompanied Phillip on his explorations of the new colony. On one of these trips Henry actually saved Phillip's life. They came across a group of Aboriginals feasting on a whale at Manly Cove. Among the natives was Bennelong, who had been Governor Phillip's 'guest' at Government House before escaping. Bennelong called out to Henry and playfully (as Henry later wrote) 'took me round the neck and kissed me' – just as he had seen Henry smooch with a woman, no doubt a convict, at Government House. The playfulness turned to danger, and young Henry suddenly found himself having to save Phillip's life when he was speared out of the blue by another Aboriginal. It could be said Phillip was 'hoist with his own petard'. At Government House he had given Bennelong a penknife blade, which Bennelong had attached to the end of his spear. Now, the twelve-foot (four-metre) spear struck Phillip deeply in his right shoulder, just above his collarbone. Henry ran to his aid, broke off the spear and helped Phillip to safety as spears flew all around them.

Henry wrote frankly in his notebook about the fears for his life: 'I immediately concluded the Governor was killed . . . he then begged me for God's sake to haul the spear out which I immediately stopped [running] to do . . . [but] could not effect it . . . just at this instant a spear came & grazed the skin off between the thumb & forefinger of my right hand. I must own it frightened me a good deal & I believe added to my exertions, for the next sudden jerk I gave, it broke short off.' Two hundred years later, I was delighted when my son Rob acquired at auction Henry's notebook, along with the penknife spearhead.

Henry was fascinated with Australian wildlife and in fact discovered and named the 'Mountain Eagle of New South Wales' (*Aquila audax*). An amateur taxidermist, his hobby was to 'stuff exotic Australian animals', no doubt to curry favour with luminaries such as Lord Sydney and Sir Joseph Banks, who were all-powerful in matters of the colony. Although he lost a large number of specimens when the *Sirius* was shipwrecked off Norfolk Island, Henry ended up with quite a collection, which was passed on through the family to my father's cousin Ella Leach.

We also heard about Henry's sailing exploits; one Christmas, he navigated a longboat over the sandbar which is now the Corso at Manly during a king tide and wild storm, making it into the harbour and avoiding the risk of being smashed to smithereens by coming through the Heads.

In 1791 Henry went back to England, where he hosted his friend Bennelong at his father William's residence in Smiths Square, Westminster. The family organised for a tailor to fit Bennelong in gentleman's finery so he could be presented to the King and London's social circuit. The tailor's bill presented to William was £6 10s – it is now held by Sydney's Mitchell Library.

Henry gallantly fought on the *Bellerophon* in Lord Howe's 'Glorious First of June' victory in the Napoleonic Wars. Just before going into battle he wrote to his father: 'We are now very close to the enemy. Every appearance bespeaks the action will be bloody. Whatever fate attends me, I beg you to be a father to little Maria [his first Australian-born illegitimate child]. I hope and pray that the Almighty will keep her under His protection.'

Governor John Hunter had also taken to Henry, and when he took up his new post he selected Henry, at the age of 23, to be his second-in-command as captain of the *Reliance*. This ship not only carried the new governor to Australia but also brought Bennelong back home. Accompanying them on board was Henry's young protégé from his recent battles, Matthew Flinders, plus the ship's surgeon, George Bass, who would both go on to etch their names in the history books as intrepid explorers and navigators.

Henry provided these budding explorers with the *Reliance*'s whaleboat and provisions for their historic voyages of exploration of the eastern coastline of Australia. Flinders later named an island in Bass Strait 'Waterhouse Island' after his mentor. In an odd twist, the French explorer Nicholas Baudin made sail for the island in 1802, desperately seeking fresh water, as the island's name implied, but unfortunately left empty-handed.

Henry captained the *Reliance* on a voyage to Cape Town in South Africa to bring back supplies for the starving colony. While there he came across Cape Town's late Commandant Robert Gordon's small flock of prized Spanish fine-wool escurial sheep, thought to be the only flock outside Spain. The sheep were not considered suitable for eating, so Henry – with an entrepreneurial spirit – used his limited funds to buy half the flock (thirteen sheep) at £4 each from the commandant's attractive widow, squeezing them on board the leaky and unseaworthy *Reliance*, some even into his own cabin. He wrote to his father: 'I believe no ship ever went to sea so much lumber'd.'

The voyage was very long – 78 days – and was one of the 'most disagreeable' passages Henry had made. But he was a great sailor; he wrote to Lord Sydney, the former colonial secretary: 'The sea became very much agitated in appearance, like the boiling of a pot, and at last began to break all about and on board the ship in a most alarming manner . . . But though we lost nearly all our sails, the most violent and sudden gale came on, which enabled us to keep before the sea, and save the ship.'

Waterhouse landed his Spanish breed at Port Jackson on 26 June 1797. These sheep were the first merinos to be imported to Australia. Henry also brought the first thoroughbred racehorse, Young Rockingham, to the colony on the same voyage, which became the country's leading stallion – his direct descendent Jorrocks, the iron horse, is said to have had more dominance over his generation than any other Australian racehorse.

Henry was passionate about the colony and sat on the Vice-Admiralty Court, trying to counter the corruption he saw developing under the New South Wales (Rum) Corps. He accumulated quite some landholdings, including the site of the Sirius Garden at the Rocks, which he later sold to Robert Campbell for his wool stores, which are an iconic landmark today. Henry also bought the famous Vineyard farm, where he bred his pure fine-wool escurial sheep, before selling them to John Macarthur when he left the colony. The rest is history: these were the sheep that formed the foundation of the Australian merino wool industry, keeping the struggling colony afloat financially.

Henry set sail for England from the colony in 1800; taking a route further south than normal, he discovered and named the Antipodes Islands. On returning, he gave his sister Elizabeth's hand in marriage to his good friend George Bass. He wrote to his father: 'You will certainly think me an impudent fellow when I inform you I this day gave irrevocably away your daughter . . . my long knowledge of the worth of Mr Bass to whom she has united herself makes me congratulate you and my mother on the occasion.'

Henry added: 'Of my own concerns I can say nothing' – no doubt alluding to his illegitimate children in the colony. My father told me how Henry never married but still did his bit for the colony's population – even if it was from the wrong side of the blanket. Henry's descendants were to experience many vicissitudes of life. He fathered three children, including my great-great-grandfather, Thomas Waterhouse, who had two children, Anne and Thomas (II). This Thomas – Henry's grandson and my great-grandfather – was born in 1810 in the colony. His father was posted overseas before becoming a farmer, and young Thomas was taken care of by friends and relatives, including his great-uncle, Joseph Waterhouse.

After Henry's death in 1812, his grandson Thomas was not neglected by his English family. Henry's father paid Master Thomas and Mistress Mary Collicott of the Orphan School in Sydney so that Thomas could live with them. Thomas did not have any formal education, but when he was seventeen, along with others from the Orphan School, he was apprenticed to Henry Cooper's timber yard at Darling Harbour. Eventually he became entrepreneurial as a timber merchant himself. Timber was a vital commodity in the colony, where demand was stronger than supply. In 1853 Thomas acquired the Greengate Hotel at Killara, signing his name with an X. He had thirteen children, naming most of them after his family back in England. He passed on to each of his children a pride in the family's heritage and especially in Henry Waterhouse's exploits.

By the late nineteenth century, my great-grandfather Thomas and his family were well established on the North Shore. They operated the ferry service between Sydney and the North Shore, as well as owning one of the first hotels at Milsons Point, which served thirsty travellers as they got off the ferry. The family also owned a coach service, which met the ferry, stopped off at the hotel and finished at the Greengate Hotel at the end of civilisation in Killara. 'Greengate' Thomas died in 1884 at the age of 74; in spite of being illiterate and partly raised in the Orphan School, he had built up a massive enterprise and raised some of the most prominent citizens of the North Shore. Nevertheless, the Waterhouse family members have always considered themselves as battlers.

Before the days of electricity, my grandfather Charles operated a large wood, coal and coke yard next to his home, the Lily of St Leonards Hotel (later the Imperial Hotel). Charles's brother, my great-uncle William, ran a boat-building yard and the ferry service at nearby McMahons Point; William was also the mayor of Victoria Borough (McMahons Point) Council. Once, he famously took all the councillors from the three North Sydney councils on his ferry for a picnic at Middle Head – all dressed in their three-piece suits and top hats! William and two of his brothers, Joseph and Thomas (III), were on the first North Sydney Council in 1890 and were featured in the 1888 Centenary Book of Sydney.

It was at the Greengate that Charles's brother John trained Peter Jackson, a Jamaican boxer who had jumped ship in Sydney. John was a well-known supporter of bare-knuckle fighting and gave Jackson a job as general hand at the hotel while he trained, and he became a great heavyweight fighter. John financed him to go overseas in search of the world heavyweight title. Jackson won the Coloured Heavyweight Championship but the world champion, John L. Sullivan, refused to fight him because he was black.

All the Waterhouses could fight. It was part of their growing up. It was an important life skill: on the coach service, patrons would sometimes say, 'Charge it to the governor!' In fact, Tommy Waterhouse junior, another of Charles's brothers, was known as the best amateur fighter on Sydney's North Shore.

In the mid-nineteenth century it was a favourite pastime for the Rocks 'Push' gang to cross to the North Shore and raid the peaceful, law-abiding citizens. One Saturday at the Greengate, some of the larrikins from the south rowdily demanded drinks and refused to pay, threatening to destroy the bar. The man behind the bar called for 'Young Tommy', a pleasant young man. Without asking for any payment, he politely asked the 'gentlemen' to leave. They found this amusing and decided to 'do Tommy over'. However, witnesses said Tommy took on the dozen larrikins, dodging their blows and landing his own punches, making a mess of six of them before they retreated.

Then ugly 'One-eyed Bourke', the notorious pugilist who led the Push gang, heard about the altercation and challenged 'Gentleman Tommy' Waterhouse to a fight – for a purse of 100 guineas. Word went out and a great crowd gathered to see the illegal bare-knuckle fight at Pearce's Orchard in Lindfield one Saturday in 1857. Before the fight started, Tommy's backers thought they had done their money when they saw the bulk of Bourke – compared with Tommy's twelve stone (76 kilograms) – and Bourke's price shortened to odds-on. They had to avoid the scrutiny of the mobile chief of the water police, Edward Cowell, and they then fought for two hours.

To the amazement of the crowd, Tommy used his fine boxing skills to dodge the massive blows of his larger opponent and Bourke shouted at Waterhouse to 'stop prancing like a bleeding gent'. Tommy then landed his own punches and knocked Bourke to the ground. They fought tooth-and-nail until dusk and adjourned until the next morning. But Bourke didn't return – he'd had enough. Tommy was celebrated as the unofficial champion of Sydney. It was the end of the continuous raids over the water by the larrikins from the Rocks.

—

My father taught my brothers and me to work hard and be entrepreneurial rather than employees. He warned us never to be complacent and always to be ready for change. He emphasised that each and every one of the family businesses had been a great success in the nineteenth century but not one was any good by the mid-1930s: the Waterhouse ferry service had been made obsolete by the Sydney Harbour Bridge, which also took trade away from our Imperial Hotel at Milsons Point; electric trains effectively replaced our coach service; and electricity meant there was no need for our wood, coal and coke yard.

When in the mid-nineteenth century my grandfather Charles (Thomas's son) bought the Lily of St Leonards, which had been named after a very attractive Aboriginal girl whose picture was painted on a sign above the door, it looked a strong prospect with its independent, non-brewery-controlled freehold licence – the only freehold licence on the North Shore. Along with the wood, coal and coke yard, the hotel had three small shops, a larger shop and a two-and-a-half-storey residential building.

When my grandfather died, the two sides of the family were still divided after his divorce. He left a one-sixth share of his total estate – valued at around £50,000 – to each of the three younger boys, and the remaining half between the five girls, which meant the girls only received about ten per cent each. Charles left out Ossie, the black sheep, altogether. Ossie was very bitter about this treatment from his father and bought a share from Violet, one of his sisters, so that he could join with his other sisters and instigate a legal action.

Ossie was the natural leader of that side, and my father, the head of the family, led the other. Over the next quarter-century, all my father's money and most of the properties went to pay the lawyers, even without anything being decided. In the end, about all that was left of the family assets was the little pub at the base of the new bridge being constructed over Sydney Harbour.

From early on I could sense my father's despair at being in the hands of costly lawyers. I realised he needed me to become a lawyer because of this long and costly family court battle, which consumed his every spare penny. It was the longest court case in the history of the Equity Court in New South Wales. When I was eventually admitted as a barrister in 1948, it seemed to me that everybody at the bar had at some time or other appeared either for or against my family. The dispute had started in 1914, eight years before I was born.

—

My father had trouble with the licensee of the Imperial Hotel and realised he would have to move in and run it himself. I was not yet four. My mother was aghast at the thought of having to go to the Imperial – she didn't drink and didn't like drunks. But eventually she did go to the hotel – she missed Dad – and she came to love it. I was only allowed to follow about two years later, having stayed in the care of my nanny, Mrs Armour, at Naremburn.

My father never drove a car in his life. He had a horse and cart, and I remember riding in it a lot, particularly from Naremburn to the hotel at Milsons Point before I moved there. He would have the horses shod along the way at one of the many blacksmiths on the side of the road – most often at the one near the North Sydney Post Office on the Pacific Highway, which was then called Lane Cove Road. You used to see lots of horses and carts, especially in Bridge Street in the city and at Circular Quay.

The Imperial had twenty bedrooms, though not all of them were for guests as we lived there too. I slept in the same bed as my mother when I was very little. Then I moved to the hotel's wide open-air veranda. Jack and I had our own beds, and we'd put the blind down to protect us from the elements when it was raining. There were two bedrooms next door, one for Charlie and one for Betty.

I vividly remember when the trains started running on the Harbour Bridge almost directly above us. It was so loud that it startled me and I leapt out of bed. It felt like the train was going to go straight through the hotel. But after a few nights I got so used to the noise that I never really noticed it again, and I became renowned as a very sound sleeper.

Work on the bridge went on 24 hours a day, with one gang simply replacing another. There had been four hotels on four corners, one of which was ours, but as work progressed, the other three hotels were resumed, demolished or relocated to make way for the bridge, until we were the only one left. During construction of the bridge we were so busy – it was a case of beer, beer and more beer. Some of the workers, mainly foremen, lived in the hotel. My mother used to do full board for 25 shillings a week, which was good value – the basic wage was about 70 shillings a week. The hotel was full of people, day and night.

I was under ten and – like just about everyone else early on – I thought there was no way the arches were going to meet. I even thought that to get to the other side you had to walk or drive over the top of them! When the roadway started to form below I remember being so pleased that we wouldn't have to climb the archway.

I was chased by the watchmen all the time before the bridge was finished. As a young boy, I climbed all over and up the bridge scaffolding. I even climbed to the top of the arch and I continued to the other side when a nightwatchman chased me. My mother was the first woman to walk over the archway of the bridge – a foreman who lived at the hotel took her long before the opening, wanting her to be the very first female on the arches. It was quite an effort but it was worth it, and she couldn't believe the view from up so high.

The opening of the Harbour Bridge in 1932 was one of the most memorable days of my life. It seemed everyone in Sydney was there. You couldn't move on or under the bridge – everywhere was jammed solid with people. It was such a big and cheerful occasion; it was a thrill to be a part of it and to see so many happy faces. I thought it would be like that every day.

I was shattered the next day when I went downstairs and there was no one in the hotel. I had just assumed all the customers we had seen the day before would be back. The naivety of a ten-year-old! The trade had been strong while the bridge was being built but times changed dramatically. One day the hotel was packed and the next day empty and desolate. It was hard on my father and mother – it was hard on everyone – to go from boom times to absolutely nothing.

I had heard vague talk about 'the Depression' and of the large numbers of unemployed, but now I felt it. The change was cruel. A great swathe had been cut through the suburbs of Milsons Point and North Sydney to make way for the bridge and its approaches. We had lost the local client base as widespread resumptions completely wiped out shops, small factories and housing. Before the bridge came, the four local hotels had the community to draw on, plus the public and the ferries that pulled in at Milsons Point. All the traffic from the city had to pass our front door. Now the bridge totally bypassed us and there was nothing. Overnight, our hotel dropped from being a strong beer house to having the smallest trade in the whole Sydney metropolitan area.

Thus, in my formative teenage years, I grew up as a product of the Depression, and without doubt my whole thinking was moulded by the harsh experiences of those times.

My father was desperate and realised the only way for the hotel to survive was by selling grog 'after hours'. In those days, hotel opening hours were restricted to between six am and six pm. If you sold liquor outside those hours, you were 'sly-grogging' and breaking the law. If caught, the licensee got a 'black mark' against his name. With three such marks, not only was his right to hold a licence automatically cancelled but the hotel's licence went as well. It was a catch-22 situation. You couldn't survive without some sly-grogging, and no matter how careful you were, you would occasionally get caught. Once a black mark was recorded things became very bleak, as it stood for three years before being erased.

Even though the hotel was flattened financially, it was still freehold and so we were not tied to any liquor wholesaler or brewery. We were the only independent in an area stretching from Milsons Point to Palm Beach and from Manly to Parramatta. Many of the police of the day would turn a blind eye, however we were treated differently – we didn't enjoy any leniency. The all-powerful brewery oligopolies didn't like our independence and did everything in their power to take us over. They made many official overtures over the years to acquire the hotel licence, but they also manipulated behind the scenes, so there is no doubt in my mind that a lot of the official surveillance we suffered was directly due to the powerful influence of the breweries over the police.

My father showed initiative and introduced Richmond Beer, the famous beer from Melbourne. This exotic brand gave temporary new life to the hotel. Patrons liked it but we now incurred the real wrath of the Sydney breweries, which saw us as a thorn in their side. Police interest in our little operation heightened, and so when the police were on their rounds I loved following them, sometimes hiding behind the pylons of the bridge, to see if they were staking out the hotel – and to make sure they returned to the police station up the hill in North Sydney – after which I would run back down the hill to give the hotel the 'all clear'. The police sometimes caught me shadowing them and I'd get a warning, but there was not much they could do.

I began to take an interest in money. I remember at the age of eleven going to the local post office in Milsons Point (the Commonwealth Bank agents at the time) and trying to open a bank account with sixpence. I was told I couldn't open an account until I was twelve, and that I needed a shilling. On my twelfth birthday I went back to the post office with the two shillings to open my first bank account. When the new Commonwealth Bank branch opened at Milsons Point I was waiting on the doorstep expecting to be given account number one, but instead it was number 43. I now set about being self-sufficient in my own way.

The main sales of beer, apart from at the bar, were quart bottles of draught beer, and you could claim a threepence deposit on the bottle. I used to collect the bottles from under the bridge. Being in the hotel, I'd know what the customer bought and watch where they were going and would collect the bottles when they were finished. I used to get up to 25 bottles a week. If someone took a girl to a quiet place under the bridge, I would keep at a discreet distance, but as soon as they left I would quickly retrieve their bottles before someone else got there. People were desperate for money in the middle of the Depression.

Similarly, my mother gave me threepence for each bag of coke that I filled up from the harbour foreshore. It was amazing how much coke was lost from ships in the harbour and floated ashore those days. Again, many people collected the coke. I also remember wanting to be a newspaper boy and a chocolate boy at the local cinema but my father carefully explained that these were regular jobs and were the domain of children whose families were in need of work.

—

From early on I looked for ways to make money, discovering there was nothing like the pleasure of actually earning my own spending money. I thrived on it. When the Royal Show came around at Easter, I always had enough money to go. I loved the show bags and the wood-chopping. The dearest bag in those days cost one shilling – I would often buy twenty bags! The Show was my highlight of the year. I always went on Easter Friday because my brothers Charlie and Jack could take me since the races were on Saturday. When old enough to go on my own, I went to the Show nearly every day.

I was very close to my brothers and sister. I can't remember ever having an argument with them. We boys were tight-knit from an early age. Jack had always been very generous. I remember when he first went to school he was given a penny to spend each day. He would have been five and I was only three and a half. Every day I would sit on the kerb at the foot of the hill near our home at Naremburn, and every day Jack would bring me home a penny sweet.

Betty probably felt closer to me than to my brothers. But I was a little scallywag. When she was fifteen and was allowed to go out with a boy, I used to go as the chaperone. Mostly it was to the movies. One day they passed me the jaffas, but as no one asked for them back I ate them all. Betty was five years older than me and was smart, good at sport and very beautiful.

I remember the greengrocer's son, Jack Taranto, a plump and shy boy, had such a shine for Betty. Jack said to me one day, 'Does your sister like chocolates?'

'Of course she does,' I told him.

So he gave me a lovely box of chocolates to give to her. I knew she wouldn't accept them from Jack, so I ate them. Next time Jack saw me, he asked me how Betty liked the chocolates.

'Oh, she loved them,' I said.

So Jack gave me another box. Betty never saw those either. One day Jack plucked up the courage to ask Betty if she liked the chocolates he'd been sending her. I can't remember his reaction but Betty was furious with me.

My father was strict on Betty with boys. She had hoped to be a movie star and had an offer from a visiting talent scout to go to Hollywood, but her life took a different turn. She wasn't allowed to wear high heels or lipstick, so she would arrange for Horrie, the handyman, to meet her up the street and sneak high heels to her when she had a date. As strict as my father was, Betty fell in love and wanted to marry at sixteen – to a man called Watson Rowland-Smith from the 'establishment' of Sydney. He was twice her age but Betty was headstrong and Dad relented, acknowledging Watson came from a good family. Dad thought she couldn't go wrong marrying into a family like that. He gave them an unbelievably extravagant wedding reception for 100 people, taking over a well-known restaurant in town near the GPO in George Street. It was 1933 and you could have bought a house for what it cost my father.

During these Depression years I grew into helping my mother and father in the hotel. I would often take on the early six am shift to open the hotel, so that my father could sleep in, until I left for school. I would pull a beer or two for the odd customer looking for an early drink before work. Helping out around the hotel and viewing people at close range stood me in good stead all my life and helped me to quietly assess the worth and depth of a person. I have no doubt that you see the real character of a person when they're drunk. Their weaknesses and true feelings will show through.

I was also getting my first introduction to the family's role in racing. My father had taken out his bookmaker's licence when he was 21. Most people are fascinated by the world of bookmakers and invariably want to know how a bookie has fared. My father, on returning from the races, would always be asked by hotel patrons, 'How did you go, Charlie?' He'd say, 'No good,' or 'Just got out,' so much so that I felt sorry for him and wondered why he persevered with such an unrewarding occupation.

At the end of each race day, my father would put the money from his betting bags in his pocket and, on returning to the hotel, would leave his bags in a back room and go to the main bar to help. On one occasion when I was about eight, Dad changed his routine by going straight upstairs to the main bedroom. I went looking for him and eventually found him, with his bed covered in banknotes emptied out from his betting bag. To me it seemed like all the money in the world. I hurried downstairs to tell the cook and kitchen staff what I'd seen, and then raced off to tell my mother in the main bar. As I burbled out my news, the whole bar stopped and listened. Needless to say, I was brought before my father, who for the first time in my life explained that you never talk about money in front of people.

—

Looking back at the Depression, everything was hopeless and yet no one ever said so. Everyone seemed to encourage one another and yet basically everyone knew that nothing was going to work. My father was a great optimist and always said that things would change one day. Being young and well looked after, the hardship didn't affect me but I was still aware of it. As the years passed and I grew older, the harsh reality of the Depression became very apparent.

I remember that vagrant families appeared under the great open park areas beneath the bridge approaches, erecting cardboard and tin lean-tos – slowly setting up 'Happy Valley' homes. After the emergence of one lean-to, a second soon appeared, then a third, and soon a small community was ensconced. Eventually, the authorities would have to intervene and the police would come down in strength. A large crowd would congregate as the squatters were evicted and their pathetic little houses knocked down. It was so sad. For a while, all would be quiet but slowly the whole process would start all over again.

During the whole of my childhood, I never heard either my mother or father ever complain or say a harsh or unkind word to each other. Both were very caring parents. I don't think I was ever smacked by either, although I do remember my father chasing me once. I don't recall ever seeing Charlie, Jack or Betty being chastised. I'm not saying we were perfect, but we were never unruly or rude to our parents. None of us was ever forced to do anything – my father would instead give his ideas and reasons. They taught us by example, and both of them simply never stopped working at some chore.

My mother was a very staunch Catholic who had married an Anglican from a bigoted 'anti-Catholic' family. Religion had never worried my father but my mother was aware of her obligations. We were all christened first in the Church of England, to please my father's family, and then as Catholics. My father had no objection to us being raised as Catholics, even to my becoming an altar boy.

My memories are of my mother running the hotel, which was a job and a half. She was an extraordinary woman, and also compassionate – it was nothing for her to quietly put a few silver coins in the hands of someone down on their luck. I don't think my father ever knew. She provided meals for the hungry, including the squatters under the bridge during the days of terrible poverty in the Depression. And she'd help those unable to pay their board – occasionally one of them would leave the hotel without having paid her, but she didn't really mind; she understood their desperate situation. My mother was loved by all the residents and she was very kind to everyone.

I was on the go all the time. I suppose today they would call me hyperactive. I was a climber – I couldn't pass a tree without climbing it. I fell once from quite a height, striking the branches as I went down. I landed on a wooden paling fence and probably broke a couple of ribs – it was excruciating but I didn't tell my parents.

I was inquisitive and in some ways a bit of a rascal. I just wanted to have fun. Jack and Charlie were different. Charlie was overweight and introverted, while Jack just loved animals.

My first school was Naremburn Public, then I moved to Greenwood Primary School, which was on the site of today's Greenwood Plaza shopping centre on the Pacific Highway, opposite North Sydney Railway Station. I never objected to school – in fact, I invariably got there early for the games and stayed late. For some reason there was often a fight on after school, and I revelled in it as I was the tallest boy. Greenwood was in a beautiful old sandstone building at North Sydney and was named after a headmaster, Nimrod Greenwood. It closed in the late 1960s but thankfully in the 1990s, when the plaza was built, the original building was retained along with the magnificent old fig trees. That was where we boys would play marbles, flick cards or have our fights.

I was a good marbles player, as well as a very good card thrower. You would have twenty kids flicking cigarette cards. From about five metres away from a wall, each would flick his card and the closest thrower to the wall had first chance to toss all twenty cards up in the air. Those cards that came down 'heads' – with the photo facing up – were all his to keep. I had a huge advantage in collecting cards, which came in cigarette packs. The packs weren't sealed, so in the hotel I could often see in advance what card was in a pack. If I needed the card to complete my set I would carefully substitute it without damaging the pack. Or when a man bought cigarettes, I'd ask him for the card – more often than not, he'd give it to me. I had the best card collection of anyone I knew. To this day, I still have many framed card sets in my office, including my favourites – the film stars and sportsmen. In winter we played a number of marble games, including Ringey and Holey. I learnt fairly quickly that you didn't play with your best marble unless you felt certain of winning. When you lost you had to hand over your marble.

It never occurred to me that it was strange to go barefoot to school until, one freezing day in the middle of winter, I heard a woman say as I walked past, 'That poor boy has no shoes!' Up until I went to high school at thirteen, only two boys in the class wore shoes. I did own shoes but only wore them when I went to church, which I did each Sunday with my mother.

The Star of the Sea Church, where I had become an altar boy when I was eight or nine, was attached to St Aloysius College. I loved to pinch the fruit from the trees in the garden of the beautiful 'Craiglea' mansion next door. Two spinster sisters lived there. I ducked out of church every Sunday while the priest was giving the sermon – I estimated how long it would last. One time I got back a bit late, which was most embarrassing – the priest was not impressed. The sisters at 'Craiglea' were strongly anti-Catholic, which was quite common in those days. To see me stealing their fruit while dressed up in my altar boy regalia was just too much, and they shook their clenched fists at me in mock anger.

Many, many years later, in the early 1960s, the one surviving sister, Miss Lee, sought me out through a real-estate agent and asked to see me. She had seen my name in the newspapers and remembered me being the 'polite' little scallywag who used to pinch her fruit. But far from being annoyed, she told me I was actually the only boy who didn't taunt her and her sister. Miss Lee said she wanted to sell the grand old house but only to me. We bought it and I told her she could live there for the rest of her life, which is what happened – she never had to move until she was too frail to stay on.

In my adult years, my spirituality has stayed with me, and although the former altar boy may not go to church very often, I still pray each night and have strong values.

Next to the hotel, the North Sydney Olympic Pool was opened in time for the 1936 Empire Games, and beside it was Luna Park, which had also opened when I was fourteen. My father expected times would change with these two new attractions. They did make some difference, especially during construction, as the workmen drank and some lived at the hotel. Once the park and pool were completed, however, it was very disappointing – Luna Park only opened at seven pm and we had to close at six. So the main benefit for us was in after-hours business. Everyone in the family pulled their weight; without this unpaid labour, the sly-grogging and the little money we earned from racing, we would have starved.

Luna Park was every boy's dream and my own personal playground. I knew every inch of the funpark and everyone who worked there. But one day a man grabbed me by the hand and wouldn't let go. I sensed danger and talked him into taking me to the House of Mirrors, which I knew backwards. Once inside, I quickly pulled away from his grasp and ran straight through the maze. Outside, I watched from a safe distance as the stranger eventually came out, still looking for me. I didn't realise then how lucky I was to escape this probable paedophile.

During the holidays I worked at Luna Park, and over the years I turned my hand to nearly every ride or sideshow. I was given jobs by the manager, Dave Atkins, a man who liked his racing and knew my father and mother, often calling into our hotel. He was a good-looking fellow with plenty of charm, outgoing, generous and perfect for the job. I loved being the wizard's assistant and wearing a costume. One of my jobs was to throw a bucket of 'water' – in reality, cellophane – over the horrified crowd. There was a show-of-strength machine in the Penny Arcade, and I delighted in tampering with the controls, making the girls register more strength when squeezing the power handle than their boyfriends.

For entertainment most people went to the movies. I made a deal with the cinema operator at the Orpheum and put up his posters on the fence next to the hotel in return for tickets. The Orpheum showed both MGM and Paramount films, and was just off the bridge exit at North Sydney. There was also a cinema at Crows Nest, which showed Fox and Warner Brothers films.

Sometimes, just for the challenge, my friend Barry Pheloung

and I tried to get in without paying. We used to walk in backwards through the outcoming crowd, thinking we wouldn't be noticed. Another friend, George Evatt (from the famous Evatt family), and I used to slip into the Crows Nest theatre through the emergency exits. We would sneak upstairs and wait to be caught when the lights came on at interval. It was fun trying to get away with it and we waited to be thrown out. Unfortunately, George was later killed in the war.

I just loved the movies. From about fifteen I used to take myself to the Lyceum Theatre or the Capitol in the city, which often had a double feature, then come home and go to the eight o'clock movie at the Orpheum. I would wear shoes and socks and dress nicely – although nothing expensive, of course.

When my two brothers, who hated school, wanted to finish after reaching the leaving age of fourteen, my father didn't like it but did not stop them. On the other hand, I thoroughly enjoyed school and had no trouble passing any exam with a minimum of study. I knew the pleasure it gave my father, who would always say, 'What did you learn today?'

He never once asked me to do law and yet I never had any doubt that I would become a barrister and take over his legal load. So, at the age of thirteen, when I went to high school I told the school registrar that I had to take Latin so I could be admitted to the Faculty of Law at Sydney University. I had topped North Sydney Intermediate before going on to North Sydney Boys High, a selective school where I came fifteenth in my year out of 150, topping Maths 1 and History. The standard was very high because it was the only public high school north of the Harbour Bridge – its top boy was often dux of the state. High school was the first time I wore long pants. Every boy also wore shoes and socks. Because it was still the Depression, we didn't have to wear a uniform.

I always had pets. Jack, too – he had over a hundred birds and fowls. Jack was almost obsessive. He bred canaries but, almost incongruously, he was also a champion cock-fighting trainer. It was illegal to fight them but he occasionally did. I was more interested in cockatoos. I had about 40 birds that had been caught in the bush. I bought them for about five shillings each. I loved to train parrots to talk. I would clip the feathers of each bird's wings, so it didn't have to be caged. I'd feed it corn and keep it in the dark in my room, where I'd teach it to speak. You need to teach a bird when it has no distractions. They loved it and never bit me. I kept the other cockatoos in a huge cage under my window at the hotel. I also had dogs, though just one at a time. My mother loved her Persian cats.

I was always mischievously looking to play a trick on my schoolmates. In my second year at high school, the class went down to the new North Sydney Olympic Pool, which was built against the side of a small cliff. The teacher – Mr Jack Quilky – was a dandy dresser. A bit of a stickler but fair and popular with the class, he taught us chemistry and physics.

After our swimming sessions, the class was to assemble at the back of the pool to have our names ticked off. Horsing around with the boys, I was suddenly struck with a good idea for a practical joke, inspired by my role as the wizard's assistant. I was already dressed and found Mr Quilky to have my name marked off. With that I ran up to the hotel, filled a bucket with water and scurried back to the railing at the top of the cliff. Looking over, sure enough I saw my class, all dressed and waiting to have their names checked off.

I lifted up the bucket and emptied the water on my school mates some twelve metres below. The cascading water was a wondrous sight and I was fascinated watching its descent, until suddenly I noticed Mr Quilky right in the middle of the crowd. With horror I realised the water was going straight at him. I couldn't bear to watch.

I fled back to the hotel, grabbed my pushbike and hurriedly rode off, not stopping till I got to Hornsby on the outskirts of

Sydney. I stayed away until the hotel had closed and waited to see if my mother had any messages for me. No – there were none. I felt instant relief and wondered if it could be possible that no one had noticed me, or rather that no one had snitched on me.

I went to school the next day and nothing happened. I wasn't called anywhere and I felt better and better as the day wore on. As it happened, my last period on this day was a chemistry lesson with Mr Quilky. I was apprehensive as the class assembled. Mr Quilky entered the classroom and immediately began the lesson. At 3.30 the school bell tolled and Mr Quilky announced, 'All right, boys, that's all for today – you may now all leave. That is, all except one. That's right, isn't it, Master Waterhouse?'

I don't think I'd ever felt worse. Funnily enough, I was pleasantly surprised at the penalty. It seemed so easy. I was given a ten-digit number to multiply by another ten-digit number. Maths was my top subject and I thought I'd knock it over in very short order. But two hours later, with no success, I was finally allowed to go home. I had multiplied it out many times but unfortunately could never come up with the correct answer. What a lesson.

3

The Addiction of Racing

I WAS SIXTEEN when I first started working at the races as a relieving penciller for my father in 1938. The meeting was at Moorefield and I had never seen anything like it: thousands of people pushing and shoving just to throw their money in the bookmakers' bags. At the back of our stand there seemed to be a continual crowd of people wanting to get paid. I remember a horse called Pure Gold won, and I thought there surely couldn't be enough money in the bag to settle, the payout queue seemed so long. At the end of the day I was frightened to ask how we had finished. As my brother Charlie drove us back to the hotel, I found we had won a motza of £10 on the day.

I was amazed. I had only been looking at the winners. We had been working on about seven Melbourne races and about ten doubles on the Sydney races. I remember thinking that if we could win on a day like this, then we would never lose.

A fortnight later at Canterbury Park Racecourse we lost over £30. I have never forgotten the day. I think it was the worst loss my father had ever had. He was desolate. I was still too raw to know what was happening, and again it was only on our way home that the catastrophic loss was revealed. I had been more concerned with eating ice-creams and watching the other bookmakers.

Interstate betting was comparatively new. It had been started by a small bookmaker, Eric Hadley, who had the idea of betting on the Melbourne flying and handicap races, as well as running his 'add-up trebles' on the local races. Hadley, like my father, was a small operator, a kindly man who only employed a penciller to record his bets, slinging his own betting bag over his shoulder to save money. He was the first on-course bookmaker to work on Melbourne races in Sydney.

Today interstate betting is a very big business. But in Sydney in the early 1930s, if you wanted to have a bet on the Melbourne Cup you had to find a friendly but illegal SP bookie, who was usually based in the local pub and would take a wager – capped with a 10/1 limit on the odds. SP bookmakers got their name from the fact that they paid out using the final prices of the horses just before the race – their 'starting prices'.

Betting on just two interstate races each Saturday kindled limited interest, but then a young and energetic new bookmaker came on the scene. Arthur Browning, just back from school in England, son of Bob 'the Polar Bear' Browning, had taken out his bookmaker's licence more by chance than intention. He had gone to pay his father's bookmaking fees. The clerk asked, 'Is this for yourself or your father?' and Arthur had promptly replied, 'For myself.' And so a new bookie, just seventeen years of age, came into being. With the enthusiasm of youth, he went everywhere and bet on everything, just as every young bookie does.

Like most before him, Arthur didn't do any good. So he decided to follow his father's path – doubles – and add to it Hadley's newfangled idea of betting on the Melbourne races. The rest is history. Instead of betting on only the two main races, Browning bet on the entire program; and instead of operating with a 10/1 limit, he offered a set price for every horse with no limit.

Radio was just emerging, and live broadcasts of the races soon became available. Hadley and Browning were in the

Paddock enclosure, but my father, who had been promoted from the St Leger Reserve to the Paddock, elected to return to the Leger. He preferred it there. My father was a very conservative bookmaker – he couldn't afford to make a mistake. But he had been a bookmaker for over 30 years by then, and although he was the bottom holder he had one of the best stands, which were based on seniority.

It was a time of large crowds, change and growth, and of increased government and racing club taxes. A typical carnival crowd at Randwick would be, say, 80,000 people, made up of 30,000 in the Paddock enclosure, 30,000 in the St Leger Reserve and 20,000 in the Flat. Bookmakers paid a fee of £1 to operate in the Flat, £2 to work in the St Leger and £5 for the privilege of working anywhere in the Paddock. They paid a halfpenny tax per betting ticket in the St Leger and the Flat, and a penny a ticket in the Paddock. Previously there had been a tax of ten per cent on punters' winning bets, which had been replaced with a turnover tax of 0.25 per cent on total holdings, which grew during the war years – firstly doubling to 0.5 per cent, then one per cent. By the 1950s it had reached two per cent on turnover.

Each enclosure was packed with 100 to 120 bookmakers, and there were long waiting lists for vacancies. At the track the atmosphere was electric. Because of the low taxes and the competition, the bookies worked to a low percentage and, accordingly, there wasn't a great deal of difference between the professional punter and the bookmaker. Both survived – some existed, some prospered. Although the bookmakers' financial mortality rate was alarming, this only added to the excitement of the game. If you ever made it to the Paddock enclosure, you knew you had truly survived: it took you approximately ten years to get there. By that time you were well schooled in your trade.

—

I soon started to absorb more of what was going on at the racetrack. These formative racing years were important to me, and I still think of the champions of the day: Ajax, Reading, High Caste, Beau Livre, Beau Vite, the good two-year-old Broadcaster and the all-conquering two-year-old filly All Love. The money was in small amounts but there was so much of it. Australia was just coming out of the Depression and there was no money anywhere – except at the racetrack. I was terribly impressed by all this loose cash, which seemed to come from an inexhaustible source.

At the Sydney races it was not uncommon to be able to listen in to more than one broadcast of Melbourne races. Eric Welsh was the official announcer on the track in Melbourne, broadcasting over the public-address system to the course patrons. This broadcast was transmitted live to the rest of Australia by one of the national radio stations. Harry Solomons broadcast on 3XY, one of the commercial stations in opposition to Eric Welsh, and was extremely popular. He was a punter and mixed in punting circles, as so many of the racing announcers did.

Solomons realised that, apart from the betting at the track itself, thousands upon thousands of pounds were invested throughout Australia on these Melbourne races. Bookmakers were fielding in Sydney, Brisbane and at countless small tracks throughout the eastern states. On top of this, most of the 3500 hotels in Victoria and New South Wales would have a cash SP bookmaker operating illegally. They all relied on the broadcasts for everything: the starters, the call of the race and finally the announcement of 'correct weight'.

Solomons came up with an idea he thought would win him the keys to the kingdom. What if he were the only man to broadcast a race? All the listeners away from the track would depend on his words, which would be accepted without question. Bookmakers at other tracks and in every cash SP joint would pay out when he broadcast the result on 3XY and announced correct weight.

The year was 1939 and the track was Ascot in Melbourne, owned by John Wren. The horse concerned was Buoyancy.

Solomons' scam was simple, and nothing like it had ever been done before. His idea was that after the horses had gone onto the track and were approaching the start, all the other broadcast cables would be cut, leaving only Harry Solomons with a live broadcast line. After the horses had jumped and the race was underway, Solomons would continue to talk and review the field, as though there had been some delay at the start.

Now, assuming that the race was 1600 metres, it was only going to take a little over a minute and a half to run. Harry just had to stall until the race had been won, when he would mention some detail about the winning horse; his accomplices would charge at bookmakers all over Australia to back the winner of a race that everyone else believed was still to be run. By the time the other stations discovered that their lines had been cut, Solomons' phantom call would be over, the winner weighed in at correct weight and the money paid out.

The betting at the Ascot track itself had no organised part in the plan. All the plunge betting *had* to be done away from the track, where interstate listeners would only lose a few minutes out of their day.

But when your luck's out, it's out. Solomons' accomplices, who had the task of cutting the landlines for 3LO and 3DB, the two other radio stations, were a fraction late in cutting Eric Welsh's wire, and Welsh was heard to shout, 'They're off!' The line then went dead. Harry Solomons continued talking on 3XY but the damage had been done.

I remember so well what followed next. My father was rubbing out his chalked-up prices from the board. We didn't have a radio but listened in to another bookie's set. When the 3DB station went silent, this bookie turned to the other stations and, of course, eventually came to Harry Solomons. Hearing that the horses weren't yet off, the bookie wrote the prices back up on his board.

My father didn't. He was cagey enough to know that something was amiss, and as a result was saved from a payout. Quite a lot of money was won around Australia on Buoyancy, which had won the race at 6/1.

Of course, there was the matter of the cut cables of the other stations. The wheels of justice may turn slowly but they do turn. Once it was established what had happened, a warrant went out for Solomons' arrest and he disappeared from view.

How he even expected to get away with it, I'll never know. He had ruined his life for ever more. Even if he were never apprehended, he could never surface again in Australia. Solomons was eventually arrested in Fiji and jailed in Melbourne for six months. On his release, he dropped from sight and I never heard of him again.

—

I came into racing at just the right time. I was in my second-last year at North Sydney Boys High, and I was just introduced to the world of permutations and combinations. I thought that doubles was a licence to print money – I had not yet absorbed that horse form could make a mockery of the figures. My two older brothers were starting to branch out with their own little bookmaking businesses. Jack obtained his licence when he turned eighteen, and off he went to work at the Lithgow dogs on Saturday afternoons. Charlie already had his provincial licence and then obtained a city licence, but only for midweek meetings.

This left me alone with my father. He was a tremendous teacher. He never lost his temper and never blamed me for mistakes, simply stating, 'They crucified the only man who never made a mistake.' He sensed my keenness with betting and probably realised it might take me away from law, yet he never told me what I should do. He regarded racing as a profession but told me only a few made real money.

My father had started out with enthusiasm but soon realised he wasn't equipped to be a major force in the betting ring, lacking both cash and experience. He was happy to be a small bookie earning a steady income. His motto was 'Little fishes are sweet'. When he took out his licence in 1898, everyone 'knew' bookmaking would only be allowed for another year or so before the introduction of the tote. He wanted to try it before it was stopped, and he would continue for 43 years. My father often warned me that the bookmaking profession would be short-lived – the authorities were constantly looking to wipe out bookies.

When I was growing up there were articles about the history of boxing and bookmaking in the old *Sunday Truth* newspaper every week. If they weren't writing about boxers Jack Dempsey or Louis Firpo, then they would be writing about bookies Barney Allen or Humphrey Oxenham and others. These fine old bookmakers were 'leviathans' – a curious old Biblical expression only used for bookmakers – and I was spellbound reading about them.

I was lucky to have had a father who had lived through these old times, and who could explain so much more of their stories. 'But remember, my son,' he would say, quoting loosely from Proverbs 23, 'gamblers shall be clothed in rags.' Nevertheless, my father never forbade me from gambling – he just gave advice.

I wasn't a punter, but as a teenager I developed a new punting system. I decided to go to the greyhounds one evening with Barry Pheloung to try it out. Barry and I were walking out the door when my father asked where we were going. We were heading for the Flat at the greyhounds – the cheapest enclosure – with our very small bank and a system that I had studied diligently. I believed it was foolproof, and tonight would be the test.

He smiled and said, 'Well, I'll give you some advice if you're going punting. Remember that if you back favourites you'll finish up without any shoelaces in your shoes.'

I nodded as I pondered this piece of sound advice, and Barry and I were about to take our leave when Dad finished with: 'Of course, if you back outsiders, you'll finish up without any shoes at all.'

This knocked the wind out of our sails. Seeing our faces, he broke out laughing and said, 'I'll be 50 per cent with you tonight in your trial.'

We attacked the bookies that evening and wiped out our entire bank. It had been the first night my system had not worked since I had been studying it. The following morning I checked to see what had happened and found that I should have won. Funnily enough, over the years I have found that most systems work on paper.

—

As my racing prowess matured, my scholastic position deteriorated. I had never had to work that hard at school and was dumbfounded to discover how far I had slipped by the end of the year. Of course, the standard was getting tougher as the weaker students dropped out. I realised that if I was going to matriculate the next year and get to Sydney University to do law, I had a long way to catch up.

At the same time, I had no intention of giving up racing. My father had come to rely on me: first I was his penciller clerk and then I took control of the business. Racing was my seventh heaven and I believed I had found the key to bookmaking success.

Bookies assess the risk of a number of runners in a race by allocating them prices, or odds. And when bookmakers take bets – normally on the many runners in a race – it is called 'making a book'. In theory, a bookmaker should lay bets against every runner at the varying odds so that, if his odds are correct, no matter which horse wins he does not lose.

Each horse's odds expresses a percentage chance of it winning. If bookmakers can field all the runners in the right proportions and at favourable odds, they will 'bet round' and win money, no matter which horse wins the race. For example, it would be good business for a bookmaker to lay a 2/1 chance (a $3 chance, in today's terms) at odds of less than 2/1.

Part of the bookmaker's skill is in 'marketing' horses well, and to that end it helps to assess the true chance of each horse. A bookmaker might assesses a horse's odds as being 2/1, or 33.3 per cent – that is, one chance in three of winning – and therefore a 66.6 per cent chance (or two chances in three) of losing. Odds reflecting the true chances of runners will add up to 100 per cent. But a bookmaker adjusts the odds, so as to give himself a margin of, say, ten per cent, which during betting competition is usually whittled down to just three or four per cent. If the margin goes into the negative it becomes a losing proposition. This margin is quite modest when you consider that a bookmaker is pleased to earn three or four per cent on turnover over a period, compared to the TAB's sixteen per cent out of every pool, which is made without any risk.

My concept was simple and really had little to do with racing knowhow. I had discovered financing. I just had to be confident I was laying the horse at a price lower than its starting price, leaving me with a profit. With no pricing service in those days, the danger was in mis-assessing the market. Punters were backing horses racing in another state. If they took 6/4 with me on a horse that might start at the longer price of 2/1, then I could lay a much larger amount against that horse if I were to offload at least part of the bet by backing that horse back at the longer SP odds, reducing my risk and gaining a clear profit with the margin.

Dad and I quickly became the top money-holders in the St Leger. It was a gigantic leap to go from the bottom to the top. To my father's credit, he never interfered with his schoolboy son's actions. He would begin the day at the stand with me but then go to sit in the grandstand. One of his friends told me later that my father simply said, 'I just can't bear it – but I think he knows what he's doing and will be all right.'

—

My father had told me that the impossible was always impossible until you saw someone do it or you did it yourself. From these earliest stirrings on the racecourse, I think my father sensed that I was going to be the gambler. Charlie would argue with Dad about taking a risk, whereas I was always given more latitude – perhaps because I never forced the issue.

When I had begun running my father's stand, I automatically experimented with my ideas, and the day came when I stood a horse for £100. The sum seemed enormous to my father because we had still not fully recovered from the Depression. Fortunately, the horse did not win – and in any case I had simply been playing up my winnings.

My father sensed the situation perfectly. Prophetically, he told me that now that I'd stood a horse for £100, I had passed a barrier in gambling and would always be able to stand such amounts. Whereas that figure had been a bundle before, now it was merely history. He was right. Throughout the whole of my career, each time I went to a new level of betting, it was never a worry going to that level again.

At all events, with this new approach, in a short time my father and I regularly had books with £100 in stakes held on a race and risked large payouts. It may not sound much today, but such large books were unheard of in the Depression. I remember earlier when a Leger bookie, Bob Adland, held £100 on a race – it was the talk of the course. But Bob had held his £100 on a feature race on a major race day – now my father and I were holding it several times a day on ordinary races. Word soon spread at the track that old Charlie Waterhouse had gone around the bend and was going to lose all his money with his idiot gambling son.

I had stayed friends with Dave Atkins, the manager of Luna Park – he loved to talk about horses. One day Dave asked me to do his business at the track. I guess he 'had a few dogs tied up' – unpaid bets at his local SP bookie – and had probably worn out his welcome. It was difficult for him to go racing in the summer, as Saturday afternoons were big days for him.

Dave told me of the great information that he had, and how he knew how to study form. But when I put his money on, I realised his information wasn't crash-hot and that he wasn't as good a judge as he thought. I was becoming very much aware of form at the time, so it was a natural progression for me to look a little harder at Dave's bets.

He would ring me with his list of bets. At first he asked me to call down for the cash but then, being busy – whether fact or fiction – said he would pay me (or receive) the cash when I returned from the races. Dave was sometimes a little slow in paying, which put me in an awkward position of funding his bets, and I didn't want to be betting for Dave with my money if he couldn't settle.

It wasn't too long before I figured that Dave was not a winner-backer, and that if I could get in front I could stay there. I started setting aside some of his money and taking the risk myself. Without thinking, I was gambling. He gave me hiccups a few times, but I hung in and, as I got in front and he owed money, the situation was different. I grew to be comfortable with £1000 risks. I still didn't consider it gambling, just good business.

A £1 punter is a £1 punter, and there is no way he will put £1000 or even £100 on a horse. He doesn't, simply because he thinks he can't. Apart from deriving pleasure from his £1 bet, he fears becoming a mad plunger. Should that £1 punter ever put £100 on a horse, a peculiar thing happens. He soon realises that there isn't really any difference – he hasn't had a heart attack, but undoubtedly he got a far greater thrill! He realises it is only money. Just as a bookmaker becomes acclimatised to risks, once a punter has bet a certain sum, he can always bet the same again.

—

I had no social life in 1939 because I had so much to catch up on at school. It was my final year and the results were critical for my future. After the exams finished I was relieved to have passed with flying colours. My father was so pleased he hurriedly took me off to see Professor Sir John Peden, the head of the Faculty of Law at Sydney University. It was an interview I will never forget. After my horror final year, I never wanted to see another textbook. All I wanted to do was to go to work in a solicitor's office where there were plenty of girls. He told us that, with my young age – I was just turning eighteen – I would be better equipped for law if I first acquired an arts degree. I was aghast. Arts was a three-year course, although I could cut it to two years by doing my third year of arts as my first year of the four-year law degree, making a total of six years if I took the appropriate subjects.

To my amazement, instead of being years of hard study, they were halcyon days. There were girls everywhere, the work was not hard and I could regulate my own study pace, selecting the subjects I loved – history and more history.

By 1940 Charlie had gone bust as a bookmaker for the second time. He was broke and demoralised and decided to hand in his licence. I already had full control of my father's stand on Saturdays and loved it. I persuaded Charlie to keep going and I bankrolled him, as by this time I had saved a small fortune. We became partners.

Charlie had a licence to work at the Harold Park trots on a Monday, the provincials on a Tuesday, the ponies on the Wednesday and Newcastle on a Thursday. I arranged my lectures in such a way that I had every afternoon free and could work with him at the races. Charlie was a good worker and he also let me have my head with the pricing and financing. We complemented each other and prospered together.

Then adversity hit the family from a different direction. War had been declared in September 1939, and my father thought it would be a good idea to get into the sheep industry. The war at that stage was a million miles away but my father knew from World War I that raw materials would become scarce. My father asked if I wanted to invest in the sheep with my brothers but, not being at all interested in the land, I declined. Unfortunately, a drought developed and didn't break, and all the sheep died. My father and brothers had lost all their ready cash. I felt terrible, not so much at the loss but because I had not joined them in the venture. I felt like a traitor.

It was just as well I was not involved, as my money kept the family going. I had been a good earner – by the age of fifteen I had saved some £100 and by eighteen I had accumulated £600. It was a lot of money and it allowed us to start up again as though nothing had happened; it was not long before we were back on an even keel.

The family had confidence in me even though I was the youngest. I took over all the family racing finances, and Dad decided we should pool everything together and all be partners.

He had taught us from a young age to stick by and fiercely defend one another against all comers. He told us you can easily break one pencil, whereas you can't break a handful held tightly together. This philosophy of the importance of family unity would drive me all my life.

Unfortunately, at about this time my sister Betty's marriage broke up. She and her husband had lived in the hotel for a while after they married. I really liked her husband – he was a nice fellow. He was a World War I veteran but he started to drink too much. Betty had never been a drinker. She got him into his brother's business but he couldn't run it because of his drinking. They separated and sadly he died soon after.

—

Then on Saturday 31 August 1941 total disaster struck. My father, although overweight, had always enjoyed good health. I had never known him to visit a doctor – he regarded all doctors as quacks and charlatans. On the Thursday of that week he became ill, and he was worse on the Friday. He said it was only a stomach upset, but that if he didn't improve he couldn't go to the races the next day. He asked me to get permission for Charlie to work in his place on the Saturday.

For the first time ever I went to the Saturday races without my father. Jack had just been granted his Australian Jockey Club (AJC) licence, and this Saturday was the first day he stood up in the Flat enclosure at Randwick.

I don't remember how we fared at the races that day, but on our return, as we parked our car in the usual area opposite the hotel, a young woman approached us. From the look on her face I knew at once that my father was dead. He was 63. He had died from acute peritonitis – an abdominal infection. He couldn't be saved – the doctor was called too late – and no one had been able to get a message to us at the races.

My mother lost all desire for living. For over a year she was little better than a zombie. She didn't laugh any more. She performed her chores as if in a dream and didn't go out. She used to pray every night to die so she could join her departed husband but, being a good Catholic, she did not think of ending her own life. I was worried about her but had underestimated her inner strength.

We were absolutely devastated by our father's shock death. He was our rock, and to lose him seemed the end of the world. I was just nineteen years of age and had relied so much on him for guidance. I was shattered but I had to consider the future. I knew I had to keep my head.

4

Making a Quid

MY MOTHER BECAME licensee of the Imperial after Dad died; Charlie couldn't because he had sly-grogging black marks against his name. Straight after Dad's death, I realised that we had work to do – and quickly – if we were to survive in the bookmaking trade. It wasn't about what I could do for myself, but more about what I could do for the family, for my mother, my sister and my brothers.

It was just as well I was around because, to everyone's amazement, I was able to organise for some of my father's prime bookmaking stands to be transferred to us. In those days the stands were decided strictly by seniority; my father had been a bookmaker for 43 years and his stands were the pick of the St Leger enclosure, so they were highly sought after.

The first thing I did was to see the bookmakers he had worked with. I knew I had to get to them quickly. They all felt sorry for us and agreed not to object to my request to transfer Dad's stand to Charlie. Then each race club had to give its permission, so I had to see all the club secretaries individually. With the bookmakers not objecting, I was able to do a deal with the officials at the proprietary clubs, Rosehill, Canterbury and Moorefield, which were owned by Claude Moore. Even though the AJC, a non-proprietary club which operated Randwick and Warwick Farm, wouldn't agree, we applied and got a vacancy immediately – although we couldn't get my father's good stand there. I didn't apply to the minor clubs of Victoria Park, Ascot, Kensington and Rosebery.

I had joined the Sydney University Regiment in 1940 and usually went to camp in the university holidays. But after my father's sudden death our situation was desperate. My mother's health was extremely fragile and she needed me to help her through the crisis. I took a short leave of absence to help run the hotel, which was an essential service, and so I wasn't at the camp when the Sydney University Regiment was sent to New Guinea after Japan entered the war.

There was a drive to train new doctors. I thought it would make my mother happy, so without any real leaning to the medical world, in 1942 I enrolled in medicine instead of first-year law. It was in the thick of the war and so it was an accelerated course. I was never that good at handling the sight of blood, and later in this first year we were already dissecting bodies from the city morgue. I had no stomach for it. It became too much for me when, in one dissecting class, some of the girls sensed my queasiness and put some male private parts between two slices of bread and passed it to me! Despite my mother's pride at her son studying to be a doctor, I realised I was definitely not cut out for medicine.

After this awful year in 1942, I was manpowered into De Havillands experimental engineering division. We were building a tropical version of the Mosquito Bomber, a wonderful British combat aircraft. It had excelled in a number of battles during the war in Europe but was no good in the humid atmosphere of New Guinea. We were looking at changing one little section of the plane to make it work in the different conditions. This was the only proper job I would ever have outside the law and bookmaking. When I started there were just three of us, including our secretary, Diane Easterbrook, who remains a dear friend to this day. I expanded the research unit until we had a staff of twenty, and I thoroughly enjoyed it. However, it was soon obvious the planes would never be needed.

—

After the war began things became scarce and, as the situation worsened, rationing was introduced. Everything was so tough. Owners of cars were entitled to limited petrol coupons with ration certificates obtained at post offices. So we bought a few small second-hand cars as a way to get petrol. I bought a Rudge motorbike to go to and from De Havillands and had enough petrol to go just about anywhere I wanted. But having a car in those days was a big deal, as was having a telephone. The hotel was one of the few businesses to have a phone at Milsons Point and people used to come from all over to use it. Our number was X3839; it later became XB3839 and still later 923839.

The rationing that hit hardest was on beer, wine and spirits. The situation was bleak. We had a hotel with hardly any trade, we were without our father, the rock, and we still had the family court case to fund. We had to find a way to make a quid and survive as best we could.

The breweries were strictly limiting their supplies and, being freehold, we naturally always drew the short straw with them. They were not about to help us when they had their own hotels to supply. Being an independent freehold had one advantage – we could buy alcohol from anywhere we were lucky enough to find it. I regularly rode my motorbike to wineries around New South Wales and Victoria. I often went to De Bortolis in the Riverina and bought 54-gallon hogsheads (kegs) of wine. This bulk wine was a pretty rough drop but we bottled it under our own hotel label. I called it 'Imperial Royal Reserve', which I thought sounded good – and so did the patrons.

That gave us surplus wine and it meant we could at least sell wine to our patrons, instead of the scarcer beer. Any beer we did get I would then sell in bulk to several clubs, including the Gallipoli RSL in the city. In those days clubs were not licensed and had to have the pretext of buying on account of customer orders and on-selling without a profit. So we would sell the beer to them for retail value, which was very profitable as we saved the labour and other costs of serving the beer while still having the counter trade with the wine.

This wartime shortage of alcohol and other items caused a huge upsurge of sly-grogging and black-marketing in Sydney and other parts of the state. In those days prices were still controlled and one was not allowed to sell anything above the set retail price. However, beer and other alcohol supplies were commonly diverted from their normal outlets and sold at highly inflated prices. Some police raids occurred but, as later events would show, many senior police either turned a blind eye or were in on the rorts. People were desperate and grateful to get anything by way of a drink.

The supply situation grew even worse from early 1942, when thousands of American troops came to Sydney as the United States entered the war. Beer, wine and spirits went illegally to the growing number of new Hollywood-style night-clubs entertaining them. Alcohol was selling at a premium, sometimes ten times the normal price. Scotch was just about priceless, selling for at least £5 a bottle, which was more than the basic weekly wage. People were even brewing their own beer and spirits, and many minor explosions occurred as bottletops blew when amateur brewers didn't quite get the formula right. Many hotels were watering down their bulk beer – using a keg of water connected to a row of beer kegs – but we didn't want any part of that.

Charlie went to auctions all the time to find supplies for the hotel and other things we needed. One day I was with him and he noticed a 36-gallon cask of raw grape spirit for sale. It was incredibly cheap but low-grade. We bought it, thinking it would be handy for something. We didn't realise at first that it was actually very high-proof, suitable as a base for brandy or even scotch – albeit not liquor of great quality.

Charlie and Jack diluted some and mixed it with brown sugar to give it some colour. To their untrained palate it tasted just like cognac. I used my schoolboy French to make a label, calling it *Maison de Ville*. I had grandly wanted to name it 'Town Hall Cognac' – *Hôtel de Ville* – but I had instead called it 'Town House Cognac'. No worries – the patrons loved it! A commercial traveller from Tooths even asked to try it and raved about its 'superb quality'. He said, 'This is cognac with a real bite.' I guess in those days they would have liked anything. Luckily no one realised the limitations of my amateurish French. However, cognac wasn't as popular as scotch – you just couldn't procure real whisky. So by amending the formula and adding less brown sugar, Jack came up with a style of scotch. This proved to be a big hit and soon the 36 gallons of raw spirit – roughly 200 bottles – were gone.

Through wheeling and dealing we had found a way to claw our way out of our tough situation. Of course, we were just bit players with a little scheme that was 'small beer' compared to what was going on elsewhere in the liquor industry. It even had a humorous side to it. At the time we had this little supply of bodgie whisky, licence inspectors came along to do a routine check on the alcohol content of our spirits. Their job was to ensure that hotel operators were not diluting their alcohol. Their testing revealed that Jack had made a minor mistake mixing his scotch formula – instead of being the standard proof it was actually about two per cent higher. The inspectors said it was the first time they had found a publican selling over proof.

Despite our unexpected success, I was still conscious of following my father's advice: 'Never be motivated by greed.' I remember Charlie wanting to buy some doubtful low-grade alcohol for a fraction of the normal price. Luckily, I didn't think it was worth the risk and, sure enough, the inspectors came around to test us.

Then we had some luck. When Singapore fell to the Japanese in February 1942, ships with English cargo were diverted to Australia. Sydney attracted most of them, being the main port and largest city. Being a freehold hotel helped us again. None of the brewery hotels were allowed to touch the English beer that ended up in Sydney, and I had no opposition when I tendered for the whole shipment. It was enough beer to last the hotel for years. The trouble was that it had an entirely different taste from our local beer, and I suddenly panicked at the size of my gamble. Then I realised I needed to go to the other large group in Sydney which I knew had the same liquor shortage as ourselves – the licensed clubs. I approached them and was given a good hearing. Soon small orders became large orders and our problems were behind us.

Our hotel patrons took to the taste and many new customers from 'dry' hotels flooded in to drink our beer. By the following year the little Imperial Hotel had gone from having the smallest turnover in the state to one of the largest. I proudly remember a picture in one of the Sydney newspapers showing a crowd estimated at 5000 people milling around outside the hotel, spilling across the road and onto the parkland under the Harbour Bridge.

—

The overnight transformation of my family's fortunes had been amazing. From the death of our father and a bleak future with the unimposing Imperial Hotel, we suddenly had a bonanza. We survived and even prospered by using our initiative, working closely together and trying every possible angle to make things work. Above all we worked extremely hard.

I turned 21 in January 1943 and my mother gave me a classic solid gold watch, engraved simply 'To Bill from Mum'. It was an unbelievable luxury at the time which I treasured. I still have the watch to this day.

We had a personal setback in about 1944 when licensing authorities raided the hotel and could have charged my mother, who was licensee, with a breach of the liquor laws. We were concerned about such a trauma for my poor mother and so were relieved when they charged Charlie instead of her. However, I realised it was serious and that if Charlie were convicted he would lose his bookmaking licence.

I was in first-year law and wanted a smart but also affordable barrister. I sought out the brightest young barrister at the bar. I came up with the young Garfield Barwick. His brilliant career was still before him – he would be knighted and become chief justice of the High Court. Garfield found deficiencies in the case against Charlie and it was dismissed. A lucky escape.

Eight years later there was a royal commission into the black market and sly-grogging, which ultimately resulted in Sydney-siders being allowed to have a drink without draconian restrictions. A big cast of Sydney identities was called before the commission. Even I had my own little scare when Mr Bill Dovey QC (Margaret Whitlam's father) asked a witness, 'And who is Bill Waterhouse?' That line made it to the front page of a Friday-afternoon newspaper. I spent a nervous weekend but my name was not mentioned again.

Our freehold hotel had good value because of both its real estate and its liquor licence, which could be relocated although only within a mile. Over the years there were often enquiries from agents and others trying to acquire the property, and I could never understand why my father had not agreed to sell. Now, with a sudden boom in business, we completely changed our thinking. For the whole of my formative life the hotel had been a hard, thankless drudge, but now it was at its best: alive, exciting and very rewarding. We decided to try to buy out all the other owners, including my warring aunts and Uncle Ossie. We offered a fortune for their share, valuing the hotel at £20,000, but were flatly rejected.

Some little time later we heard by chance that the other side had approached a brewery and, just to thwart us at the urging and instigation of Ossie, were selling their half for £6000 – much less than the £10,000 we would have paid them. I had not yet got my teeth into my law degree but felt they had made a legal mistake, so I went again to Garfield Barwick.

In the ensuing court battle, the family fight was finally put to rest. The Equity Court ordered they sell their share to us for £6000. My father's wish had come true – an end to the family dispute – the longest running equity suit in the history of New South Wales. Regrettably, after we had fought so long to gain control of the hotel, it would soon be pulled from under our feet.

—

Betty was still young and beautiful and married a second time. Unfortunately, she found another fellow who liked his liquor. Leo came from another well-established family on the North Shore, but we didn't know he was the black sheep. They, too, lived in the Imperial for a while, then moved around the country a bit. He proved himself a bastard – he hocked her jewellery, hocked everything, even my mother's jewels. When I found out I tried to buy everything back but the pawnbroker's story was that he had sold it all at auction. Leo was a low fellow, a real no-hoper. The marriage only lasted a couple of years and was over by the end of the war.

It was so sad. Betty was a gorgeous and intelligent girl and she had twice fallen for the wrong man. Then she began seeing a man who was married. He promised to get a divorce but I strongly advised her against him. However, I think Betty really loved him and so I always felt sorry I had intervened. I decided that from then on I would never interfere in any relationship again.

—

The war had completely changed racing. Apart from drastically reducing meetings to just three Saturdays a month, interstate betting was abolished and would not be reinstated until after the war. The only alternative was to bet on the local Sydney races – either 'straight out' (for a win or a place), or on doubles. I was fully aware of the vast gulf between away betting and locals betting, which required far more skill, more knowledge and, most importantly, more self-control.

Interstate bookies were by that time already using betting boards to display all the races of the day: they wrote their prices on them in chalk. Locals bookmakers, however, didn't have boards and only bet 'off the book', which made it difficult for interstate bookies to adapt to fielding on the local races. It was also hard for the locals bookies to follow one another. The skilled bookie who understood the chances of each runner from its form had a real advantage.

My father had schooled us well in doubles, but my brothers and I now decided we would go 'straight out' on the local races. It may sound a simple decision but it certainly wasn't. Bookmaking can be a quick money-making business but, more likely, it can be a money-losing business. There is an old truism that there is always an end to a winning trot but there may be no end to a losing one. You can go broke while putting your poor gambling down to bad luck.

Funnily enough, Charlie and Jack were not at all keen on the races during the war years, preferring the hotel with its steady profit. I liked the money from the hotel but far preferred the challenge of racing.

—

Working at De Havillands, I realised I was too comfortable. I knew instinctively I had to leave; I felt I was becoming a robot, having staff and not having to think for myself, and receiving wages each week. After a year I realised that if I didn't make a move then, I might never want to. So I enrolled in Arts III and Law I, fulfilling my father's original but unspoken wish.

The law faculty was completely unlike arts. In 1944 there were only 41 students in my year, half of whom then failed. The remaining ones were a bright bunch and the standard was high. Among them were Neville Wran, later to become premier of New South Wales; Lionel Murphy, later the leader of the government in the Senate and a justice of the High Court of Australia; Lionel Bowen, who became the attorney-general and deputy prime minister in Bob Hawke's government; Adrian Roden, a future justice of the Supreme Court of New South Wales; Dennis Mahoney, who would become a justice and president of the Court of Appeal; Robert Minter of Minter Ellison; R. W. Millar, who went on to the boards of corporate giants like Caltex and Tooheys; and Chester Porter and Frank McAlary, who would both become prominent QCs. Chester and Frank had celebrated in the streets of Sydney at the end of World War II; the Movietone news captured Frank dancing in the street and he later became known as 'the dancing man'. I easily recognised him from the photos when they appeared in the paper.

Adrian Roden and I quickly became firm friends. One day he came riding pillion with me on my motorbike to the Riverina to buy wine for the hotel. Adrian fell off on a straight but bumpy dirt road – luckily he wasn't hurt, but he didn't quite see the humour in the mishap and refused to get back on. We had to wait to catch a lift to the winery and he insisted on going home to Sydney by train.

The hours at law school were different from any other

faculty. Lectures were between nine and ten am, then there was a break, with lectures again between four and six pm. In between lectures you had two alternatives. If you intended to practise as a solicitor, you became an articled clerk to a law firm. If you wanted to become a barrister, between lectures you were expected to go to one of the courts – to watch, listen and learn the art of advocacy.

On my first day at law school I was recognised as being one of the bookmaking Waterhouses and was asked if I might be interested in a game of poker. It was the custom for a small group to have a game in one of the lecture rooms. I had never gambled for money with cards in my life, but when they said they were playing four shillings blind, I knew I couldn't lose much. I quickly learnt better.

To speed up the action the group played with a euchre deck (with cards only numbered seven or higher) and their blind was something else. The first hand dealt to me didn't even have a pair. The first player said he was playing. I was the second and also said, 'Playing.' The third player said, 'Limit,' which meant he raised by two shillings. The dealer then said, 'Sixteen shillings.' The first man said, 'Play,' and – in for a penny – I again said, 'Play,' thinking that the limiting would stop. No! The third player said, 'Thirty-two shillings,' and then the dealer said, 'Sixty-four.'

I had no choice but to accept. I was in for £3 – around the basic wage. And all this was before I even drew a card. In the end, I drew four cards, still didn't make a pair and so had my first initiation to law. We broke for lunch – sandwiches – and then went back to poker until 3.59 pm.

—

My friends Adrian and Ambrose Bundy were always devising new and different ways to gamble. We loved our racing and came up with an interesting variation. Each Monday the race clubs would issue the weights for the following Saturday's meeting. Because of the sparseness of racing, there were always packed fields and it was common to see 50 or so horses weighted for a race. This field would be reduced to between ten and sixteen by Thursday.

We decided that after weights were issued at lunchtime on Monday, each of us had to frame a betting market, working to a ten per cent margin. We would then make bets based on one another's prices. Each morning we would look at the track gallop results, adjust our prices and again exchange them. After Thursday, over half the field would have gone and, if you were fortunate to have 'laid' – accepted a bet on – one of the scratchings, you cleaned up, because the betting was 'all in' with no refunds for non-starters. It sounds simple enough but, gambling-wise, it was like playing Russian roulette with money.

This silly exercise stood me in tremendous stead in later years. I have never been a good form analyst but have always had a great grasp of prices. After a bit of practice, it was surprising how on a Monday you could accurately pick the actual field for the Saturday and, unbelievably, get very close to the actual starting prices. Of course you made mistakes, but invariably the others playing would not pick the errors. A lot of times you would grit your teeth, cross your fingers and trust to luck.

I was soon given a wonderful chance to test my ability on my own at the local races. I had wanted some bookmaking experience while studying at university but it was not acceptable for a lawyer to also be a licensed bookmaker, so I convinced Uncle Tuck to take out a bookmaking licence so that I could work the stand. The locations were poor but I did well. Then Jack took almost a year off from the races to concentrate on our hotel, and I received permission to work his stand during his absence. Jack had much better stands and by now was a 'locals' Paddock bookmaker at Rosehill, Canterbury and Moorefield, and a Flat bookie at Randwick.

I must have been crazy. Whereas Jack had been content to follow the other bookmakers' prices, I formed my own markets without any pricing service and audaciously opened up the betting on each race, being the first to call the prices. Mathematics was something I never had to study – I knew figures backwards. But I was still a raw novice and surrounded by all the top professionals in the top enclosure. My clerk was Adrian Roden, who would himself have made a top bookie. He enjoyed it as much as I did.

Of course I made mistakes. Jack's Paddock stands were in the back row. When I opened up the market, everyone in front would look around and listen. As there were still no betting boards, you had to call your prices – but you could go through the field at your own pace. If you called a price and saw the whole crowd swarm towards you, you knew you had made a blunder and would only let the first punter on before cutting the odds. It was very hard to make an impact and compete with other bookies, and it was exhausting. I wasn't sure whether I could survive. The bookies who knew and understood the odds could run rings around the rest. I was well prepared with my mathematical leaning, my father's training and of course my university pals' exercises in forming a market.

Then overnight I sensed how I was handling it wrongly. I was laying the favourite first, like everyone else did. I was calling, 'Six to four the field,' or 'Seven to four the field,' which meant the favourite was 6/4 or 7/4 with the rest of the field at longer odds. I suddenly realised that to work out the price of the favourite, it was much smarter to work out the prices of the other horses first. So I did the reverse. I began to call and lay the outsiders first: 'Twenty to one Rainbird . . . Ten to one Proctor,' and so on.

It was a good marketing exercise. People would come up to

me and ask the price of a horse simply because they had heard me call out a horse other than the favourite. I also knew it was a good strategy. As a teenager, when I helped my father open up the hotel early, I'd had lots of time to kill before school. I liked to open the paper to check the race results from the previous day, along with the starting prices. I enjoyed analysing the SPs of the horses that won the most. I kept a record, and over time it was clear to me that it was better to lay the longer-priced runners – as the longer the price was, the better the margin. Through this I worked out the now widely recognised 'favourite/long-shot' bias.

So I had a bit of a monopoly on laying the long-priced horses. Other bookmakers described me as 'putting the roof on first without foundations', but it was a very sound practice, giving a better margin on turnover. Punters loved it as it opened up opportunities for them away from the short-priced favourite.

I became supremely confident but was still able to control my ego, and suddenly money began to pour in. I won nine straight Saturdays and was about £6000 ahead after all expenses, which was a fortune in those days. More importantly, it proved to me that I knew what I was doing and could work out a way to handle the locals in top company.

It was a time of huge crowds and packed betting rings. The bookies in the Paddock were the top of the crop and had served their apprenticeship over the years, driving the country circuit then the provincial circuit, followed by a minimum of three years in the Flat, and at least three years in the St Leger before attaining Paddock status. If you weren't in the top three or four in the Flat or Leger, you found it very difficult to get a promotion to the Leger or Paddock, respectively.

The leaders of the ring at that time were Ken Ranger, 'Sharkey' Dwyer, Bill Mulligan, Harry 'Doc' Austin, Eric Welch, Lionel Bloom, Ernie Vandenberg, Jack Shaw, 'Gentleman' Jim

Hackett and Joe Mathews, plus 'Snakes' Nathan, who was the king of the St Leger. What names! I got such pleasure from just working on the periphery of these giants. I was also becoming better known in the racing community. I had joined the City Tattersalls Club when I was twenty and conducted race settling for the family each Monday. Now that I was operating on my own, without Jack or Charlie, it was different. I received recognition and respect in my own right.

Jack returned to the track at the end of the year and I had my law exams to pass. I had not done any work through the year and so I had to cut myself off from the world during the month before the exams. The only break I had was for Saturday racing, but for the rest of the week I started study at six in the morning and finished at six at night. From seven to nine at night I would phone other students. It was full-on occupation.

I got through without a 'post', or second-chance exam, and swore to myself it would be different the following year – that I was going to change my ways. But the next year and every subsequent year was exactly the same – traumatic hell. I still managed to get through without a single post.

One year I was nominated as the student representative for my year but, doing the gentlemanly thing, I voted for my opponent. He voted for himself, which led to a tie. I was also active in the Law Society, although my good friend Neville took a tongue-in-cheek jab at me when he wrote in his law column of my 'months of indolent conduct' – for missing four consecutive Law Society meetings. University was a lot of fun, and the charming, good-looking Neville and I were the closest of buddies.

My dear sister, Betty, married for the third time in about 1944 to Commodore Norman Hall, a ship's captain for the Swire Yuill line. Sadly, Betty had three bites of the cherry but had found yet another man who liked to drink. She wore the pants but there was no bitchiness in her. Betty and Norman had two children, Neville and Cathy, whom she adored.

—

Around 1946 we had trouble of a different kind, caused by an unscrupulous local member of parliament, Jim Geraghty. The Liquor Act allowed hotel licences to be moved anywhere within about 1.7 kilometres. Geraghty came to see me. He had a block of land at Crows Nest, just inside the zone, where he wanted to move our hotel licence. Geraghty's estranged wife was the licensee of the Crows Nest Hotel, the second-largest hotel in the metropolitan area. But Geraghty wanted to start up and run another hotel in competition. When I wouldn't go along with him he wanted to buy our hotel licence, and then he unsuccessfully tried to force me to sell the Imperial to him.

Then suddenly the minister for housing ordered the resumption of the Imperial Hotel site in order to build a hostel for wharf labourers who worked on the other side of Sydney Harbour! It turned out to be just a set-up. I was approached by a third person – on behalf of Geraghty – who said that for £5000 they could have the resumption cancelled. Much to their surprise, I refused to deal with them.

After having fought so long, and having bought the hotel at a value of £12,000 for the land, the hotel and its licence, we were now only offered £2000 in compensation – later increased to £2800 – for the resumption of our twenty-bedroom hotel, the disused wood, coal and coke yard, four vacant and dilapidated shops, and five three-storey residentials on an acre of land – all at a prime habourside location. It was a ridiculous valuation. I doubted that we could win a long and expensive court battle against the government, given my father's earlier experience. He had owned land which was resumed for the Milsons Point train station; he fought the lowly sum offered and won – the only problem was that the whole of the compensation was needed to pay the lawyers. Despite this, there was still no way that I was going to pay the £5000 bribe money.

In a strange 'coincidence' at the same time, Willoughby Council resumed our ancestral home and ten-acre estate at Naremburn. I think we received about £1400. The council thought it would make a fine addition to the adjoining parklands. Some 60 years later, the land is basically in the same state as it was when it was resumed, except our home, the stables and the orchards are all gone. I still feel poorly done by. Today the land would be worth millions.

Incredibly, a third resumption occurred in the same year. Jack, wanting to get out of the city, had purchased just under six hectares of land at Dundas, a quiet suburb about twenty kilometres away. He built a lovely two-storey home and became a hobby farmer. All his life Jack had yearned for farm life. At one stage we owned around 80 thoroughbreds; he also bred Charolais cattle, goats and pigs. If he didn't make a nickel or a dime out of it, it didn't matter – he just loved the life.

The Department of Main Roads resumed the farmland, allowing us to keep only the land the house was on; they took away Jack's dream. Worse, we had paid £40 a hectare for the land and yet the government paid us just £32 a hectare, saying that the land on which the house stood was worth more than the rest. To this day, the road still hasn't been started.

I have no doubt that Geraghty was behind at least two of these inexplicable resumptions – all because he had wanted our freehold hotel licence and wanted to put pressure on us. Geraghty later came under a cloud and was expelled from the Labor Party for corruption on other matters.

Over the years it has been said I had political clout. I wouldn't say that, but when these cruel resumptions happened in a row, I certainly swore that there would be no more resumptions without a fight. In the late 1940s I heard that

Willoughby Council was contemplating resuming the land we had bought as a proposed hotel site at Chatswood, for a council car park. I went straight to the premier, Joe Cahill, who was also the minister of lands, and told him of our plight and how we had suffered by the recent series of resumptions.

I'll never forget his words: 'Don't worry, son. Go home and relax – no one's going to resume that land for any car park whilst I am still the premier.' That was the end of all resumption talk.

In the mid-1940s we were continually prodded into vacating the resumed Imperial site, as the department said it was eager to start building. However, this was just a sham, as it never developed the site – instead the land was made into a nondescript little park. Not until 50 years later was part of the land used to extend the North Sydney Olympic Pool.

We had acquired a small duplex 100 metres up the road at 54–56 Alfred Street, and we won an application to put a temporary hotel licence there so that we could keep our licence alive. We then called for tenders to build a temporary bar on the front lawn, making as little change to the back as possible. The lowest tender was £5000, which we thought extortionate – and ironic, given that it was the same figure to stop the resumption. However, we were all united on not paying a penny to the politicians.

We decided we would try to build the bar ourselves, hiring tradesmen directly. Charlie was positive he could do it for less than £5000, even though we had never had any experience.

That was to change our lives completely. We completed the building for about £2800 and, for the first time in his life, Charlie found something that he did well and gave him a reason to get out of bed early each day – he thoroughly enjoyed it. And our goals as a family changed from simply trying to win at the next race meeting to looking at property and building.

The bar was only temporary, however, and we had to find

a site on which to erect our permanent new hotel. We were also aware that it would be a far bigger challenge to build a complete hotel. Overnight a tremendous opportunity opened up with the abandonment of licence relocation restriction. We could now move anywhere we liked in Sydney. The only catch was that it had to be approved by the licensing court and the new location passed by the local council, after considering objections by local residents or any other interested party.

I quickly found a site at Spit Junction. I was supremely confident that we would soon be on our way. How wrong I was. At the licensing court the objections that came in showed brewery influence everywhere. I had never expected foul play from a big company, but I had a very rude awakening. They didn't dirty their own hands but had no compunction about hiring others to do their dirty work. One brewery agent said, 'I'm sorry to do this to you, but I'm just doing my job.' We lost that battle.

The fight showed me that to succeed at council level we would have to mount a long, hard campaign. We were looking for an area which already had a top-trading hotel. We didn't want to go somewhere where there was no trade. For the next year all my available time was spent searching the Sydney suburbs for likely sites. I checked the census figures and the hotel licence turnover numbers. At that time there were approximately 2000 hotels in New South Wales, which had a population then of around four million people – or one hotel to every 2000 people. Eventually we settled on the Chatswood area, where there was just one hotel to over 60,000 people – by far and away the best figures I could find. The existing Chatswood Hotel was also the only hotel in the whole of the metropolitan area whose trade had not dropped during the Depression.

The next thing was to find and buy a site. It took a year, but after plenty of door-knocking at homes on suitable sites – I would simply ask owners if they wanted to sell – we eventually acquired two cottages. They were on the wrong side of the railway but big enough for the hotel we wanted to build. We then went back to the licensing court and spent another year in countless hearings. The main objection was from the giant brewery Tooth & Co., which owned the Chatswood Hotel. We won the case in 1948, and ours would be the first new hotel licence to be allowed into the area for over 50 years. We were not home yet. Gaining council approval would then prove an extraordinary ten-year saga.

Meanwhile, elated with our success in building the small temporary bar, my brothers and I decided to build three houses on land in Sans Souci which had been left to us by our father. If we could make a success of this, we could further assess our chances of building the new hotel at Chatswood. After all, our plans for Chatswood, at that stage, were not too grand – it was only a small site. Charlie was to supervise the building and I was to look after all the administration for building, racing and the hotel, as well as chase building supplies and liquor. These were both in short supply and hard to get.

We also bought a small country hotel at a town called Neville, some 25 kilometres out of Blayney, and Jack was to take control of this. This was very hard on Jack, as he had to drive to Sydney twice a week for the races – on Saturdays and Wednesdays – 1600 kilometres every week.

We also invested in properties in Milsons Point, North Sydney, Willoughby and other areas, but none was better than the glorious 'Greencliffe' site on the Kirribilli waterfront. It was the last harbourside site close to the bridge that had not been resumed to make way for the bridge. However, this was in the days before Sydney Harbour featured the world famous Opera House, a time when Kirribilli was not regarded as an exclusive area. Having learnt to swim right in front of 'Greencliffe' in the harbour, we knew the large site well. We had also rented a garage on the property. When Mr Kleemo, the jeweller who owned 'Greencliffe', came to us looking to sell, we knew we had to buy it – at its price of £8500.

Although it had a rundown block of flats on it, I always knew the 'Greencliffe' site was destined to be something special. In the decade after World War II rents were controlled, but even after that we let the little block of flats there run itself, with rents remaining low. Eventually they were so low that they qualified as low-cost housing – enabling all the special-rate concessions that came with that – despite the fact that 'Greencliffe' had one of the best views in Sydney!

Every now and then I still run into people who say, 'Remember us? We were your tenants at Kirribilli when we first married. It was just fantastic to live there so cheaply, with the best view in Sydney.' I can only agree, as this site was to become my home 50 years later. Every day I still appreciate the amazing views of the Opera House, city, bridge and harbour.

—

Running all the business affairs, I held the family purse strings – and I was quite tough on Charlie, Jack and myself. I wrote everything down and kept a tight rein on expenses, tallying each of our accounts. However, I was single and quite frugal, so I didn't have anywhere near the expenses of Charlie or Jack with their respective families. Soon the books became quite imbalanced, and I realised it was a stupid exercise that could only cause tension later. We were either partners in everything, or not at all. I decided to tear up these drawings reconciliations, and from then on I never worried about what either of my brothers spent.

The three cottages at Sans Souci were built for £2500. Charlie was a tremendous self-taught builder. He was slow but thorough, would pick up his own materials, check everything and pass nothing by his tradesmen if it was not 100 per cent correct. We had not set out to make a profit but to gain building experience, but we ended up selling the three cottages for approximately £9000, earning us a windfall profit. What a bonanza.

Things at the races were improving too, even though in those days we had no pricing service. Then Mick Bartley – or 'Melbourne Mick', as he came to be known – arrived on the scene. He approached me and offered a pricing service to give us the fluctuations on all the Melbourne races, asking a staggering £20 fee per meeting. This was a time when the basic wage was about £5 a week. Both Charlie and Jack immediately dismissed it, but I was interested to see more. Mick offered me a free trial for one day and it proved a great success.

Mick had runners at the Melbourne courses who would write down the markets from the bookies' boards, run from the track and cycle to a nearby house, where these price fluctuations would be phoned through to a Sydney house near the course. From there, another small team of runners would bring the pricing information to us on course. This would happen eight or ten times a race. Mick's pricing service became very important, and this was the beginning of a long friendship with him.

Jack, who had found his niche in bookmaking, was the first to get to the Paddock at Moorefield, Rosehill and Canterbury. He was soon followed by Charlie and me, and both of us were then promoted to the Paddock at Royal Randwick in 1949. It seemed to us that we had gone just about as far as we could go. We were successful at racing and were in the top enclosures. We had our hotel licence approved for relocation. There was no trouble anywhere and we were 'on top of the world'. Jack, having had his home property resumed, had settled in well in the country, and Charlie had found his niche in building.

And I was now a practising barrister-at-law, keeping Wednesday afternoons and Saturdays free for racing, where I worked on the stand with Charlie. When I graduated in 1948 my mother and the rest of the family were so proud. I was the only Waterhouse to have attained a university degree, and over the years Jack would often say, 'Don't ask me, talk to Billy – he is a BA, LLB!'

5

An Innocent Abroad

IN 1950, I was 28 years old, six-foot-four tall (1.92 metres), dark and had a smooth patter – but I had never been serious with any girl. My two brothers had married and were producing heirs. Most of my friends were either married or else forever falling in love. Neville Wran was my best friend. With every new girlfriend, Neville would come up with stars in his eyes and say, 'I'm in love, I'm in love – this is the real thing!' I enjoyed a girl's company as much as anyone and would cheekily flirt with any woman I fancied, but I had never been smitten.

I think the reason was simple. Unlike all of my friends, I had never taken a girl out in the daytime. I usually went out on Saturday and Sunday nights, but I always spent the daylight hours on Saturday at the races, while on Sunday most of the day was spent balancing the books and preparing the turnover tax and the clients' results for settling on the Monday. I had stumbled on the secret of a perpetual life of bachelor bliss.

On one settling day, Jack Muir, a bookmaking friend, tried to force my hand by giving me a return cruise-ship ticket to London instead of the cash he owed me. I was taken aback and asked what in the hell he thought he was doing. He replied that I had never had a real holiday in my life, that he was going to England in June with a solicitor friend and that I should join them. After a few days, I decided to accompany them. In all my life I had never once thought of travelling anywhere, least of all overseas. I had lived on work, work and more work.

But ten days before our departure, my mother had a stroke. The ship sailed without me. Thankfully, two or three days later my mother's health improved and soon she was fully recovered. I was disappointed at missing the ship and doing my money cold.

Later that week I had a free morning from court and was striding down Elizabeth Street from my legal chambers when I bumped into another friend, Lionel Murphy, who was also then a young barrister.

'Where are you off to?' he asked.

'I'm going down to Thomas Cook & Son to book a passage to England!' I told him.

At first he thought I was kidding but when he saw I was serious, he impulsively decided to go with me. Together we went down to Martin Place and booked our passage on the P&O liner *Strathaird*, which was due to leave Sydney on the second-last Friday in October. I picked that date because I had never won on Melbourne Cup Day, the first Tuesday in November, and I wanted to be well away on the high seas.

The weeks slipped by and Jack Muir came back and enthused over his trip to London. Then the fickle finger of fate intervened. Jack was married but separated. His estranged wife had had a car accident and was charged with manslaughter. As a young barrister, I was delighted to be offered the case, but I told Jack he should get someone else as I couldn't miss the boat a second time. He asked me to start the case anyway, and someone else could finish it if necessary.

The case started on the Monday and I was assured it would last two days at most. The ship was due to sail at midday on Friday. However, the case had still not finished by Thursday night but only required a few arguments on Friday. My sister, Betty, had packed my clothing in a large travelling trunk – 1.5 metres high and 90 centimetres across. I took it down to the wharf on Thursday evening with Lionel.

I assured Lionel I would catch the boat but was still in court when the ship sailed – with my trunk on board. I got bogged down with racing the next week, so in the end I flew to Perth a week later, where I found Lionel, who had expected me in Melbourne and then Adelaide, packing to leave the ship as he had given up on me. He was homesick and lonely but needed little encouragement to stay. I heard Comic Court win the Melbourne Cup whilst on the Indian Ocean.

The next month was idyllic, full of fun and excitement. Lionel, like me, had a large wardrobe. In those days you dressed for dinner every night, in either a dinner suit or white tuxedo, and every evening was a party night. The ships were always full as air travel was only just starting. A first-class single cabin cost £300 from Sydney to London, the same price as an air ticket.

The trip from Perth to London took four weeks. We travelled via Colombo, Bombay, Aden and Port Said, the Suez Canal and Marseilles – passing the erupting Mount Etna on the way – then sailed on to London. Visiting these places topped off a marvellous, glorious month.

On my first morning at sea Lionel asked me over breakfast what my plans were. I was quite definite: 'Nothing – absolutely nothing. I'm going to go up on deck, find a nice comfortable deckchair and just sit there and watch the water and the world go by.'

Lionel just gave a half-smile and said, 'I'll be in the lounge with a book if you want me.'

I headed for a deckchair and settled in for the morning. After just five minutes I couldn't take any more inactivity. I went looking for Lionel, who had been waiting for me. He knew me better than I knew myself, and he'd been on his own for ten days before I arrived. I realised I was a stranger to the art of relaxation. The ocean voyage taught me a tremendous lesson: how to unwind. By the end I actually could go and sit in that deckchair and enjoy watching the ocean blue.

Lionel was a great chap – kind, considerate, a brilliant brain and a good conversationalist who could talk on any subject with his tremendous general knowledge. He was shy and most conscious of his large nose, but he had a beautiful speaking voice, which gave him a good start in any female company. We knew each other well, he loved meeting pretty girls when we went out together in our undergraduate days, and we complemented each other well.

When we reached Marseilles I phoned home and found that my mother had had another stroke. This time she was desperately ill and not expected to live. Betty told me that she was unconscious and would probably not last more than one or two days.

I phoned all the airlines to get on the first flight home, which turned out to be leaving London the following Wednesday. Our ship was due in London on the Sunday evening, so I remained on board. I had an awful problem with my large travelling trunk. It was too big to take on a plane and P&O would not take unaccompanied baggage. I slipped the ship's agent £5 and he fixed it for my baggage to go back on another ship leaving London on the Tuesday.

Arriving in London, Lionel and I went to the Regent Palace Hotel near Piccadilly Circus. The tariff was £1 per night, including a full breakfast. I phoned home that Sunday night and my mother was still alive, but her condition was unchanged. There was nothing I could do. I had two days – Monday and Tuesday – in which to see London. I walked everywhere. I have since been back to London many times over the years but I think I saw more in those two days than on any other trip.

I phoned home again on the Monday evening and Mum was just the same. I rang again the next night and was overjoyed to be told she had passed the crisis and was miraculously out of danger. Betty told me not to come back, that our mother was fully alert and had insisted I finish my holiday.

Then I realised I had no clothes – my trunk had gone on the ship that same day – I had just an airline overnight bag with two clean shirts, two sets of underwear and shaving gear. And an airline ticket, which had taken a great deal of wrangling to obtain. I spoke to Lionel and we decided to continue our holiday and eventually fly back to Australia. We'd hire a car and spend a fortnight driving through England, Wales and Scotland, and then have a month in Europe and a month in the United States, arriving back in either late February or early March.

We enjoyed our trip through the British countryside and were scheduled to arrive in Dover late on our last day in England to catch the boat-train to Calais that night. We had met two Australian girls, dentists, on the ship to Europe and had agreed to meet up in Paris. I had done most of the wintry driving from Edinburgh down to near London as I knew Lionel wasn't an experienced driver, but finally, exhausted from late-night partying with a pretty girl, I let him take over for the last part of the night drive to Dover. I fell asleep in the front passenger seat.

I awoke two days later in a specialist hospital. Ice had formed on the road and Lionel had run off into a brick wall built to stop cars going over the cliff. Being asleep and without a seatbelt, I had gone straight through the windscreen. The locals had pulled Lionel from the car – he wasn't too badly injured, but they had looked at me and said, 'He's dead.' They left me half in the car and half on the bonnet. The ambulance arrived and the officers were told I was 'gone'.

The snow, however, was to save me. A village policeman who was checking the wreck noticed that the snow near my nose and mouth was melting. He realised I was still breathing.

He quickly stopped the ambulance from leaving and I was placed inside. I was unconscious and looked pretty bad. You couldn't touch anywhere on my face where it wasn't lacerated. My facial flesh was completely severed in two places and you could put your fingers through the holes. My right jaw was shattered in five places, and I had lost teeth, broken several ribs and injured my kneecap. The local Maidstone hospital didn't want to touch me with my serious injuries and sent me to East Grinstead Memorial Hospital.

I was so lucky as East Grinstead was just the right place for me. I was under the supervision of a New Zealander – Dr Sir Archibald McIndoe, a medical legend and pioneer in plastic surgery. He was known even in Australia, as was this air force hospital, which specialised in burns, broken jaws and plastic surgery. It was for the RAF and only took a few emergency civilian cases.

To the day I die, I will never forget the morning I came to in the hospital ward. I couldn't move. I had no feeling anywhere in my body. My eyes eventually focused, and in the beds around me I saw the weirdest collection of 'monsters'. The ward was mainly plastic surgery cases, all of whom looked horrific. One poor individual had fallen into a vat of boiling oil.

After an eternity I gingerly managed to get one hand up to my face because I knew something there was terribly wrong. My hand found the wire that was holding my jaws together. I just couldn't bear to touch the rest of my face. I panicked. I couldn't feel my feet – I thought I had no legs. I realised my life was ruined and I would have to live the rest of my life in a wheelchair – if I was lucky. No, I decided, I would rather be dead.

Lionel, meanwhile, had accompanied me in the ambulance to hospital. He had a few bumps on him and, on examination, reference was made to his nose. The upshot was that they decided to operate and perform cosmetic surgery on his unfortunate nose. Lionel couldn't believe his luck. The dressing was to stay on for three or four weeks.

It was mid-December, and one of the girls whom we were to meet in France came down from London to see me. She was told my ward and bed number but didn't recognise me and was about to leave when a nurse pointed me out to her.

At first it was dreadful. Around five every afternoon I would get a slight throb on each side of my head, just above my ears. Each throb would move up my head and be a little harder than the one before, until they became two sledgehammers at the crown of my head. It was excruciating and unbearable. At that stage I couldn't talk at all, with my jaws wired together and in such pain, but when I pressed the bell the sisters would come and wheel me to an isolation ward where they would inject me with morphine. That did not stop the sledgehammers but it stopped the pain, and I remember thinking how we had tricked the demons in my head. Yet I worried each time that I would become a morphine addict.

With my jaws wired up, I had to 'eat' through a rubber tube. I was fed soup – three courses of soup. The trouble was that whilst I knew the rubber tube must have been hygienically cleaned, I also knew it would have been in any and everyone's mouth. The thought was enough to make me physically ill, and this was the real worry. If a jaw case were to be sick, the wiring would have to be cut very quickly to avoid choking. Each time a meal was brought to me I would sit and look at it and say to myself over and over, 'I will not be sick, I will not be sick,' and then slowly – ever so slowly – I would start to eat, or rather suck, my meal.

We spent the festive season in hospital. However, disaster struck Lionel. His dressing moved. The nose should have been immediately reset but all the senior surgeons were away for Christmas, and by the time one of them returned it was too late. Poor Lionel had had enough and left with his nose in a far worse state.

—

After six weeks I was gradually improving and I asked permission to have a break in London. Although walking with a limp, I felt fine and the doctors agreed – on the condition that I came back in a couple of weeks to have some more plastic surgery on my face. I never made it back there. As my cockiness got the better of me, after a day in London I decided to fly to Paris. Lionel was going to join me two days later.

It was Friday night in Paris, and so I went to the Folies Bergère. The show had started with its beautiful girls when I nearly passed out. An awful realisation struck me: I should never have left the hospital. I felt I had to return immediately. I had overdone it by flying to France and going out the first night. I somehow made it back to my hotel.

When I woke the next morning I felt terrible. I couldn't move. I was sweating and shaking and couldn't get out of bed. I actually thought I was dying. I wallowed in self-pity and didn't move from that bed all day and night. The next morning I was still as weak as a kitten but I knew I had to eat. I made my way along the corridor, holding onto the wall for support, into the lift and down to the restaurant, which fortunately was part of the foyer. I dropped into the first chair I saw and ordered an omelette. I could only eat a little but immediately I felt some strength returning.

Lionel turned up. I was on the mend and so early the next week we decided to travel by coach – the cheapest way – to the French Riviera. It was the middle of winter and quite chilly but we loved it. We went to the fabled Monte Carlo Casino. I won on the first night – not much, but enough to cover my costs – whereas Lionel did his bank. He wanted to know how I had won when he had lost. Lionel was one of the most intelligent people I had ever met, but a gambler he was not. He had been one of the worst poker players at university and he was no better at roulette. He had gone to the table to win, whereas I had only wanted to buy time to enjoy the night by playing the odds – if I lost my money it would be the price of our enjoyable evening.

In continental roulette, with only one zero, the house has less than 1.5 per cent margin going for it instead of the normal three or even six per cent. Playing on the law of averages and waiting for, say, three odd numbers in a row, or three black or three under, I would then wager a small amount on the opposite. I accumulated a small pot and then having watched a certain number – say, the house zero – I would place a small part of my winnings on that number. During the night, with a little luck, I had managed to win on three of these selected numbers. As they paid the odds of 33/1, I finished comparatively well in front.

Lionel was fascinated to learn that my only gambling was with the 'house' money – that is, with my winnings. I had gone there not to win but to allow for a gradual loss, so as to last as long as I could through the evening. On this occasion, however, I had won.

As we left I tried to explain percentages to Lionel: that red and black were very close to a 50 per cent chance each, just like an even-money shot at the races. Lionel was wide awake and wanted it explained in detail, however I was tired and worn out from concentrating on the numbers all night. I suggested we talk about it in the morning. At breakfast, Lionel told me he had stayed up and worked out all the odds for himself. And he was absolutely correct, showing his truly brilliant brain.

Our next stop was to be Rome, but I wasn't that well and decided to let Lionel go ahead. I wanted to go where I would be forced to do nothing – just relax and rest. Lionel flew to Rome and I flew to Geneva. I went to a travel agent to book into Saint Moritz, which seemed the perfect place as I had never skied and certainly couldn't now, but the agent talked me into going to Davos, saying it was more fun for the younger generation. So I went by train to Davos and the beautiful Palace Hotel.

I had never seen anything like it. The hotel was luxurious and the town a picture postcard. In the morning I was put at a table of British skiers, who were good company. But as soon as breakfast was finished everyone disappeared. As I didn't ski there was absolutely no one to talk to, drink with or even look at.

Looking out the window, I saw the beginners' ski school on a very gentle slope. I decided to join the class, bad knee or not. I had to hire everything. Usually you can't hire your clothing but they made an exception for me. I then hotfooted it across to the ski class. It was marvellous. I fell but it was impossible to hurt yourself in the soft, powdery snow. I was a quick learner and by the end of the lesson I wasn't falling that much – I couldn't wait to get back for the afternoon session.

Back at the hotel, when I went to get my room key there was this very attractive green-eyed brunette, Gretel, on reception. She handed me my key and said I was the only Australian registered at the hotel, then she asked why I'd come to Davos. I couldn't help my mischievous humour and replied that I was the Australian skiing champion and that I had been asked to come to Europe to teach them some new tricks as their standards had slipped, probably because of the war. I didn't for a second think that she would believe me.

On the contrary, Gretel was immediately impressed and said she would like to go skiing with me. I suggested we discuss it over dinner that night. But no, she would be working on reception that night, and the hotel did not like staff fraternising with the guests. After a little coaxing, it was agreed that we would have dinner at a little restaurant she knew, some other night after we had skied. I felt as though I had won the lottery.

Shortly after, Gretel phoned my room to say that she had arranged to have the afternoon off after all, and we could ski and have dinner that night. I nearly came through the phone agreeing. Immediately after lunch, I was ready and waiting and we set off into the wild white yonder. Of course, I had no intention of skiing – I just wanted to take Gretel out. When the time came to ski, I would find some excuse to avoid it. We walked along the quaint little streets until we came to the small cable funicular train that takes you up the mountain.

Gretel took me on a ski lift to the top of the Parsenn, then the world's longest ski run. Novices would not dare go anywhere near the Parsenn. I was taken to the top because Gretel believed my baloney that I was a ski champ. Riding the T-bar was no trouble with Gretel and I holding onto each other.

The top of the Parsenn was like the top of the world. Through a break in the clouds, you could see land far below. But I couldn't look down because to me it was a sheer drop.

I knew I had to get out of this situation. I took out my finger, wet it in my mouth, held it up and timidly said, 'I can't ski today – I'm a perfectionist and the conditions are not right for me.'

Gretel looked at me in amazement. 'But there is no other way down!'

Turning, I saw the T-bar of the ski lift disappearing over the precipice. It was freezing but I was sweating profusely. The slope looked almost sheer but there was no choice.

Following Gretel, I gingerly started off with my left knee – my injured knee – almost touching my chin. My shoulder became my brake. Whenever I fell, all I had to do was take my shoulder out of the snow and I'd be upright again. My real worry was that if I ever *really* fell, I would finish up as the biggest snowball ever.

I don't know how long it took to get down, but I would never have made it without Gretel's support. She was furious, however, and once we got back she wouldn't even look at me. Needless to say, there was no dinner.

Completely crushed, I decided to head for Rome. Lionel and I had no set itinerary except that we had to be back in London around the end of January to leave for New York. So I went to Rome on my own, walking, or rather limping, everywhere. I had studied Roman antiquities at Sydney University as part of the Latin course and had found it unbelievably boring, but seeing all this in person was exciting. I loved history and could almost imagine myself back in olden times.

I stayed at a hotel on the world-famous Via Veneto near the Spanish Steps and got talking to an attractive young lady while in the cocktail bar on my first night. We got along splendidly, although I didn't speak Italian and her English was very weak. Three hours later, I discovered I had wined, dined and seduced a 'lady of the night'. She must have thought I was the strangest nut she had ever met.

The next day was Sunday and, thoroughly chastened, I decided to walk around parts of the old walled city. Off I set, and eventually I was accosted by a chap who spoke to me in Italian. When I shook my head he addressed me in French. Now, my French was poor but I had studied it for five years at high school. I had been able to make myself understood, although poorly, in both Paris and Nice. The man asked me, of all things, where Rome's black market was. He was from the country and wanted to buy things unprocurable in the countryside and had only two days to do it. I apologised that I was a foreigner and didn't know Rome. He went on his way and I on mine.

Half an hour later I was in a poor section of the city and was approached by an American. He said he was a seaman who had to leave later that afternoon. He had a half-a-dozen suit lengths that were unprocurable in Italy and worth a small fortune. He had to sell them as he was short of money, and this was his only chance. Could I help him? I began explaining I was a tourist, when who should be walking along but my earlier 'friend'. I told the American this chap was seeking the black market but was Italian and didn't speak English. In my limited French, I asked the Italian if he could help the American.

The two men were very able, smooth and extremely logical. Unfortunately for them, I was a young barrister who had spent around twelve years at the racetrack and recognised all the signs of a good con. They were relying on my greed and trying to get me to act as a middle man: to give the American money for the suit material and then to wait for the Italian to turn up the next day. Of course, he would never turn up and I would be left with the worthless cloth and out of pocket.

Having nothing better to do, I decided to play the role right out. They asked me to join them for a drink to try to work something out. With hindsight, I realise how crazy I was, but to be in the middle of a classic con with real professionals was too much for me to resist. We came upon a quiet little *ristorante* and for the next two hours I accommodated them by translating all their questions and answers to each other.

I let them play the scene out to the end, thinking that perhaps they would produce something like a rabbit out of a hat. Of course, they had nothing else – the trick had to work quickly or would not work at all. I'd eventually had enough and said I had to go. I had succeeded in wasting their best working day – Sunday – and by their demeanour I belatedly realised that they probably felt like doing me over. I was young and tall but, despite my injuries, I made sure I walked away firmly, feeling hatred behind me. I decided never to be so foolish again.

—

I'd had enough of Rome and headed north. I wanted to see Wiesbaden because my maternal great-grandmother had emigrated from there, and I also wanted to see the carnival at Cologne. To get to Wiesbaden I flew to Frankfurt, staying overnight to catch the coach at midday.

Something was about to happen that would change my whole life. I might sound like a lecherous womaniser, but this wasn't the case. It was as though I had been let out of school and wanted to play. All my life I had rigorously regimented myself. I had never allowed myself the luxury of female company for company's sake. I was even 21 before I lost my virginity. It was not that I didn't try, but work came first. Now, on holiday, I was completely without any work obligations and all I had to do was have fun.

I went to the bus stop about twenty minutes before the Wiesbaden bus was due. No one was there. After ten minutes an attractive young lady turned up and we had a friendly chat. Then about 50 people appeared just as the bus pulled in. After being the first there, I was last onto the bus, which was now pretty full, but as I walked down the aisle I saw the young lady, Ilse, had saved me a seat next to her.

During the trip I got to know Ilse Lehtpere quite well. She was the sole survivor from her family. Her father, mother, brothers, sisters, uncles, aunts and cousins had all died, either at the front, through Allied bombings or through concentration camps. The German people had also suffered badly in the war, with seven million dying, including one and a half million civilians. Ilse had one distant relative left and was visiting her in Wiesbaden. Work was rationed and Ilse could work just one week in two. She had the day off and was returning to Frankfurt at 11.30 that night. She agreed to join me for dinner and a visit to the casino before she left.

I checked into my hotel and did a rapid run around the delightful old town before meeting Ilse at six. We had an early dinner and went on to the gambling tables. I soon tired of Ilse's idea of gambling. I was winning, but not as fast as she was losing. It was the old story – she wanted to win, and the odds are stacked against this type of amateur player. So, after the allocated bank had disappeared, I suggested we go and see the rest of the town. Once outside, I told her I wanted to go back to my hotel.

'What for?' Ilse asked.

'I'm cold and want a scarf.'

We went back to the hotel lobby, but Ilse soon realised my ploy and refused to accompany me to my room to get my imaginary scarf. In a firm but friendly voice, she said, 'No!' She meant it and I knew she meant it.

Now, if ever I am to be awarded marks for a good facet of my character, it will be that I have an even temperament with girls. A true gambler accepts any loss with equanimity, but at the time I felt dudded and wanted to cut away. It had been an expensive and fruitless night. We went walking and came to a small bar and went in to have 'zwei cognacs'. Ilse asked when I was leaving and I naively made a shocking blunder.

I said I was off on Saturday to Cologne for a week and suggested she come along. Having been rejected by her only a little earlier, I knew there was no way she would accept, otherwise I would never have asked her. I could think of nothing worse than going away with a girl and being one-on-one with her 24 hours a day. I had always gone home alone after a night out.

I felt like a stunned mullet when, slowly, carefully, and obviously thinking deeply, she replied, 'Yes . . . that might be good for me. I have next week off and there is a train from Frankfurt to Wiesbaden on Saturday morning. I am sure I would enjoy myself.'

All merriment left me. I had only wanted a one-night stand and had no intention of going away with Ilse.

I eventually took Ilse down to the station, politely put her on the night train back to Frankfurt and arranged to meet her on the Saturday morning, when she would come by train.

I went back to the hotel feeling quite miserable. I wasn't going to turn up, yet I knew she was looking forward to her holiday. All Friday I worried. I didn't have a phone number to ring and stop her, I didn't have an address to write and apologise, but I knew there was no way I would be meeting that train. I certainly didn't want to be tied down with a girl for days on end.

However, at ten on Saturday morning I found myself with my bag packed waiting at the station. My only hope – which grew stronger all the time – was that Ilse would have had a change of heart and not turn up. She was obviously not a loose girl.

Ilse bounced off the train with the first batch of people, and when she saw me her face broke into a beautiful smile. I didn't know until later, but this was her very first holiday. I hadn't even bought train tickets, but she had phoned and reserved them so we went straight to our private cabin on the train. It was obvious she was not going to let anything happen in the cabin; far from being annoyed, I was actually relieved as I felt uneasy being one-on-one with a girl in daytime.

Ilse must have sensed something wrong and suggested we have a drink. I produced a special bottle of wine I had fortunately bought in Italy to take back to Australia. She was flirtatious all the way to Cologne, but every time I responded I was gently but firmly rejected.

Approaching Cologne, Ilse asked where we were staying. I said I had not booked anywhere and we could pick out the nicest hotel we saw. A look of horror came over her. She couldn't contain herself and blurted out, 'You fool! Don't you know that Cologne was almost destroyed during the war? There are so few hotels that you must book well in advance!'

I told her not to worry, that we would find a room somewhere. She was distraught. She said this was impossible, absolutely impossible. She then said the hotel I had stayed at in Wiesbaden was the finest in town and would not have let me go to Cologne without a booking. I told her they had indeed suggested a hotel, the Excelsior, and wanted to book it for me, but I had declined.

Nevertheless, Ilse insisted we went to the Excelsior and, sure enough, I had a reservation there – a beautiful suite. It was the most luxurious room I had ever been in. There was also a little second bedroom, obviously for a travelling maid. My admiration for German efficiency was cemented that day. Without Ilse I never would have gone to that hotel, and without that booking we would have been finished, as the town was indeed booked out.

Ilse wanted a bath and of course closed the door behind her. A few minutes later, to my amazement, she called out, 'Willy, could you please scrub my back?' That was the turning point in our relationship and Ilse was a beautiful lover.

When we went out on the town that evening, it soon became apparent that after the war there was a shortage of men and a surplus of girls, and that Ilse was prepared to repel all assaults on me – now her property. I had a truly marvellous time.

Later, back at the hotel, despite our new intimacy, Ilse said, 'Now you will want to sleep on your own – I will take the second room.' There was no way I was going to allow that. Yes, I did want to go to sleep on my own but beds meant nothing to me, and I quite firmly insisted that she take the big bed. Ilse was determined. She slept in the little room and joined me in the morning for breakfast.

We then went out to see the sights. The remarkable thing about Cologne was that almost the whole city was flattened, with one exception. The beautiful Dom, the cathedral that took 600 years to complete after work began in the Middle Ages, was not badly bombed and stood out in stark contrast to all around it. Climbing to the top, you could see for kilometres – and for kilometres there was desolation. I was in awe of the Allied bombers' precision in avoiding it – until an Australian wartime bombardier back in Sydney burst out laughing and told me it was simply that they couldn't hit it.

I found that when I was walking with Ilse people were very friendly to me. In London I had bought a trenchcoat that had a military bearing, as it was modelled on the 'great coat' used by English soldiers in World War I.

Ilse laughed gently and said, 'They think you are a German officer, a hero who has been badly injured during the war.'

I suddenly realised she was right. My face was badly cut and scarred, and I was walking with a limp. It was the sign of a proper Prussian officer to have a sabre scar on his face, as a mark of courage, and I certainly had enough to satisfy anyone. I played this up and loved using my best movie German, such as '*Jawohl*' and '*Gute Nacht, meine Damen, meine Herren*'. I would also click my heels in the best tradition of the cinema.

After four or five days, Ilse had to go back to Frankfurt. If she lost her job there would not be another. We exchanged addresses and promised to write. I took her to the station and put her on the train. Seeing her off, I was pleased to be on my own – I could have a ball. Of course, the train had hardly left the station when I realised I missed her. I missed her dreadfully. I was lonely and decided to pull out the next day. Even though I was almost 29, perhaps for the first time in my life I was in love. I would sincerely have denied it at the time, but never having experienced the symptoms, how was I to know?

Getting to know Ilse over those five days, I realised I had found a woman who was not only attractive but also strong, proud and intelligent. She had lost everything but had kept her dignity. She had earned my respect.

Ilse changed me forever. If it wasn't for Ilse, I don't think I would have ever married. It was the first time I had spent time with a girl day and night.

—

After Ilse, I decided to take an international train, crossing Germany and finishing up in Copenhagen. I then flew back to London to meet Lionel but was four days late. Instead of having a week in London before flying to the United States, I had only two days. I had asked a young lady I had met in Durham if she would like to come to London for the week before I left. She apparently had come down but, of course, as I had not returned to London on time, could not reach me at the hotel. I had no way of contacting her or knowing where she was. With only two days in London I went to the Prince of Wales Theatre in Leicester Square with another young lady, whom I had met by chance at the hotel. She had been principal 'boy' in one of those fabulous London pantomimes and was full of fun.

We arrived at the cinema after the film had started. The theatre was in near darkness, and before my eyes became accustomed, I felt uncomfortable – like something was boring into me. I looked to my left and found a pair of angry eyes belonging to the young lady from Durham. What were the odds not only of going to the same cinema but of actually sitting beside her? I gulped, speechless – but really, what could anyone say? And the young lady I had come in with now was wondering why I was not watching the screen. I felt terrible and had to sit through the whole show in a state of funk.

The next day, Lionel and I flew out to New York, which we found very expensive. England and Europe had been good value, as things were much cheaper than in Australia, but America was the reverse. We decided to go to a show on Broadway. We bought the last two tickets to *South Pacific*, with Mary Martin in the lead. The only problem was one seat was up the front and the other right up the back. I offered Lionel the chance to toss a coin for the good seat. He won and sat up the front. Despite my cramped location up 'in the gods', I loved every minute of the show – I had never seen anything like it and was thoroughly enchanted.

Lionel decided to head for home early and, armed with the extra currency which I had been able to buy from him, I spent a month touring the States, which I thoroughly enjoyed.

When a taxi driver heard I came from Australia, he said, 'Buddy, how come you speak American so good?'

He was satisfied when I replied, 'I have been practising.'

I went by train to Washington up to Philadelphia, across to Chicago. I visited all the museums and loved them. In Chicago there was a mining exhibition underground in an old disused mine right in the middle of town which was fascinating.

I then went on to Denver and Aspen, then Las Vegas, Los Angeles and finally San Francisco. I enjoyed all the cities, although Los Angeles was a bit of a disappointment. I made a mistake in picking a hotel in the centre of the city which was fairly dead, compared to Beverly Hills, and to top it off I had gone to Santa Anita and not backed a winner all day.

I flew out of San Francisco in a Qantas Constellation, the newest aircraft of the era. It took two days to reach Sydney, and on the flight I actually went to bed in the evening. What is now the overhead luggage compartment dropped down and formed a bunk. There were three stops: Hawaii, followed by then the smallest island imaginable – an atoll called Kanton Island – which was just a runway with a shed, and finally Nadi in Fiji.

The first things that struck me when I arrived back in Sydney were the customs officers' Australian accents, and the smallness of the office buildings in the city. I had thought they were so much bigger.

6

Love and Marriage

I CAME HOME to some disappointing news. Both my brothers had been demoted at the trotting track from the Paddock enclosure to the St Leger. No reason was given, but obviously the authorities suspected – but could not prove – unwanted liaisons between trotting stables and bookmakers. Over the years the trotting authorities had to battle with a bad public image, with the trots often referred to as the 'red hots'. After trotting had switched over to night racing in 1948, they tried hard to improve public acceptance. The demotions were obviously intended to show the authorities meant business, but they achieved nothing, except to draw a further division between the controllers of the sport and the bookmakers.

It wasn't that different to the position in New York State in 1936 when the authorities banned bookies from that arena forever. The sport had apparently deteriorated, and the authorities wanted to monopolise bookmaking through their totes to the punters' disadvantage, which only made things worse. Rather than abolishing bookmakers outright, the authorities should have sacked themselves – they were in charge but did not understand their industry.

Similarly, the trouble in Sydney really came down to the fact that amateurs were trying to run a professional sport. Completely underestimating the contribution of bookmaking to racing – the thrill of the battle between bookmaker and punter – these controllers simply looked upon the bookmaker as a necessary evil. He was there to be policed, punished and taxed. Bookmakers are not lilywhite and can certainly look after themselves in most situations, but usually they are not so stupid as to be crooks.

My father never tried to teach me anything about winning but he did teach me about not losing. One of his main lessons was to be on guard about the 'dead-un' tip. According to my father, far more money had been lost by bookmakers laying dead-uns than had been won. Unscrupulous punters often used the ploy simply to get better odds. The bookies I have known who departed suddenly from the game often did so through laying a supposed non-trier that won.

Contrary to what is so universally imagined, in my experience bookmakers are never the principals or organisers in a scam. Most punters blame their misfortune on anyone or anything but themselves. Some undoubtedly lose money on non-triers, but in my experience when a punter names a losing horse as a 'non-trier', nine times out of ten he is just trying to rationalise his own error of judgement.

I had no doubt that our trouble at the trots had been caused by a winning commission we had placed earlier in the season. There was a horse called Fellon that was owned, trained and driven by a young man named Lindsay McIntyre. McIntyre was a one-horse man and a battler. I had appeared for him as a barrister in some little case and he had told me about his trotter, which he had entered in the feature harness handicap at the Sydney Show on Easter Friday. I saw Fellon clearly beat Dixie Beau in the final, but since it was the Easter Show there had been no betting.

McIntyre had asked me then if I would put a commission on for him. He wanted me to place his bets when he was ready to back Fellon at a Harold Park meeting. I soon forgot our conversation. Two years later, Lindsay McIntyre knocked at the door of my legal chambers and said tomorrow was the night to run the commission on Fellon.

I strongly advised him against backing it, as I knew it hadn't run a place for over a year. McIntyre just laughed and said, 'I'll win for sure. I've had trouble with its legs but I've got the horse right at its top again.' I still asked to be relieved of my obligation and tried to persuade him not to put his good money on his nag.

He simply said, 'Remember the time Fellon beat Dixie Beau? I could beat him again off the mark.'

As it happened, Dixie Beau was also entered at the same Harold Park meeting. Whereas Fellon was in the weakest race of the night, Dixie Beau was the clear favourite in the strongest – the feature race. If McIntyre was right, then his horse was the greatest certainty ever. I realised that I had the opportunity of a lifetime. The commission was only £650 and I was the only person who knew.

I contacted everyone I could think of who might be interested in helping. I think I had about 50 people. There were three enclosures in those days, all with plenty of bookies. We backed the horse in from 33/1 to 5/2. In the race it was last with a lap to go when he made his run along the outside rail – he ran around the field and bolted in by almost half the length of the straight!

There was an immediate uproar. The next day, *The Sydney Morning Herald* spoke of the largest plunge since night trotting began. There were murmurings of a ring-in, boat race, doping, fix and so on. When the smoke of battle had settled, I had a good talk with my brothers and we decided to not take commissions to back a horse with on-course bookmakers ever again. Although we had a batch of winning tickets, McIntyre's bets were entitled to be paid the top odds. To my mind, our winnings – what was left over – were not commensurate with the bad publicity, innuendo and demotion that came with it.

The five leading bookmakers who had backed Fellon, including my brothers Jack and Charlie, as well as Jack Muir, were demoted to the St Leger. It took a full year and I had to do a lot of PR work before the trotting club relented and reinstated the demoted bookies back to the Paddock.

I feel sure that my decision to avoid commissions saved me from untold troubles later on when I became a licensed bookmaker. Bookies are a hard, tough, capable lot and know how to squeal if you touch the nerve in their pockets – especially if they think they have been tricked. Most of us love to hear a little scandal, and many are too ready to believe what they are told. Once it goes to the next level – the stewards and even the racing committees – it becomes very dangerous, as they are in a position of complete power over your livelihood, not only in the allocation of stands but in the issuing of licences. You can quickly find yourself having to prove your innocence – even though you are not in any way involved in any skulduggery.

—

Trotting was a side issue. My brothers and I were establishing ourselves at the races and concentrating on our two small hotels: the temporary bar of the Imperial at Milsons Point and the Neville Hotel, which Jack looked after. We were experimenting with building and I was also working as a barrister.

We were very busy but contented. I was not married but had great friends. Neville Wran and I were very close in the city, and Jack Muir and I, through the Fellon incident, became closer at the track. And I shared barristers' chambers with Johnny Milford. They were all very different men, so I had a varied and interesting life. Milford had gone through law school with me and had worked as a clerk at the races, along with my other university pals. Of all my mates, Neville was fiercely loyal and was my closest friend.

Neville had settled in with a good firm of lawyers – Bartier, Perry and Purcell – and was becoming established. Around this time he excitedly told me he had heard a new singer. When I said I'd never heard of him, he replied, 'Nobody has, but I'll guarantee he will be as big as Crosby or Sinatra. I think I'll start a fan club. It'll be huge.' Not being the least interested in this, I pooh-poohed the thought. The singer was Elvis Presley.

Neville had no political allegiance, but over coffee one morning we were talking of our futures and how to get legal work. It was a time when a few barristers were also standing as political candidates and being elected into parliament. We were discussing joining a political party when I said I thought that not only would the Labor Party give us a better chance of running for a seat in parliament, but it would also be more likely to give us legal work. That was the clincher. Whereas I never got around to it, Neville joined the Double Bay branch of the ALP the next week. From there he went on to become one of the longest-serving and most successful premiers of New South Wales. I sometimes wonder what would have happened if we had decided to join the Liberal Party.

Funnily enough, I had also recommended the Labor Party to Lionel Murphy. It was not that I was such a Labor man myself, but I sincerely thought the opportunities with the ALP would be much better for us young barristers.

An incident occurred in the early 1950s which could have brought me undone, but for my father's teachings. My barrister mate Johnny Milford had an 'in' at the Sydney Town Hall, where some aldermen were running a racket with the granting of fruit barrow licences in the city. Johnny told me he could arrange some barrow licences for a backhanded payment. Initially, I jumped with excitement at the chance of easy money. Then I thought of what my father had often told me: 'If greed is your motivation, don't do it.' As greed could be the only reason, I knocked it back.

Just as well. A few months later there was a public scandal as the racket was exposed. Police moved in and charges were laid.

—

1951 and 1952 were years of great activity for my brothers and me. At the time we thought we had arrived but, looking back, I realise that we were simply laying the groundwork for things to come.

Charlie and Jack operated from the same betting ring in the Paddock on interstate races and were continuously in competition with each other. They also had great rivalries with other bookies, especially Arthur Browning, who had done so much to popularise interstate fielding.

The clubs decided to put in one interstate bookie's stand on the Rails, which was offered to Jack, while Charlie stayed in the Paddock. Everyone thought Jack had made a mistake in leaving the other interstate bookies in the main ring, but he was to prove them all wrong. Incredibly, in a short time Jack's holdings grew to be the greatest on the racecourse, which meant he was the biggest bookie in Australia. Freddy Angles told me he thought Jack was the biggest in the world. Jack pioneered the big betting era in Sydney. When he put a price against a horse, anyone was entitled to back it to win £10,000, no matter what race, or price. In those days £10,000 was a hell of a bet.

We were still having trouble all this time with the relocation of our Milsons Point hotel. Whilst the licensing court had approved of the transfer of our licence to Chatswood back in 1948, Willoughby Council rejected our plans fifteen to nil. I couldn't believe it. Then I learned that the mayor was spending a lot of time at the local brewery-linked hotel, the Hotel Chatswood. It began a tough, long decade of campaigning. I lobbied at the next three council elections and spent countless hours with numerous and prospective aldermen. For years this tedious, boring grind just became more laborious, but I believed perseverance would overcome even the toughest opponents. We finally won council approval in late 1958. We started building the Hotel Charles at Chatswood immediately.

While this seemingly endless fight was continuing, we had bought an old, burnt-out hotel in Coonamble in central New South Wales. Its licence could be moved anywhere in the state except the Sydney metropolitan area, so Charlie and I sought out a good regional hotel site. I finally found a few weatherboard houses and vacant paddocks at Fairy Meadow, a growing suburb of Wollongong, south of Sydney.

To save money I did the legal work to move the licence. This meant I regularly had to take a light plane to Coonamble; it arrived at the dirt airstrip at around 9.30 am and left an hour later. As it was usually just a short court hearing and the airstrip was about ten minutes from town, I would always try to get back for the plane, but never once did I catch that return flight. I would then spend the day sitting on the big, wide country hotel veranda, which had a view right up the main street. It was like being on a movie set, watching young men wearing Akubra hats and riding bareback race madly up and down the street, yahooing and shouting just for the fun of it.

Strangely, our Fairy Meadow application went smoothly through the licensing court and the Wollongong City Council. We were getting more confident with our building and decided that as we couldn't get permission to start our hotel in Sydney, we would begin the hotel at Wollongong. Charlie had started work on a duplex house at Lane Cove and also a small block of flats at the harbourside suburb of Woolwich. We started planning for what would be a big job.

—

In the early 1950s I had bought my first new car. The Jaguar XK120 roadster had just come out. It was billed as the fastest production car in the world – the 120 referred to its top speed in miles. I fell in love with its graceful and stylish lines and wanted it in white. Only an iridescent blue one was available, and the next order would be subject to a £50 price rise, so I happily settled for the blue one. At the time, it was one of only three in Sydney. The car cost around £1900 – the average wage in those days was around £4 a week. I could have bought a small house for what the car cost – yet I still knew it was worth it.

I was never a 'rev head' but I did like to drive fast, and this was a matter of style – which no doubt also helped my chances with the girls. I had the XK120 for about five years, until my daughter, Louise, was born. I then bought a big American Dodge. I liked the spaciousness of the American cars and I thought they were good value for money. I later bought second-hand Cadillacs for their value and had them converted to right-hand drive. When I had the Jaguar I could take it to town, park it anywhere near my chambers and leave it there all day long. For that matter, you could park anywhere in the city – there were no parking police or restrictions and there was always plenty of parking space.

I was leading the life of Riley. I was a young bachelor with the best car in town, out nearly every other night, and usually with a different girl. I had some lovely girlfriends, including the gorgeous Maide Hahn, who was runner-up in the Miss Australia contest.

I worked hard, seven days a week. I happened upon the ideal profession in law, as it allowed me to regulate my work around the races. In those days a barrister was inaccessible to the public – appointments had to be made through a solicitor. In court, the barrister could decide if a hearing date was suitable. Obviously, I avoided setting down matters on Wednesday afternoons. Saturdays were always racing, and Sunday was the day not only for settling but also to keep up on the business bookwork.

One day I left my brief at home, realising only when I arrived at court. So in a matter of fact tone, I asked my client to tell the court his name and address, and then to describe his case in his own words. I stumbled through and won – neither the client nor the court realised my lack of preparation.

I loved the law, its challenges and the pleasant lifestyle. All you were doing was arguing one side of a case in court – but at times you had to bamboozle to try to get your client off. That was your role. Young barristers were rarely entrusted with serious matters but occasionally you might fluke a good case. Lionel Murphy, for instance, had a murder case for his first court appearance, an unbelievable start to a brilliant career.

Barristers are expected to act impartially, whether they suspect their client is innocent or guilty. In criminal matters the barrister should identify anything in the accused's defence and also any mitigating circumstances. In some cases this may be sufficient for the accused person to be released and set free, but at the same time, a barrister is bound by the instructions given. If a client admits guilt, then the barrister cannot plead 'not guilty' on the client's behalf.

I once had an alleged bank robber as a legal-aid client. I looked upon it as a godsend – the chance of a lifetime to make my name as it had made the news. Two police constables had called on an assistant scoutmaster in a poor outer suburb about unpaid fines for traffic offences. On seeing the two police officers, he had blurted out, 'Oh, you've come at last. I'm glad. This has been on my conscience now for over two years and I'm glad it's all over, and I've been caught.'

All the constables wanted was the paltry few pounds, so rather than sit down to hear the man's troubles, the senior constable simply said, 'Give us the money and we'll be off.'

The scoutmaster then replied, 'I can't – I've spent it all – the last went over six months ago.'

At this, the two constables suggested that the scoutmaster tell the whole story in his own words.

I remembered reading about the robbery. A masked bandit had held up a city bank with a gun (a toy one) and had stuffed his pockets with money and carried more in his hands. On rushing out of the bank he had collided with first one and then another passing pedestrian, strewing money about, before finally escaping on a pushbike.

Having told the constables his story, the man was promptly arrested and charged. He had no money or friends, so the Crown allocated me – a junior barrister – to represent him. He was worried and nervous but to me seemed to be a decent enough young man – no street ruffian. Certainly not the type to be a bank robber.

Before he could speak, I said, 'You must listen to me first. I am briefed to act on your behalf but I am bound by what you tell me. If you have done this hideous crime then I cannot allow you to plead not guilty. While I am aware that it is alleged you made a confession to the police, I will not believe that until I have heard it from your own lips. Now I want you to listen to my question and answer that and nothing more. My first question is: did you hold up that bank?'

He said no, and I quickly replied that I knew he hadn't. When I asked if he had confessed just because he wanted to see his name in the papers, he said yes. I had checked with a psychiatrist whom I had called in another case, and he agreed that the notoriety complex could be a valid motivation. Apart from his admission, there was no evidence against him. The case was listed for mention, and the accused was called and asked how he pleaded. I stood up and said I was appearing on the accused's behalf, and that my client would be pleading not guilty.

This was a Monday and the matter was stood over till the Friday, when the court would determine a date for the hearing. As it happened, I was due in court on the Friday on a minor matter at Parramatta, a suburb some twenty kilometres west of the city. There was no way I could do both cases. The bank robber case had received a small mention on the front page of *The Sydney Morning Herald*, something that every young barrister craves, yet I did not want to forgo the Parramatta case.

I approached my client and asked if he thought he could handle the listing without me, and I explained that all he had to do was sit still in court. The prosecutor would then say that he had arranged with me for a certain date for the hearing. The judge would then ask my client if that was all right, and he just had to say yes.

My client said it would be no trouble – as simple as falling off a log. I went to Parramatta and returned soon after lunch. I phoned the prosecutor to verify the date set down for the hearing and was greeted with the news that my client had confessed again – this time to the judge. The case was relisted, now for sentencing. I made as good a plea for leniency as I could, but the judge was not a man for leniency and my client was removed from society for several years.

I also had some good wins. I was very pleased that I was able to get Jack Muir's ex-wife off a manslaughter driving charge after I argued the mitigating circumstances of her difficult situation. I took whatever work I could, and I also did my share of rent-control board cases, which were commonplace after the war. My articled clerk at University Chambers was Ken Hall, who was also the clerk for luminaries such as Gough Whitlam and Sir John Kerr. Ken became one of the most famous long-serving clerks in the legal world.

As a barrister, I was no longer allowed to work as a licensed clerk – but that didn't stop me from going to the races and helping on Wednesdays and Saturdays. Of course, I was still deeply involved in running all our family interests – bookmaking and real estate. I arranged everything in racing for my two brothers. I paid the fielding fees, bought the betting tickets, printed the interstate race fields, hired and fired the staff, arranged their cash or working bank, banked the proceeds, got the pre-post betting prices, scrounged for information, balanced the books and worked out the settling figures. I also paid the tax and represented them in the Tattersalls Club at settling. It may sound a lot, but it was a labour of love – and we were partners.

My brothers and I were also more engrossed than ever with building our many projects. We sold the hotel at Neville and bought the Tattersall's Hotel in Blayney, which we immediately set about renovating – this time under Jack's supervision as he loved living in the country.

—

Both Jack and Charlie were raising their respective families but I was still the confirmed bachelor – although I had never really settled back into my carefree ways since returning from overseas. I remember going to a party one Saturday evening at Jack Muir's place at Palm Beach and being bored, even though he had arranged a 'Dance of a Thousand Veils' with the latest troupe of showgirls.

My old mate Barry Pheloung did not like Jack Muir or the fast set of girls he thought we took out. On Good Friday in 1952, he asked me to his home and had casually invited a girl to join us for tea, a Manly girl from a very respectable family. Suzanne was beautiful and had a determination and spark about her. I actually remembered seeing her about six years earlier when she was just sixteen – I even could recall the colour of her dress. This was most unusual for me, because

I was normally oblivious to everything around me except my work. A girl might have caught my attention but not for what she was wearing.

When we did go on our first date I told her I was a rat. I didn't really want to get tangled up with any girl and I wanted her to know where she stood – and that I was not the marrying type. I told her I was a confirmed bachelor just out to have a good time. That didn't faze Suzanne, who'd had a string of boyfriends herself, including one who had given her his university pin. I thought I was safe, and so – without realising it – I fell in love.

I first noticed that something was amiss when we met soon after for an early dinner at a city restaurant. Apart from the two waitresses, I was the only person in the restaurant when Suzy arrived from work and walked towards me. The waitresses both laughed spontaneously. They said they couldn't help themselves because of the idyllic look of bliss on both our faces. I immediately reminded Suzy that I was a confirmed bachelor, never intending to get married – never intended even to have a serious relationship with a girl. She agreed. We were engaged within six months and married exactly one year later.

That was a funny year. I *knew* I would never marry, as did my mother, Betty, my brothers and all my friends. But Suzanne was the first girl I had ever gone out steadily with – and in the daytime. I am sure that if I hadn't by chance met Ilse in Germany after my accident, I would never have known the feeling of falling in love.

Every Sunday after settling, Suzy and I went out for the day. Suzy had had many boyfriends, but nothing prepared her for me and my antics. When I asked if she liked driving fast she said yes – so when I saw a sporty MG on the road I took off after it. To me, an MG was like a red rag to a bull. I had to give up in the middle of the race when Suzanne screamed 'Stop!' – she was terrified.

Suzanne was a beach girl. I thought this was great as I liked the surf and the beach, although I must admit I was so thin – just twelve stone three pounds, or 77 kilograms – that I didn't have the physique to show off. My idea of being on a beach was to skylark and bury her in the sand or frolic with her in the surf. She had never had sand in her hair before and thought I was a barbarian. Once, when we went rowing on a lake at Terrigal on the central coast of New South Wales, I thought it was fun to maroon her on a little island and pretend to row away. I was incorrigible. On one date Suzy wore a fashionable strapless dress with a stretch bodice. I couldn't resist pretending to pull it down with a little tug as we drove along, but much to my chagrin, I overplayed my gag and down came the dress. Suzy was mortified that I had revealed her undergarments. Gradually Suzy smoothed out my rough edges as best she could.

Suzanne had come from a strict Presbyterian family. When we decided to marry, Suzy told me she could not possibly marry in a Catholic church. I was not a strict Catholic but my mother was a staunch member of the church, and she was now paralysed and in a wheelchair. I knew that if I was ever to marry, it had to be in a Catholic church. Suzy was under pressure from her family and would not budge. And, because of my mother, I couldn't either. Eventually, Suzy suggested a neutral church. For fun, I nominated a mosque, which she accepted – but she quickly changed her mind when I joked that, under Islamic law, all a husband had to do to divorce his wife was to say to her, 'I renounce thee, I renounce thee, I renounce thee.'

In the end, we were married at St Canice's Catholic Church in Kings Cross. It was a small wedding. Suzanne's father, still not happy about the church, only decided to come a few hours before the ceremony. Her mother made her wedding dress, and Betty, now a milliner, made her a wedding hat. Betty was driving Suzy to the church but unfortunately had an accident on the Harbour Bridge. Now in her mid-thirties, Betty was still beautiful and, after working some of her charm, they ended up with a police escort to the church.

Neville Wran was my best man. He and his wife, Marcia, were the only non-family guests. Suzanne's father held our wedding dinner party at the old Wentworth Hotel, and the following morning we went by flying boat from Rose Bay to Nouméa for our honeymoon. We left at six am and the flight took eight hours; today it would take less than three. We stayed in one of the large, French-style bungalows at Anse Vata, which are now long gone, replaced by modern hotels.

We had a honeymoon of ten clear, fun-filled days. I had actually taken a Saturday off racing. We arrived back on a Friday evening and Suzy moved in with me to our home at Waverton, which was also the family hub.

The next morning my brother Jack was expecting an early breakfast, having come down from the country the previous evening. Soon Charlie turned up with his father-in-law, Charles 'Chicka' Schramm, and two friends and sat down. Suzy had never cooked anything more than a grill in her life and was completely unprepared for this invasion. To me it was all normal and I didn't realise her predicament.

Breakfast was all race talk, which continued until all of us, except Suzy, decamped for the races. Without my noticing, everyone had ignored Suzanne or, at best, treated her as a waitress. After the races we all came back to the house, where I kept all the racecourse gear. Jack stayed with us for dinner – luckily, my mother's nurse, Mary Abdoo, called in and helped Suzy cook a giant turkey which Jack had brought from the country – and then he set off back to Blayney.

That was when Suzanne poured out her troubles. She had never worked so hard or been treated so offhandedly, and she would not put up with it. I realised what I'd done to her. I had been raised in a hotel, was gregarious and used to people arriving unannounced. Suzy was not.

I also knew that, sooner or later, we would have to move. The Waverton house was a rambling old home that we had bought when the Imperial Hotel was resumed. I loved the house but I could see that Suzanne would never be able to keep up with it. It had six bedrooms, a dining room, a lounge and a massive enclosed veranda, which was itself probably as big as a normal house. Later I arranged for the Waverton house to go to Betty, who then sold it to buy her own home near the water at Greenwich. It helped set her up for life.

I had a great friend, Jock Rorrison, a bookmaker who had emigrated from Scotland during the Depression. He looked like a real battler. At first he was an SP bookie, operating in a pub in Double Bay. As a Scotsman, he was very tight with his money. He became a bookmaker at the dogs, and then in the Flat at Randwick, where I met him. We became lifelong friends.

His wife, Billie, was a stylish woman who was the fashion buyer for Mark Foys department store. Jock always told Billie that things were tough and he had no money. He omitted to tell her about the £65,000 he had in safety deposit boxes. When the taxman found out, he wasn't the only one annoyed. It was front-page news, which Billie only saw when she arrived at work. She had great trouble coming to terms with it, since she had always been scrimping and saving. The tax office took most of it, but Jock, in true racing style, just shrugged it off and said, 'Oh well.'

Jock never asked me for anything; rather, he always wanted to help and we enjoyed each other's company. He was a lovely guy. He was one of my true friends in racing.

As it happened, Jock, who lived in Clifton Gardens, was moving. He heard I was looking for a house, and so invited Suzy and me to see the place he had been leasing. It was a fairytale house, built on a large block of ground in a quiet cul-de-sac on a waterfront reserve. At the end of the road was Ashton Park Trust, hundreds of hectares of bushland that abutted Taronga Park Zoo. The house had been built by Warwick Fairfax, the newspaper magnate, for the beautiful European ballerina Madame Hélène Kirsova in the late 1930s. During the war many American warships had been based in Sydney Harbour. Rumour had it that when Warwick was absent, Madame Kirsova lit a red lamp on the top floor to show one particular American navy commander it was convenient to visit.

The house had three storeys and was built on a slope. The bottom floor had a large ballroom that Madame Kirsova had used for her ballet classes. The living area was on the middle floor, which was almost level with the street. The top floor had an indulgent master bedroom which we loved, with its own stone fireplace so large you could stand upright in it, and a veranda overlooking the front garden, which ran down to Taylors Bay, one of the quietest and most secluded inlets of Sydney Harbour.

Suzy and I both loved our new home and the tranquillity of the suburb, and we soon made new friends, including Jenny and Armand George, who – incredibly – also had a Jaguar XK120, although silver. We got on very well with the Georges and became godparents to each other's children. Away from the frenzied pace of the Waterhouse racing home-office at Waverton, Suzy was in her element and soon was expecting our first child.

My bizarre sense of humour got me into trouble with my serious-minded lawyer friends in 1954. It was a time of conservative values, and Suzy was still, as she would say, trying to 'polish her rough diamond'. She was heavily pregnant when we went to Lionel Murphy's wedding. One of my law-school friends, Bob Packam, looking at Suzanne's expectant state, said in front of a group, 'I didn't even know you were married.'

With a straight face I replied, 'Oh yes, all of three months now.'

Instead of laughter there was silence. The line went down like a lead balloon and everyone moved away, leaving Suzy and me standing alone. I looked down at poor Suzy and said, 'Sorry – I can't say it was a joke now, can I?'

7

Fate Takes Over

CHARLIE WAS IN HIS ELEMENT with our various building projects, but in the early 1950s his health began to give him trouble. He was grossly overweight – 130 kilograms – and, like our father, he suffered from diabetes. Charlie had also developed gallstones. He was only 38 when his doctor advised him to go on a diet before being operated on for his gallstones. Charlie tried but found it almost impossible to lose weight because he liked his food too much. He kept delaying the operation, hoping his symptoms would disappear, and dreading the surgeon's knife.

Charlie collapsed in January 1953 and I feared he was going to die. I had backed him financially when I was just a youth and we were very close. He knew I kept my distance from Patty, his wife. I did not feel she was a good wife to him. So I was surprised when Charlie said to me, 'Billy, if anything happens to me, I want you to look after Patty and the children.' He sincerely and honestly loved her. It moved me and I realised that, whatever my own feelings, I had to respect my brother's wishes. It completely changed my attitude towards her and their relationship.

Charlie improved, and after a short time was back into his normal pattern. He controlled his diabetes, or at least some symptoms of the disease, but of course he could not cure himself of the gallstones or the pain. I didn't know then that he was in the habit of relying on my mother's nurse to provide him with large doses of the painkiller pethidine – without a doctor's approval – so that he could sleep.

By mid-1954 we were at our busiest. We were building at Woolwich and Lane Cove, and having finally decided to make his home at Northbridge, Charlie was building a mansion there, which even included a room for his previously bachelor brother, and also a huge walk-in safe. We had also started building the new hotel at Fairy Meadow. Charlie worked long and hard. He was always at one of the jobs before his men and back again before the end of the day. It was hard because we were building without the luxury of outside finance.

Towards the middle of the year we struck financial rock bottom in our racing. Whether bookmaking or punting, there always comes a period when whatever you do, you can't win – and to make it worse, you feel as though you'll never win again. The pressure was on all of us, Jack, Charlie and myself, and there is no pressure like money pressure. While we could regulate both building and bookmaking, we could not put either into limbo. We still had to find wages each week with our building teams, and we had to be able to lay bets on each race.

Exactly thirteen years after our father's sudden death in August 1941, Charlie was stolen from us too. At three am Patty phoned me and hysterically screamed out that Charlie was dead. Taking my mother-in-law, Mrs Dart, a former nurse who was recuperating at our place after a breast cancer operation, I threw a coat over my pyjamas and raced over to their house. I couldn't believe Charlie was dead and I thought I could still save him.

Of course, it was all too late. Patty had tried to help his pain by giving him the pethidine medication. Charlie had given a sudden start, moaned and rolled out of bed. He was dead from a massive heart attack. He was only 39.

My father's death had devastated me, especially as I was still a teenager. Charlie had been ill, yet I still couldn't believe he was gone. He was so overweight, and was under so much pressure, as we had suffered seventeen consecutive losing days at the track. Adding to the trauma was that Charlie had four young and helpless children – Charles junior, the eldest, was only eight, and the youngest, Julie, was just four months. Jack had two young children: John, also eight, and Margaret, six. My firstborn, Robbie, was just six weeks old. I had no idea what to do. I was completely overwhelmed by my personal loss. I just couldn't imagine life without Charlie.

—

Bad news travels fast, and later that day I got a call from the foreman at Fairy Meadow asking if we intended to continue with the hotel. I automatically replied that he was to continue, but I felt like a ship without a rudder. We had buildings underway in five areas and we had lost our builder. Charlie was an able builder. He had known the detail on every project but no one else really did. He didn't keep much paperwork as it was all in his head. Charlie didn't use architects – we preferred to save money with draftsmen – and so we had no idea where to pick up. We also stood to lose nearly half of our income without us having Charlie's bookmaking licence.

Jack and I knew hard decisions had to be made. We decided that Jack would come down at once to Sydney, leaving his wife, Gwen, in Blayney until the Tattersall's Hotel could be leased. I decided to take a year's leave of absence from the law to help build the hotel in Fairy Meadow. I also applied straight away for a bookmaker's licence to retain the income stream.

My wife had married a barrister who was now a bookmaker. I told Suzy it would only be for a year; I would finish the hotel and the other projects and then go back to the law. I started

110

working at the Wentworth Park dogs the following Saturday night, and a fortnight later was granted a licence in the St Leger Reserve at Randwick, where I started on the first Saturday of the Spring Carnival in late September 1954.

I had spent a fair proportion of my life on a racetrack by this time. I was 32 and had been a clerk since I was sixteen. I had done just about everything that could be done on a bookie's stand, so nothing was really new to me. Nevertheless, it was a totally different feeling. For the first time I was working as a licensed bookmaker in my own name, not a clerk. I had a very limited bank, since most of our little money at this time went to Jack on the Rails in the Paddock. However, I felt supremely confident and bet to the limit all day. I bet blind because of the large crowds but knew I was keeping in front. I was told that my holdings that first day were the biggest among all the St Leger bookmakers, local or interstate – something no beginner had done before. I worked at the dogs that evening and finished around midnight, exhausted but in seventh heaven.

—

For the building projects we found an able architect, Foss Van Breda. He proved to be a tower of strength. Jack and I had decided to share the building workload, but I hated every minute of it. Apart from having to be in Wollongong at six in the morning, I was doing something that I did not understand and so felt out of my depth. On the other hand, Jack had already had a little building experience in the country and now found he liked it. Fortunately, we were winning at the track. Right from my first day our luck had turned, and for the next year it was a novelty to have a losing day – or at least that was how it seemed.

Jack and I had another problem to consider. Charlie had left a respectable estate worth about £42,000 before death duties – on paper a fortune and a lot for those days, but we knew only too well that his family would receive just a fraction once death duties were paid and if the estate were liquidated by the executors. We were in a growth period and our shared assets included many half-finished buildings. We knew we could apply to the court to pay out Charlie's one-third share of our joint assets, but Jack and I both realised that, without our help, Patty would go through Charlie's legacy and wouldn't have enough for school fees and other necessities, let alone to provide for the children's futures. Jack and I both felt strongly for Charlie's four young children, and I had an obligation to Charlie from when I had promised the previous year to look after Patty. I thought, 'What would I want to happen if I had died and left my wife and small child?' Suzy agreed that we had to help them.

Jack and I decided we should carry on as though Charlie were still alive and still working in the partnership – in effect, we would gift the estate one-third of our future income. We would finish off the hotel and the other projects with his estate as an equal silent partner. Our goal had been to have three hotels and three homes. If we could do that, it would mean Charlie's children would be set for life and we would have fulfilled our moral obligations.

So we called a meeting with Patty and her father, Chicka Schramm. He had been a baker but had left his position to work with Charlie as a racecourse clerk and handyman on the building jobs. He was a good and loyal man. Jack and I outlined to Patty what we were prepared to do for the children, and the effort we would go to. We explained that it would make for tough times for us all and asked if she accepted our offer. She readily agreed and we were committed.

When I told Neville Wran, our solicitor, of our intentions, he was aghast and earnestly tried to dissuade us. He was very firm, advising that, whilst it was an admirable motive, such an idea never worked in the long term. He said that Charlie's children were too young to realise what was being done for them, and that when they grew up there would be no gratitude. Rather, they would expect more and finish up suing us!

Prophetic words, but Jack and I had made up our minds. Foolishly, we ignored Neville's advice. We reasoned that if either of us had died, we would have wanted our surviving brothers to do the same.

And so we began our golden age. Everything clicked. We finished off the house projects in Sydney and also completed the hotel at Fairy Meadow. It was extremely successful – it achieved the top country-area liquor sales in the state for many years.

I wanted to name everything after our late brother because we loved him, and Jack agreed. The Fairy Meadow Hotel became the Hotel Charles, and we were to build two more hotels with the same name. We erected a couple of small four-storey office blocks in Milsons Point – Charles House – and converted a house in North Sydney at 194 Miller Street, firstly into a residence and then into offices – another Charles House. Later we built the high rise St Charles units in Upper Pitt Street, Kirribilli, and we acquired a farm in Wallacia, which we also called St Charles. We also named our family companies after Charlie – Charles Properties, Charles Holdings, Charles Magazines and so on.

However, while we were honouring our late brother's memory, our gesture would be interpreted very differently by Charlie's children as they grew up.

—

Freed up from the legal profession and with Jack supervising the building, I focused my efforts on racing. I knew I could take on the interstate ring in the St Leger because I had spent years building up the business with my brothers. I wanted to be able to hold my own in any field, so I started a pre-post doubles book, where I took bets in advance. We would combine the odds for two races from the upcoming Saturday meeting – the flying (sprint) and the handicap – and send out tables with the odds for winning both races. The runners of one race would be listed down the margin and of the other along the top – in effect, the odds of winning one leg were multiplied by the odds for the horse in the next leg. Our charts would be printed in time to be taken to the GPO by midday on Thursday, which meant some punters would receive them the same day and the others by Friday morning, before the Saturday.

I worked at the city horse races, the trots and the dogs, and also at provincial courses such as Hawkesbury and Kembla. I was surprised when I soon led in every area. For the first time, I began to think of fielding on the Melbourne Cup Carnival.

When I started out as a clerk in 1938, several fielders would come from Melbourne to work on our carnivals and a few Sydney bookies would go down to Melbourne for theirs. This generated great rivalry between the two betting rings and ensured strong betting duels. The big bookmaker from Melbourne who came to Sydney was Bob Jansen, and the Sydney bookies who went south were our leaders, including Jim Hackett and Jack Shaw. I remember one wet Wednesday when Jansen, fielding under a tree to avoid the rain, laid a bet of £10,000 to £1000. Jansen was standing the horse for what was then double the first prize in the state lottery, and double the first prize of the Melbourne Cup.

Now that I was a bookmaker in my own right in 1954, no Sydney bookmaker was working in Melbourne, and Albert Smith was the only Melbourne bookmaker who came to Sydney for the carnival. I knew there was no use applying unless I made it into the Paddock enclosure in Sydney, but I hungered to throw my hat into the Melbourne ring.

—

I remember a punting incident not long after I had taken out my own licence and begun to stand up in my own name, I was working on interstate races in the St Leger at Rosehill, and Jack was in the interstate Paddock. The race clubs were not concerned about providing a service either to patrons or bookmakers on 'away racing' – they were interested only in their own event. As a result, the patrons and bookmakers had to provide everything for themselves. Arthur Browning arranged for the race club to allow him to broadcast the race calls for each of the Melbourne races over the public-address system at the Sydney track, which also gave the first official indication of starters in each local race. It was a terrific advantage for him to be in control of the information source, as he was the only one aware of all that was happening before each race.

The first race on the program was for two-year-olds. It was early in the season and it looked like a match race: 5/4 for one horse and 7/4 for Guncotton. Arthur's commissioners charged through the interstate rings, taking 7/4, then 6/4, backing Guncotton all the way to 2/1 on.

It was a hell of a back-in. I had been doing business with Arthur one way or another since 1938, so I was wary.

The opening favourite had blown out from 5/4 to 2/1, at which point the commissioners charged back into the ring and backed it, taking the 2/1 back to even money. This in turn forced the price of Guncotton back out to 6/4. Arthur's commissioners now charged back into the ring, this time again attacking Guncotton. They took the 6/4 and again backed it into 2/1 on!

The bookmakers looked at their books and thought that they had never had it so good. Arthur had backed both the favourites, taking short odds for much of the money. They thought they had no risk, as no matter which horse won, they couldn't lose. But I knew Arthur was anything but silly, and I smelt a rat.

Sure enough, just two minutes before the race, the announcer – courtesy of Arthur's broadcast – went through the actual runners. The original favourite was not listed – it had been scratched. This news hit like a bombshell, and all hell broke loose among the bookies, who would have to refund the money they were holding on the scratching. Now they stood to lose a fortune on Guncotton. They would not even receive any deduction on Guncotton's payout, as the early favourite had been scratched before the betting had started in Melbourne.

Arthur, who had exclusive access to the pricing service and controlled the broadcast, knew the horse was a scratching – but he hadn't informed his fellow bookies. Arthur had the bookies in a vice-like grip and, through his manipulation, he had placed his bets at odds of up to 2/1 when Guncotton's real price was long odds-on.

Guncotton won the race by many lengths, starting at 5/2 on. I hadn't really laid Guncotton, as I had been cautious of Arthur, but most of the interstate ring bookies had been hurt, including my brother Jack, and they lodged an objection against paying.

The club ruled against the poor manipulated bookies and they had to pay out in full, with no deduction to make up for the scratching. Also they had to refund all the bets made on the scratched favourite. Although no law or race rule had been broken, it was sharp practice. Following lobbying, which I spearheaded, the clubs took over the race broadcasts themselves, thus ensuring this type of manipulation could never happen again.

Back then turnover was booming. Bookies in the St Leger enclosure still worked in pounds, shillings and pence, so they issued tickets in shillings. But I was a gambler and wanted to imitate the bigger Paddock and Rails bookmakers, so I changed to clerking in pounds.

—

In the late 1950s Jack and I also started up an off-course SP betting office. This was illegal but no one worried much about that at the time. The race clubs were aware of the fact that many of their leading bookies had SP offices but they tolerated it, thinking that at least it was a service to patrons unable to attend the track. It kept up interest in the horses and was just part of the culture.

This attitude changed with the introduction of the TAB in the early 1960s, when running an off-course SP betting operation became a more serious criminal offence with jail terms. It meant that I and most other bookies gave up our SP businesses. In those days the race clubs couldn't have been doing too much wrong, when you consider that the three enclosures at Royal Randwick were always full of people and bookmakers. Randwick would attract 70,000 people at the two major carnivals, and 50,000 at the Villiers–Summer Cup meetings in the early 1960s.

Because there was so much off-course SP betting in those days, I don't believe the introduction of the TAB can be blamed for the reduction in race attendances over the years. I don't think that even today, in real terms, the TAB has yet reached the figures of the old days for betting off-course.

—

Punters all over the world are the same. You'll recognise the same expressions and hear the same throaty roar when the favourite hits the line. Yet they do fit into different categories.

A lot of phone punters are commission men who seek out clients wanting to have a bet and bookmakers who will take those bets. They live by carving a commission on the bets from one or both sides. The reason the commission operator exists is simple: it's because a professional punter finds it hard to get set for his money. No normal bookie wants any part of this 'tough' money. The hard, full-time professional operator doesn't mind paying a commission if he can get set for his money. The bookie gets business, the operator gets his 'com' and the pro gets his money set. All parties' interests are served. To earn his commission, however, the agent has to guarantee both ends. He guarantees to pay the bookie if the horse loses and he guarantees to pay the professional if the horse wins.

Our SP office was run by Mary Abdoo and 'Melbourne Mick' Bartley. They were as unalike as you could imagine but worked well together, as their interests didn't clash. Mary was a nursing sister for my mother. She had never made a bet in her life but was fascinated by all the race talk in the house. She was as honest as the day is long, and completely dependable. Melbourne Mick was a true racing professional. He lived, slept and dreamt racing. He was a reliable and tireless worker and had unbounded belief in his own ability.

Looking back, it was logical that Melbourne Mick and the big punter Freddy Angles would become associated. The softest thing about Freddy as a gambler was his teeth. He had come up the hard way during the Depression, working for his mentor, the fabulous Rufe Naylor. Naylor was a remarkable entrepreneur who had staged match races for professional runners in South Africa, established a chain of theatres, started a racing newspaper, stood for a seat in federal parliament, become a registered bookmaker for a short while and also promoted boxing and cycling. Naylor ran foul of racing authorities and was warned off, and he unsuccessfully took his appeal to the Privy Council. Nevertheless, Naylor was still a big punter. He had been the first man to study photos taken at various points around the track and produced films of races using hand-wound movie cameras. He had employed agents at every track and had men working on the weights and measures for every runner. Naylor had had no real opposition and was held in a position of awe.

When he died suddenly in 1939, Freddy was working for him and so stepped straight into his shoes. Almost overnight Freddy became the biggest punter in the country, employing 'Hollywood' George Edser and others for ten years to place his commissions at the track. He would often back three or four horses in every race. Freddy took Naylor's approach further, mixing it with inside knowledge.

Freddy couldn't go onto a racecourse, as he had been banned by racing officials – without explanation – for several years, so he needed to find SP bookies with whom he could place his bets. It was the track's worst-kept secret that he was unofficially in partnership with Ken Ranger, the leading locals bookmaker in the Sydney ring. Most people thought that whatever Freddy did was hot, but he had a natural ability and was blessed with a talent for gambling on horses. Freddy was no angel, but he wouldn't be guilty of half the accusations against him. However, Freddy certainly was involved in some pretty sharp practices, and I saw firsthand his manipulation of both the horses' chances and the betting. I realised after one incident that taking his business was dangerous.

In 1959, on his own initiative Mick agreed to run a commission through our SP office for Freddy on a horse in the Canterbury Guineas on a Saturday. Gemsbok had been assessed as the 5/2 pre-post favourite. Its trainer was the redoubtable Bob Meade, one of Freddy's men. Bob was a paradox. To meet him he was a nice guy, but on the racecourse he changed into Mr Hyde. He was ruthless, believing that no one had a right to know what he was doing. If anyone ever stole his 'market' or price, he would 'pull up' the horse without compunction and wait for another day.

The day before the race, Meade approached Dougie Weir, a top jockey, and asked him to ride Gemsbok in the Guineas.

Dougie was surprised, as he did not usually ride for Meade. Meade explained that Gemsbok would probably open as the favourite but wasn't quite fit, and instructed Dougie not to knock it around during the race.

Dougie readily agreed but was very much aware of Meade's reputation as a plunge trainer – put simply, there was no 'hotter' trainer at large. Dougie had a large following of punters. He warily informed them there was the opportunity of a punting bonanza. Dougie knew that Meade would have to tell him if Gemsbok was trying. If Meade changed his instructions just before the race, Dougie would immediately signal to his punters, and they could then attack the bookmakers and get the cream of the market. If the horse wasn't trying, they could 'pick up fruit for the sideboard' by laying the horse to lose with bookmakers.

When the betting opened half an hour before the race, Gemsbok, instead of being favourite, blew like a gale. It was a hard horse to lay – the punters hadn't seen the stable's men backing their horse. The moment of truth arrived when Dougie Weir had to mount. All of the jockey's punters watched closely as he received his instructions from the trainer.

Bob Meade got straight to the point. 'Now, Doug, I've told you Gemsbok is not fit and can't win. That's true, but I don't want you to get into trouble with the stewards, as I've noticed the horse has blown out in the market. Make sure you jump him with the field, and use the whip if necessary to have him up with the leaders, or at least in a forward position. See if you can keep him there till you get into the straight. They'll pass you there, as the horse simply hasn't done enough work to finish on.'

Dougie realised Meade had been truthful and signalled his punters accordingly, then trotted out onto the track. In the betting ring Gemsbok went for a real bath, led by Ken Ranger, and its price blew right out to 25/1.

Jack Thompson, a leading hoop, waited for Dougie to bring his horse alongside on the way to the starting gates. 'Now, Doug,' he said. 'You've been told you were riding a no-hoper. That's not true. You're on a certainty – it will win by ten lengths. If you miss the start, we'll wait for you and you'll still win. But if you jump and lead early, we can all do our best to catch you. If you do as you're told, there'll be the odds to £500 for you.'

There was no way out for Dougie. He was hooked, but at least the sweetener was substantial. Of course, Gemsbok jumped straight to the front and the further they went, the further it strode ahead. It won with consummate ease, beating Thompson's mount into second place. Even a blind man could see what had happened – an SP coup had been landed. Angles made an absolute killing and Dougie earned £12,500.

I hadn't been working on the race as I was fielding on the Melbourne races in Sydney, so I was largely unaware of what had happened. I was furious when I heard that rather than the pre-post price of 5/2, Gemsbok's starting price was 25/1. By extending the odds too far, Angles and Ranger had put the finances of all the illegal off-course bookies in jeopardy.

If an SP bookie takes a bet of £1000, expecting to pay out £2500 if the horse wins, he will grit his teeth if it comes in at 10/1, but he will manage to cover the additional £7500 loss. But if the horse wins at 25/1, you put him and yourself in grave peril. The bookie now has to pay out £25,000. If he hasn't got it, he's unlikely to pay you anything – he'll welsh on the whole bet.

Being the commissioners for his bets, I was horrified as we had to guarantee Freddy his winnings, regardless of whether the SP bookies could pay us or not. Nobody – and I mean nobody – would want to be exposed to anything this stupendously dangerous. I was most apprehensive about not being paid. Thankfully, the SP bookies all settled in full, but I still sacked

Freddy from having any future 'coms' with us, and I lost faith in Mick as our man.

Despite the experience, I still liked Freddy Angles and I'm sure Freddy liked me. He was a hard man to beat and an even harder man to catch out. I did a couple of times, but he'd merely smile with an affected grimace and say, 'You dirty bastard – you've got me again.'

In the early days of photo-finishes, I was working at Kembla Grange and Freddy, finally allowed back at the track, was standing nearby. Two horses flashed past the post, wide apart as they hit the line. To the naked eye it looked as though the outside horse had won. But I had a friend who was a 'nob' on photo-finishes; he signalled to me that the inside horse was the winner.

I knew the only way I would catch Freddy or anyone else betting on this photo-finish was if I appeared unsure. So gingerly, I called, 'I'll take 10/1 on the outside horse,' which was bookie speak for 'odds-on of 1/10 if you want to back it'– a punter had to outlay £10 to win £1. I made it so very short to give the punters the impression I thought it was almost a foregone conclusion that the outside horse had won, but also that the outside horse was a good result and I wanted to take some insurance. It was a calculated risk – the real price for the outside horse in the photo-finish would have been about 6/4, and 1/2 for the inside horse. Even hardened punters like Freddy were bluffed, and he jumped in with £2000 to win just £200 on the outside horse.

Outlaying £2000 to win £200 may sound like a sucker bet, but if a punter is sure there's no risk, he thinks it is easy money. Having got Freddy's bet, I continued to call the same odds, trying to attract other business.

That was enough for Freddy – he knew he'd been taken and said in good humour, 'You bastard!' As he would say, 'Good sports don't grumble and good mugs don't tumble!'

Freddy and others didn't know about my photo-finish man, the old-time journalist George 'Chips' Breen, who was sitting up high in the stand, directly above the finish line. He was cross-eyed and wore glasses, but he was a 'dead-eye Dick' on photo-finishes.

Even though you can never completely wipe out corruption or trickery where people deal in money, you can at least control it on a racecourse as everything is on open display and sharp practice is soon apparent. I had to laugh one day when told in Las Vegas they didn't have to ban any jockeys or trainers in the United States because all horses were always trying. Ridiculous!

—

I looked up to some giants in my early days. Towards the end of the war, the late Bill Mulligan had won £5000 on a race. A 20/1 shot had been a 'skinner' – that is, he'd laid no bets at all on the winner and so kept everything. It may not sound much today, but it was a fortune then and it certainly excited me.

That soon became chickenfeed when it was reported that Ken Ranger had held over £130,000 one day. I admired Ken's sangfroid, and I was always fascinated by his daring and impressed that he never seemed to get rattled and would lay gigantic bets without a flicker of emotion. He was not that long at the top – he had a heart condition and had actually collapsed a couple of times at the track. The pressure on a big-gambling bookie is all-consuming, and rarely can one man hold the top spot for long. But Ken had certainly made his presence felt.

He brought a tremendous amount of public interest to the racecourse, but he also smashed a psychological betting barrier. For the first time, here was a bookie regularly betting not in thousands but in tens of thousands. I never dreamt that I would be as big a gambler as Ken Ranger, but if I modelled my future on anyone, then it was him.

8

Lured by Melbourne

THE YEAR 1959 was to be the most momentous of my life. It finally decided that my future was bookmaking. A vacancy appeared in the Paddock interstate ring and I was promoted, thanks to my high turnover. It was the first vacancy in five years and, until then, I had thought I would never make it there. As soon as I was registered as a Paddock bookie in Sydney, I applied to work at the carnivals in Melbourne. I was accepted – the first successful applicant in ten years.

An old-time Sydney bookie, Jack Mandel, congratulated me on my decision to have a crack at Melbourne but added some advice: 'I'm glad you're trying Flemington, but remember this. Not one of us has ever made a success of it. Have a go, by all means, but don't get carried away by it or they'll pick you up in pieces.'

After thanking him for his consideration, I said, 'I promise you, Mr Mandel, I may not win much but they won't get my money.'

He gave a kindly smile and only said, 'Remember what I've told you.'

It was also in 1959 that my brother Jack and I finished the hotel at Chatswood. After the interminable delay in gaining approval, the building shot up incredibly quickly. We had started in late January 1959, and the hotel opened while I was in Melbourne for the racing carnival in November. It was an instant success. At the last minute we also decided to buy another adjacent block, this time anonymously – to keep the price down – so that we could build a modern liquor drive-through. This was the second hotel drive-in in Australia and was extremely popular, with cars queuing right around the corner in peak times. It was the key to the hotel's marvellous growth. We had also built the longest public bar in the metropolitan area, and a lounge in which we could seat a thousand people comfortably.

Almost overnight, all our expectations for the hotel had been surpassed. Jack and I had hoped we could make it into the top ten licensed hotels in the state. Instead, after just one year, the location and the innovative concept meant that we had the top sales not only in New South Wales but also the whole of Australia.

—

Even when you are the biggest holder on the Rails you can be plagued by 'hard money' from the pros, as my brother Jack was in the late 1950s. This can inhibit you so much that you lose confidence and go back into your shell. However, not every move a big gambler makes is lethal, so it is to the pros' benefit to place a smokescreen around their real intentions. The odds may be in your favour but you will still sweat.

As Jack and I were partners, it was to our joint advantage to overcome any obstacle impeding either of us. I suggested we sort out his punters. I decided to take the hardcore pros so that he could handle the remainder more aggressively and offer them top or extended odds.

I approached most of the tough-money brigade and put a proposition to them: if they came straight to me in the Paddock, bypassing Jack on the Rails, I would set them what they wanted. This was a great opportunity for them, as usually, once a commission starts and the punter has shown his hand, the odds offered have a tendency to drop quickly and drastically. The pros may not get the rest of their money on and certainly only at reduced odds. Jack and I figured that as most of the big money was to be made on his Rails position, it would be to our mutual advantage if I could manage the tough players; we would both be content if I could break even with the pros.

The idea worked well. Relieved of the tension, Jack shot ahead, betting very big and handling himself well. I found that I could manage the crafty group a lot better. They respected me for allowing them to get set, and I realised very early on how vulnerable they themselves were. It became a little like swimming – once your feet don't touch the bottom, you find you don't sink and it becomes fun. While Jack grew and prospered – to our mutual surprise I did also.

Big bookmakers are made by big punters, and big punters are made by big bookmakers asking if they want more. I had read with relish of the betting duels on the Australian turf and also in England and the United States. I had always been fascinated by them and yet never once envisaged myself in that arena.

My initial stint in the Melbourne betting ring, however, was quite a let-down. I finished the carnival just behind but was terribly disappointed by the betting. I had been handled by the licensing committee, which allocated me an unworkable betting stand. The only hope was to gamble up and try to attract the turnover. Despite my appalling stand, I managed to have the largest turnover and was considered the biggest bookie at Flemington that year. In Melbourne they drew stands annually, so I spent the next twelve months lobbying, trying to move from my wretched position.

I had by then formed a phone friendship with a small Melbourne punter named Joe Metz. When I began to work in

Melbourne we became close friends. Joe was also close with Sir Eugene Gorman, who was a truly remarkable man. Through Joe, I got to know him and we got on marvellously together. Gorman was getting on in years but had lived a very full and successful life. After serving in both World Wars, he rose to be the leading criminal barrister in Melbourne. Gorman was appointed chairman of a number of company boards and a committeeman of the Victoria Racing Club, which was then the controlling body for all the racing clubs in Victoria. He had one of the most lucid and clearest brains I have ever known, but I didn't realise his devious side until much later.

Gorman was fascinated by big gambling. As a young man he had been generally feared in the ring, but punting was the one field where he had failed. He always wanted to know how the big punters were faring, what they backed and my opinion of them. With hindsight, I think he actually wanted them all to lose. But Gorman was wily and quite conniving and gave no hint of his resentment.

Years earlier Jack Phillips, a Rails bookie, had served with Gorman in World War I and considered himself a friend. One Wednesday during an Easter carnival, Gorman phoned Phillips and said, 'Jack, I can't get to the races today. The trainer only gives this horse of mine a very rough chance, but will you put £100 on at the starting price for me so I can give the jockey and trainer something if it happens to win?'

Jack was a man who could look after himself on the racetrack, and he knew how crafty Gorman was. Here Gorman was telling him the horse was trying, and yet obviously there was no wrap on it. The horse was assessed as 7/2 second-favourite for the race. When betting settled there was no support for it, and the horse's odds lengthened; eventually it started at 8/1. The horse won. Jack lost on the race as he had kept Gorman's £100 and had not backed it back. It was logical, as he knew the horse was not greatly fancied.

Walking off the track, Jack was bemoaning his luck. He said that although it should have been a winning day, he had lost through knowing too much.

Another bookie replied, 'I'm in the same boat. I thought I should have won but I was unlucky because Eugene Gorman phoned me this morning and asked me to have £200 on his horse. He didn't fancy it but wanted a bet, "just in case".'

Jack Phillips stopped in his stride. He checked with the other Rails bookies and found that Gorman had phoned them all and outlaid over £1000. This was a fortune in the Depression, and with the high starting price – more than double its assessment – he won far more than if he had used an army of commissioners.

This little caper gives a good insight into Gorman's thinking. He hadn't told the truth but he hadn't told a lie – he had traded on the natural greed inherent in so many of us. If I have tried to teach my children and grandchildren anything, it is to be aware of the vices, especially greed. I have always insisted that you should never enter into a deal motivated by greed.

—

I had a secret friend at this time: Harry Slamen, the 'Black Prince'. He was without a doubt the most feared punter in Australia. Our relationship was not long yet I had tremendous respect for the man and his ability. He died about a year after I first ventured to Melbourne.

The Black Prince was anything but popular. It would be a toss-up whether the fear and hatred he earned from bookies was worse than the loathing and detestation he got from punters. Yet he kept to himself, sought no advice, asked no favours and paid his debts. He was a self-made man who owned a chain of bookshops in Melbourne.

I had met Harry through our SP office in Sydney. Melbourne Mick had left to start up his own business and Mary Abdoo was now in charge. We had become a very powerful force in the SP world and we were not punters. A Sydney punter – 'Big Jim' Pollard – had approached me to do an SP commission for 'a friend'. We did it and it was successful; the horse blew in the market and no money got back to the track. From this I first met the Black Prince.

Harry flew to Sydney to see me. He was a man of about 60 years of age and had been involved in racing most of his life. He told me that the 'com' we had done was the most successful that he could remember because there was no talk after the race. This after-talk can be quite disastrous for any stable, as it can put the spotlight on them.

We got on famously from the start. Harry believed he had found the keys to the bank vault with me – a big gambler who had access to every racing market available, one who turned over big money and yet was not interested in punting. But in life things very rarely work out as we imagine. With hindsight, meeting me was probably the most unfortunate thing that happened to the Black Prince.

Harry owned a string of horses and a farm, complete with a training racetrack. Everyone thought his runners rarely tried in a race, as he always wanted better odds. It was said that he expected 10/1 at a bush meeting for a horse that should have been 2/1 in the city. Now with me he could bet whenever he wished, and since there was no money coming in through me from off the course, the price stayed at attractive odds.

I think I was about the only person he really trusted. He went to extraordinary lengths to maintain secrecy and planned everything well into the future. He never once looked for the spotlight and the big prizes. He had a great horse that could have been set for the Melbourne Cup, but that never interested Harry. He would rather give a few easy runs and set the horse as a certainty for a minor race.

Once during the Melbourne Cup carnival, I called to see

Harry at his office. He told me he was setting a horse for a maiden race at Cranbourne in the country in late January. This was in early November, and he was planning for this ordinary race two months ahead. He told me the name of the horse and said that when it came to race day, he would merely say the amount of money that he wanted to bet without disclosing the name. To me, this exemplified the unbounded trust that he had come to place in me.

Probably only one horse in ten of his was in his name, all the others being registered under dummy names. Racing was the only leisure Harry had – apart from an attractive young wife – and so his racing had to pay its way. He was the only big betting owner I ever knew who not only wasn't interested in publicity but studiously avoided it. A lot of wealthy owners say they avoid the spotlight yet undoubtedly still want the recognition. Harry wanted to win, and I am sure that money was not his main objective.

Harry had an incredible perspective on the psychology of people. His book business had shops all over Melbourne, and all were connected by a telephone exchange in a small shop near Flinders Street Station. Invariably Harry would be working in the back room, answering the phone. Very early in his career his telephone girl had taken suddenly ill and Harry filled in for the day. He caught a thief that day and so continued in the role – he said it was the most profitable work he did in his organisation. He had learnt of so many ways that people could steal, and of trusted employees being anything but honest, taking advantage of the business or seeking other jobs; even husbands and wives cheating on each other. It gave him an incredible, if twisted, insight into human nature.

I respected Harry's judgement on a person's character more than anyone else's, and I couldn't help asking if he knew Sir Eugene Gorman. Oh yes, he knew him well. He said that if I was to get ahead in Melbourne, it was essential to have

Gorman well and truly on side. Gorman was a man who would do nothing unless he had a benefit, yet if you offered him money you would insult him or, worse still, cause him to accuse you of trying to offer a bribe. The best thing to do, Harry told me, was to say you had put £500 on a winner the previous Saturday for him. Apparently Gorman would accept this without question.

Sure enough, it worked like a charm. Harry told me I would need to do this regularly, and even then I would have to be careful with Gorman because he could be very jealous. Harry warned me never to appear to be too successful. Gorman's brain was too brilliant to let anything be simple, and Harry cautioned me that he was very mistrusting.

Sir Eugene himself once told me his philosophy: 'In racing, make sure you keep yourself in the best of company and your horses in the worst.' When I told the Black Prince about Gorman's remark, he laughed heartily and said this fitted Gorman, but only his public image. Harry believed that Gorman mixed with every milieu of society – the leading citizens went into his chambers by the front door and the worst criminals by the back.

Nobody realised that I knew the Black Prince. When he placed a com, as far as I was concerned, it was set. I did not intend to back the horse for myself; indeed, if not all Harry's money was placed I was prepared to stand the balance myself.

In the past, Harry's commissions would not be placed until seven or eight minutes before the start of the race – so it would be more difficult for any of the commissions to be sent back to the racecourse. But despite these precautions, Slamen had never known whether the whole of his commission was placed. The advantages he gained by doing business with me were manifest. His money was definitely on and payment was guaranteed. Immediately, there was far less organising and no concern about trustworthiness.

The Black Prince had such a reputation for success that other stables were very aware of him. If his horse was considered a trier, they might decide to wait for another day for their own. If Slamen was not thought to be trying, it was a different matter. However, not even the Black Prince wanted to pull horses up for no reason, but now, with no money coming for his horses at the track, it invariably appeared that they were not trying, and so Harry encountered much more opposition than he had in the past.

I had changed his tempo. He was putting on money all the time because he got the good odds, but his horses didn't win all the time. It was the worst thing that could have happened to the Black Prince. Suddenly he was starting to chase money in a losing run, and he was breaking the cardinal rule: money lost is lost and gone forever – you should never throw new or good money after it. No one knew he was losing except me.

Harry Slamen died in strange circumstances during my second year in Melbourne. Rumour had it he had been murdered by a relative who had lost all his money backing Harry's tips. He drove his car into a tree at high speed. The car disintegrated and both men died instantly. It was a straight country road and apparently no other cause could be found for the accident. As no one knew Harry had been losing, I could well imagine the ruined relative thinking Harry had set him up.

—

As we moved into 1960, I felt on top of the world. Suzanne and I had three beautiful young children, and my brother Jack and I were told by the accountants we were the third-highest individual taxpayers in Australia. Everything we touched seemed to fire.

The birth of one's children is always a special time. I remember when Robbie was born I was delighted to have my son.

When Louise was born, I was thrilled to have a girl – she was a beautiful baby, with lovely features, including beautiful lips. Suzy and I would slip in to watch Louise sleeping, with her perfectly formed hands up on either side of her face. I remember the day she was born, I'd had a terrible result at the races but I told everyone I had won the lottery: I had my little girl. With my bookmaking and racing commitments, I hadn't been able to get to the hospital. I had the races on Saturday and the dogs on Saturday night – and then settling on Sunday. Suzanne was disappointed but I couldn't just leave my stand for a few hours to get to the hospital, and settling had to be done. I was excited that I had a daughter but I just had to wait.

Six weeks after Louise was born in 1956, my beloved mother passed away. After her first stroke five years earlier, she suffered more strokes and was paralysed. When we gave the house at Waverton to Betty, my mother lived for a while in a house we bought right on the beach at Narrabeen. We thought it would be lovely for her but she couldn't stand the incessant crash of the waves. Being paralysed she couldn't escape the sound. Then we bought a beautiful but rundown mansion, 'Fern Hill', at 57 Upper Pitt Street, Kirribilli, and I moved my mother into part of this lovely old home; she was entranced by the continual activity on the harbour. I would visit her every day and usually twice, and she loved it when Suzanne and I would bring the babies, Robbie and Louise, for her to see.

Suzanne and I felt two children were enough at that stage, thinking we would wait a few years and have two more, but then David came along. It was hard for Suzanne having three children under four and all in nappies. Although David was a surprise, he was a joy. Unlike Robbie and Louise, who were both difficult eaters, David loved his food and so he was a pleasure at meal times.

I was always proud of my children and I felt we brought them up well. My philosophy, which I learned from my own father, was to not be autocratic but rather to regard the children as young adults, and to treat them with respect and try to explain the rationale behind what I said. They were taught to respect other people's property and be considerate of others' feelings, to work hard for what they wanted, and to respect law and order and authority – but also to stand up for their rights. I always felt that the three of them listened to what I had to say. I cannot recall ever having to smack any of them for misconduct, rudeness or unbecoming manners. Yet they certainly weren't three little angels, and each had a mind of their own.

My approach to child-rearing wasn't always perfect. I remember one funny example when Robbie was about nine years old, Louise seven and David five. It was winter, cold and bleak. Suzanne and the children would rise between six and six-thirty to get ready for school, while I would stay in bed, getting up nearer eight. Suzanne would then drive the children off to school while I had coffee and toast.

On this occasion when I got up, I noticed that a wireless, several lights and the electric blankets were still on, even though the children were dressed and downstairs. I was annoyed about the wasting of power and money, and I called the three into the lounge. I sat them down and carefully explained the folly of waste, and that I was really only looking after their money for them: they were simply wasting their own money.

Not being so concerned with logical facts but striving to prove my point, I continued: 'Now, let's look at the position. Assuming each power point uses electricity at a cost of two pence an hour, you are wasting 40 pence per hour. If you multiply this by 24 hours, and then by seven days for a full week, and then by 52 weeks, you come to a figure of £1456 for a year. Over twenty years, you will have wasted around £30,000. This is *your* £30,000, wasted and gone forever.'

I watched three little pairs of eyes looking at me. I had their complete attention. When I finished they all went and systematically turned off every powerpoint. I showered, dressed and felt so pleased with myself.

When Suzanne returned from taking the children to school, I couldn't contain myself as she came through the kitchen door. 'Well, I fixed that problem without any excitement or raising my voice. If children are treated as young adults, they will respond accordingly.'

At that Suzanne burst out laughing. 'You fool!' she said. 'You simply don't understand children. Do you know what happened after you finished with them? The three of them were arguing about what share each would get when you died. They couldn't agree on who would inherit the house and who would get my jewellery.'

I was completely crushed, slurped down the dregs of my coffee and crept out the door.

When the children were young, I had unexpectedly moved into the hotel at Chatswood, and I revelled in its spectacular growth. Jack's wife, Gwen, had been the licensee, but in 1960 she walked out without warning. While Gwen and Jack had run the hotel at Blayney quite well, there was a whole new dimension to running a top city hotel. Understandably, Suzanne hadn't wanted to come with me; with three little children it would have been difficult.

Hoteliers could not be bookmakers – the government wanted the licensee to be on the hotel premises, not at the races – so I couldn't transfer the licence to myself. I chose another woman, Shirley McLean, a top barmaid, to replace Gwen. She worked the bar and her husband worked in the cellar. Like Gwen, she was one of the early female licensees in Sydney. At that time few women worked in managerial roles; they were mainly secretaries and in other support positions. It was a gamble but I thought she had talent.

At first Shirley didn't want to take the job – she didn't think she could handle it. I told her she could do it and I would show her how. Shirley accepted the authority I gave her and suddenly she went from working the bar to being in charge of this big hotel. She flourished and did a marvellous job. It was simply a case of someone needing to be given the opportunity. One day, however, her husband suddenly quit – he didn't like her telling him what to do. He wanted her to go with him, but she wouldn't. To her credit, she told him she was the licensee and had to stay. The marriage was done.

Successful as the hotel was, there were some areas that didn't fire. I had introduced one of the first smorgasbords but could never make any money out of it. People would pile up their plates with food – and then leave most of it there. It would break your heart to see the waste. We had to employ a full-time handyman just to repair the chairs that people had wilfully damaged with their knives. I couldn't believe it; the patrons would steal things and break things – even toilet seats. They could be very destructive.

The children would often come to the hotel on a Friday night. They'd go swimming at Frank O'Neil's training centre and then come for dinner in the hotel: pink lemonade and chicken in a basket. Then we'd go to the drive-in movies at Frenchs Forest; the kids really looked forward to it and we'd have a great time.

—

Jack was keen on country properties. I liked these sites too, but mainly because of their development potential. I wasn't really a country man. Our first farm, St Charles, was about 50 acres at Wallacia. It was a piggery with a weekender house; we acquired it from Jack Muir in 1961, when he had a cash-flow problem and was unable to settle. As always in cases involving debt settlement, you end up paying 'over the odds' for the property, but you are glad to get paid.

I have many happy memories of our farms. Back in the early days, we used to send all the scraps from the Chatswood Hotel to feed the pigs at St Charles Farm. It probably cost us more in labour and petrol but, being Depression boys, Jack and I couldn't stand to waste food. An employee used to drive a truck up every few days with all the scraps. On one occasion he took his wife with him. The couple had lunch at the farm and decided to go to the famous lion park near Warragamba Dam. The trouble was, when they drove into the park the lions could smell the truck and came from everywhere, surrounding them. They couldn't move and were scared out of their wits.

A few years later we bought another much larger farm at Wallacia, named Elizabeth Park. We then tried to buy more adjoining land but our friend Ray Fitzpatrick, a property developer, said it was too expensive and we should wait to get the price down. Ray was trying to help, but we missed out and I learnt a lesson – if it is a great property you are better to buy it, even if the price seems a little much. We did manage to buy another adjoining property of 222 hectares called Pemberton Park, bringing our Wallacia holdings to 1000 acres or 400 hectares – within the boundaries of Sydney.

Jack and I decided that investing in and developing properties was definitely the way to go. I realised early on that one had to always go for the best location, and I loved Kirribilli and Milsons Point. Once, strolling along Kirribilli Avenue, I found a terrific waterfront site with a little three-storey block of flats – the 'For Sale' sign was overgrown with vines. The asking price was £8500, which would have been too high originally, but now, two years later, I thought it good value.

One agent who helped me a lot was Bill Halliday – a Dickensian character who was overweight and bald and always wore a black suit and pork-pie hat. Bill thought the Kirribilli Avenue property a bargain and said he could sell it for a profit of £2000. This was appealing as it would have been a capital profit – tax-free in those days – but I said to Bill, 'I don't want to sell because I could never replace it.'

Halliday said, 'I'll get you the site next door.'

Incredibly, he came back and said the next site could be bought for £9000. We were short of funds and the bank couldn't help us, but it did introduce us to a private financier, and we bought this house next door, which later became my home. Needless to say, I still wouldn't let Halliday sell the first site.

Halliday helped us sell another property at Gore Hill. We couldn't find a buyer at our price, but he said, 'I'll get it sold for you.' I agreed that he could keep whatever he achieved above our asking price, the government valuer-general's assessment. Bill found there was a burst pipe that was making everything damp, and when he sold the property he couldn't believe I honoured the deal with his bonus commission.

In the early 1950s we had bought five shops in Penshurst Street, Willoughby, for £11,000 – a fortune. They were strictly under the rent control which affected most properties after the war, and so ten years later, although the government valuation was high, there was no way you could sell at the valuer-general's price with such low rents. I commissioned a design for their redevelopment and went to each of the tenants and told them my plans, explaining that I didn't want to have to redevelop but that I didn't really have much choice – unless, of course, they would like to buy their own premises at the valuer-general's price?

All the tenants said they wouldn't have the money, but they jumped at the chance when I offered that they could pay a deposit and then pay the shops off in their own time – or I would even guarantee them at the bank if necessary. It was a great deal: they became masters of their own destiny, and we obtained a top price of £23,000. I saw it as no real risk to us, because if they defaulted we still had recourse to the property. A few years ago I was delighted when one of the old shop-owners came up to me at the races to thank me; she said I had changed their lives with my support and faith in them.

Jack and I had built two hotels and struck the jackpot twice, but we still wanted the third hotel we had dreamed of before Charlie had died. We approached Tooheys for a new hotel licence. We were hot property in the trade now, and accordingly were offered a new licence and site for £20,000, to be paid after completion of the hotel. The £20,000 represented the book value of the land and licence, which had been held by the brewery for over 50 years.

The site was at Bronte, directly opposite the proposed Bronte railway station – proposed since 1910! I had the land and licence independently valued at £50,000. I was pleased to receive this valuation and did no more checking. This would turn out to be a major mistake. Tooheys may have been good at brewing beer, but we were to learn the hard way that they had little idea of sites.

Meanwhile, we needed financial relief. We had decided to build a block of home units on the site we owned in Upper Pitt Street, Kirribilli. We wanted it to be the tallest building in one of Australia's densest suburbs, at least ten storeys high and with glorious views of the city and right up and down Sydney Harbour. We had always tried to build without an overdraft; now, for the first time, we borrowed £200,000 to build the St Charles home units.

I was about the first to introduce strata titled units with the St Charles development. I had heard about this modern concept, which gave people ownership and legal title to their own 'unit of living space' rather than a shared company title, and in 1961 I had lobbied the Labor state government for its introduction – just in time for our fabulous new project of 88 units.

Halfway through building the units, we began work on the Bronte Charles, which we decided to extend to 88 rooms.

Midway through 1960 we had sold 60 of the Kirribilli units and our financial risk was well covered. Then came the 1960 credit squeeze and almost overnight these 'sales' evaporated. We were left with 75 vacant units for more than a year. The state government then decided not to extend the railway line to Bronte. It was too late to alter our plans, so we were to dawdle and take two more years to build the hotel.

—

At Flemington, I was put in the draw with the other fielders for the 1960–61 season, and so managed to escape from my awful fixed stand. It is hard to explain, but there was a world of difference between the two stands. Now I raced away from the other bookies, with my turnover increasing at each carnival. I worked the Melbourne carnivals from the Cup in 1959 right through to the Newmarket (held in late February or early March) in 1968, and my turnover was never surpassed.

Going from one city to another is far harder than people realise. To go down to Melbourne intending to take over would have been the action of a fool. I went simply because I had always wanted to field there. I'd read about the trainers Lou Robertson and Jack Holt, the bookies Wallace Mitchell and Manny Lyons, and Eric Connolly, the biggest punter in Australia, who died in 1944. I just couldn't get there quickly enough, and once there – especially after that first year – I loved every minute of it.

I didn't mix socially with the other bookies, basically keeping to myself. On the stand I showed little reaction to what was happening around me, but I stood tall, which probably helped earn me my lifelong nickname, 'Big Bill'. Some people may have thought I was half-asleep at times, but I was always concentrating. I was never without a cigarette in my hand – it was normal for me to smoke 100 on a race day. My other vice was my boyhood love of ice-creams, and I'd often be seen licking one on the stand.

In Melbourne, once I got in front I decided to let myself go and gamble. In Sydney, we were always short of money and I didn't want to add to the burden. We had the Bronte hotel and the Kirribilli flats to finance. We had enough other expenses with the schooling and day-to-day lives of our three families, including Charlie's children. I had decided that although I would limit my losses, I would not limit my wins – any winnings could be played up. When I had told Jack about my intentions for Melbourne, he'd just laughed, but I truly believed I could look after myself.

I never took much money to Melbourne; instead, I took my bank manager, George Thorley. George enjoyed himself as much as I did. If I was short for settling on the Monday, George and I would go around to the bank for a refill. It may sound silly not to take much money, but it helps to check rapid losses, and that's all you need. You don't bet any less, but you do bet far more carefully.

Melbourne made me a big bookmaker; it made me think big and prepared me for the massive betting duels that were around the corner. In a three-year period I did not refuse any bet offered to me in Melbourne, and not once did I back a horse back.

I also kept working in Sydney – both in the city and at the provincial horses and trots. Joe Taylor was probably the biggest punter in Sydney at that time. He part-owned Thommo's Two-Up School, had operated numerous nightclubs – including Checkers – and was to run some of the city's largest illegal casinos. On his day there was no bigger punter. He would bet and, if the horse won, would put the winning ticket on his next selection. He was a big man and completely fearless – in his youth he had been a professional boxer.

By the Melbourne Cup Carnival in 1961, Joe had built up a credit with me of at least £50,000. I was unbelievably tight:

the credit squeeze had hit, the Kirribilli building had to be kept going and I had been losing. I had made up my mind that I would call it a day with Joe after I came back from Melbourne. I would pay him off and take no more business from him for six months. I had never done this before. Early in the carnival there wasn't much in it either way. I couldn't whittle Joe back much and he couldn't increase his winnings either. It came to the inaugural Provincial Cup, limited to horses that raced extensively in the provincial or country areas, horses that were perhaps a grade below the average city runner. The prizemoney for the race was quite substantial, and there was also a fine cup to be won.

The race had been Sir Eugene Gorman's idea – to support country racing. He had also set a horse of his own, Prince of Baghdad, to win the race even before the concept was approved. Accordingly, his horse avoided city racing, running only in the country areas. When the race came on Oaks Day, Prince of Baghdad was in prime condition; Sir Eugene told me it was a 'lay-down misère'. He and I were extremely close at this time, and he made me promise that I would not lose when his horse won. He invited a host of us to a 'victory dinner' at the Hotel Australia in Collins Street.

The race was difficult to price. Horses from various parts of the state would be meeting for the first time and it was hard to assess their form. I knew it would probably not be a big betting race, as punters would no doubt have the same problem, so I had no intention of getting heavily involved. It had all the hallmarks of a plunge race. Knowing what I did about Sir Eugene's horse gave me an extra incentive to pull back, as I knew it would shorten in the market.

Sir Eugene's horse opened with some 6/1 money but mainly at 5/1. Not wanting to lay it, I offered 4/1, being prepared to shorten this as soon as I saw the 5/1 disappear. But Joe Taylor was in front of my stand and in a belligerent mood.

'What are you trying to do to me?' he complained. 'Why have you got 4/1 up for Prince of Baghdad when there's plenty of 5/1 and even 6/1?'

'I don't want to lay it – go and back it elsewhere.'

'I don't want to go elsewhere – I do all my business with you and you've got all my cash. If you don't want to lay me a fair price I'll take my cash and my business elsewhere.'

I couldn't argue with that. Joe did do all his business with me, to the exclusion of all other bookies. I was not offering a proper bookmaking service to a good client. We settled on a bet of £20,000 to £4000 each-way – a hell of a bet for such a race at the time.

No sooner had I laid the bet than the price began to tumble. The 5/1 went to 9/2, then 4/1, 7/2, 3/1 and then 5/2 the ruling price. Finally it started as 9/4 favourite. I couldn't credit my position. Here I was standing the one horse that I didn't want to lay, the one I knew all about. I knew Sir Eugene must have also tipped the horse to Joe. I hadn't been winning, was short of cash and now had been caught where I should never have been.

The race was over a mile (1600 metres) and the track was very heavy. One horse, Barham Duke, came into the straight about fifteen lengths ahead of the field. It's a long straight at Flemington – over two furlongs – and it can seem to take an eternity to run. Barham Duke started to shorten stride and a horse came out of the pack after it – Prince of Baghdad. Half a furlong out everyone could see it was going to be a photo-finish: one horse was well in front but tiring, and the other horse was flying.

Prince of Baghdad and Barham Duke hit the line locked together, with the roar of the crowd deafening. The result went up: Sir Eugene's horse had finished second, just missing out.

I hadn't won on the race but I had saved a small fortune. This was the turning point of my carnival. When I returned to

Sydney the next week, Joe's entire credit had gone and I was firing again.

It's funny, but all my life it has been the same – when your luck is in, you can't go wrong and when your luck is out, no matter what you do, nothing will work. Jack and I paid off our building overdraft and suddenly we had cash again.

—

I worked in an entirely different manner at each track depending on the situation – whether a certain track was known for big punters, where the stand was situated, what percentages I expected to earn, and so on. I had to adjust my thinking and style of operation.

In Melbourne I was never at the top of the market because I felt the percentages of the other bookmakers' odds were too liberal and margins were too tight. I put up my own market that gave me a better margin, and so I was only betting big at a price I thought was good value. I was able to stabilise the market because of the magnitude of the betting. I was prepared to take the full bet of any punter, which is one reason I always led in turnover.

In Sydney it was totally different. I was still working on the Melbourne races, but I was protected from the well-informed home punters by 1000 kilometres and armed with a pricing service from Melbourne. I could be top of the odds all the time and prosper.

The early 1960s was a time when racing was booming; my fingers would get tired from 'punching cardboard' – issuing a betting ticket. I wrote these by hand in crayon, showing the wager and the horse's name. For over ten years in Sydney I didn't write fewer than 3000 betting tickets at a Saturday race meeting. My record was 4800 handwritten tickets – on two occasions. That might not sound much but the average meeting lasts about four and a half hours from the first race to the last. At the peak time, you are issuing 500 tickets a race – most of them in the ten minutes before they jump. Now, with computers, we would be lucky to write 1000 tickets per computer operator – on our busiest days.

Laying bets is very, very fast work and the tickets had to be legible. Unusually, although I wrote the tickets very quickly they were still clear enough for the clerks to pay out on without having to check the ledgers – and no one could write faster than me.

Back then I had two of the fastest and most efficient clerks in the country – they were legends. Len Tovey was on the bag, taking the cash, calling the bet and giving change. My penciller was Bill Peters, who recorded each bet and kept a running tab. Each bet required a series of figures to be entered in the ledger, which then had to be tallied to show the take-out for each horse. Peters was an arithmetical genius – no matter how frantic the betting, he would know what I was up for at any one time, and he would have everything completely worked out by the time the race had been run. There has never been anyone like him – before or after his time.

Len Tovey was the equal of Peters on the bag. He could take the cash for the bets and count the money with both hands – all at the same time. He would find the change from other punters having a bet rather than losing the time to dig into the bag. In the days when cash was everything, a fortune in notes would go through his hands. At the end of the day, Len's money would be all perfectly bundled and – most importantly – accurate. One day in a packed betting ring a 'dipper' slipped his hand into the bag to steal money; Len closed the bag on him with one hand and thumped him with the other.

In Sydney, after a race day I would return to the office with three or four large betting bags either empty or so crammed full of money that we had difficulty closing them. With four people helping, it could take an hour to count the money, and sometimes even that wasn't enough time. The money would be put in our hotel safe and banked the next day.

During these years I didn't use a 'runner' – a clerk who watched and reported on what other bookmakers were laying, what the leading punters were backing, or who could finance any horse that had been overlaid. I wasn't being big-headed – I was just confident in what I was doing. I was not interested in following anyone else, especially when I didn't know his motivation, and I did not 'bet back' any bets or finance my book. If I didn't want to lay a horse, I didn't reach to lay it by extending the odds. If I laid a bet, I kept it. If the bet was too much, then I only took what I wanted. I was never a punter.

The nearest thing I had to a runner was a little old World War I veteran named Alfie. If you ever saw Charlie Chaplin's character 'the Little Tramp', then you were looking at Alfie. He would stand and watch me work on a Saturday with hero worship shining out of his eyes.

In Sydney and the surrounding provincials, racing went on nearly every day and night. Alfie was at them all. At the provincial meetings, as the days were not busy, Alfie always asked if he could get me anything. Having a very small bank, he lived just to back a winner. If Alfie lost, he borrowed his fare back to Sydney or bummed a ride. Alfie and I both knew he would never pay it back, but we preferred to give him the fare as his body odour was always quite intense.

Gradually, over the years, Alfie worked his way into being our tea man. From this he promoted himself to price-watcher. What he was really doing was merely asking my opinion of a horse's price or chance – looking for the tip. One day, just before we headed to Melbourne for the Cup Carnival, Billy Peters said to Alfie, 'Why aren't you coming to Flemington? The boss misses you down south.'

Peters was fooling, trying to make old Alfie feel good. Two days later, as we walked on to the track at Flemington, who should be waiting for us but Alfie, resplendent in his scruffy suit, in the best tradition of a gentleman tramp. He had 'jumped the rattlers' all the way from Sydney. After that we always gave Alfie a return ticket to Melbourne, and his gratitude was boundless.

In the middle of the afternoon, Alfie would go to the cafeteria and get a large tray, and fill it with cups of tea and plates of cream cakes. On Alfie's first trip to Melbourne, I saw him in the middle of the afternoon weaving his way through the crowd. Sitting on the stand between races with my settling clerk was 'Mercurial' Michael Pitt.

Michael was a diminutive man in stature but a giant in the betting ring. He was a successful self-made businessman who had emigrated from Poland. Michael had been the biggest punter in Melbourne for more than twenty years. He never missed a meeting and bet on every race, backing not one but several horses. He would make what is called a 'punter's book'. It would be hard to estimate how much money Michael lost punting over the years, but it would have been staggering.

Alfie approached us with his laden tea tray. To see the concern on his face as he carefully balanced the cups was worth the price of admission. About ten metres away from us, Alfie tripped and lurched forward. I can still see the scene clearly: Alfie dropped the entire tray over Michael Pitt's head and onto his lap, before sprawling on top of him.

Michael leapt straight to his feet, furious. Although he was a gentle, kind man, his patience had been stretched to the limit. But Alfie was oblivious – all he wanted to do was to brush off Michael's face and clothes. Realising he was only making things worse, he reached into his pocket and brought out his soiled handkerchief.

It was this sight that completely did Michael in. A look of horror appeared as Alfie's grubby handkerchief approached his head. He turned and fled to the gentleman's washroom. But to prove his mettle as a punter, Michael continued punting for the rest of the day as though nothing had happened.

Who said there was no fun at the races?

9

A World Outside Racing

M Y LIFE WAS BECOMING more and more attuned to racing. Jack and I bought the racing newspaper *Newsletter*, and then the old sporting paper *The Referee*. Barry Terry, a top racing analyst, ran the *Newsletter*, while Ron Casey, who later became a prominent television and radio personality, was the livewire editor of *The Referee*. We incorporated *The Referee* in September 1963 and began trading in 1964 as a newspaper publisher.

The Referee was printed on its trademark pink paper and we assembled a group of racing experts, including a bright young Kingsley Shaw, Bob Curtis, John Schofield and Max Grey, who wrote in-depth stories analysing recent runs and the form for the upcoming races. From this experience I developed a healthy respect for newspaper publishers – with their deadlines and the never-ending need for fresh news stories to fill their pages.

To help circulation I ran various promotions through *The Referee*, including 'Pick the Card', in which readers, using a free voucher, had the chance of winning £5000 if they could pick the winner of every Sydney (or sometimes Melbourne) race on the Saturday. Luckily, no one ever picked it, and only later did we realise how foolish we were – we had not placed a cap on the winning pool. This meant that if more than one punter picked the card – which could have happened, if well-fancied horses had won every race on the day – we would have been facing a payout of hundreds of thousands of pounds.

I wanted the newspapers not so much for profit but as a means of increasing my racing doubles business, which was bumping along quite well. At its peak we had thousands of clients to whom we would mail out the doubles charts. Punters loved the doubles in the same way that they loved soccer pools and Lotto later on, because for a small outlay of even just £1 they could get odds of 1000/1 or more.

In fact, in the mid-1960s the journalists Fred Imber and Des Corless took a $1 doubles bet – backing What Yours in the Caulfield Cup with Now Now in the Melbourne Cup – to win a million dollars. It made for a good story: Imber billed it as the 'biggest single bet ever recorded', but still admitted: 'Actually our million-dollar bet does not represent "value" as the chances of either of the two horses running is remote . . . But Corless and I might have made racing history . . . and doesn't the betting ticket look lovely?'

Try as I might, I couldn't increase the circulation of *The Referee* more than marginally. The paper was 90 per cent racing and had a good following, but the losses were mounting. Although it was a good paper, I closed *The Referee* in 1965. I always meant to go back to newspapers – I hate a failure – but never did.

—

As the Charles Hotel at Bronte was drawing near to completion, the bills mounted. The bookmaker Jack Muir was my closest racing friend at this time, and I had helped him in times of financial shortage. He always paid me back. He asked me for help at around this time but I didn't have the wherewithal and thought I should insure against giving a direct refusal by crying my own shortage in advance. If a person needs cash, it's no use saying you've got nothing to spare if you are building an 88-room hotel, especially if he's not asking for much and is desperate.

No multi-storey hotel can open without a working lift, so I bemoaned to Jack that the operators would not install the lift until they were paid. The lift had in fact been paid for and installed. Having made my point, I promptly forgot my white lie.

The Charles was due to open in November 1963. About a fortnight before the opening date I received a phone call from my solicitor, the well-known and highly regarded John Rothery of Freehill, Hollingdale and Page. That morning John had bumped into the police hotel licensing superintendent and had a curious conversation. The superintendent had asked how the Bronte Hotel was coming along. When John told him everything was okay, he was then asked about the lift. John was at a loss to understand why. As the superintendent left, he said, 'Get Bill to ring me – if there's trouble with the lift, we'll work something out, but get him to ring me.'

I assured John that everything was okay. I had known the superintendent for twenty years – we had been quite friendly, but then he had done me a gratuitously bad turn. I told John I would not be ringing and not to worry. I wanted no favours.

A few days passed and John Rothery rang again to tell me the licensing superintendent had phoned again to say that if I wanted to open the hotel without a lift it would be okay, as long as I told him when the lift would be delivered. Now John wanted to know the story of the lift. I told him I didn't know what he was talking about – the lift was working perfectly.

Suddenly it hit me between the eyes. I had forgotten what I had told Jack Muir. He and the super were friends – I had actually introduced them years before. I was stunned to realise Muir's treachery in reporting that I was opening the hotel without a lift. Of all the people I was friendly with, Jack was the last I would have suspected of betrayal. I had told a fib to get respite – he had believed my story and then tried to cause me harm and embarrassment for no gain.

Needless to say, that was the end of our friendship. Human nature can be devious and I have never ceased to be astounded at what people can do to one another, no matter how strong a relationship might seem. Unfortunately, Jack Muir turned out to be an outright and poisonous enemy.

We opened the Charles Hotel at Bronte on time and without trouble. It was our biggest financial outlay but was to prove a real lemon, due to the promised Bronte railway station never being built. We got by with the influx of American soldiers on R and R. We would give taxi drivers a bonus for every new guest they brought us from the airport.

It was a large hotel with panoramic views of the ocean. We had been used to drinking hotels or pubs, so an accommodation hotel was a whole new ball game for us. In an avant-garde step for the time, Suzanne decorated the hotel with an Australian theme, choosing rust-coloured Australian motifs to tone with earth-brown carpets and redwood furniture. She used wooden panels with great effect instead of cement and tiles.

We had problems with the management and so I moved to the hotel late in the year to run it until we found the right person. It was an effort for Suzanne and the family, especially as the children were now so far from school. To help out, Mo Reynolds, a well-known ex-bookie, would drive the children to school in his large Cadillac. Mo had been a major force in provincial and trots bookmaking. He was also skilful at pre-post betting and had built up a business supplying prices to a large client base. He had hit hard times and attempted suicide, and I wanted to help. I bought his pricing business but still allowed him to keep his own clients. He also helped me put together and send out my daily doubles charts.

—

Around the time we opened at Bronte I received a call from a friend in Melbourne, Arthur Abrahams, who asked me if I would be interested in going in with him on the twenty-storey Sydney Chevron Hilton, which had run into trouble with the credit squeeze. It had cost £8 million for the stage-one construction, and there was still a gigantic hole that was to be the main building. By 1963 an official liquidator had been appointed. Although I was not at all interested, I saw the liquidator and found the property could be bought for £3.5 million.

Jack and I agreed that there was no way we could afford it. We decided I should put in a silly offer of £2.5 million. I was dumbfounded when my offer was accepted and the Chevron Hotel was mine.

I contacted a young architect, Neville Gruzman, and explained that I would try to form a group to finish off the hotel. I wanted him to draw up an artist's impression of the completed project for only a small fee, but that I would recommend him as the architect. He accepted and we signed an agreement, which was very fortuitous. Ignoring many restrictions and limitations, Gruzman produced a magnificent design. Now I looked around for partners.

I had an interesting new racing client. Robert de Lasala, a wealthy newcomer from Hong Kong, who had settled in Sydney and was keen on thoroughbred racing. He was a remarkable man with an incisive brain. He owned 43 ships and was considered the third-wealthiest citizen in Hong Kong. Robert was attracted to the glamour of horseracing and was soon one of the leading owners in Sydney. We became firm friends and I told him of the incredible opportunity. He took the Chevron deal to three prominent Chinese businessmen in Hong Kong; they were excited and came to Sydney to inspect the site and do a feasibility study.

The Chevron project had had a lot of publicity over the years. It was to be the first new international hotel erected in Sydney for almost half a century and was the brainchild of Stanley Korman, the hottest entrepreneur in Australia at the time. Before the 1960s credit squeeze, everything that Korman had done was a success, with properties all over Australia, New Zealand and even in New York. But when the squeeze hit he came unstuck.

Korman came to see me and couldn't believe the sale price of 'his' Chevron. When he found out that I had nothing in writing with Robert or the Chinese, he offered me £250,000 to transfer the deal back to him. I refused, as I had a gentleman's agreement and wouldn't go back on my word. To a gambler a man's word is everything. Korman then offered me £50,000 for our share. I declined this too, but he asked me to think it over and not be too hasty in refusing.

I phoned my brother late at night and told him of the offer: £250,000 capital profit, tax-free – it was one hell of a deal. Jack agreed that we wouldn't want to earn the odium of the commercial world. Instead, I took the offer to our new partners. They just laughed, saying they would not sell for double the purchase price.

It is amazing how things change. The Chinese loved Neville Gruzman and he loved them. He had been used to penny-pinching clients like me, and now he had clients to whom money meant nothing. The project was completely revamped. I made several trips to Hong Kong. On my first trip, the English realtor Ronald Collier booked himself a seat on our plane so we could talk. But he travelled in first class, while Robert and I were in economy. We both always travelled that way. If anyone asks why I travel second-class, I reply, 'Because there's no third class.'

Our Chinese partners looked after us so well: we were offered the choice of a brand-new Rolls-Royce or Lincoln

Continental for our use, but we preferred to walk the hundred metres from our hotel to our meetings. Our hosts took us to dinner each night. There was a certain amount of good-natured banter but, more importantly, we gained an insight into one another's characters.

I remember one discussion on how few people would ever see a million dollars, and what the money represented. Eddie Chan said that if one spent a dollar a day since the birth of Christ, then one would have spent less than $750,000. And at that stage you could have lived in most parts of the Far East on a dollar a day.

Another of our hosts looked at it differently: 'You are all wealthy men – you need never work again in your life. On waking in the morning you should sit on the edge of your bed and meditate for two minutes, asking yourself the question: "What can I do today to make myself happy, without hurting anyone else?" It is simple, yet not one of you will do this. Instead you will go out, plan, scheme and plot about how to make more and more money. As a result none of you can claim full or ideal happiness.'

Pang Kwok Chang, another partner, had an entirely different approach: he said, 'To my mind, no man is wealthy unless he has spent a million dollars on himself.' Pang was the picture of sartorial splendour. Beautifully groomed, with impeccable taste, he was in complete contrast to Robert, who you might think had slept in his suit. To drive his point home, Pang said, 'Robert, by my theory you are undoubtedly the poorest man here.'

I had several more trips to Hong Kong and enjoyed myself even more each time. Slowly but surely, however, I felt the harmony evaporating between Robert and Pang. They were on a collision course.

Meanwhile, the Sydney City Council rejected the plan because it didn't comply with its building codes. The relationship between the partners had soured and I couldn't get them to agree to anything. On top of that we received a huge bill from Gruzman. Fortunately, I had the letter of appointment.

After the Chinese application failed, I met Pat Hills, the deputy leader of the governing Labor Party, at a function. When he also inquired about the Chevron, I replied that I never wanted to hear of it again. He laughed and said that the government wanted the gaping hole in the ground filled. I asked if they would approve a casino on that site, and he said they would consider it favourably.

I was electrified by the thought of being granted a casino licence in Sydney. There was a state election due in New South Wales in ten days' time. Pat told me I should put a proposal to the government immediately after they were re-elected. This would mean that it would not be an election issue and that the new casino could be open and operating before the next election came around. I went to London, where I quickly arranged the necessary backing for the casino. I returned to Australia two days before the election.

I also knew the opposition Liberal Party's leader, Bob Askin, well because he enjoyed his racing. I liked Askin. Early that year he had been going to throw in the towel but I convinced him to have another go. He really was the only one with any dash. I told him then that he would one day be premier. I was later astounded when Askin said in a victory speech at the Trocadero that he respected two people, and number one was Bill Waterhouse.

Along similar lines, I remember once when Neville Wran became a QC in 1968 and was thinking of going into federal politics, I talked him out of it. I told him there were much better opportunities in New South Wales. He was elected to the upper house in 1970 and became premier in 1976. In the mid-1990s I encouraged John Howard to run for the federal opposition leadership once again and told him I was convinced he would become prime minister. I guess I've had a good nose for political careers.

Anyhow, before the 1965 state election I had told Askin of the government's interest in supporting the Chevron and the proposed casino. He also liked the concept and said that if the Liberals won the election the proposal would be quickly passed. He even said he was prepared to move it as an opposition motion, should his party be defeated.

I can't recall when I have ever been more confident of a project. Both political parties supported the issue. Labor had been in power in the state for over twenty years and there seemed no likelihood of them losing power now. The only significant issue was that the state Labor government was introducing an off-track betting totalisator service. This had alienated the whole of the illegal betting community. In Australia every man and his dog likes to have a bet, and thousands of bookies, one in every pub, catered for these clients, not to mention the many thousands of employed staff. A lot of people were affected, and so it played out in the election, which turned out to be a cliffhanger.

When the dust settled, the Liberal Party had won government by one seat. The Liberals had not expected to win and now wanted to do nothing in the least controversial. When I went to see Bob Askin, he was friendly, effusive and grateful, but quickly sidestepped the question of introducing a casino. 'Wait a year,' he said. 'When we've settled into government, we'll look at it again.'

The issue was always politely sidestepped and so I knew I was swimming against the tide; ultimately, I had to let the matter drop.

I knew Bob Askin right through his political life and after he retired. Since his death, a lot of scurrilous accusations have been levelled at him, which obviously he cannot answer. I can honestly state I never heard him ask for a bribe or suggest anything nefarious. He stood up for causes even if they weren't necessarily popular. When the AJC wanted to raise the turnover tax on bookmakers, Askin put himself on the line to help us and the tax went unchanged – for his term of office, anyway. Askin bet with me over the years and never asked for over the odds or even time to pay; he always settled. I could name a few politicians who haven't. Askin was not a saint but he was certainly not a crook.

That chain of events was the swansong for me with the Chevron. It was so disappointing to turn down a quick profit, and then to see it all come to nought. But Robert de Lasala had opened up the world of business outside Australia for me.

—

Jack and I decided to share some of our success with a few charities. We gave £10,000 to the Camperdown Children's Hospital and £5000 to both the Monte Sant' Angelo Convent and the Melbourne Lord Mayor's Fund. Over the years we made many other donations to worthwhile causes, including the Mater Hospital in Sydney.

It was around this time I was sought out by Brother McCallum, a truly remarkable man of the cloth. I allowed him to use the Charles Hotel at Chatswood for Sunday evening charity nights. He had boundless energy for his charity ventures, but died suddenly of a heart attack. Years later I visited the Strathfield Marist Brothers and found a commemorative plaque to myself. He had never mentioned this to me, but it showed the man's genuine appreciation.

—

After Charlie's death in 1954, Jack and I had kept going as though he were still alive with our original intention that each family should have a share of the income from the three hotels as well as a fine home. With the completion of the Bronte Hotel in 1964, we had now achieved that. After ten years of gifting

Charlie's children a one-third interest of our income from racing and including them in our projects, Jack and I ceased including them in new business activities from the middle of that year.

I had tried hard to be a father figure to the four children and made sure they went to the best schools and were well provided for. It wasn't easy as there were troubles. After a decade of working hard and sharing our profits with them, Jack and I felt we had fulfilled a moral obligation – in fact, we had made them all wealthy in their own right. Their father's estate, after probate, was estimated at £25,000, including a one-third share of the half-built hotel at Fairy Meadow and the un-built-on site at Chatswood. If Charlie's share of assets had been sold up, it would have realised much less than that valuation; although it would have lasted the family a few years, it would certainly not have given the children the start in life we had now achieved for them. We felt Charlie would have been very pleased with what we had done for his children.

I worked six and a half days a week, and Sunday afternoons was my time with my children. We'd usually go for a nice lunch at one of the few restaurants that opened, such as Laddie's Place at the Spit, or the Rock Lily at Mona Vale, or Jonah's at Whale Beach. Laddie's was owned by Laddie Gordon, whose father had once been Sydney's leading bookmaker but had died of a heart attack. Gambling does put people under pressure and sometimes there are sad cases like this. Laddie served deliciously fresh oysters and huge wooden platters of lovely fresh fish.

One time, my friend Joe Metz was up from Melbourne and joined us for lunch. He loved to eat and was very fat. He ordered six dozen oysters and two platters of fish and relished it. After lunch, however, all he could do was to stagger out onto the beach in front, and lie down for a sleep.

We'd usually also go for a drive in the afternoon and visit one of our building sites. Although the children were young,

I felt it was good for them to see what was going on. I would then take them to a park for a play on the swings. After we bought farm properties at Wallacia, we'd often go up there for the day for some riding or to play with the farm animals. Sometimes Suzanne would take the children there on the Friday evening and I'd join them on the Sunday afternoon.

In 1965, the landlord of our Clifton Gardens home decided to sell. Although I sent someone to the auction, the price of this lovely waterfront reserve home was beyond my expectations. I was used to buying property as an investment, so the price had to be right. We decided to move into one of the homes we'd bought at Kirribilli, right on the waterfront and opposite the Opera House – which was then under construction. Understandably, Suzanne was lukewarm about the move, as we were going from a cul-de-sac in an idyllic, quiet family suburb to the hustle and bustle of Kirribilli.

I gave Suzanne the choice between the beautiful old 'Craiglea' mansion in Upper Pitt Street (as by now Miss Lee had died) – which was in such an original state that it had no electricity or running water – and the less imposing but well maintained waterfront home in Kirribilli Avenue. I was glad when Suzanne chose the more modest waterfront home.

We ended up completely restoring 'Craiglea'. Our building team spent more than a year bringing it back to its former glory, and it became Jack's glorious home. It meant that instead of making way for a high-rise development, 'Craiglea' was preserved as an historic home – well before a heritage listing was even thought about.

Suzanne and I had always encouraged the children to have a go at everything – so they could see what they were good at. Although Suzanne couldn't ski, she took the children to the snow because we wanted them to learn most sports. They loved skiing so much. One of the first times they went to Perisher,

Robbie wanted to catch the first flight and head straight to the slopes – he couldn't wait. They all arrived at Sydney airport dressed in parkas, pants and even wearing ski boots.

From an early age, Robbie was quite grown-up and accepted responsibilities well. He was almost like a father to Louise and David, and at times perhaps a surrogate partner to Suzanne when I was busy. Once in the lead-up to Christmas when Robbie was about five or six, he ran ahead from the car to the front door and saw that a tricycle and other toys had been delivered. He ran back and said, 'Mummy, Mummy, the Christmas presents have arrived – stop the children!' He quickly moved them away, and we realised he obviously knew there was no Father Christmas.

When Robbie was just eleven he wanted a boat to sail; I told him he couldn't have one until he could swim a mile. Ron Casey, who worked for me as the editor of *The Referee* newspaper, was Robbie's swimming coach at the time. There was a major swimming competition, for the Wattriama Cup at the North Sydney Olympic Pool, where contestants had to swim more than 30 laps on handicap against competent swimmers, including an Olympian. Robbie entered and just wouldn't give up – he swam and swam. I was so proud to see his determination. Halfway through, Casey surprised me by saying Robbie was leading on handicap. Unfortunately, I had to leave before the end as I had to fly to London, but I was amazed on my arrival there to hear from Suzanne that Robbie had kept up the effort and won on handicap.

In the second half of that year, Suzy had suggested we take the children on a world trip. I thought this was a great idea. It was a good time for the children to go, as they could travel at reduced rates until the age of twelve – Robbie was still eleven. I was to meet them for Christmas in London and we would continue together. Travelling overseas was not common then, and indeed Suzy herself had only been on two brief trips

– our honeymoon in New Caledonia and a short visit with me to Japan.

The worldly Sir Eugene Gorman encouraged Suzy and recommended a travel agent who would put together the itinerary, complete with all the hotel bookings, transfers and tours. When one travelled, everything was planned and one did it in style. Like others, Suzy held a drinks party in the airport lounge for all the family and friends who had come to see her and the children off.

Everyone was amazed at Suzy's spirit of adventure, setting off into the world on a ten-week trip with three young children. I knew she would be fine and planned to join them in a few weeks. They had a ball, travelling through the United States and seeing all the sites, starting off with Disneyland and Universal Studios in Los Angeles and finishing with the Empire State Building and the Statue of Liberty in New York.

I guess it was optimistic of me to think I could get away from racing – in any case, I didn't want to express any doubts for fear Suzy might cancel the trip. Unfortunately, the family had to have Christmas in frosty London without me, and they continued for the remaining five weeks around the Continent. They went to Paris, Amsterdam, Brussels, Vienna, Salzburg, Rome, Venice, Florence, Naples and Athens. Suzy even took them skiing at Saint Moritz. It was brave of her. She was taking the kids to strange places where they didn't speak the language – or know the food. But it really was the making of the children. Robbie became the protective male figure, Louise was inspired by what she saw, and David returned as a confident young boy.

I had stayed at home in Kirribilli, which at the time had one of the highest burglary rates in New South Wales. Before we moved there, our house was burgled nineteen times in 21 months. The man responsible for many of them was eventually caught by the water police as he tried to make a getaway by boat. A couple of nights before Suzanne returned from overseas with the children, I was lying in bed half-asleep, and opened my eyes to see someone climbing in the window. I don't know who was more surprised – him or me. I jumped up, shouting abuse, and before I could grab him he escaped.

When Suzy returned she decided to get a watchdog. She found a handsome brindle great dane, which had been bred as a show dog but couldn't compete in Australian shows because his ears had been mistakenly clipped by his American owner. He was called Fury of Weydane, and he was like a small horse. I was amazed to come home and see this huge dog – Suzy really meant business. No one burgled us again while Fury was in charge. I've always loved dogs, but Fury was the first amongst equals. He was intelligent, had a very kind nature and was very protective of us all. He really was man's best friend, not just to me but to each of us.

—

I had a hankering for an overseas venture. Harry Akhil, an Indian Fijian, ran a small manganese mine in Fiji. Harry was interested in racing and owned a few slow runners. In about 1964 we got talking on the track and Harry suggested a mining deal in Fiji. My brother Jack was very interested and suggested we have a look. Jack brought Ray Fitzpatrick to Fiji with us. Ray was an enormously successful man and an experienced road-builder in Australia. He in turn brought along Ben Dickinson, a leading geologist.

We drove from Lautoka, where Harry was based, which is on the western side of the island, near Nadi Airport, across to the capital, Suva, on the other side. The trip was approximately 240 kilometres, although just 80 kilometres by air. It was the worst road we had ever been on. Ray passed his comments on to government officials, who told us that the World Bank was in the process of allocating £9 million towards the cost of a new road.

Ray called me aside and said he could build the road for as little as £3 million. He said that if I could win the contract, we would be partners and have a good profit. I approached the authorities and offered to build the road. They had to wait until the World Bank supplied the money. It was suggested by the speaker of the Fijian parliament, Sir Maurice Scott, that I set up a local business enterprise, as they would call for tenders for the road contract when the time came, and local businessmen would be given preference. Since I was a bookmaker, Sir Maurice suggested I open a betting agency in Suva.

A firm called Pearce and Co. already acted as the Fijian agent of a very old Sydney betting firm called Hackett and Williams. The process of having a punt was very slow. Bets were taken by the firm in Suva by ten in the morning. They were then airmailed to Sydney, where the accounts were calculated and then posted back to Suva. The operation took ten to fourteen days.

I realised that if I was ever going to get that road contract, I had to commit to Fiji. I decided to start with a modernised betting agency in Suva, and I invited Sir Eugene Gorman to come across to help me sort out the red tape.

Taking Sir Eugene was a masterstroke. He was probably about 70 at that time, retired but very well known and respected by all the colonial authorities. With Sir Eugene's direction, and help from Sir Maurice Scott, who had also been the leading lawyer in Suva, they worked out a way for the licence to be issued.

I was quite excited at the new venture. I had formed a friendship with a man named David Crompton who was based in Suva and was interested in racing. He asked if he could manage the new betting shop with a friend of his, Francis

Grant – a well-regarded Indian Fijian. Both were working for Burns Philp, the leading trading company in the South Pacific. David was in charge of the credit department and Francis was his debt collector.

It was obvious that David was going to be the organiser and Francis the worker. They were to be paid a commission on all the business and took bets up to midday on Saturday. The clients were paid out on Monday morning. It was a big improvement but still primitive. I was amazed at the response. There was no racing on the island, and very few of the local people had even seen a racehorse, let alone been to a racetrack, yet they crowded into the betting shop. The indigenous Fijians were fascinated.

Anyway, as the business settled in Fiji, David Crompton dropped out because of other priorities and Francis took over entirely. I was unsure if the venture would survive as I didn't know Francis, but the Fiji betting shops very soon were achieving extraordinary results.

I thought that if the results were this good in the towns they would be even better in the large resort hotels, as most of the tourists who came to Fiji were from Australia. I thought they would love to bet on Australian racing with us. If they won, it could pay for their holiday; if they lost, they could settle their debt back home.

Without exception, the resort shops were disappointing. I was amazed and yet, when I looked at it, it became patently clear. As a rule, the person who went on a holiday didn't leave Australia to have a bet with Bill Waterhouse; he could do that very easily at home.

Meanwhile, we had opened in each of the large towns and invariably these were all a success – because in these places we were providing the people with something that had been lacking – a low-cost leisure activity. A local could pick up a form guide, study it during the night before the races, go to the betting shop the next day and make, say, a two-dollar bet. It was an inexpensive pastime.

We soon had agencies all over the island, and our clients were the locals rather than the tourists. In those days overseas betting was still extraordinarily difficult logistically. The form papers would be on sale on Friday in Sydney around midday. We had to arrange for these to be collected, driven out to the airport and sent on the plane to Nadi, Fiji – where they would be sorted out and sent around the island. They would arrive in Suva on the Saturday morning, if all went well. Many times the papers were not offloaded at Nadi but taken on to Honolulu.

Francis soon became a full one-third partner with Jack and me in the Fiji business and went on to be involved with me in ventures overseas, and over the years we travelled extensively together. Francis eventually became a millionaire in his own right. For almost half a century, though we had our ups and downs, we remained firm friends.

—

In the late 1960s Jack and I also became involved in mining in Western Australia. And why not?

Everyone in Australia seemed to be interested in mining at that time. After we returned from Fiji in our initial mineral search, Ben Dickinson suggested several ventures in Australia. I was not overly keen but Jack was, so we formed a small partnership with Ben and also Harry Akhil, the owner of the mine in Fiji. Before we got underway we added another partner, Joan 'Coco' Money – who was a legend in her own time. A widow, young and beautiful, she successfully ran an extensive business in Western Australia and was both well known and respected throughout the west. Without her efforts I doubt if we would ever have got far with the Mines Department in Perth.

We finished up with a large area to be geologically surveyed in the Kalgoorlie area, which Ben thought could be good for nickel. He suggested an exploration agreement with a large North American company, International Nickel (Insel). Foolishly, we signed what we were advised was the standard company exploration agreement; if any minerals were found, a new agreement would be entered into with our syndicate, which we had called DAWM (using the first initial of each of our surnames).

And then the nickel boom started. The fabulous find at the Poseidon mine set the scene for a stock exchange explosion the likes of which Australia had never before seen. The whole country plunged into a mad minerals gamble. As it turned out, our lease abutted the nickel find. Billy McMahon, the federal treasurer and later prime minister, told me ours was one of the choice mining leases in Australia. The shares of Poseidon shot up from a few cents each to hit $280. It seemed every mining lease was floated on the stock exchange and shares were oversubscribed overnight. However, we had entered into an agreement with International Nickel and our hands were tied.

Further, we had been assured by Insel that we would be paid the identical royalty received by the West Australian government. It turned out that although our royalty started at the same level of 0.5 per cent, there was no allowance for our royalty to change; the government royalty rates later rose to 2.5 per cent and Insel refused to amend ours.

I went through the agreement line by line and found a possible out. I sought Neville Wran's advice. The agreement was subject to an option that had to be exercised within two years. Insel had to notify DAWM before 31 December 1969. It was early May – there were seven months to go.

As the deadline drew near, I became more and more confident that they had overlooked this requirement. However,

I made a fatal mistake. Ben came to see me towards the end of the year and I told him about my discovery, and that I was sure Insel did not realise the provision existed. We now only had to sit tight and the mine would shortly revert to us.

Then out of the blue, just two weeks before the deadline, the company exercised its option. The curious aspect was that the notice of extension was sent directly to Ben Dickinson at his home address, rather than to me at my office at Milsons Point, even though I had the carriage of all dealings between DAWM and Insel. I realised then that Dickinson must have warned Insel. Although he was our partner, he was interested in other business ventures with Insel. We were stuck with a one-sided agreement and an under-market royalty, which probably cost us a small fortune.

10

All Gamblers Die Broke . . .

IN 1963 I WAS ACCEPTED to field on the Caulfield Cup. It is run two weeks before the Melbourne Cup, which meant I would have approximately one month's stay in the southern capital. It had not been easy and may not have happened without the support of the Victorian Amateur Turf Club (VATC) chairman, Sir Maurice Nathan. I was again afforded the 'luxury' of a specially allocated stand. This stand was 1A – right at the far end of the Rails, away from the grandstand and crowd and in a narrow bottleneck past the winning post. I missed the 'cream' business as the average punters were not going to push their way down to me to take the same price as offered elsewhere.

Yet I did have something going for me – I was by now known in Melbourne as the leader of the ring, and I knew that as long as I didn't make mistakes, I could handle the stand. As well, there are always 'stargazers' who go to the races just to see the person they have been reading about in the newspapers. So I always had a group of onlookers, which in itself helped attract business.

And I had the inside running in one other area – the large gamblers knew that they could get on in one go with me – which enabled me to still hold the turnover figures and ensure I was the leading fielder.

When I finally escaped this Caulfield stand a couple of years later and was included in the draw, I was again amazed at the general business I had lost. The general public, just out for a day, do not generally shop around for prices. People simply compare the closest three or four bookies. If all have the same price, they go to the nearest to make their bet. With this type of business, there is no need for any worry. All you have to do is to punch cardboard and your margin percentage from your betting board will look after you.

Looking back, I realise that I had become a well-rounded bookie. I wasn't right all the time, but I didn't make a big mistake and get caught at the wrong odds. At the same time, my prices were competitive with the market. If I had a punter, I didn't lose him by being under the odds.

As you go along, you get better in your judgement and prove yourself. You start to know the punters and suddenly you are a much more astute operator. I could work out the odds quickly and I liked gambling. For me it was a matter of overall ability and, using the form I put together, I worked out my prices and away I went.

Part of my skill was in being able to 'dress' my betting board to attract customers – similar to window-dressing in a retail store. I tried to make my prices appealing and competitive, while at the same time ensuring I was just under the odds on horses that I liked on form.

I had developed my own style. Early on I decided I wanted to be fearless in my betting. This doesn't mean I didn't care if I won or lost, but rather that I didn't want my punters to know what was going on in my head. Just as a good card player develops a 'poker face', I prided myself on the fact I would take a bet without flinching or showing any other reaction, although I stood to win or lose a small fortune on the result.

Over the years punters said they had increased their bets just to challenge me, waiting for me to cut them back and so acknowledge that their bets had found my limit. It was this style that gave rise to the huge betting duels which were just around the corner.

—

With the two kinds of big punters, professionals and amateurs, the difference is as great as between the sky and the sea. The amateur can still be difficult to beat, but he is not as price-conscious – he relies more on the 'tip'. He just wants to back a winner. The professional who is well organised often beats you on price, whether he backs a winner or not, which in big wagering ruins the balance of your book. If you're trying to bet big on your way up to being a top bookie, it can be completely demoralising to be shot down in a second by one of these pros.

If a horse was to figure in a plunge and firm from 100/1 to 14/1, this would be looked upon as a sensational plunge by the general public. To the bookmaker's book, however, the difference is just six per cent – exactly the same difference as between 5/4 and even money, yet that sort of shortening is seen by the public as nothing. In bookmaking it is important to catch the favourite at the shortest price possible.

The Paddock is the most expensive public area of the racetrack and attracts both the biggest backers and the biggest bookies. The Rails section runs along the fence, dividing the general paying public from the members' stand, and bookies have two-sided stands: one for the public and the other to serve the members. The members and their invited friends are regarded as the upper echelon of the racing world.

Right up until the mid-1970s women were not allowed in certain areas of the members' stand, including near the main Rails bookmakers. On Sydney and Melbourne courses a line was painted on the ground, over which ladies were not allowed to pass. It was considered unladylike for a woman to bet – and besides, they certainly shouldn't know what their husbands were betting.

This members' inner sanctum also contains the 'birdcage', which is only accessed by the licensed and registered persons who are involved in the next race to be run, and the connections (owners) of the runners. Here the starters are paraded, trainers give instructions to jockeys, and the jockeys mount their horses before going out on the track. After the runners have left for the starting gate, you will often see a punter rush from the birdcage back to the betting ring to place their bets. The advantage to a serious punter, whether amateur or professional, of being close to the birdcage is obvious: it is extremely useful to see the horse's condition and temperament at close range immediately prior to the race.

—

From early on I realised there was a hell of a lot of truth in Damon Runyon's observation that 'all gamblers die broke'. The big bookie during and after World War I was the flamboyant Andy Kerr – the 'Coogee Bunyip'. His fame was widespread, but he went broke in 1930 and spent the next 25 years a broken man. He tried to recover by fielding at the dogs but it was too late to come again, and of course there was the inevitable new young brigade. His downfall had been the Caulfield and Melbourne Cups double of 1930 – the most disastrous doubles result ever to befall the Australian bookmaking fraternity.

Joe Mathews and 'Gentleman' Jim Hackett both were big bookmakers too, and both died very wealthy. But Mathews was not a gambling bookie and Hackett had inherited a fortune from his father, who was also a bookie. Two other big bookies were Charlie Howie and Reg 'Dopey' Donovan. Both died without a feather to fly with.

Apart from Ken Ranger, Bill Mulligan also influenced me. He was a bluff, gruff man who hit the headlines before Ranger. I was staggered by his betting during the war years. I thought Mulligan was the next best thing to a genius. He had a rough tongue and a quick wit. I remember a conversation he once had with a country grazier who had just come to Sydney for a holiday. The pair got talking at the Tattersalls Club. 'What do you do?' asked Bill.

'I'm a sheep farmer. We've just finished shearing and I'm down for a few weeks.'

'How often do you come to Sydney?'

'Usually once a year – after shearing.'

'Oh,' replied Bill. 'How many properties do you have?'

'Only one – that keeps me going enough.'

It was obvious the man was extremely wealthy, but Bill couldn't help himself: 'Only one property! Well, I have four, and I shear my sheep at a different one each week.'

The grazier looked at Bill and smiled. 'You're joking, of course?'

'No, I'm not – my farms are Randwick, Warwick Farm, Rosehill and Canterbury, and *my* sheep get sheared every Saturday!'

However, when I got to work beside Mulligan for several years in the late 1950s and early 1960s, I soon realised my idol had feet of clay: he was a man of limited racing ability, relying on bluff.

Arthur Browning was another big bookie of my time. A few years older than me, he made a big impact. He had charisma and was a lion for many years, having a big say in the ring. Apart from being a bookie, he enjoyed the punt himself – as I had seen from the Guncotton incident back in 1954. Arthur considered himself a gentleman and wouldn't get up on his stand – he preferred to stay beside it on the ground. On occasions when he lost badly on a race, he would climb up on his stand, throw down his hat and jump on it in frustration! He was a wise fielder who retired wealthy in the late 1970s and spent most of his retirement travelling the world.

Chris Jenkins was a well-known old Melbourne bookie. He was a great guy with a tolerant and generous outlook on the world. He only bet doubles and had no peer. His mailing list covered the whole of Australia and he would hold £250,000 in bets on a big double, which was a hell of a lot of money around 1960.

The main double of the year was the Cups double – offering odds on winning both the Caulfield and Melbourne Cups. Chris would lay doubles bets at long odds to win huge amounts – up to a million pounds. With these very large lays he had the option to immediately refinance or 'bet back' with another doubles bookmaker or, alternatively, wait until after the first leg was run, as most of the horses entered wouldn't even start – which was a powerful advantage, as it meant he kept all those stakes for the non-runners.

If the first leg of some of the doubles bets he'd taken got up and he was facing exposure for the second leg, he could still refinance the risk, using some of the pool of funds he was holding to cover his potential liability on the second leg by backing the high-risk horses. So either way he should still be in front.

The real danger was when the same horse was backed to win both legs. I had come to know Chris around 1956, when I was in awful trouble with Redcraze for the Cups double. Chris warned me then that you must never let yourself into trouble on the double with the same horse. If a horse wins the first leg, it almost automatically becomes favourite for the second leg. So any chance of backing the horse straight out to win the second leg to get out of trouble disappears – the price is just too short.

So it was for me with Redcraze. After winning the Caulfield Cup it started at 7/4 in the Melbourne Cup, a price I could not bring myself to take to cover the exposure. Fortunately, it was beaten by a half-neck by Evening Peal.

I swore that I would never get into trouble with the one horse in a feature double ever again. The next year, the punters took the very low odds offered by the bookies about Tulloch winning both cups. I couldn't resist. When Tulloch won the Caulfield Cup I was suddenly in deep trouble, as he also looked a certainty for the Melbourne Cup. Incredibly, Tulloch's owner, E. A. Hayley, controversially scratched him from the Melbourne Cup, much to the chagrin of his trainer, T. J. Smith, and the punting public. Tulloch was only a colt, and Hayley felt he was too young for such a gruelling event. If Tulloch had started, he would have no doubt won at odds-on – and I would have been crushed. It was a tremendous lesson for me.

Twice I had escaped by the skin of my teeth, and I was never again to lay the one horse to win both legs of a feature double. Incredibly, an outsider did win the Cups double in 1962. I worked on both races and remember it well.

Even Stevens was owned by the New Zealand industrialist James Wattie, who produced Wattie's tinned and frozen groceries. The horse was the greatest certainty ever to start in either race – for those who knew all the facts. He was a five-year-old thrown in with seven stone eight pounds (48 kilograms) for the first leg and one pound (half a kilogram) more for the second. This was almost at the lower limit of seven stone seven pounds (47.6 kilograms) and yet he was later revealed as the best horse in Australia, beating Sky High, the Australian weight-for-age champion, after winning both cups.

The plan was brilliantly laid out – almost too brilliantly. Even Stevens had won a minor cup in New Zealand as a four-year-old and then was hidden away, starting only at picnic meetings where he was beaten, hence the low weight and long prices on offer when the cups weights were issued. The Even Stevens Cups double was sent out at 1000/1, and it wasn't long before money for it started pouring in.

The horse had been left in New Zealand until the last minute, when he was brought across by the inaugural Qantas Horse Flight. Almost overnight, from being an outsider and likely non-starter, Even Stevens sensationally firmed to become one of the favourites.

Only eighteen horses start in the Caulfield Cup, and the first horses eliminated are the poorly performed horses with little hope of winning – the bottom or low weights, which included Even Stevens. So his only chance for a start was to go into the ballot. Here he was lucky and drew the third emergency. This still meant he could only get a start if three of the confirmed starters were scratched, so it still looked like Even Stevens would not be getting a run. The connections had outsmarted themselves as the horse did not have enough weight to force his inclusion in the field. Then fate took a hand.

It poured rain all the Friday evening and it kept pouring on the Saturday morning – the track became a quagmire. Horses which were poor mud-runners started to be scratched, including the favourite, Aquanita – eventually giving Even Stevens his unlikely start in the race.

He started the Caulfield Cup at 6/1 and bolted in. He was then given the maximum ten-pound (4.5-kilogram) penalty for the Melbourne Cup. In a large field of 26 runners and starting from a wide barrier of 21, Even Stevens started at 3/1 and was never under pressure. He went to the lead 'in a canter', and won untroubled by four lengths.

Chris Jenkins had seen the awful change in his fortunes all the way along with Even Stevens. He had been wary of it for both legs of the double from early on, but when the Even Stevens double shortened to 50/1 it seemed ridiculously low for a horse which was probably not even coming over from New

Zealand to win both legs. So he broke his own rule and took two wagers of £50,000 to £1000.

Further, in a cruel twist of fate, his clerk had mistakenly thought the wager had been erroneously repeated and so only recorded the one bet. Only after the races were run was the blunder discovered – the ruinous blow in an already disastrous double. Chris paid out the extra £50,000 without a murmur; in fact, no one in Melbourne was even aware of the dreadful mistake. Chris kept on going but was only a shadow of his former self, ruined by the one thing that he had tried to scrupulously avoid.

Adopting the hard and fast rule of not laying the one horse in both legs of the double was to save my skin in a different way a few years later.

—

My father had drummed into me how bookies came and went, and that it was rare for anyone to stay at the top for a long time. The pressures of the trade were enormous, and any weakness – such as fear or ego – had to be carefully controlled or it would spread and consume you.

I do think that I was incredibly fortunate. Firstly, I was extremely well trained before I actually took out my licence. I was 32 when I started, yet I had been a bookmaker in everything but name since I was a teenager. I had no inhibitions, and I didn't need training or testing – and I had the necessary ability. Further, I had other activities – we were building hotels and developing other projects. Funnily enough, any pressure I felt came almost solely from this quarter, which is probably why I loved and hated building.

As well, I was able to adapt. My father had given me a solid grounding in doubles and trebles. I soon realised that the three different betting codes – thoroughbreds, trotting and dogs – needed to be handled differently, with distinct techniques.

I developed an in-depth understanding of interstate betting. When I later went to work at the Melbourne carnivals and then the United Kingdom, again I had to adjust swiftly and efficiently in order to survive.

By the mid-1960s I was regularly called a 'leviathan bookmaker', under headlines such as 'They're never too big for Big Bill'. But reporter Bert Lillye wrote in the *Daily Mirror* on Melbourne Cup Day in 1965 that it was not just the punters who were doing their best to batter me down. The government was getting its share from me, with more than £60,000 a year in turnover tax. Des Corless quoted me as saying my biggest personal concern was not losing money but my nerve: 'If I lose my nerve, I am finished as a bookmaker.'

My resolve to never show any reaction or fear about a big punter's bet sometimes meant I would take the bet and then nonchalantly extend my odds a little, especially if I felt like 'giving it a stand'. This caused some to see evil and land me in hot water.

One such example occurred at the Harold Park trots a week before the 1965 Melbourne Cup, when it was suggested that I had more than luck on my side when I stood the 2/1 favourite, Koala Dan, to lose £13,000. It ran fifth. Len Smith, the highly respected chief steward at the trots, launched an inquiry, examining my sheets and questioning me at length.

After the inquiry Mr Smith announced: 'Mr Waterhouse's pattern of betting is most unusual and I took the step to hold the confidence of trotting followers in the administration of the sport. It was disclosed that Mr Waterhouse is a gambling bookmaker who often makes an unbalanced book, depending on his assessment of a horse's chances or the persons who back horses in a race.

'Further, his books disclose no pattern of over-laying horses from certain stables and that horses he overlays are often successful and give him a bad result.'

Bert Lillye wrote that Mr Smith's conclusions coincided with his own observations of me over the previous ten years: 'He is a fantastic gambling bookmaker who is a magnet even to the non-betting onlooker. They regard him as the James Bond of Australian bookmakers.'

—

The Melbourne Cup usually draws around 100,000 patrons to the Flemington racetrack. The action starts early in the morning when the car parks fill and people set up their picnics beside their cars. Champagne corks pop and chicken is devoured throughout the day. The ladies are in all their finery with hats (and, in those days, gloves) and the gentlemen in top hats and morning suits. The betting ring is always packed to the limit and there isn't a vacant seat in the grandstands, and the last revellers are put off the course well into the night. All this, of course, because of a horse race.

Each year I would throw a party for local and visiting VIPs at Maxims, the leading restaurant in Toorak, taking up the whole top floor. It would be a black-tie affair, and on display would be a large solid-ice horse with a hole where the saddle went which was filled with caviar. Mary Jane Pratten, my terrific secretary, would organise everything, with help from my friend Joe Metz. Suzanne would be there as my charming hostess. We would also have friends down from Sydney. They were lovely times.

The Melbourne Cup Carnival starts on a Saturday with the Derby, and – after the Cup on the Tuesday – continues with Ladies' Day on the Thursday, featuring the Oaks, and finishes the next Saturday with the George Adams Handicap (now the Emirates Stakes). Betting takes place over the four days. The leading punters come from all states and as far away as Perth.

In 1965 the Victoria Racing Club invited the English model Jean Shrimpton to be its official guest at the Cup Carnival.

She introduced Australia to the miniskirt, causing a sensation. To top it off, she didn't wear a hat or gloves. The critics were horrified. Ms Shrimpton must have wondered what had struck her, such was the reaction at the nation's holy grail of racing.

That year I had again represented the Sydney betting ring – the strongest in Australia – and my holdings, still in pounds, were big. Under the headline 'Bookie Holds £1/2 Mil.', Des Corless wrote: 'Sydney bookmaker Bill Waterhouse staggered Victorian racegoers at the V.R.C. carnival with his colossal wagering. Over the four days he held nearly £1/2 million – only £180,000 less than . . . all TAB agencies in NSW . . . Waterhouse's turnover created an Australian record . . . more than ten per cent of all money invested at Flemington.' Des went on to say that the big winners were the Victorian government and the VRC, which shared in the £8000 turnover tax.

I was the only 'guest' bookie working on the course, which meant that every visiting punter was drawn to me. This had its pros and cons. Soon after I had started in Melbourne I had a big day, winning a massive £20,000, and took about £10,000 into the club in my pocket. I remember walking out of the settling room flat broke. My money had been won from interstate clients, mainly Sydney, but they wanted to settle when I returned to Sydney. Worse, they relied on me to pay their other losses for them with the Melbourne bookies. This sometimes also happened in reverse: after having a bad losing day, I have had tens of thousands foisted on me for safe custody.

When you're holding somebody's money – or even when you owe a small fortune – a camaraderie exists between bookie and client. Invariably a punter playing up his winnings or chasing his losses will ask, 'When do you finish your market? Can I phone you and get an idea of what you think the market will be?' I have never claimed to be a puritan, and even though in earlier years – before the introduction of the TAB – I had an SP business, I have never asked anybody to phone up and bet pre-post with me.

But the progression is a natural one. You have a good client, someone you do not want to lose. Of course you'll give him an idea of the price a horse will be later that day on the track. If you quote a price of 4/1 and the punter thinks that's a fair price, he will then logically ask if you will be laying it at that price. Of course you'll lay a wager: it would be both childish and unrealistic to do otherwise. Once this has happened, it will happen again and become a regular thing. It is an advantage to any gambler to know in advance what price a horse will be, and to the bookmaker what price a punter will be prepared to take.

It sounds quite simple to assess pre-post prices but it is anything but. It is exceedingly difficult to get an accurate professional assessment of a horse's chance that is reflected in its price; it is even harder to come to a price that the public will accept. The two must somehow be blended together, and a miscalculation in either direction can be disastrous. For example, if you assess a horse as a 2/1 chance, what do you do if, when you offer that price, no one wants it? Do you extend it until you receive a response? What if the extended price is 4/1? And how does your new price affect the prices of other runners, since now your margin is reduced with the extended odds? Your answer to that question is the difference between being a percentage bookmaker and a gambler.

The big professionals who would bet pre-post in the morning were important to me. By gleaning their opinions on the prices of the horses they were backing, they enabled me to frame and finetune a very accurate market. If they thought the price I offered was not on the mark, they would react to it – either by taking the price if I was too high, or by negotiating for a better price if they thought I was too low.

Melbourne man Les Brougham – known as 'Possum', since no one saw him during the daytime – was one of the best form judges I knew, and a professional punter who never lost over a period. I valued his opinion very highly and so would accept his pre-post bets without limitation, which gave him an extra edge. He was sensible, bet modestly and was a great help to me in Melbourne.

Betting on the morning of a race is undoubtedly the most dangerous form of wagering, as far as the bookmaker is concerned, but if he can handle it, it is also of inestimable value. I built up a substantial early-morning market while in Melbourne, which meant that when I went to the track I had an excellent assessment of the form for all races. By the time I stood up in the betting ring I was very confident about each horse's chance, and also about what price the punters were prepared to accept.

—

In those days my carnivals program was marvellous. Early spring was spent in Newcastle in New South Wales for the Newcastle Jockey Club's Cameron and Cup Carnival. After that I would fly to Melbourne for Show Day in mid-September at Caulfield, then back to Sydney for the AJC's Epsom–Metropolitan Carnival, then to Melbourne for the Caulfield and Melbourne Cups. This would all take a little over two months, and by the time the Melbourne Cup Carnival was finished, I had had enough racing and wanted to go home.

I thoroughly enjoyed Melbourne as I always continued my strategy of limiting my losses while playing up my winnings. I bet big but I never chased business. There has always been rivalry between Australia's two biggest cities, and I was very much aware of it. After a while the bookies came to realise that I wasn't after their blood, that I was not a quotation-buster, nor was I trying to steal their business. I don't think they ever came to love me but they did accept me and treated me well.

After the final day of the Cup Carnival, Suzy and I would

catch one of the large cruise liners back from Melbourne to Sydney. We'd have a couple of hours after the last race to catch the *Oriana* or *Marconi* and would arrive in Sydney on the Monday morning. This was tremendous. It capped off the Carnival beautifully and I unwound, arriving in Sydney ready to fight the world again. The Europe–Australia run was coming to an end and this lovely way to travel would soon be no more.

Rough seas were soon to appear on the racing horizon. Although real trouble was still a couple of years away, the scene was about to change and I would be caught up in the vortex.

11

Giving Myself the Needle

B OB 'CHICKENS' INGHAM ran up to me at the Canterbury Park races one day early in 1966 and excitedly burst out, 'There's a guy down on the Rails with Jack betting like mad! You've never seen or heard anything like it!'

Bob himself was as big a punter as any, and already one of the wealthiest men in Australia. At that time he was betting in the new dollar currency in amounts of around $10,000. Now he was watching a man betting in amounts of $40,000 and $50,000. Gambling for Bob and others would never be the same.

My clerks and I were intrigued, as none of us had heard of the mystery punter, whose name was Frank Duval. He had been racing before without flexing his punting muscles. Now his name began rippling around the track like the water lapping on a lake that signals a coming storm.

Frank Duval was a country boy from Narrandera in the Riverina, a wheat town on the edge of the Murrumbidgee Irrigation Area. He fought in World War II and became a captain. He liked the army and, rather than returning to the farm, volunteered for the Australian Army of Occupation in Japan.

After serving out his army term, Frank set up an office in Tokyo. Steel and iron ore were then in short supply and expensive – this was before the iron ore explosion in Australia.

Frank came to Sydney looking for opportunities. It was the time when Sydney was replacing its trams with buses, so all the old tramrails were being pulled up and sold as scrap. Frank was on the spot, tendered for the lot and was on his way.

Overnight he was a wealthy man. He became interested in mining companies and, because he was in on the ground floor, he had it made in Japan. Others found it difficult to crack the tough Japanese market but for Frank it was easy. It was like being in the vault of the bank – he had just what the Japanese needed.

I don't think Frank ever thought of himself as a gambler, or that he had a problem with liquor. He just enjoyed life – he worked hard and took time off regularly to unwind. Every year he would go tiger hunting in India, spend a week playing the tables on the French Riviera, and once or twice a year he would come down to Sydney to do a little business and play the horses. Win, lose or draw, he would then get on a plane and fly back to Japan. Rarely did he have more than a day or two at the track on these visits.

The day he clashed with my brother Jack in 1966 was an ordinary race meeting. There were no major races scheduled and it was early in the year. Frank had a horse running and had merely gone out to see it go around. After a few drinks – he could demolish a bottle of hard liquor in the time I took to smoke a pack of cigarettes – Frank moved into the ring to make his wager.

Jack was still at his peak at this stage and took all of Frank's bets without hesitation. He hadn't met Frank before – hadn't even heard of him. Jack was given no guarantee for Frank's betting but did not query his ability to settle. This impressed Frank, as did the fact that he was not restricted in his betting. Ego plays a tremendous part in a gambler's make-up. Like a weed in a garden, ego contributes little but is very hard, if not impossible, to control.

I think Frank wanted to bet big, but I also think he expected to have his bets cut back. He started betting halfway through the race meeting – his first bet was $60,000 to $40,000. It lost. He then had $100,000 to $50,000 and lost. Then he had $90,000 to $40,000 and lost again. On the last race he bet $150,000 to $60,000 – and won. Frank had lost $130,000 and then won $150,000, so he finished $20,000 in front. He was pleased. He'd had a pleasant and profitable day.

No man had bet like this ever before in Australia, either with us or anyone else. One bet, although it may be talked about, doesn't make a man a big punter, but to bet that way all afternoon was unheard of. People said he wouldn't be back – he'd had a few drinks, had the adrenaline pumping and probably let things run away. I hadn't seen him but both Jack and I knew he would be back. Jack put it succinctly: 'He's tasted blood now – he'll come back for sure.'

Duval had backed four favourites. A horse is usually favourite in a race for one reason: it has the best form, which is widely exposed. Accordingly, favourites carry the most public money, invested by the largest section of the punting public. Because it looks the winner, a favourite represents the biggest threat to the bookie, who will offer lower odds. Big gamblers will back favourites because everybody likes to be on a winner, and that old truism still applies – any price is a good price about a winner.

It's only natural to look for value away from the favourite. The professional punter will look for another horse with less exposed form. If such a horse is fit and has a chance, it means the punter can win more with a smaller outlay. A man who backs four straight favourites indicates strongly that he is only a favourites-backer; and if that is indeed the case, he is not to be feared. This punter has no surprises for you, as you have more than a good idea of what he's going to back.

Frank was the exception to this rule. After this particular

race day he returned to Tokyo, but his presence lingered. He'd been unexpected and so he hadn't received any publicity, but he had created an impression in the ring. People like Bob Ingham, who abhorred publicity and shunned the spotlight and were aware that big gambling attracted publicity like a magnet, nevertheless still loved to gamble. Now suddenly they realised that they had only been playing. This had been serious betting.

—

Frank Duval came to Sydney again in the middle of 1966. It was nothing sensational, but it appeared Frank was different from most other punters in at least one aspect. Most punters have price and amount in mind when betting. Frank had neither. If he decided to back a horse, that was it. No doubt he compared the prices on offer, but price was not his main consideration. Neither were the amounts Frank invested.

I only ever saw him bet with two or three bookies. If a bookmaker did cut his bet, Frank never quibbled and never went elsewhere to get the rest of his money on. He simply turned and left the betting ring. These two traits were exceptional, and I had never encountered them before in a big gambler. They were the hallmark of an exceptionally wealthy man to whom racing was a diversion and betting was a sport – an extremely rare animal.

I flew to Melbourne on the Thursday before the 1966 Melbourne Cup Carnival. I was staying at the new Southern Cross Hotel, and I planned to have a couple of days to relax and then go to the Victorian Club in Queen Street. Here I'd mix with racing people and learn who was firing or going poorly. The interstate high-rollers would be surfacing and I would start to psych myself up for the betting at the carnival.

On the plane going down to Melbourne was Frank Duval with a few friends. We nodded to each other. I must confess that I felt my body tense up. It was just the way he looked: friendly, contented and confident, just as a mongoose looks at a cobra. I already had tremendous respect for Frank, as he had done what no one else ever had. I sensed respect emanating from him, too. Unbeknown to me, he said to his companions when I was out of earshot, 'I'm going to take that man to the cleaners at this carnival.'

Up to that point only one bookie hadn't limited Frank – my brother Jack. This must have rankled with him. I guess that, as much as winning, he wanted the feeling and recognition of power in his betting duels. Money is as good a medium as any to wield power, and if a gambler can cause a horse's price to shorten dramatically, he is happy. Frank hadn't achieved this in his duels with Jack. Now I wondered if he was coming to Melbourne for a showdown. I was already the leader of the Melbourne betting ring – the biggest bookmaker in the country – and although not yet widely known, Frank was the biggest punter. Soon the whole of Australia would be electrified by his betting.

Seeing Frank on the plane put a different complexion on the carnival for me. I immediately became excited but also apprehensive. I knew I would have to attack the meeting differently. In your own town, it doesn't make a great deal of difference in the overall picture whether you win, lose or draw on a particular day. What you lose today you can win back tomorrow. My philosophy in Melbourne was still not focused on winning but rather on controlling my losses. I knew if I lost to Frank, it could be months before I had a chance of recovering it.

The Spring Carnival was a very big betting occasion and was covered by the whole of the national media. I was more than happy to see my Melbourne stints as a good PR opportunity. Now I felt it was going to be difficult, or at least different.

A gambler needs to regulate himself. A punter can control

his actions. For a bookie it's harder; he must have a plan and know how to react. Of course, any self-respecting gambler can think under pressure and adjust himself for the changing conditions, but it can be like going into a French exam after studying for Latin.

Although Frank was a favourites-backer, I still went through the fields to find any connections. Sure enough, there was a horse owned by Frank called What Fun, a good three-year-old filly from Sydney. She was entered on Saturday's Derby Day in the Wakeful Stakes, a race for three-year-old fillies over ten furlongs (2000 metres) and then in Thursday's Oaks – the major race for three-year-old fillies in Australia.

Now I knew there could be an onslaught by Frank on the Saturday, so I apprehensively studied the fields. The carnival's opening day is always a dangerous one. Five of the races on Derby Day are at 'set weights': the Wakeful Stakes, the Smithfield (now the Carbine Club Stakes), the Maribyrnong Plate, the Mackinnon Stakes and the Derby. Set-weight races are ideal for favourites, as none of the horses are handicapped. It surely was Frank's day, as if you follow favourites, form counts for everything.

On Saturday Frank came down to my stand and had $48,000 to $3000 about What Fun in the Wakefield. The horse ran a creditable race without ever looking like being the winner. This was a nothing bet for him and it was the only bet he had all day. I had expected him to appear at any time, yet because of the nonstop betting I had forgotten about him. If Frank had really started to bet, then I would have ignored everyone else to focus on him. However, it was not to be.

As usual during the carnival, I had been invited to be on a local television station's Sunday sports program to be inter-viewed by Jack Elliott, the racing editor of the Melbourne *Herald*. Elliott asked me whether there were any large interstate punters at the meetings. I said there was the normal attendance, but there was also another person who, if he opened his shoulders, would make the Melbourne ring sit up and take notice. I did not mention his name publicly but told Jack after the show. Being in Melbourne, Elliott had not heard of Duval and was unimpressed.

Monday was not a race day but was still part and parcel of the Melbourne Cup scene. All the racing fraternity congregate at the Victorian Club to do their settling for the previous week's business, and also to discuss the next day's Melbourne Cup. It is the opportunity for all the interstate visitors to surface, so they can arrange betting credit facilities with the bookmakers, renew acquaintances, discuss the horses' form and any gossip. I expected Duval to turn up, at least for a drink, but he didn't.

The next day was Cup Day, the biggest day of the year. Funnily, it isn't the biggest race in bookies' turnover, but it is in the number of bets. Bets from all over Australia swell the turnover of the totalisator, but not of the betting ring itself. The Melbourne Cup is very hard for punters because it is a handicap. Also, big punters don't enjoy being pushed and shoved around, so Cup Day, although high in volume, usually doesn't bring out the huge bettors. Frank did not have a bet and was not seen in the betting ring.

After the running of the Cup, most on the course appear intent on an alcohol-led frenzy of self-destruction. Traversing the members' car park is an unbelievable hassle. Everyone wants you to have a glass of champagne and chicken leg with them. I could think of nothing worse. I was always on a tight schedule. I had to finish the settling figures as quickly as I could, because I was always due at some function and the next day was settling day at the club.

Thursday was the next race day – the Oaks. I had looked at the form guide closely and the horse I liked for value was What Fun. I had done the filly's form in detail for the previous Saturday's race and had thought she couldn't win, but she'd run a good, honest race and had made up a lot of ground on the leaders. She'd be suited by the Oaks' longer distance. The more I looked at the form now, the more I was attracted to What Fun.

On arriving at the track, I noticed Clarrie Stickland, a neighbouring bookie, working early on the feature event. He had 12/1 up against What Fun and I couldn't help approaching him and saying, 'Clarrie, I don't want to poke my nose into your business, but I do think you have What Fun over the odds. If there's a horse in the race for the bookies to watch, this is it.'

Clarrie thanked me for my gratuitous advice but paid no attention. Anyway, I had Duval out of my calculations, thinking he might have just come to Melbourne for the social outing and had probably returned to Japan. That was my big mistake.

—

Most people think that professional gamblers are a trust-to-luck, hope-for-the-best, easy-come-easy-go, indolent bunch of people. Not so. They may not spin or weave or work by the sweat of their brow, but they have a professional approach to their work. A select few have natural advantages that are denied to others, such as photographic memories that can be priceless when doing form, panoramic vision when watching a race, or mathematical magic with figures. With the majority it's a question of application. Many factors affect a gambler's decision. They may not fancy the program, the track conditions, the weather, the rider or the barrier.

There are many sayings in racing with an element of truth. 'Never chase bad money' – you should never try to win back your losses by betting bigger. 'Frightened money can't win' – a person scared of losing allows too many inhibitions in his thinking and so never wins. One old gambling phrase that applied very well to me on Oaks Day in 1966 was 'Giving yourself the needle' – for a gambler who loses his logic and is stampeded into making decisions contrary to his intentions, as though under a drug. While aware of what is happening, you cannot respond normally. It's the one thing a gambler dreads and guards against.

This state of flux is contrary to a bookie's training and thinking – yet it can happen. When it does, the only saviour is good old plain Lady Luck.

Oaks Day, the traditional Ladies' Day of the carnival, has always been a heavy betting day. It's a day for gamblers to gamble. I had been through the program and had firmly set my mind on what I was going to do. I could see value in 'saving' a couple of the runners on the day because of the prices. They weren't favourites – in fact, they were at or near double-figure odds and so could easily be 'lost in the book' if I wanted to reduce their odds. The two horses I wanted to save were What Fun in the Oaks and Yootha in the earlier Provincial Cup, which was trained by a very astute country trainer, Arthur Smerdon. He was as capable as any trainer in Victoria, but he was like an oyster – no rumours escaped from his stable. When he moved he had the respect of both punter and bookmaker.

Remembering Sir Eugene Gorman's horse in the Provincial Cup several years earlier, I was on guard. Smerdon had given Yootha a similar preparation and I sensed it could almost be a certainty. I wasn't going to leave myself open; if either of these two horses won, I would not lose on the day. I did not foresee the coming events.

The opening race saw good betting but nothing outstanding. I held only $8000 and felt the meet was going to be more like a social day. The next race Frank made his start, successfully backing the favourite, On Par, to win $62,000. Then he took an even $40,000 on the next favourite, Legal Boy, and I knew the battle was on: two bets in a row. I really wanted the favourite to lose, because there was no way Frank would not be back for the next race and the races after that. But Legal Boy won; now I was feeling a little seedy and was $100,000 in the hole.

The next was the Provincial Cup with Yootha. It had been listed as an 8/1 chance in the morning assessments. When opening a market, bookmakers tend to open with about the same price. A few opened it at 8/1, but the majority of the betting ring had the horse at 6/1. I did something I never do. I opened the runner at 4/1 as I just didn't want to lay it. There were two good reasons. It was an unusual race, and the fairly new idea by the club to bring together horses from all over the state made it difficult to assess the relative form. And if Smerdon, who was a death adder in the betting ring, declared Yootha, then I knew it would be heavily supported and would shorten and come right into the market. It was better to be safe than sorry. I didn't want to get involved and so took the only protection that a bookmaker has: to be under the odds.

After I had put Yootha's price up – which was at least three turns under what was still available elsewhere on the Rails – I didn't expect to lay it at all. The 8/1 had been taken, but there was still 6/1 everywhere, so I knew my 4/1 wouldn't be touched.

But Frank was in front and playing up his winnings. From the edge of the crowd, he called out, '$20,000 to $5000, Yootha!'

Hearing him shout such a big bet, the crowd swayed noticeably, turning to catch a glimpse of the man. There is always a small gathering of punters around the leading bookmakers, looking to see what to back or simply to enjoy watching the struggle between bookmaker and punter. To call out like that was almost unheard of for a large punter. And he was prepared to take significantly under the odds. I took his bet and cut the price to 7/2, which made the price collapse throughout the ring.

I was nonplussed. This had never happened to me before. Usually a punter, if he's a client, will point out how you are under the odds and will suggest at least a compromise on prices – just as Joe Taylor had done with Gorman's horse in the Provincial Cup a few years earlier in 1961. No one, but no one, would ever knowingly and deliberately take under the odds unless there is one hell of a reason.

Frank was out for blood: my blood. Unaware of this, I thought he must have drunk a little too much champagne and had not checked out the prices. His bet put me in a quandary. I liked the horse. The price now blew to 9/2 around the ring. I could back my way out, refinancing the horse at a profit with the other bookies still offering better odds, whether the horse won or lost. I noticed Duval heading towards my stand a second time and did a stupid thing and turned the price out to 9/2. And Frank claimed me for another bet to win $30,000.

Duval was later quoted in *The Age* as saying he had challenged me after I 'didn't blink an eyelid'.

I had originally allowed for my own high opinion of Yootha's chance by massively cutting the odds, but now, by extending the odds, I had effectively dared Duval and was facing a significant risk of $50,000.

If I had not blown the price and instead cut Duval's bets, I am sure I would have broken his spell. Duval wanted to win, but more than this, I think he wanted to see me back down and admit his bet was too big for me. In the punter's mind, it is important to establish yourself with your opponent. To have me cutting his bet would have meant a lot to Frank – it would have shown that he was in charge. If I'd realised this I would have cut his bet quickly, but I was not to know.

Yootha won narrowly and the effect on me was devastating. Instead of 'saving' the horse I had identified, I had lost badly and was now looking down the barrel. Very soon I would have to steel myself; rather than cut any of his bets, I was about to 'give myself the needle'.

—

Big betting duels between two adversaries rarely start as this one did. Usually when two men decide to lock horns, it takes time and a certain ritual is played out. Both parties in the initial stages carefully regulate their betting in order to observe the other's reaction. Both are looking for weaknesses, the reaction to pressure, and how to unbalance the other. They may not like each other but, without exception, there will be mutual respect. Without this respect there can be no duel – a possible fight to the financial ruination of one.

If two gamblers lock horns in a duel, only one will survive and the other will be crushed. Once a man's gambling nerve is gone, that's it. It doesn't come back. Any betting after that is just for the fun of it.

I should never have become involved with Duval like this at such an early stage. I had a good, cool temperament and would have backed off without the slightest embarrassment. If Frank wanted a betting duel then he could have one, but on a ground more of my choosing. Here I was in peril.

I have found over the years that to come out on top of any serious punter, you must take your time to learn how he thinks and reacts. To do this you have to close your mind to everybody around you and ignore every other client's business. Only then can you put yourself in your opponent's mind. You think as he thinks, and you reach the stage when you foresee how he's going to bet. More often than not, you even know the horse he's going to back and – more importantly – whether he's going to plunge or not. Once you get to this stage you are ready for him and his chances are slim. At least, that's how you as the bookie see it – no doubt your opponent is equally confident.

I would rather never have put myself through this sort of thing, but if you want to be the top gun, you must expect to draw challengers. When all this is going on, you can carry on a conversation with your other clients and take their bets, but really you are oblivious to them. You can't properly concentrate on anything else, which is very risky, particularly if one of your other clients starts to run hot, because at this stage you cut nobody back. Betting with Duval that day was like being in a trance.

At one point that afternoon, my bagman, Len Tovey, who knew me backwards since the days when I was an up-and-coming bookie, burst out laughing and said, 'Do you know who you were speaking to just then?'

I didn't.

'You've just had a conversation with your wife, and I knew you didn't even notice!'

I was completely unprepared for Duval, even though I had broken all records with my increasing holds in Melbourne in the early 1960s and was confidently betting big. If Duval had started on the previous Saturday he might have given me hiccups, but I would have been in charge. Now he was about to take control.

—

The next race came along and I waited for Frank to come back. He was now way ahead and his horse, What Fun, was about to run. I didn't know if Frank was betting based on tips, relying on connections, or if he just picked a horse.

In Sydney he had been a favourites-backer, but the horse he had just won on had been genuinely assessed as an 8/1 chance. You always mask your feelings when you're on the stand, but beneath the facade I was in a filthy mood. I was ready to pick a fight in an empty house. I knew the wheels were coming off but I also knew there was nothing I could do about it.

I had been caught off-guard by Frank's bets. The market price, although not under the odds, can quite often be beaten, and if you're backing a favourite the price is incredibly important. Frank didn't give a hoot in hell about the price – he just took what I offered. I was now losing a fortune – around $150,000 – of which Frank had won nearly all. I was aware there was no way out and should have been following my own rules: 'That money is gone and lost forever – start over and begin again – limit your losses – don't throw good after bad.'

What Fun had been assessed as a 12/1 shot before the first race. The bookies now had the horse on their betting boards at 8/1 or more. I liked What Fun and was aware that Frank owned her; I knew the position I was in, and I knew he would back the filly again. And I certainly didn't want to lay her. The only thing I could do was put up such a short price that Frank would not accept it. Even if What Fun won, I was determined not to lose on her.

By this stage a very large crowd had gathered around my stand. Word of Frank's betting had spread around the racecourse like a fire. Duval was no longer a nobody in Melbourne, thanks to his moderate punting on Derby Day. As he tried to distance himself from the big betting, the reporters relentlessly followed him. It reached the stage where every time he made a bet it was broadcast over the national radio. The press were attracted to me too, and if there was anybody that I didn't want to talk to at that stage, it was a newspaper reporter.

I hoped Frank would back the favourite, Star Belle, and then have a saver on his runner. I didn't like the favourite at all and was in the mood to give it a good old-fashioned stand. I put up odds of 5/1 about What Fun, fully aware that the odds on every other board were 8/1. The crowd was now thickly packed around my stand, watching but not moving, and effectively impeding anyone making or trying to make a wager. Who would want to push through a dense pack of people to make a bet when you could go anywhere else and place your bet at better odds and without any hassle?

The tall figure of Frank Duval could only get to the edge of the crowd, but in a loud, clear voice he called, 'I'll have 100 to twenty, What Fun.' He was at least six metres from me, so our business was anything but private.

It was a huge bet and I had to verify what he wanted, so I heard myself calling back, 'You have $100,000 to $20,000, What Fun, Mr Duval.' That's what he'd asked for, and I had not cut him back.

I should have either cut his bet or else started to finance it, but I believed that if you took a bet, you kept it. Besides, it was all too late by then, as reason, logic and common sense had gone straight out the window.

Duval didn't know it, but he could have asked me to set him for a million and he would have been on. Emotionally, I may have been swept out to sea, but Duval too was losing contact with the sand and was drifting into deeper water.

At this stage, Jack Elliott came up as excited as a schoolboy and declared, 'I've just checked our newspaper records, and that bet you laid is the largest bet ever recorded on any racecourse in the state of Victoria.'

I thanked him very much, but I would have been just as interested if he had told me his cat had just had kittens. After Duval had taken his wager, I reduced the price of What Fun to 9/2. Apart from Duval, I was still trying to bookmake. I didn't like the favourite one little bit and so I extended its odds, but the crowd around the stand was making it impossible for me to get any general business.

About ten minutes after his initial bet, Frank reappeared at the back of the crowd, this time the general public side, trying to get closer. He claimed me for his second bet. 'I'll have 90 to twenty, What Fun.'

'You've got $90,000 to $20,000, What Fun, Mr Duval,' I replied.

His betting on What Fun was now mammoth. The crowd around me had heard every word and the mood was electric.

Clarrie Stickland then tried to do me a favour. He knew what trouble I was in. He leaned across from his stand and quietly said, 'I know the connections of Farmer's Daughter and it hasn't pleased them since last Saturday. It's lost condition and they don't think it has any hope of running out the distance.'

Farmer's Daughter had been the second-favourite for the race on the morning line, and now I was being told that it couldn't win. I still didn't like the favourite at all and was beginning to feel trapped. I had no way out. The wagering was now too large to even contemplate backing back. Even if I'd wanted to bet back, the bets were so big I would have caused a stampede by the watching punters on the price of What Fun.

After I had laid Frank's second wager I reduced my price about What Fun to 4/1. Once again he resurfaced, this time from the members' reserve, and called out at the back of the crowd, '$100,000 to $25,000, What Fun.'

I replied immediately. 'What Fun, $100,000 to $25,000, to Mr Duval.'

Duval had outlaid $65,000 to win $355,000 on What Fun. It was an unbelievable situation. No betting at this level had ever occurred before. Duval had not just smashed the old betting record, he'd soared right past it. The most disquieting thing for me was that never at any stage had I read Duval correctly. To this day, he is the only serious gambler I have found who wasn't influenced at all by price. This is the bookmaker's main defence, and I had used it about as much as I could – but it had made no difference.

Sydney *Sun* journalist Bill Casey, who'd overheard the bets, immediately approached Duval to confirm the details. Duval replied, 'Give us a go,' and then smiled and said, 'I know nothing about the big bets. Leave me out. I only had $10 on the filly.' However, Casey named Duval the next day and outlined the big bets. Another newspaper story carried a picture of Duval with the tongue-in-cheek caption of 'Mr Duval, $10 bettor'.

Bill Casey wrote next day that 'the support for What Fun was amazing and over the century, Flemington has never seen anything to equal this wild plunge'.

You can't imagine the impact I felt on finding myself in this predicament. The horse I liked – the horse I had intended to save – had been backed in from a quote of 12/1 to 9/2 and second-favourite, and now I was standing it well out of my depth, for a sum far greater than I had ever stood before. If it won, I would be the best part of half a million dollars behind, with half the program still to come and with a wild punter on the rampage and firing. In my mind, I had put the brand-new 88-room Charles Hotel at Bronte on the line. I felt sick and reached for yet another cigarette. I was already on my fourth pack.

I rethought the race. Candy Floss, ridden by George Moore, had the best form, but I didn't like her. Now that Farmer's Daughter was under a cloud, I suddenly realised that What Fun was almost a good thing! But I couldn't do anything. I decided to sit on my book as it was and let the chips fall where they may. Besides, my general business had been stifled by the crowd. Try as I might, I found it next to impossible to get money out of laying Farmer's Daughter.

It was hell on that stand waiting for the race to start. Time seemed to have stopped. After Frank's last bet I dropped What Fun's price to 7/2, fully expecting him to claim me again for another huge wager, but he did not return. Post time finally came but I didn't want to watch the race; I knew I would simply die a thousand deaths. So I went for a walk, relying on the club's broadcast for the result.

The VRC Oaks was a 2500-metre event for three-year-olds, the fillies' equivalent of the Derby. All the horses carried the same weight. The race starts in the straight, goes past the winning post, then on around the course and back to the winning post. Listening to the broadcast was terrible and things just seemed to get worse. The favourite, Star Belle, never seemed to be travelling well, and by the time they got to Chicquita Lodge at the back of the course she'd had enough and was the first horse beaten out of first place.

Farmer's Daughter was about four lengths in front of What Fun, who was travelling nicely. I couldn't believe what I was hearing. I was being done like a dinner. I had been told fairly late in the betting that Farmer's Daughter could not win, and I myself had picked What Fun as the best staying filly in the field. I'd figured that if she could be near the leaders coming into the straight, she would swamp them. Now here she was, second into the straight and with only an unfancied horse in front of her.

But luck's a fortune, as they say. Just as Sir Eugene Gorman's horse had not been able to run down the leader five years previously in the Provincial Cup, now What Fun could not reduce the lead all the way down that long, long straight at Flemington. Rather than folding, Farmer's Daughter hung on and won easily, with What Fun second and Star Belle a close third.

What a sudden change in my fortunes! I should have had a catastrophic result but instead it was a good win. However, for the first time in my life I had felt out of control; it was the only time I'd had no command over the gamble.

This was the middle of the program, and even after winning Duval's $65,000 on the Oaks, I was still in the hole for $135,000. While I was still having a bad day, I had at least broken his run. I felt like a new man. I knew I was committed to the gamble and was aware that Frank was dictating the pace. I also realised that the Oaks had been his king hit and he would now have to rethink. Frank was well in front, but he still had to finish it off. His ego wouldn't let him leave now, and I felt my chances were improving.

The next race was the Batman Stakes. It was a consolation race for horses beaten in the Derby and invariably a favourite's race, as at that time there were no weight penalties and the best Derby loser had an advantage. Pharaon had run second to Khalif in the Victoria Derby on the Saturday and looked a sitter – a sure thing – for the race. It was at a certainty's price, too: 5/2 on (you had to put on five dollars to win two). It was not a horse to plunge on. Because Pharaon had stifled betting, there was very little public action. People just stood around the stand, watching and waiting and expecting. They knew something was going to happen but they didn't know what.

I then made the biggest bookmaking mistake of my life. It cost me $90,000 – enough to buy two or three houses in Sydney at the time. Frank appeared at the back of the crowd, calling out, 'Bill!' He put up his hands showing ten fingers and shouted, 'The favourite!' – which was Pharaon.

I was polite, and although I thought he meant to bet $100,000, I called back to him loudly, 'Pharaon, $10,000 to $4000 on, Mr Duval.'

I called it back clearly because I knew it wasn't consistent with his betting pattern, but I thought it presumptuous to interpret it as $100,000 to $40,000 on. Yet for him to bet to win just $4000 made no sense at all. I waited for him to correct me but he didn't, so the bet stood.

You must always expect the unexpected on a racecourse, and Pharaon was beaten into second place by the 8/1 Magic Flute in a photo-finish. Before the horses were back into the mounting yard, Frank charged back, ashen-faced. 'Would you repeat the bet in the last race, please?' he asked.

I replied, '$10,000 on Pharaon at 5/2 on.'

He breathed an audible sigh of relief and with a grin said, 'Yes, that's right, but I wasn't sure what you had recorded.'

My good friend Jock Rorrison was near the stand, and he said to me, 'You know he thought he had $100,000 on that?'

'I realise that,' I replied, 'but what can I do?'

Jock was right, and I had mishandled the situation. I had called the bet back to him clearly, but he was at the back of the crowd and it had gone over his head. After the 'certainty' had been beaten, he thought he had lost $100,000 and was a very relieved man to discover his mistake. Of course, my mistake not only cost me $90,000, but if the horse had won, no doubt Frank would have expected me to pay him $40,000. And, as he was a good client, I would have paid. Later, Duval confirmed to journalist Kevin Perkins what a blunder I had made and laughed at his luck.

After the Batman Stakes, both Frank and I were in better shape. I'd had a fair result on the race, and Frank, although he'd lost, was $90,000 better off than he should have been. To any punter that would be almost as good as backing a winner.

The last race on the program was a handicap; the favourite, Bastille, was 7/4. Frank came up and claimed me for $70,000 to $40,000 about Bastille. I shortened the price to 13/8 and he came back and now claimed me for $65,000 to $40,000. Why he didn't punt the $80,000 in one bet I don't know, as he should have realised I wasn't in the frame of mind to cut him back. So now he had a total of $135,000 to $80,000 about the last favourite. For each of us it meant the difference between winning and losing on the day, with Frank set to win a total of $215,000 if Bastille won.

I watched the race. Bastille and Lord Palford were neck and neck to the line. It was a photo-finish, but Frank's luck had started to run out. Bastille was pipped at the post and placed second. Frank had lost $80,000 on the last race and had just about broken square on the day. If his last three 'seconds' had won, he would have been over three-quarters of a million dollars ahead.

In the last three races he had lost $155,000, and all up I had finished just ahead on Oaks Day. I held more than the Flemington tote on the day – $398,000 for the seven races, compared to its $325,492. At the end of the carnival my turnover was well over a million, and my turnover tax nearly $30,000.

As a memento I still retain my Oaks Day racebook for Thursday 3 November 1966, showing Duval's bets written in ink and signed by me on the day for verification. This had been the greatest betting duel ever witnessed on an Australian racecourse. It was given extraordinary media coverage through-out Australia, and news of our betting even flashed around the world.

When Duval struck me in the Oaks, my brother Jack was working at a small meeting at the Kembla Grange racetrack. Jack told me the radio coverage of Duval's betting was broadcast over the public-address system and the crowd's mood was electric. Everybody at Kembla Grange felt as though they were at Flemington. This national coverage continued throughout the day.

I was completely unaware of all this, and when I returned to the hotel that evening I couldn't understand why everyone was looking at me in the lobby. I felt like a wrung-out sponge and was surprised to find Suzanne waiting anxiously for me. It was only then I realised the events had been given national coverage. The newspapers that evening and the following morning were full of it, as was the television news. For the first time betting was a hot topic among the general public, not just among racing fans. I suddenly found myself with a national profile as a 'leviathan bookie'.

I wrote my own newspaper column a couple of days later, in which I tried to keep faith with Frank by referring to him as 'the Sydney bettor', not naming him. 'Banks don't disclose their clients' names and how much they have, and I use the same code,' I wrote. However, the editor put a stop to that nonsense by inserting a par: 'Jack Elliott says the punter was Mr Frank Duval, known in racing circles as "The Hongkong Tiger."'

The press seized upon the sobriquet 'the Hong Kong Tiger', which was really a misnomer, as Frank was strictly a Tokyo man. Caricatures appeared in the press of a tiger's tail hanging out the side of my betting bag; in another paper there was one of me fainting off my stand when told Duval was back. The nickname, however, was to be with Frank for the rest of his life. I think he both revelled in it and hated it. It meant he could never have a small bet – people expected him always to be daring. Every time the Hong Kong Tiger surfaced at the races, his movements were always faithfully recorded in the press.

However, I knew that Frank and I would never lock horns again in a serious confrontation, although in essence very little money was won or lost between us. I think Frank might have been $10,000 or less behind overall. Sure enough, over the years he would come to Sydney and have a bet, and these bets would still make the news. But it would never be for the same amounts and would usually be on a horse he owned or had an interest in, or following a tip from his stable.

When I look back over Frank's career as a punter, it's amazing to say it but he never lost his money betting on the horses. His two biggest forays cost him nothing. He is the only big punter I can recall who was prepared to take under the odds. I feared him more than any other because I couldn't read his mind – he was unpredictable. Although I knew he would never come back as a gambler, he brought an uneasy fear to me every time he was at the track.

More important was Duval's impact on betting. From that first day, he was the talk of the racing world. He caused punters to be more adventurous and think in higher numbers. He lifted me to a new and bigger dimension in my bookmaking. I hadn't cut him in any of his wagers, nor had I backed any of his horses back. Over the next three years I would accept every bet offered me on a racecourse, and not once did I back a horse back.

Funnily enough, Frank had not actually been the biggest investor at the Melbourne Cup Carnival of 1966. 'Mercurial' Michael Pitt had easily outlaid more money. Pitt bet on each day, on every race, often selecting two or three horses to back, and he practically bet with the whole ring. Yet outside the small racing world, few people would know of Mercurial Michael. He was a serious punter who spent all of 50 years jousting with bookmakers, whereas Frank was a plunger – and one of enormous depth. He caught the publicity and betting rings were never the same again.

Duval's name will be remembered as long as people talk about betting.

12

Colourful Characters

D AMON RUNYON IMMORTALISED the knockabout racing characters of New York's gambling scene. For me, looking back, many similar figures stand out in Australia. Most of them have never been called by their actual names, adding flavour to their character.

Racing people meet in a sporting leisure activity without the normal formalities. A bond forms between people from all walks of life that could never occur anywhere else. Symbolic of this camaraderie, regulars and prominent personalities usually find they are landed with a light-hearted nickname.

Sometimes it's the way they look: the Polar Bear was old Bob Browning, Arthur Browning's father, who had a mop of white hair on top of a massive body, and Black Bart (Bart Cummings – who had jet-black hair). There was also Skinny Bernie (Bernie Bennett). The nicknames also referred to how they performed, as with the Legal Eagles (Clive Evatt, who combined at various times with Michael McHugh, Bob Charley, Morgan Ryan and Don Scott), the Little General (T. J. Smith), the Walking Titanic, the Bermuda Triangle, the Cocktail Cavalier (Tony McSweeney), Ming the Merciless, Brian the Liar, the Swamp Rat, the Goose (Bill McKelvie, a leading bookie), the Candy Pig (a trainer), the Ant (Brian Mills), the Ginger Cat (Pat Murray, a top Randwick trainer), the Meat Skinner (Brian Schaeffer),

Jockey Jack, the Emu, Dave the Dasher (Dave Segenfield), Evil George, the Birdman, Chickens (Jack and Bob Ingham), and Poultry Pat (Pat Barrett).

Most nicknames were incredibly appropriate, or at least pithy. Arthur Browning was Raffles, after the fictional character who was a gentleman thief. Les Tidmarsh was Hundreds and Thousands – always talking in big figures. Jack Muir was known as Mother Muir since he was a merciless gossip.

'Silent' Leo O'Sullivan once told me over a drink about one of his great tricks of the turf. In a match race trial between his horse Gay Vista and a horse trained by Jack Green, he fooled everyone. Gay Vista was soundly beaten in the trial but went on to win by four lengths on the race day, beating Green's horse and allowing Silent Leo to land a betting coup. As he later told me, the secret was that he had fitted Gay Vista with a heavy set of lead shoe plates for its trial run.

Hollywood George was one of the most strikingly good-looking gamblers that strode the Australian racing scene. A big gambler with a strong nerve, he was a snappy dresser who really looked like a filmstar. Jimmy Jenkins was the Silverfish for getting inside bookies' bags. In the 1950s no one bet bigger than Jimmy, who had a slick mane of silver hair. Other names could be a little cruel. The Wild Duck was so named because he would never settle. And of course there was Lou the Pest.

Lou was a cockney from London who had lived in Australia for many years. Always immaculately dressed, he invariably attached himself to a leading bookie. On one occasion he was connected to the flamboyant bookmaker Jack Shaw. Jack fancied himself as an expert in assessing horses' form through watching them run. At the end of betting he would go to the front of the grandstand and, with no seats left in the stand, would step up onto a stool to see the race. It was Lou's job to bring the stool. On one occasion he forgot.

Without a second thought, Jack looked at Lou and said, 'Down, Lou. You have to take the stool's place.'

Lou, without hesitation, went down on all fours and Jack, supported by his other clerks, stepped onto Lou's back and watched the race. Curiously, no one criticised Jack, as he was relying on Lou for a service that had not been provided. In the racing world there is a different set of values.

All bookies were given names. I was known as the Serpent, a nickname coined by Hoppy Hopkins, because he said I seemed aloof at the track, biding my time until I was ready for the poisonous pounce. Johnny Spooner was known as the Egg for continually saying a horse was already 'laid'. There was the Doctor, who always told a punter he could get better (odds elsewhere), Mischy the Pig, the Coogee Bunyip and so on.

Dopey Donovan, who was before my time, got his name by occasionally arriving at the track somewhat the worse for wear from drinking. Obviously intoxicated and unaware of what he was doing, he would get up on his stand and call out the wrong price for the favourite. The punters would try to take advantage of his condition but Dopey was usually not as dopey or drunk as he led people to believe; he got away with this subterfuge on countless occasions to avoid laying the favourite.

The media also coined names for some punters when they were enthralled by their betting exploits. They named both the Hong Kong Tiger and the Filipino Fireball (Felipe Ysmael, whom I encountered soon after Frank Duval). The media, and therefore the public, interest wasn't just because of wealthy men indulging themselves; rather, it was a fascination with the big-boy game played by the punter against his opponent, the bookmaker – duelling for money for the sheer thrill of winning with a kill.

—

Much has been written over the years about the evils of gambling. There will always be the extremes where trouble is caused by somebody's weakness, but this is very much the exception, not the rule. Gambling on horses is a vice, but it is a soft vice, just like having a beer, and can be a low-cost entertainment. It can give a great deal of satisfaction and pleasure as a social leisure activity.

The average punter is a $2 bettor. Although he may hope he is going to win, in his heart he knows the percentages are against him. He studies the horses' form for the field, gaining stimulus and the satisfaction of making his own decision. When he invests his $2, who knows? He may strike the daily double. Some people want to go to the bar and drink, others to the cinema; if you get drunk it can be quite expensive and destructive, and if the movie is not to your satisfaction you don't get your money back. You never see a drunk or a fight in a betting shop. Everyone is too intent on trying to win.

On the other side, the hopeless gambler is usually just plain hopeless. But they are only a very small percentage of all gamblers, and once you realise who they are, you don't want to do business with them. Whenever I knew someone was really down on his luck, having lost heavily, I would tell him that what he was doing was foolish and warn him to stop. However, once you let him on, often after a while it is very hard to refuse him credit – in his mind, you are denying him a chance to win his money back.

Over the years I have been approached by fathers, brothers and also children of hopeless punters asking for help with a family member, and I would always try to help, although it was very awkward at times and involved some very high-profile people.

One of the most notable was Bob Ingham. There had always been big punters around, but after Frank's onslaught they became much bigger. Duval had blazed a new path in betting boldness and Bob followed right behind. His betting also became huge, without publicity but not without problems.

Bob and his brother Jack were friends of mine, with a high profile in racing. They were partners in the well-known business called Inghams Chickens. I had helped them out in the early days of their business when they were short of funds by lending them $200,000, and I knew both Jack and Bob well. After Bob became a big punter in the wake of Duval, he ran into a losing trot. It was a very awkward situation.

Jack, the elder brother, came to me because he couldn't tolerate the betting any more. 'Please don't let my brother bet any more,' he said. 'It is threatening our partnership.'

I warned Jack that Bob would just bet with others if I denied him credit and, understandably, he would feel wrongly done by. Bob had to learn the lesson himself. Wanting to help my friends and seeking a solution to their problem, I suggested to Jack that I should still let Bob on for his bets but in a side account, on Jack's behalf. In effect, Jack would be Bob's bookmaker – if Bob's bets won Jack would have to pay his brother, but if Bob lost, nothing would be paid. I had nothing to gain and, although this was against the rules and not being straight with Bob, I genuinely thought it was the only way to help in a very sensitive and difficult family situation.

Jack was extremely grateful and, sure enough, six months later, a large bill of around a million dollars in losses had accumulated. When Bob found out he really didn't owe the money both brothers were very relieved to have saved a fortune, and the tension between them was gone. I have always found Bob a true gentleman of the turf and I was glad to have been able to help.

Another person who suddenly became a big punter after Duval was a young Kerry Packer, who quickly ran up a loss of $105,000 with me. I let it sit, assuming I would be paid eventually. I was surprised to be called in one day by his media mogul father, Sir Frank. He asked me how I was and if everything was okay.

'Yes, fine,' I said.

'Does Kerry owe you any money?' he asked.

'No,' I replied, not wishing to cause trouble between father and son.

Sir Frank then said, 'I know Kerry has been betting with you and he owes you. If you had told me, I would have said you will have to wait until he can pay you. But now you've said he doesn't owe you, I'm going to pay you the $105,000. But I don't want you to let Kerry on any more.' Sir Frank then wrote out a cheque.

Although he was betting with other bookies, it was a few years before I let Kerry back on for a bet. By that time Sir Frank had died, and Kerry's betting would soon become world-famous.

In a friendship with a professional or even a serious amateur punter, no matter how much you relax, underneath it all you are unconsciously on your guard, forever probing, looking for weaknesses. During a carnival or even after a meeting, how do you relax with a guy whom you've slain or who, conversely, has taken you to the cleaners?

I have been friendly with all my big punters, and some have been good mates, but there is not one with whom I have gone out with socially on a regular basis. I have always maintained that to bet big with anyone, you have got to respect him and be respected in return. You may not even like each other, but that is not important. What is important is the respect: without it there can be no big betting.

There is another category of people connected with racing: the conmen. I was never free from these pests, especially when I was in Melbourne. Everyone was aware of where I was staying, so nearly every day I'd receive some call at the hotel offering a get-rich-quick scheme. I suppose every trainer and jockey had to put up with some rascal using his name, either looking for a punter to put money on a horse or a bookie to lay a supposed non-trier. Every conceivable concept of racecourse chicanery has been offered or suggested. Occasionally I also heard from friends that someone purporting to be a representative of mine had offered lucrative pickings for a trainer or jockey – to give information about a mount, or else to 'stop' a horse. These things never worried me, as I had no control over them anyway.

Contrary to popular opinion, gamblers are mainly responsible individuals, fully aware of what they're doing. The bank teller who bets with embezzled money is not a gambler but a crook. He's going to steal anyway – gambling is simply an investment that allows him to hope that, by backing a winner, no one will catch him. But popular opinion assesses him as a 'gambler falling to temptation'. This generalisation is the cross that regular gamblers have to bear.

In nearly all countries, gambling debts were and still are unenforceable. The gambler owed money is denied access to the due process of justice and relies solely on a gambler's word of honour. In the late 1960s I had lobbied the premier of New South Wales, Bob Askin, about the inequity of not being able to sue. Askin had been involved with SP betting in his early days, and was very aware of the difficulties in the racing world with non-payers. I found a receptive ear, and New South Wales led the world by changing the law to allow the gambler to sue and, of course, be sued. Dire predictions of a rash of litigation ruining lives were made, but nothing really altered when the new law was introduced, except that it stopped a little blatant cheating, as in the case of a punter called Ian Caldwell.

Caldwell had come to prominence a few years earlier at the Inglis Easter yearling sales, when he paid the record price of 15,500 guineas for a colt, Columbia Star by Star Kingdom. Anybody doing this receives good press coverage and acceptance throughout the racing world. Although not much was known about Caldwell, no one queried his betting credentials. He had been a small punter, but in March 1967 Caldwell decided to have a punting splurge. If he lost, so what? He had no intention of paying. He couldn't be sued and the worst that could happen was that he would be warned off racecourses.

Caldwell read that legislation to make gambling debts enforceable in law had passed the New South Wales Legislative Assembly but was still being read in the Legislative Council. The newspaper on the Wednesday morning reported that objections to the bill were made by Clyde Packer, who was then a Liberal Party member of the Legislative Council, which in those days still had some members who were appointed by the government rather than directly elected by the people. The press report said the Act had not yet been approved, and there was a backlog of legislation.

On this Wednesday there was a race meeting at Canterbury Park. Caldwell decided it was time to move. Parliament would soon be adjourning for a month; if he was fortunate, he could operate each day until he ran out of credit. But when your luck's out, it's out. He bet with only two bookmakers – my brother Jack and Aussie Austin. This gave him more credence, because a punter who is going to 'take the knock' will often bet with everyone.

Caldwell decided to 'martingale'. He would bet and then, if he lost, he would increase his next bet to cover both any previous losses and his desired win amount. This would continue until he backed a winner. At that point, no doubt, Caldwell intended to stop for the day, collect his winnings and begin again at the next meeting. He would continue on in this way until he lost, when he would then default, keeping his previous winnings.

He bet with Aussie on the Sydney races and with Jack on the Melbourne races. On this Wednesday he arrived at the track halfway through the program and backed two losers, one in Sydney and one in Melbourne. He then backed a winner in Melbourne, which put him ahead. With that he started to leave. He walked out through the interstate ring, where I was working.

I didn't know that Caldwell had been betting but I happened to be watching him as a local race was about to start, and here he was leaving the racecourse. At that moment an announcement came over the public-address system that the winner of the previous interstate race had been disqualified as it couldn't draw the correct weight. Caldwell obviously heard the announcement and, without halting or seeming to change his step, turned and walked back.

He was too late for the next local race but had $40,000 on the favourite in the last race in Melbourne with Jack. The race was a five-furlong (1000-metre) sprint at a provincial Victorian track; whatever horse was first out was usually first around the bend and first home. The horse Caldwell backed did everything asked of him. A very speedy horse, he jumped first and increased his lead to the turn. The favourite was 'leading by four lengths and going easy', as the announcer called. As often happens, it tired and was beaten in a photo-finish. Caldwell had lost.

It certainly had not been his day. He hadn't intended to go to the races but had been influenced by what was happening in parliament. Worse was to come for him.

Contrary to what the newspapers said and unknown to us all, the bill had eventually been passed in the wee small hours. On that very morning Bob Askin had sent the bill to the governor, Sir Roden Cutler, for his signature. When Caldwell made his wagers at Canterbury that day, he was doing so under the new law and so could be sued for his debts. Once Jack and I knew our good fortune, Aussie joined us in bringing an action against Caldwell.

We were the first to sue under the new legislation and in May 1967 *The Sun* ran as its front-page headline: 'Bookie to sue losing owner'. Of course, Caldwell didn't have any cash to pay us, so we had to settle for some disused land in the Blue Mountains, which turned out to be the original site of the Chateau Napier, the first guesthouse in Leura, and a small hotel out west. We had to pay Aussie out as he wanted cash, but we still own the Leura land, which looks down the Jamison Valley.

Caldwell didn't get into trouble by gambling but by trying to steal. His was a calculated piece of trickery that had nothing to do with normal betting.

—

I have seen the martingale system ruin so many gamblers. It is simply a concept of increasing your bet after a loss, in order to recoup losses and win something. However, each time one loses, one has to increase the next bet by enough to win back the losses and still make the target profit. It's one of the favourite systems for gamblers with no understanding of racing. The only thing that it guarantees is that if you win, your win will be small and certainly not commensurate with your losses when they come – and come they will.

To my mind, the martingale system is totally flawed and dangerous because it can get you into trouble very quickly. It only works in one situation – if the punter doesn't intend to pay. In fact, most martingalers end up not paying as they get themselves in far over their heads. In my experience, a person who embezzles from a bank or a trust is inevitably a martingaler – they never set out to lose that kind of money but find themselves in a desperate predicament, and the only way out is to steal.

An old punter of mine, Len Shapiro, was of Russian extraction. He was a very tight businessman and racing was his hobby. On the track he mixed with all classes of people, whereas off the track, with his thick Russian accent, he was not so widely accepted. Len loved going to the races each Saturday and Wednesday and, using the martingale system, he would bet with the goal of winning or 'stealing' $100. He would famously hold up his $100 as he was leaving the track with his winnings for the day. This went on for years and everyone thought he was a genius. One day, however, he had a 'martingaling' disaster, and instead of winning his $100, he lost around $300,000! He lost about half of it to my brother Jack and the rest to Bobby Deverall. Bobby panicked as he had backed much of Shapiro's business back with Jack and, no matter what, he would have to pay Jack out. To Len's credit, he paid his debt in full.

One man who bet opposite to the martingale system was the young future media baron Rupert Murdoch. Some people are loser-backers but Rupert was a winner-backer. He only bet with me over the 1966 Melbourne Cup Carnival, but he won every day. I don't know if he had big money then – I was not privileged to see any of it!

Rupert started betting moderately, then slowly increased his wagering as he won, playing up his winnings. This is the correct way to go. His winnings from the four-day carnival were just under $100,000, more than substantial for a beginner.

I do feel that Murdoch would have made a real success of punting if he had kept at it. I recall that he had a fearlessness in his eyes when he made his bets. There was none of the urgency or anxiety one sees in some punters. Murdoch never returned to punting after that one foray, obviously saving his gambling exploits for big business, where he successfully built up his world media empire.

No doubt a man of enormous ability, Rupert was an undergraduate at Oxford when his father, Sir Keith Murdoch, died. When Rupert arrived back in Australia, the main asset left after death duties and probate was a small-circulation newspaper, *The Adelaide News*. His first expansion was acquiring the Sydney *Daily Mirror*, founded by Ezra Norton.

Norton was one of the last survivors of the group known as the 'wild men of Sydney'. These men controlled great wealth and power. Norton had an intense rivalry with newspaper proprietor Frank Packer, and the two had featured in a famous punch-up in the members' enclosure at Randwick Racecourse on Derby Day in 1939.

—

One of the great legends of punting was the brilliant form genius Don Scott, who was the brains behind the betting syndicate known as the 'Legal Eagles'. Don had been dux of his and my old school, North Sydney High, dux of New South Wales and had won the University Medal. Yet he couldn't drive a motorcar. And poor Don was liable to awful spells of depression. He told me he had been enrolled to become a church minster at a Protestant theological college in Sydney's eastern suburbs, past Randwick. One day in 1949 he had caught the wrong tram and ended up inside Randwick Racecourse, in the middle of the AJC spring meeting. So Don, with £2 in his pocket, paid his way into the St Leger enclosure and was thrilled to see a row of bookmakers, a parade of horses and a race. I can just imagine him being amazed at what had hit him. Don had five bets – the first four lost, but he won on the last and was hooked.

Don said he'd had the best time he could ever remember, mixing among all those people who used their skill to pick winners by studying the horses' form. He enjoyed it so much that the rest was history. As part of the Legal Eagles syndicate, he began an assault on the bookies throughout Australia. Clive Evatt, a leading Sydney barrister, was the face of the group, which also included the solicitor Morgan Ryan. Don had one of the best racing brains I have known. I never saw him seek a tip or complain about his horse being pulled. Scott was always satisfied to back up his own opinion with cold hard cash. I regard Don Scott as having had the single most important influence on the understanding of racing form in Australia. He wrote several books on the subject that became big sellers and revolutionised the way people looked at form.

However, I believe that his greatest advantage and contribution to racing was his 'staking system'. Far more important than his formula for form, it introduced a vital concept for limiting losses. In racing, if you can control your losses, your winnings will follow.

It was a little like Isaac Newton being inspired by an apple to develop his theory of gravity. One day at a meeting at Newcastle in the 1950s, Scott thought a race was a match between two horses. One was the favourite at even money and the other's price was 10/1. Don went into the betting ring and had £200 to £200 on the favourite and £200 to £20 on the other horse. At that stage Don's method was to support his selection to win £400. As he had had two selections, he had divided his bet to back each to win £200 and had an outlay of £220. The outsider won by a whisker from the favourite. Don's judgement was spot-on and yet he had won nothing.

Obviously this was not the way to go to get the result he wanted. What then was the correct method? All his thinking had been focused on the amount to be won, not on the amount staked. There was obviously a defect here and Don took a step back and looked at the possibilities. He came up with a revolutionary new staking system that was to become the model for a whole new generation of punters.

Scott's system was quite simple. He decided each stake based on the amount he wanted to 'return', relying on *his* assessed prices for the horse in the race. The return goal initially selected might be, say, £500, including the stake. His system meant he would have to stake according to his own prices on the amount that would return him £500, should the horse be successful.

Let's assume he'd assessed the price of each of the two horses in the Newcastle race at 4/1. Based on these prices, he would take, theoretically, £400 to £100 for each horse, a stake of £100 and a return of £500 on each.

If one of the horses is betting with the bookies as an even-money chance, under Scott's new system he should not back it; it represents no value, since he had assessed it as a 4/1 chance. However, if the other horse, which he had also assessed as a 4/1 chance, is 10/1 with the bookies, then under his new system Scott should have the same stake of £100; with the odds at 10/1 his bet becomes £1000 to £100. He should make this bet because the odds represent good value.

Under the old system he would simply have broken square on the race – now he wins £1000 if his selection is first to the post. Even if he had put £100 on the favourite as a saver, he would still finish £900 in front.

It is so important to be in control of your betting. With his new system, Scott was completely in control. His betting became regimented and all worry of staking disappeared. It capitalised on the principle of value – the yardstick of all gambling.

This style of staking is like a simple form of the Kelly Criterion, a concept which was later adopted around the world for punters, blackjack players and hedge funds.

Scott applied his system and it was a sensational success. He had abolished 'bad value' betting. No more would he take 2/1 about any horse like that beaten favourite at Newcastle because, whilst 2/1 rates it as being able to win one time in three runs, or a 33 per cent chance, Don had assessed it as only 4/1, or one time in five – a twenty per cent chance. Provided Don's price assessment was correct, he realised he had the keys to the bank vault. However, as soon as the spotlight found Don and as others followed his lead, his value started to evaporate. After all, gambling is not so much about finding the winner as winning the value.

It's just like the coin tossed in the air – if you get better odds than even money about either heads or tails, there is value in betting and you must win over a period.

Unfortunately for Scott, as more attention was focused on him, he found it increasingly difficult to place his bets at the value price. His whole operation had centred on value. Once his commissioners started backing a horse at a particular price, other punters immediately latched on and backed the horse themselves. Unlike Scott, they were concerned only with the tip – for them the price was secondary. The copycats stifled all the value from the selection. Scott could no longer get set for the full amount at the odds he wanted.

Don Scott was a classic case of the spotlight cruelling the punter's advantage. As an unknown, he was able to get set without any trouble, but once people followed him, what had been easy before became hard overnight. There have been many groups that have tried to emulate Scott, including one led by Jim Mason, one led by John Rome, and yet another led by Michael McHugh QC (later a High Court judge). These punters have all stood the test of time.

13

Rolling the Dice in England

I LEFT MELBOURNE in November 1966 after my duel with Frank Duval and went back to Sydney, not with a lot of money but with a tremendous public image. I'd always had my share of publicity in the racing world, but now it was different.

I was writing a weekly racing column for Jack Tier, the editor of the Sydney *Sun* newspaper at the time. My betting duels had captured the imagination of the public and, after writing a feature or two in 1966, Jack has asked me to write regularly. When he suggested payment, I told him to donate what he thought I was worth to the Royal Blind Society. I had expected to do the column for a few weeks but kept it up for over three years, firstly with *The Sun* and then with Sir Frank Packer's *Sunday Telegraph*.

The column had a real following and I loved writing it. I would write about a punter or the bets I was taking, or I'd give my thoughts on the upcoming racing or a comment on the industry. I was told these articles helped create an aura around the bookmakers' and punters' exploits, intriguing the readers.

After Melbourne I felt different – I wanted to take on the world and try out the English scene, where bookmaking had begun some 200 years or so before. I mentioned my idea to Jack Tier and he thought it would be a great challenge and said *The Sun* would support me with coverage for the trip. I vaguely knew Stanley Wootton, the Australian-born English trainer, owner and breeder who also owned a racetrack, and knew he was coming to Australia on his annual visit. I approached him and he was most enthusiastic about the idea. He bitterly bemoaned the state of gambling in the United Kingdom and the nature of the English bookies, and he thought I could breathe some fresh life into the game.

It was extraordinarily difficult to arrange. The English bookies didn't want any outsider to enter their ring, least of all an Australian. There were so many obstacles that the attempt appeared doomed, but I came up with the notion of working under an existing English bookmaking company licence. I was finally accepted in early May 1967, and had only a couple of weeks to arrange my trip. The English Derby is usually run on the last Wednesday in May or the first in June. I was very excited.

Stanley Wootton, the 'Squire of Epsom' who was in charge of racing there, had organised everything in England. A friend of his, Wilfred Sherman, from the famous Sherman football pools family in England, operated 147 betting shops at the time but was not on the track. Stanley arranged for Sherman to take out a track bookmaking licence and for me to be the 'operator', without Sherman having any financial interest. His company name was Wilfred Sportsman and I was to be his track operator, with my own name displayed. I was now on the Rails at both Epsom and Ascot.

The Australian media gave a lot of publicity to the trip. It was billed as 'Betting at the English Derby with a Rails fielder representing Australian bookmakers'. It had never been done before.

Before leaving Australia I'd applied to the Reserve Bank to take funds out of the country, as there were still currency restrictions in place. I had asked for $250,000 to be available in London. I was shattered by the response – I was allowed only $50,000 in total, and only after I undertook to bring all my profits back to Australia. With such a small amount, there was really no point in going, as it could be lost on the first race I worked, but because of all the preparations I couldn't back out now. With real fear and trepidation I set off.

I left Sydney with two friends, my close bookmaking mates Jock Rorrison and Les 'Hundreds and Thousands' Tidmarsh. Les asked if he could have a small interest in the venture. This suited me down to the ground. Even if I had been allowed to take more funds, I knew I should not tackle the United Kingdom head-on. I went there not to lose. If I won, so much the better, but I wanted the experience to acclimatise me. If it was as good as I hoped, then I could consider a more aggressive attack next time. Even with plenty of funds, I would have given Les an interest. Now I welcomed it and invited him to have whatever he wanted. He wasn't greedy and took two shillings in the pound (we were working in English pounds), which represented a ten per cent interest. Jock took the same. This increased my bank to $62,500.

We arrived on a Thursday morning and took a cab to the Hilton in Park Lane. As I entered the foyer I immediately heard: 'Call for Mr Waterhouse.' I went to the house phone and it was Wilfred. He said he was in the lobby near the front desk. I looked around but couldn't see him anywhere. It was quite strange. Then I felt a tug on my coat – and there was a tiny but perfectly groomed and elegant man all of four-foot-eleven (1.5 metres) who came up to my midriff. I was six-foot-four (1.92 metres). We must have looked an odd couple.

We introduced ourselves and he said, 'Well, let's go – I'm running late and I've got to work on the first race at Sandown Park.' I declined, explaining my tiredness, but Wilfred had me in his luxurious Rolls-Royce in a matter of minutes. I didn't unpack, change clothes or even shave.

Tired as I was, I was glad I went, as it gave me some indication of what to expect of English racing. I met several Australians who had based themselves in England. Probably the most interesting was John Mortimer Green, known internationally by his sobriquet of 'the Butterfly'. (Years later John was caught up in the Fine Cotton betting scandal and was warned off for a year.) There were several Australian jockeys there – Breasley, Hutchison and Williamson – who had attracted quite a select group of Aussie punters around them.

When we met in Wilfred's office next morning the first thing I wanted to know was who did his form. This is one of the cornerstones of bookmaking. If you don't know the correct form, how can you assess the correct odds? Wilfred told me he did his own form.

I could not believe my luck to think that the man whose pitch I was using was also a form man. I wanted to sit down then and there to go over a race with him to ascertain the way he worked, but he said, 'No need to do that today – we'll look at it tomorrow.'

I planned not to start until the Tuesday at Epsom, the first day of the carnival, telling Wilfred that I had been limited to $50,000 in funds and would have to cut my cloth accordingly; I didn't want to be put out of business before I really got started. Wilfred then generously said he would be 50 per cent with me, which doubled our bank.

Funnily enough, I ended up with only four shillings in the pound (20 per cent) in my own venture. (The other two shillings in the pound were taken by another friend, Albert Smith, a leading Melbourne bookie who was also in England.) I didn't mind – it meant that the bank was increased to $250,000 – but I thought I was handing out diamonds. It was just as well that I wasn't greedy, as those diamonds would turn out to be glass.

—

On the Saturday Wilfred took me up to Newbury. Ray 'Hoppy' Hopkins came along too. Hoppy was about 30, dark-haired, extremely good-looking and very intelligent. He had been dux of his school and had a ton of ability. He was a punter and probably the most respected judge at that time, and very few bet bigger.

We had our cold pork pies and champagne and tried to untangle the meeting. Different in most ways, English meetings usually had six races beginning at around two pm, with 30 minutes between races. No Rails bookie put up a price until the horses were saddled and out on the track. There didn't appear to be a great deal of excitement. We bumped into Des Lake, an Australian jockey who was riding in the main event, which had a field of only three runners. He gave his horse a good chance but didn't seem to want to declare it a good thing. I decided to 'oppose' it.

In England, a punter can approach a bookie and either back a horse to win or alternatively oppose a horse, laying it to lose. I could see no harm in this. At the time, this was not allowed in Australia, although it was allowed for a while in the 1990s but banned again as part of the fight by officialdom against the new style of betting epitomised by Betfair.

Lake's mount was on the bookies' boards at 7/4 and there was no trouble to lay £2000 to £1000 against it. Wilfred followed suit and also laid the horse. It was a straight mile (1600-metre) race – the first I had ever seen. It is about as far as you would want to look, as it takes all your concentration just to pick up the horses. The three runners appeared to be locked together all the way, and that's how they came to the post. There wasn't a length between them at the finish, but Lake's mount was beaten and I had some expenses money.

Wilfred was really more a punter than a bookmaker, and he finished up well in front. Driving us back to London, he called into a stud and showed Hoppy and me a yearling he had just acquired. In a good mood, he said he would call the colt 'Bill Waterhouse'. I was aghast as I could think of nothing more embarrassing than having a horse running around a racecourse with my name. I needn't have worried; Wilfred eventually sold it to Norwegian interests, where it won their Derby.

Wilfred was the most generous, thoughtful and fun-loving host you could possibly imagine. Every night he insisted we go out, and he took us to all sorts of places that we had read about but had never thought of seeing. Yet we still hadn't done the form and my first meeting was getting closer.

On the Monday, the day before I was to start, I said, 'Wilfred, I've got to talk with you about tomorrow's races. I need to know how and why you have assessed the horses. Without this I'll be flying blind.'

'Not to worry, old boy, we'll have plenty of time tomorrow.'

There was no point in arguing, as I knew Wilfred was set in his ways. What I had seen at the tracks had been instructive. I wasn't frightened by the other bookmakers and I knew I would not let the team down.

On the big day, Jock and I arrived early at Wilfred's office. I knew that it was too late to worry about form but I wanted Wilfred's prices. He hadn't done them! I could not believe it. He said he would do them soon. I pestered him, as I did want to compare his prices with the newspapers' assessments and a very rough set I had done.

Eventually he said, 'All right, I'll do them for you.' He picked up a *Sporting Life*. He made a 5/1 shot 4/1, and a 2/1 chance perhaps 9/4, then he handed the paper over to me after about three minutes work. 'There you are,' he said. 'You'll find they will be quite close.'

I almost went into shock – I was speechless. I realised only then that I would be going into the meeting as cold as a spud. Wilfred obviously had not had the slightest idea of what I wanted all along.

Although it scared the pants off me, it didn't make much difference in the end. There simply was no money at the races. Even on the Wednesday, with a massive crowd for the Derby, I only held about £30,000 ($75,000). Wilfred, who promptly found a very large box to stand on beside me so he could talk into my ear, told me this was the top hold. I had expected to hold up to a £250,000 ($625,000) on the Derby and felt completely deflated.

Royal Palace was the pre-post Derby favourite at 7/4. The market was well settled – the bookmakers had bet pre-post on the Derby for the best part of the year. It was to be ridden by the leading Australian jockey, George Moore. The Rails bookies in England were not allowed to have any boards displaying odds and had to call out their prices to attract punters. I was given the honour of being allotted one of the two 'tick-tackers' just so he could run my prices to the other bookmakers. Tick-tackers, in the absence of betting boards, were a time-honoured tradition. These men signalled price changes using their hands. It was an archaic and completely out-of-date system, but no problem due to my experience as a young bookie.

I was calling 7/4 about Royal Palace when my tick-tacker said that it was now 6/4: the price of the favourite had shortened. I hadn't laid Royal Palace and so was delighted to think I could perhaps lay it at a shorter price. So I now called 6/4 Royal Palace, still with no reaction from the public. Next the tick-tacker called that Royal Palace was now 11/8. I was delighted. I did not like the horse and meant to stand it.

The shorter Royal Palace's odds became, the more reasons I had to give it a good stand. So I hurriedly made the call of 11/8 for Royal Palace. I was making myself hoarse with no result, when the tick-tacker said that Royal Palace was now 5/4. I was a bit hesitant but Wilfred urged me on: 'Quick, make it 5/4'. I did.

The only trouble was that, after calling 5/4 for a couple of minutes, I still had not taken one penny for the horse, so I called 11/8 again, with the same reaction. This caused the whole process to reverse, as my tick-tacker signalled my price to the other end of the betting ring and the general price of Royal Palace went back to 11/8. I took Royal Palace out to the original price of 7/4 before I could lay it, and even then it was for very little money. The horse started at 7/4 and won easily, but I did not lose much.

I invited all the Aussies, including the writers based in London, for cocktails at the Inn at the Park Hotel that night. There was a great camaraderie and we shared a few laughs about the Pommy newspaper treatment of us 'cobbers'. The journalist John 'Strop' Cornell, who was the London editor of the *West Australian* newspaper, said 40 years later that the night had stuck in his mind as a special memory.

The next day the bookmaking firm next door told me, 'You're the most hated man in England. You caused Royal Palace to start at 7/4 when the bookies all expected to pay only 5/4.'

All the betting shops controlled the bookmakers on the course. They had incredible power and looked upon the race-track as a kind of benevolent society for themselves. They had held bets worth millions of pounds off the track for Royal Palace, which meant the betting shops had to pay out nearly 50 per cent more as I had blown the horse's starting price out from 5/4 to 7/4. I had cost them a fortune.

—

The English led the world in bloodstock and once showed the way with their betting. Now it was in trouble. In my view it was simple: the race clubs didn't get their fair share of revenue from the off-course betting taxes. The government took the lion's share, leaving the race clubs with only about 0.75 per cent. In Australia the clubs get about five per cent of the TAB's turnover.

In my view there should be little or no tax paid on race-course betting. Unless you get people back to the racecourse, the industry will decline. I realised what was wrong with the bookmakers at the course in England. I don't think I encountered one self-employed bookmaker working on the Rails. This was nonsensical. The clerks running the stands were all working for wages. A clerk is not interested in sticking his neck out to make a bet that means little if he is right, but his job if he is wrong. I knew that the English bookmakers weren't going to listen to a colonial.

However, there were a lot of headlines in the English press about 'Big Bill'. One newspaper headline read: 'Place your bets, cobbers'. I attended two memorable functions. Firstly, there was the Derby lunch hosted by Lord Beaverbrook (Max Aitken) for all the owners of runners in the big race. I was fortunate to be invited as a celebrity, and was seated next to the legendary William Hill. I was fascinated to meet this larger-than-life man, who had led the English betting ring in the 1930s, 40s and 50s and who had then established a vast chain of betting shops.

Bing Crosby was at the lunch and was introduced to Hill by a friend, who said, 'I want you to meet the biggest bookmaker in England.'

I suspect Bing was kidding, but he came out with: 'Oh, hello, Mr Ladbroke.'

It brought the house down but only a sickly smile from William Hill. The rival betting chain, Ladbroke's, had just been taken over by the young energetic Cyril Stein; it was a sore point.

I was also invited to the Racehorse of the Year dinner. Every-one in racing was there. Suzy Volterra, the owner of the Folies Bergère and the Casino de Paris, travelled to the dinner from France, and Bing Crosby went as well. To me it was fairyland.

Despite the social side, I finished off the four-day Epsom carnival financially dented, physically tired and demoralised. I was off to Europe for ten days as there was a fortnight's break before the Royal Ascot meeting, but I had to work the next day at Kempton Park. I would have left on the Saturday morning for Paris, but Stanley Wootton, also the chairman at Kempton Park, had invited me to field so I had no choice. I arranged for Hoppy to get my bags and meet me at Heathrow, and to book us on the first flight to Paris after seven pm.

Albert Smith and I had been invited to the pre-race luncheon. I was 44 at the time. Albert would have given me about twenty years but was still my equal in heart and stamina. He used to go socially each year to England and hadn't missed an English Derby or Ascot Gold Cup for many years. He was a very generous and kindly man who, if he couldn't do you a good turn, would never do you harm.

Like the other functions I had attended, the Kempton Park lunch was a delightful presentation of racing, and the guests were lions in the sport. I was seated next to Captain Boyd Rochefort. I'm tall, but I felt small beside him because he sat so straight. He was the trainer to the Queen and a fascinating conversationalist. I was enjoying the lunch so much that I didn't want to go to work at 2.30. Old Stanley kindly marked my card to help me with the program, and he proved a good judge. That was all I needed.

I remember there was an odds-on chance that Stanley had thought would find it hard to run the last furlong. I offered evens and the crowd thought I was mad, but the horse weakened in the last furlong. My mate Jock Rorrison said, 'You've got a lot more respect from the bookies now.' At all events, we won something on the day, although I lost my voice calling the odds. I couldn't get to Heathrow quickly enough.

—

The three of us reached Paris around eight or nine o'clock in the evening – Albert had made a spontaneous decision to join Hoppy and me. Like schoolchildren on vacation, we couldn't get out fast enough to see the town. We went around to the Champs Élysées to find something to eat. I wanted to go back to bed after this as I was tired, but Albert walked us up the street until we came to the Lido.

There was a queue stretching into the distance waiting for the last performance. Albert borrowed a brick – £10 – and disappeared. The next thing, he reappeared with the doorman, who was all smiles. 'Ah, Monsieur Smeeth, it has been so long . . .'

We were taken into the empty nightclub and seated at a table almost on the stage. A bottle of champagne appeared. After a few more minutes the doors opened and the people, some of whom had obviously been queuing for an hour or more, were let in. I appreciated Albert's savoir faire.

Albert was as able a bookmaker as I've ever seen. He wasn't a gambler but a legitimate odds-maker. Hoppy was a different kettle of fish, a punter. The three of us got on famously, yet Hoppy was our natural opponent at the track.

Hoppy had been my biggest and most regular punter for over ten years. Our fortunes had fluctuated and, unlike with most clients, we rarely settled with each other. Rather, we would work either into credit or debit. Hoppy had just about the best memory of anyone I knew. He could recall what he had backed in a race eighteen months earlier, telling you not only the prices but the placegetters and the beaten favourite – he was probably the most complete gambler I have ever encountered.

Hoppy had a credit with me in excess of $100,000 when we left Australia for Europe; within six weeks of our return, he had replaced his credit with a debit of close to $800,000. He typified the continual battle between bookie and punter as each tries to find out what the other has in his favour, whilst concealing his own advantages.

We decided to motor down to the French Riviera and hired a car. Hoppy parried and probed endlessly at me, and soon we were betting. Albert, as a wily bookie, knew what was going on but was unconcerned. He was not a gambler and had no interest in the pure gambling of head-to-head betting between individuals. We arrived at Cannes and went to the Palm Beach Casino that evening. Albert, a long-standing member, made us both members. The casino was well patronised and had a bevy of beautiful girls, as indeed did the whole of Cannes. Albert told me that any girl on her own was 'in business'. This advice was to prove misleading and embarrassing when I visited Cannes with Neville Wran another time.

We walked back together along the beachfront from the casino to the hotel. It was a balmy night and we must have encountered 50 beautiful young ladies of the night, all out exercising their well-groomed poodles. You could travel the world and never see so much pulchritude in one place.

—

Time was running out and I would soon have to return to England for Royal Ascot. So we left the Riviera and went to Spain. After a few days in Madrid and a visit to the Alcázar of Toledo, we headed back to England. I had my voice back again but was still wary of the meetings. The Royal Ascot meeting is the social event of the English racing season, and the Ascot track near Windsor Castle is owned by the Queen. The royal family are driven down the track in their carriages and into the royal enclosure. Apart from being the social event of the racing calendar, the meeting also attracted the best horses and – I was told – the biggest betting.

The meeting certainly was a vast improvement on the Derby, but it was still a very tepid affair. I would hold more in one race in Australia than I did all day at Ascot. The English betting tax not only killed off punters but also the bookies, who now served only the interests of the off-course betting shops.

I saw an opportunity in the Gold Cup. The favourite was a French horse, Danseur, at the very short odds of 9/4 on. It was ridden by Yves St Martin, who used the shortest stirrups you could ever imagine. I knew the horse had been outstanding but had not started for a long period. It was huge and the race was over two and a half miles (4000 metres).

I called, 'I'll take twos,' meaning I was offering odds of 1/2, and someone laid me £2000 on to win £1000. After attracting no more business, I then called, 'I'll take 15/8,' and an Indian Prince approached.

'I'll have £1500 pounds to win £800,' he said.

There was no more interest and I was about to call 7/4 on but Wilfred could take no more of this foolishness. 'This horse is a certainty,' he said. 'It's an out-and-out champion and you shouldn't be standing it at all.'

I stopped laying the horse. Wilfred did have 50 per cent of the business, and he had been a great pal. Also, I had been wrong so often. Danseur broke down, didn't finish and never had another race.

The English venture had been a financial fiasco, but it was still worth it. I'd lost my money but that wasn't the point. As I wrote in my column in the Sydney *Sun*: 'I believe my activities attracted considerable interest, not only here in Australia but also in England, where I was given good coverage by the press and was interviewed by the BBC.'

My losses had been limited to $50,000, thanks to the Reserve Bank and my friends who had wanted an interest. 'Perhaps the most rewarding feature was that I was asked to stay on and continue working at the races after Ascot,' I wrote.

However, I hadn't been able to work in the manner to which I had been accustomed in Australia, and I'd wanted to show English racegoers a different style of bookmaking. Stanley Wootton asked me if I would return the next year and I accepted. I planned to take across a newfangled Australian betting board – and my own punters. I was to be allowed the punters but not the board!

—

While in London I had met Charles St George, a managing agent underwriter at Lloyd's of London insurance, and we formed a very close and long-lasting friendship. Charles was also a leading owner on the British racing scene; his stable included Ardross and Rhinegold. He was an elegant man in the top level of English society. A former Guards Officer, Charles had the most beautiful and gracious wife, Christine. He was a charming host on my subsequent visits to London, invariably providing his luxury 'town apartment', Claridge House in Mayfair – complete with a full-time butler – when I or the family came to town.

Through Charles, I became the first Australian-based Lloyd's insurance underwriter in 1968. I was advised that all the underwriters joining this exclusive 'club' took on the insurance risks with unlimited liability. As Charles had told me that claims on the underwriting members had only ever been made twice in Lloyd's history of over 200 years, I regarded it as a very good bet.

Over the years I invested a large amount, made my family members, and encouraged many of my friends into this illustrious society. Many other prominent Australians, such as Malcolm Fraser, would later become Lloyd's members. The time when I joined was a golden period, and I had years of splendid results. I didn't touch my dividends but ploughed them back, increasing my investment and bringing my family in as members.

I joined many of the famous syndicate operators, including Peter Cameron-Webb and Tim Sasse. Tim and I became friends, and when his son Duncan, who wanted to be a horse trainer, came to spend a year in Australia I arranged for him to work with T. J. Smith and Bart Cummings. Duncan trained the winner of the Eclipse Stakes in his first year as a trainer in England.

—

After the four-day Ascot meeting was over, I flew to the United States to have a break. Hoppy came with me. We stopped for a couple of days in New York and went to a race meeting at Aqueduct, and then the Roosevelt Park Paceway, where I knew the owner, Marty Rosenbaum. The next stop was Las Vegas.

A large percentage of Charles St George's business was in the United States, and when he learnt that I was going to Vegas he insisted I stay at the Stardust, which was the world's largest resort hotel with 1500 rooms. Anyone who has been to Vegas will tell you that the city is like a giant neon sign. The Stardust seemed to be a kaleidoscope of gyrating moving lights and signs. I went inside to check on the booking. The foyer of the hotel was an ocean of slot machines. At the reception desk was the longest queue of people I had ever seen. I certainly had no intention of spending the next hour in a queue.

I turned to leave but then I noticed a solitary person at the far end of reception. I went up but he snapped, 'I'm sorry, all enquiries must be from the queue.' I turned away, and as an afterthought he asked, 'What name is it, sir?'

I replied, 'Waterhouse,' and began walking away.

The clerk called out, 'Hold on, Mr Waterhouse, we do have a reservation for you.' He snapped his fingers and two bell hops appeared. Hoppy and I were taken to a magnificent luxury suite with two master bedrooms and a lounge with a cocktail bar on the top floor with a view along the strip.

The next morning I received a call from Moe Dalitz, the senior partner and biggest shareholder in the hotel. He would have been around 66 at the time. Moe had been a prominent gangster in Cleveland. He had packed his bags and moved to Vegas, where he built the Desert Inn. Moe had been one of the first into Las Vegas after it was opened up by Bugsy Siegel with his Flamingo Casino. Bugsy, along with others from the east-coast mob, funded the Flamingo but the Mafia investors didn't get the return they expected. Bugsy met an early demise.

Moe had been the head of the Cleveland mob and still had a bullet buried deep in his body as evidence of his tough background. Moe wanted to ply his trade legally and so had moved to Vegas and financed Wilbur Clark to build the Desert Inn. I'd visited the Desert Inn in 1951, and now I was excited to meet the man behind it. Through the publicity I'd received in England, Moe had heard I was the world's biggest bookmaker.

Moe and I hit it off immediately. I liked him and our friendship stood the passage of time. I visited him in Las Vegas every year, and he also came out to Australia to visit me. He was fascinated by my world of bookmaking, since bookies had been outlawed in the United States back in the days of Prohibition, and so American bookies had lost their expertise in the art of making a book.

Moe told me once, 'You name it and I've done it. I've broken just about every law in the book, but all that is a quarter of a century behind me. I haven't broken any law since I came here in 1950. Yet I'm still written up as a gangster.'

He probably did more for Clark County, Nevada, than any other man. He built the hospital and helped build synagogues for his own faith and also churches for every other denomination. Around the Desert Inn he built one of the finest golf courses in the United States and started the famous Tournament of Champions. With the golf course, he built a first-class country club. During his reign at the Desert Inn it became the Mecca of the rich and famous. Howard Hughes lived in the top two floors and ended up buying the hotel because he didn't want to move out for the high-rollers at Christmas.

Dalitz had earned tremendous respect from everyone in Vegas. Wherever he went he was given the red-carpet treatment and the best table for the shows. Charles St George had given me a huge build-up. This reputation stayed with me in Las Vegas for many years, and I was always given the best suite on my stays, and I was never once given a bill. I never sought or expected such favours, as I'd been brought up in a hotel and automatically expected to pay my own way.

I loved Las Vegas and decided to have another crack at a casino licence back in Australia.

14

The Mystery Punter

BEFORE I WENT to England in 1967 I had been puzzled by a bookie working in the same ring as me. Bill Deverall, an old-time fielder with 30 years' experience, was backing back horses with me for thousands of dollars. This was peculiar – it wasn't Bill's style. He was not a big gambler. He must have been getting some big bets from someone, and – more importantly – he must have thought the business was good as he was paying turnover tax on the bets and guaranteeing those bets he laid off with me. A bookmaker in those days paid a two per cent turnover tax, perhaps half of his profit margin. Also, as Bill would be liable for the bets with me, he had to be confident he would be paid by the punter.

Each day Bill would bet with me and each day I would peer through the ring to see if I could detect anyone who might be the mystery punter. After the next bookmakers' draw for stands I found myself beside Old Bill. I couldn't have been more delighted. I felt certain I would find out the identity of this unknown punter.

For six months Bill bet back with me and, believe it or not, I still didn't know who the punter was. When I wasn't busy I focused on the stand next door, but to no avail. I knew that, for a bookie of Bill's calibre, a bet back should be made quickly, for fear of a price drop, which could be disastrous for him.

Every time a bet was made, you would expect to see a punter, any punter, I even looked for a woman. Often there was no one near Bill when he bet with me, and I couldn't fathom it. Being in a betting ring is somewhat akin to a local fair, with people all around – but you would expect to recognise a regular face. When the stands changed again I almost gave up hope of ever unearthing the identity of this punter.

Then around Easter 1967 a man approached me at Rosehill Racetrack and identified himself as Peter Hunter. I vaguely recognised him as a man who had bet with me occasionally for cash a few years earlier. I had not seen him at the races since. I sensed at once that he was the mystery punter.

He explained he'd been betting with Old Bill but now wanted to bet in larger amounts and couldn't get his bets set. He preferred not to shop around in the ring seeking the top odds, as this usually created interest among other punters, which could cause a horse's price to drop. Peter said he hadn't bet with me because, as the leading bookmaker, I attracted too much attention. Racing for him was purely a hobby, and he didn't want any publicity to affect his business.

Peter didn't want credit and would bet in cash, but he didn't want to hand over cash each time. He preferred to pay a sum before the first race and to bet until either it was depleted or he had finished betting, to avoid drawing attention. I would pay him either in cash or cheque at the end of the day. Peter said he had been more than satisfied with Bill Deverall, but felt forced to bet with me for larger amounts. He said he was an accountant in partnership with his two master builder brothers in Canberra.

Peter gave me $12,000 in cash. 'Please don't count it now, but check it after I've gone,' he said and walked away. He came back just before the first race. I heard a voice from the back of my stand. With his mouth close to my ear, he whispered, 'The favourite, $2000 at 5/2, please.'

I called the bet to my credit clerk in a low voice and turned to acknowledge the bet with Peter, but he was already on his way. I was surprised how far he already was from my stand. In a matter of seconds he was lost from view. I now understood why I had never been able to spot this mysterious punter.

The horse won and he approached me for the second race, having $5000 on a 5/1 shot. Again, Peter disappeared almost like a wisp of smoke, causing not the slightest disturbance to anyone. In the whole time I would know Peter, I never saw him talk to anyone. Nor do I recall ever seeing him standing still. On a racetrack everybody talks to the people around them, but Peter was the exception.

At the end of the day Peter had lost $2000. He came back and I gave him $10,000. He thanked me and I thanked him; we both agreed it was a pleasure doing business with each other. He left, saying, 'I'll see you next week.'

The following week the meeting was at Warwick Farm. Again Peter put $12,000 in my bag very early in the day and we both observed the same ritual. This went on for several months; each week a similar sum of money was put in the bag and we settled after the last. Then one day after the last race he said, 'I won't take my money today – I'll leave it there for next Saturday. I don't like taking that amount home over the weekend.' So the scenario changed a little.

This bank of about $16,000 lasted a few weeks and was wiped out one day with one race left. Peter came to me and said, 'I've exhausted my bank – can I have a $4000 credit bet on the second favourite, please? I'll pay you next week.'

I said yes, and I knew that would be the end of Peter. Give a cash punter credit and he never pays you when he loses. I didn't expect to get my $4000 and was resigned to losing a good client. I would willingly have given him the $4000 as a gift rather than lose him, but of course you can't do that.

He turned up the next week with my $4000, plus another $12,000, and so we went on until May, when I went to England to work at Epsom and Ascot. I arranged with Jack to look after Peter's business. I instructed Jack to bet whatever he wanted and to cut him back on nothing – I would take full responsibility.

Jack was ecstatic. 'You've lost him now – he will never leave me!'

'Okay,' I said. 'I'll be back in about six weeks'.

—

It was July 1967 when I arrived back in Sydney. I had been travelling badly before London, and although the amount lost on the Derby was not great, it was another loss. A gambler wants to see an indication that his luck is turning.

Things had not been that good during my absence either. Jack greeted me with, 'Thank goodness you're back! You can have your punter back – he's going to give me ulcers if I continue with him'. I had half-forgotten about Peter Hunter.

Hunter had increased his betting and won consistently. All Jack had done was pay and pay, without ever receiving. Hunter also had left a credit 'in the bag' of about $20,000. So we locked horns once again in much the same fashion as before England. After a couple of weeks he phoned me and said he would be unable to be in Sydney the coming Saturday as he had to go to a meeting in Melbourne. Would it be possible for him to phone me from Melbourne and have a few bets? I said yes and told him to phone me at ten in the morning. I didn't like to do this, but I considered it part of the service and didn't want to lose him as a punter.

On Saturday at ten am the phone rang and it was Peter. 'Hello,' he said. 'I'm in Melbourne, and it's rainy, cold and miserable. I'll be pleased when my business is finished here.'

After the usual pleasantries, he invested about $14,000 and hung up. I noticed later in *The Australian* that the weather had been just as he described it. Peter won on the day but, more importantly, he had created a precedent. Now he needn't go to the races to bet.

Sure enough, at ten am the next Saturday he phoned, this time from Darwin. He told me it was hot – around 100 degrees. And sure enough, the newspaper had it 101 degrees in Darwin. Peter's betting now substantially increased, but I didn't worry: I was holding his cash – around $40,000. He also was now betting on two states, Sydney and Melbourne. He just lost on the day.

The next week the same thing, only this time he was in Cairns in the north of Australia. He had a reasonable credit but outlaid a little over $200,000. I pointed this out to him but he replied, 'No worries. I've got a credit of $35,000 and I'm sure I've got a couple of winners there, but if not, I'll be at your office at five on Monday afternoon.'

I accepted this, knowing that he did look as though he had a couple of winners there. One winner or even a couple of placings would shorten the disparity rapidly. He had rarely bet each-way, usually concentrating on the win option. This time he had taken several bets on horses at middle-order odds – some of $10,000 to win and others of $5000 each way.

Peter and I were in the period in which two protagonists sound each other out: the courting time of gambling. It was the first day that he had upped his bets in such a dramatic fashion. It was also the day he didn't get a return and he lost the lot. He had converted a $35,000 credit into a debit of $180,000. I was distressed by the result, just as he must have been. I would have been happy to wipe out his $35,000 credit. To have won $10,000 above this would have been a bonus.

A debit of $180,000 was an utter disaster. It was an absolute fortune, enough to buy several of the priciest houses in the best suburbs of Sydney. I didn't know if Peter would – or could

– pay. I had no way of contacting him, as he was so concerned with his privacy. Since he hadn't wanted credit before, I didn't know his telephone number either at home or at work. I was nonplussed. This was still Saturday, and I was in for an awful weekend as I waited for Monday.

George Thorley had followed my dealings with Peter from the beginning. He loved the atmosphere of big gambling and revelled in the telling of the actions. When I told him on the Monday morning what had happened, his face dropped. 'Oh, you fool, you bloody fool! You gave him $180,000 credit without knowing anything about him? Oh, how mad can you be?' I took it all day from George as I knew he was right.

My brother was entirely different. To him, it was just bad luck. Like spilt milk, it was over and done with.

The hour between four and five pm was very long. Five o'clock eventually came and the girls left the office, but no Peter. George, with the saddest possible look, asked, 'Well, are you just going to sit there or are you going to go home? He's not coming. He never was coming.'

I replied, 'Whether you're right or not, I'm staying here until six. Hunter told me he was catching the afternoon plane from Melbourne, and it may have been delayed.'

George had solid reasoning on his side. 'He knows your phone number, doesn't he? He would have phoned you if he was delayed.'

Before I could answer this unanswerable question, there was a knock at the door and Peter Hunter's head showed around the corner. 'Sorry I'm late,' he said, 'but I couldn't get a taxi at the airport and the traffic was terrible. I was frightened I might miss you.'

He then handed me a certified cheque for $180,000 drawn to the Rural Bank of New South Wales. He explained that he had phoned the bank from Melbourne and they had the cheque ready when he arrived from the airport by taxi.

George had waited in his own office while Peter was with me. Peter didn't stay long – he thanked me for the trust and didn't seem upset by his large loss. He left after ten minutes, saying that he had to catch a plane back to Canberra.

A moment later George burst into my office. The transformation was remarkable. He was like a boy released from detention. He hadn't expected the whole of the debt to be settled but knew something substantial must have been paid. His astonishment was complete when I handed him the cheque.

'I've got to apologise,' he said. 'You were right – this man is extremely wealthy. To get a bank cheque of this size shows the bank regards him as a most esteemed client. They wouldn't do that for anyone under any condition unless he was an exceptional client. You can take it from me that Hunter has great wealth and you can bet him unlimited.'

As much as anything, the $180,000 signified a change in luck, like rain coming after a long drought.

—

My luck didn't last. Things began to hot up with Peter and after a couple of weeks he had credit of about $60,000 again. He phoned me the next Saturday, saying he'd been waiting for a horse and wanted a good bet. The horse, Regalano, was the favourite in a wide betting race in Melbourne. I was working at Rosehill in Sydney and didn't expect to hold much money on the race.

Peter asked the price and I told him 11/2.

He said, 'I want $275,000 to $50,000, please.'

This was an enormous amount – like a Frank Duval bet, except that Frank's were at the carnival and this was only a minor race. I took Peter's bet.

As we were driving to the track, I told Jack what I'd done and he said I was crazy. We weren't travelling that well and a big loss like that could be disastrous, whereas if the horse were beaten, we wouldn't get that much benefit.

'It's difficult to beat a sole punter just one-out,' Jack said. 'There's a limit to what you can win, but no limit to what you might lose.'

I had to agree. So, for the second time in my betting career, just as I had decided to quit betting Joe Taylor six years earlier, I decided that if the horse won, I would pay Hunter and tell him I wanted a break from betting him. Little did Jack and I realise it, but this was the Rubicon for both Peter and me. Unknown to me, Peter was also intending to quit if the horse won and to finish with betting altogether.

I meant it when I told Jack I would quit. The race now took on a different complexion for me. At 11/2 the field, Regalano was a long-priced favourite. On track, the race was a tame affair; I was naturally under the odds on Regalano and so the public was not greatly interested. I think I only held about $6000 at the track.

Listening to the race was a nightmare. Regalano was a strong sprinter and always a good chance, which was why he was the favourite. Under pressure and in the firing line, he won the race narrowly in a fairly close finish.

I was numb. I've always tried to mask my true feelings after a race. I have a good poker face, and if I show emotion, you shouldn't take it at face value. I have deliberately looked wounded after a big win and smiled after a heavy loss. This day I did neither. I felt the weight of the world. My racing staff, not knowing about the bet, saw that I had had a good result even though the favourite had won. They thought I had won about $5000, whereas in fact I had lost $270,000. Of course, I couldn't let on to them.

Then came an announcement over the PA system. A protest had been entered on the race! It was by the second horse against the winner. In Australia in those days, protests rarely succeeded. After what seemed an interminable delay the protest was upheld and the winner was relegated to second place.

I just couldn't believe my luck. I showed no emotion whatsoever, yet in an instant everything had changed. 'That's bad luck, Bill,' said one of my staff. Within me, my heart sang.

Driving home with Jack, I declared that Peter was finished now and would never be a threat again. The heavy blow would be an eternal nemesis for him. To have won $275,000 only to see it turn into a loss of $50,000 would be unimaginable for anyone. Even a hardened pro would have trouble accepting it. A man can steel himself to accept a loss of $50,000 – but here he had to accept a shock effective loss of $325,000. I knew it would completely shatter Peter.

—

That minor Melbourne race was Hunter's turning point. It emerged later that at the time he was in the hole for $250,000. If Regalano had won he would have been out of trouble. Hunter had been through hell and would probably have learned his lesson – but after this loss it was a different story. He still thought he could 'get out' but instead went further and further out of his depth.

After the loss the man I knew as Hunter was in a desperate position. He approached me and complained that having to make his bets so early on a Saturday morning was an obvious handicap for him. He asked me if I could give him a number to ring during the afternoon. I had closed our SP business a few years earlier when the race clubs cracked down on all off-track bookmakers. The clubs had made an ultimatum – any bookmaker who persisted with an illegal off-track business would be disqualified and lose his licence. Both my brother and I enjoyed our racing too much to jeopardise our futures, and the off-course business, although profitable, was hard to control. So we had closed up shop.

Hunter had now placed me in a quandary. I liked him as a man. He had a true gambler's nerve. I could appreciate his dilemma. I wanted to keep his business because he was not in front and I felt in the ascendancy.

I then made a seriously wrong decision. I agreed to his request and arranged for him to phone Mary Abdoo. After we had closed down, Mary had kept her own small but profitable SP business going, which gave her a nice living. I knew she was completely trustworthy.

Matters now began to get out of control. When Hunter bet with me I at least had some semblance of control. With Mary he had no rein on his weakness. It was like allowing an alcoholic into the cellar of the local hotel. He bet bigger and bigger, his losses mounted. The harder he tried, the more he lost; the more he lost, the more he had to put on. He paid me a cheque for $300,000 after a heavy bout studded with losses, and I thought this would be the end. It wasn't.

We were no longer settling each week but were allowing his account to run until it reached a sizeable figure. I think he paid another $300,000, the last amount I received from him. He continued betting, got in front, then lost and got behind, fluctuating all the time. A colossal amount of turnover was involved.

I remember one bet Hunter had during this period: $50,000 on a horse called Windsor Park that won at the good odds of 11/1. He won $550,000 on the race – a record bet at the time – but of course no one knew. Even this win didn't put him in front. Soon after this he just stopped ringing and of course left owing me around $700,000. I still didn't have an address or contact number for him, as I'd always respected his wish for complete privacy. I couldn't have chased him even if I'd wanted to.

Strange as it may seem, I was relieved that Peter was gone. The excitement had left his business and I felt sure he was getting into trouble. All the time I was expecting a call from his brothers, thinking he must be draining the family's assets. Most importantly, I knew what I was doing was against the racing rules, and I had placed my licence on the line. I had won a fortune from him – far more than I ever expected – and I felt a strong sympathy for him. How different it would have been if Regalano had kept the race and not been disqualified. Peter had waited for the right race and had found the winner, but even then it was not enough. His luck was against him.

The tragedy that would eventually unfold was so bizarre that I don't think it could have been scripted. Although it was not known at the time, Peter Hunter was not Peter Hunter at all, but one Peter Huxley. He didn't live in Canberra but in the seaside Sydney suburb of Harbord. He was not working in partnership with his brothers in the building industry, but held an important position as the secretary of the Rural Bank of New South Wales – he was the second-highest executive. It would be another two years before Peter's double life and the scandal became public. Only then would the depth of his deception be made clear, and the wrath of society and officialdom fall on his head. And on mine as well.

Few swindlers ever set out to swindle, but they become victims of their own greed when they try to cover up the shortfall. Not at any stage did Hunter consider that he was stealing. A brilliant man with a lucid brain, he had started to dabble in the stock market, had got his fingers burned and had used the bank's money as a temporary expedient. Not a great deal of money was involved in the beginning – only a few thousand – and I believe Hunter saw it as a temporary measure. Hunter had covered his tracks well with me. He had always appeared to be travelling, although all the time he was actually still in Sydney.

It came as a huge shock when, in early 1970, I picked up the afternoon newspapers in my office. The story of a charity embezzlement was on the front page. I didn't take a lot of notice until I saw the photo accompanying the story – a photo of Peter Hunter but with the name Peter Huxley. He was charged with embezzling almost $2 million from the Rural Bank.

I felt sick, but I also knew I had nothing to fear, for I had no knowledge or suspicion of what he'd done. I was totally forthright with the investigating police and provided all the records they asked for. Of course, it wasn't long before the tax department came calling as well, but they found that every cheque from Hunter/Huxley had been declared for tax purposes, and they were satisfied.

What was reported in the press was dreadful. Huxley had been on many boards and set up dummy accounts, from which he 'borrowed'. It was appalling when it was revealed that he had taken a large sum from a Freedom From Hunger account, amongst others. The sum mentioned in the press was being overstated as between $7 million and $9 million. Those amounts had been illegally moved around, with one account being used to pay another. In the end, the total amount missing from all accounts was still the staggering amount of $1.8 million, and the revelations shocked all of Sydney. The Rural Bank's insurers made good the full amount to their customers and no client or charity lost money.

The extraordinary thing in all this was that Huxley did not expect to be caught or charged. He'd always claimed he wanted to pay the Rural Bank back but the burden was too great. Confident his duplicity had succeeded, he'd left the bank, joined a pastoral company and was a highly regarded investment advisor.

When he was caught and the authorities wanted the money repaid, Huxley told them he had lost the money to four bookmakers. However, I was the only bookmaker to stand up and say that I'd won from Peter. The others all went for cover and denied it. I confirmed that I had been paid approximately $700,000, and that around $700,000 remained unpaid – in my mind I had already written that off.

The story in the media was sensational. The massive betting, much of it off-track and against the rules, was featured through-out the press and I was most apprehensive. The authorities threw the book at Huxley because of his executive position and his betrayal of trust. He was given an eighteen-year jail term with a twelve-year non-parole period – more than some murderers. Of course, I felt extremely sorry for him; I abhorred his actions but accepted that he was a victim of his own greed and naivety.

After sentencing, he was called back to be examined in the Bankruptcy Court. Here I was also given a thorough going-over. All his bets were brought out and I realised that I was going to be in strife with the AJC. I hoped they would understand I had been caught in a vortex from which I couldn't extricate myself. I heard nothing officially, but was relieved to be told privately that the racing authorities were sympathetic, realising that, with Peter having lost so much, I could not have refused him a chance of getting out.

All the bookies who bet with Huxley also went to court but the others either denied betting with him or professed that he had won from them. I was the only one to acknowledge that I was ahead of Huxley, and all the records were there for them to see. If Huxley had lost the missing $1.8 million and I was paid only $700,000, it was obvious that others must have won as well.

If I'd known Huxley was stealing I would have had to pay the money back, and I'd have been charged as an accessory. The liquidators wanted to claw back money wherever they could but it was clear that I had no knowledge or inkling that Hunter was Huxley, and that although I was curious about him, I had no suspicion of any criminality. So that was where the matter rested.

The other bookmakers who either 'could not remember' betting with Huxley or said they had lost to him had no trouble with the AJC. However, I suddenly felt a hardening from the AJC committee, and when the season drew to a close in 1971 I was asked to 'show cause' why my licence should be renewed.

Neville Wran had acted for me at the Huxley bankruptcy hearings but he wasn't really a racing man. We both felt it would be better if Sir Jack Cassidy QC, whom I had known over the years and who was experienced in racing, acted for me with the AJC committee. I realised very quickly that the AJC had a closed mind on the Huxley matter. They had been embarrassed by the adverse publicity for the racing industry through the Huxley hearings. They declined to renew my licence for the 1971–72 season but gave no explanantion. The chairman, Sir Brian Crowley, said I could apply for my licence the following season. I took this to mean I had been given a one-year suspension. Naturally I wasn't happy, but I felt I couldn't complain. However, my licence was not renewed in August 1972.

Meanwhile, between my finishing with Peter Huxley and his court case, a new performer had arrived on the scene who was to be the biggest horse-backer the world had ever seen.

15

The Babe

FELIPE YSMAEL WAS KNOWN as 'the Babe' because of his boyish looks. A Filipino of Spanish extraction, he was approaching 40 at the time I met him. Educated in the United States, he came from a fabulously wealthy family. His grandmother, who ran the family and kept him in check as a young man, had vast interests in the Philippines, and had donated a large part of Quezon City to the people as the seat of government. Ysmael Steel had a monopoly, with the sole right to manufacture refrigerators, radios and other electrical goods.

Felipe also held the tobacco-importing concession, and I was told his timber concession alone was worth a billion dollars – unheard-of wealth in 1967. He was not tall but was a keen athlete. He had won the world amateur jai alai championships in Spain a few years earlier. Jai alai is said to be the fastest game on earth and is the top sport in Spanish-speaking countries around the world. Felipe was interested in all sports, but especially racing, and he had the punting urge from an early age. Even while at college in the United States, Felipe loved going to the tracks and attacking the totalisator.

Ysmael had his own horseracing string in Manila, and as he grew up he travelled the world to visit the racing countries. He was disenchanted with American racing, unimpressed by its control and the government's harsh views on betting.

He enjoyed racing in England but couldn't stand the English bookmakers, because he couldn't get set for enough money and it drove him to distraction. He then found Australia and loved our racing, making Melbourne his second home. He spent a fortune on a house with extensive grounds at Dandenong, just outside Melbourne, and on a beautiful country property.

The Babe did nothing by halves. I remember walking down a Melbourne street with him and his local man, Frank Ford. The Babe decided he needed some more cars, so he just walked into a car showroom, picked out a large Mercedes and said, 'I'll take that.' Frank, of course, had to make the arrangements. The Babe didn't wait.

Then we went into another showroom and bought a new Pontiac for his German wife, Hildegarde, a former world-class ice skater. Frank, out of breath, arrived just in time to be told what had been bought; and the Babe went to a third showroom, where he bought a four-wheel-drive Range Rover. I don't know how Frank kept track, but the three cars were delivered promptly the next morning.

Felipe hit Melbourne like an exploding volcano. Extremely volatile and quick-tempered, he also had a very gentle and generous side. He settled into the local scene and started betting, and the city would soon hold its breath. Felipe probed gently at first but there were some tremors felt in the betting ring. When his commissioner or trainer queried the size of a bet or a price to be paid for a horse, he told them that they weren't to concern themselves as he treated $1000 as they would one cent. He wasn't joking.

At this stage the Babe was at the peak of his powers. In 1966 he had supported a relatively unknown young lawyer, Ferdinand Marcos, to become president of the Philippines. Felipe had poured a fortune into the propaganda machine to help Marcos' campaign, and personally led a large election parade down the streets of Quezon City. Marcos had been an underdog and, against all predictions, he'd got home. Felipe had backed a winner.

In Australia, although Melbourne was his chosen city, his first horse trainer was Graham Heagney in Adelaide. Ysmael came to Sydney for the Cup Carnival, had a few bets with my brother Jack on the Rails and then went back to Melbourne. The only other bookie he bet with in Sydney was Albert Smith. Jack told me he had found another big punter, but we didn't realise just how big.

Then some curious events started to occur in Melbourne.

If a top professional assesses a horse's chance at 4/1, the figure is usually quite accurate. In a pure (100 per cent) market, that horse has a twenty per cent chance in the race and should win once in every five starts. As a punter, you would, theoretically, be square after five races. To survive, a professional punter has to get a longer price than 4/1 for that horse, and a bookie has to convince a punter to take a shorter price. The difference, of course, is the bookie's margin.

If a trainer manages to keep a horse's improvement on the training track secret, this is a bonus for him and his connections. The horse may now actually be a 2/1 shot – that is, it should win once every three starts. The trainer and his backers now will eagerly attack the bookies until the price shortens to 2/1. The bookmaker is aware that there are certain grey areas where his knowledge is limited, and the weight of money plays a role here.

Usually, when the 4/1 chance does race, it performs as you would expect a 4/1 chance to perform. Whether it wins or loses, when analysing the form after the race the professional assessment is invariably borne out. If a horse is backed in from 4/1 to 2/1, then that horse will usually perform better than expected.

What was happening in Melbourne was that some horses were being backed in to very short quotes for no apparent reason. A horse assessed at 4/1 would be backed in to start at 5/4. This is a colossal shortening and might happen only two or three times a year on a city track. Suddenly it was happening in Melbourne on a regular basis.

The horse that started at 5/4 ran not as you would expect but more like the 4/1 chance it was. A 5/4 short-priced favourite should go to the line very strongly but this wasn't happening. These horses were not even filling a place. While one poor run by a horse or a mistake by an analyst can be forgiven, something is wrong when it happens regularly. What I didn't know was that there was a huge new punter affecting the prices.

Ysmael never personally approached any bookie in Melbourne or placed a bet himself. He used a small army of commissioners, controlled by his close associates. His main adviser was the genial Frank Ford, reputably one of the best judges of horseflesh in Australia and an honest man. That's no doubt why he lasted so long with Ysmael. Frank was no gambler – he knew little about betting and hated the responsibility. He valiantly tried to curtail his boss's betting but he may as well have tried to hold back the dawn.

The bookies were having a field day with these bets. Even if unaware of what horse was the 'pea', all they had to do was wait for the first move and then rapidly shorten that horse's price. For example, if a bookie was asked by a commissioner to lay $40,000 to $10,000 about a horse, all he had to do was to say, 'No, I'll lay it $4000 to $1000,' and then shorten its odds to 3/1. Then he might lay $3000 to $1000, followed by $2000 to $1000. When the price reached, say, 6/4, he could lay $10,500 to $7000. All this would mean that, instead of laying $40,000 to $10,000, he had now laid $19,500 to $10,000. The bookie can thus win the same amount of money but stands to lose $20,500 less.

Similarly, if he is aware of what's about to happen, he needn't lay the horse at all in the early proceedings. He can have his odds so much the shorter, and then, when they drop to 2/1, could lay $40,000 to $20,000. His risk is the same as if he'd laid $40,000 to $10,000, but now he can win double the amount if the horse is beaten. Never in their bag-slinging history had these bookies found themselves in such a clover patch. I was to change all that.

For a multitude of reasons, I altered the pattern that had stood me in good stead for ten years in Melbourne. In both the Spring and Autumn Carnivals there, I had never once looked to upset my Melbourne cousins. In Sydney I would take on the punters without regard to the other bookies, extending my prices when I wanted to lay a horse. Melbourne was different. I fell into line price-wise with the other bookies. I didn't want to antagonise them or open myself to greater risks as, until Duval, I had always set out not to lose my money. Having the local bookies offside had been at least one of the reasons for the downfall of all my predecessors.

For ten years I had not trodden on any corns in Melbourne. I had no enemies there at any level. I was the golden-haired boy, invited to all functions and regarded as a major asset to the carnival. Now I wanted to approach the meetings in a different, more deadly manner. I was to achieve what I set out to do, but I was to pay a horrendous price, and would keep on paying it for many years.

Unbeknown to me at the time, the Babe had already antagonised some powerful people in Melbourne. Apart from buying horses, Felipe also bought part interests in others. Gordon Skuce, a popular and able racing man, had brought to Australia an unsound English horse, Don Juan, which trained well on the track; Skuce told the Babe it had the potential to become the best sprinter in Victoria. The Babe loved champions and eagerly purchased a half-share for a very high figure, giving Skuce a large profit. However, Don Juan broke down at its first start after he bought it. I don't think it ever raced again.

The Babe had bet plenty of money on Don Juan too, so his loss was twofold. A suspicious man, Felipe was convinced Skuce had known the horse was a dud. He accused Skuce not only of cheating him on the purchase price but also of cheating him out of winnings on his bet. Skuce had placed the Babe's commission and took offence at the accusations. The upshot of all this was that Skuce refunded the Babe's purchase money and the friendship between the two was severed.

Skuce was also partners with a fellow called Brian O'Brien, who was extremely close to Sir Eugene Gorman: the three of them were together in the Don Juan venture, even though the Babe thought he was dealing only with Skuce. When the Babe realised he was being handled, he dropped Skuce like a hot potato. Felipe had unknowingly sealed his own fate, as Gorman never forgave him for abrogating this transaction.

I had also fallen out with Gorman's man Brian O'Brien over a betting incident, although I didn't know they were partners and I didn't hear about the Don Juan episode until much later. I knew Skuce but he never mentioned it to me. Neither did Felipe. If I had only known these machinations, I would have saved myself a hell of a lot of trouble. I would suffer from Sir Eugene's machinations myself, even though it was from behind the scenes.

Sir Eugene loved being a powerbroker in racing, as well as the recognition that came with his former position as a long-serving VRC committeeman. He enjoyed mixing with the cream of the crop, whether bookies, trainers, owners or punters. Sir Eugene was fascinated by these individuals, both good and bad. He always wanted to know who was betting, how much and on what.

Felipe had become influential and high-flying in Victorian racing. However, Sir Eugene's ego and jealousy meant Felipe's future in racing in Australia was in peril.

This was about the time in 1967 that I had gained the

ascendancy over Peter Hunter, and I had just received his cheque for $300,000. For almost twelve months I had been betting on a very large scale. Duval had electrified the racing world with one day's betting. Everywhere, my punters were betting bigger and bigger. With Hunter beaten, the challenge of a new punter was something I was looking forward to with an almost uncontrollable hunger.

I felt I could have a pleasant romp, as with Hunter's $300,000 Jack and I had some spare cash, and our main building commitments were completed. I had no idea of the magnitude of betting that would unfold. I had always tried to keep a rein on my ego and had deliberately refrained from openly challenging a punter or embarrassing him in any way. But after hearing that there had never been a punter of his dimensions before, I felt a tremendous yen to get at Felipe.

—

One of the opening salvos of the Melbourne Spring Carnival is the mid-September Show Day meeting at Caulfield. Then the focus turns to the Sydney Spring Carnival, and back down to Melbourne for the two Cup Carnivals. I went to the 1967 Show Day meeting aware that just as I knew of Ysmael, he would know of me. Although I had never met him or his commissioners, I knew they would find me. I deliberately didn't make any overtures for their business. I simply went to the track and waited. I felt a little like a spider waiting in his web.

My plan was simple. I was aware that Ysmael's commissioners were having trouble getting all their money set, and that the bookmakers were only taking slices of the action and then reducing their prices, hoping to lay the largest portion at the lowest odds at the finish. I decided to take Ysmael's bets without cutting the amounts, and then add fuel to the fire by not cutting my price.

This is something that no big punter can bear. Half the punter's thrill is to see the bookie writhe with fear or apprehension and frantically race for cover behind shorter odds.

I didn't have long to wait. Frank Ford approached me. I knew his name but that was all. I could see at a glance he was no gambler. He was well dressed and wearing a hat, and he had an open look on his sun-deepened skin. You could see all his sins were on his face. Instinctively I trusted him, which was most important, as apart from the money there are many tricks that can be worked on a bookie at the track.

I saw this man looking at the names displayed on the top of the bookmakers' stands. He was obviously looking for me, for as soon as he saw my name he came over. This was a small but important point. Any half-decent professional would know exactly where his opponent would be and what he looked like. Frank didn't.

His first words were: 'Mr Waterhouse, my name is Frank Ford. I've got some commissions and would like to place some bets with you. If you tell me whom you'd like to ask, I'm sure they will give me a satisfactory reference.'

I replied in a friendly but clipped manner. 'There will be no need for that, Mr Ford. I know of you – your credit is unlimited.'

'I want $10,000 on the favourite,' he said. 'How much of that would you like?'

'You have $20,000 to $10,000, the favourite,' I replied, and deliberately turned my back on him. On the Rails you have business coming from both sides of the stand. It doesn't stop. With a big punter, you might pass your tickets to a clerk so he can write while you talk to the client, but I wanted to give Frank Ford the impression that I regarded his bet as I would a newspaper boy's. It had the desired effect.

Within a few seconds, Frank gently pulled my sleeve. 'That was $10,000 on the favourite, wasn't it?'

'Yes, $20,000 to $10,000,' I said courteously, and again gave my attention to other patrons. I was certain Frank would be taken aback, especially as the price had not been altered. This was most unlike the treatment he had been copping from the Melbourne bookies.

I knew I was confusing Frank, but I was taking a hell of a chance. I also knew that a team of commissioners would be placing bets for Ford and the price could collapse like a deck of cards. But I was the leader of the ring, watched very closely by the other bookies. They would have seen Ford had backed the favourite, but if I could stand pat, I thought I could stabilise the price. The only worry was that if other professionals followed the money with other bookies, then the price of the favourite would quickly be swamped, blowing the odds for the rest of the field and throwing my market into chaos.

Every nerve in your body, every bit of training tells you to shorten the price in this situation – it's only common sense to try to lay the horse at its shortest odds. The favourite's price wavered momentarily with the other bookies but soon came back to my 2/1. The danger was past. My thinking had worked.

Looking back, I know what Felipe was probably thinking back in the grandstand. As an incredibly suspicious man, when told by Frank that I'd taken his whole bet without cutting the price, he would have thought immediately, 'Oh, Waterhouse must know this favourite can't win.' Probably the bookies also thought that I regarded the horse as a fair risk. If so, they too were wrong – the favourite won the race.

Up came Frank again before the next race. 'I want $10,000 on the second-favourite, at your price or whatever part you want of the bet.'

'You have $35,000 to $10,000 about the second favourite, Mr Ford,' I said, and turned away to the public side of the Rails.

Again, within a second or so Frank tugged my sleeve and said, 'That was $10,000, right?'

I replied, 'Yes, Mr Ford – you have $35,000 to $10,000.' Again I didn't alter the price but left the 7/2 on display. I was very apprehensive, however, as his first horse had won and once more I was concerned that the price might yet collapse. I was taking a dangerous risk. To me it was almost as important for the price to hold as it was for the horse to get beaten. If the price dropped, the race was ruined for me. The gamble was in the value of my prices for the whole field on the board, and therefore my odds as percentages had to stand up.

My ploy held once more. I managed to stabilise the market and the horse stayed at 7/2. Felipe's doubts were probably dispelled in that race – although the horse didn't win, it ran a creditable race and finished in the places.

This went on all through the day. The bets increased but were substantial rather than big. On each occasion I treated the bet as though it were a mere bagatelle, and each time Frank tugged my sleeve and checked the bet.

It was a traumatic day, like playing Russian roulette. I'd lost badly but felt like I'd won. My strategy had worked: I had taken all of Ford's bets without affecting the market, far exceeding my wildest hopes. I knew it was something that Ford and Ysmael would never have expected. Unintentionally, I had wrecked the day for the other bookies. They were expecting some good pickings and there weren't any. No horse that the Babe had backed had tightened in the market.

Ford came around after the last race to collect his winnings, which isn't the correct procedure. If you bet for cash you get paid immediately, but if you bet on credit you have to wait until settling day. My nephew John was working with me. A young man of 22, he naturally did not want to pay. We hadn't worked out any settling and he wanted to follow the normal procedures.

I was following my own script in the drama. I asked Ford what figure he made it and told John to issue a cheque for that amount. I explained to Frank that I didn't do business this way and I hadn't worked out his account, but I would take his word on the figure; if it didn't tally with mine, I would contact him. I thanked him for his business and said I would see him in a month's time.

I now had a month's respite back in Sydney before I faced up to the two Cup Carnivals in Melbourne, and I knew that in those four weeks before I came back to Melbourne, Ysmael would be handled by the local bookies again and again.

—

When I arrived back in Melbourne a month later it was the Tuesday before the Saturday start of the three-day Caulfield Cup Carnival. I hadn't been in my hotel room long when the phone rang and a voice asked, 'Mr Waterhouse?'

'Yes?' I replied.

'This is Felipe Ysmael. I would like to get together with you if possible. Would you be free for lunch at my house in Dandenong tomorrow?'

I replied that I would be delighted. Dandenong is about 30 kilometres or so from the city centre. Ysmael apologised for dragging me so far but mentioned that he abhorred publicity. By going to his house, we would be away from all prying eyes. I said my business manager, George Thorley, was in Melbourne with me, and Ysmael politely suggested he join us.

I put the phone down in a state of bliss. I couldn't believe it. I understood that Ysmael never dealt personally with bookmakers, and yet here he was phoning me and inviting me to his house. It meant he had been waiting for me and checked my arrival. I hired a car and floated out to Dandenong on cloud nine.

The house was a large bungalow, beautifully finished with all the latest touches. It was set in spacious grounds that took up several hectares, surrounded by a high fence. Present were only Ysmael, Frank Ford and both of us. We went into the lounge room and talked pleasantries. The Babe soon got onto racing. He told me he had been surprised and impressed with my betting over the Show Day meeting and explained the difficulties in getting set for his betting. Also, he had been handled by some of his commissioners, who were working in with the bookmakers. He said he knew this would not have happened with me.

Ysmael offered me all his business. I couldn't believe what I was hearing. This was what I had been seeking, and it had fallen into my lap so quickly and so easily. I had no doubt that Frank Ford was responsible for Felipe making the move. Ford had never been happy trying to control all the betting. Now it would be simple. The four of us sat there agreeing, all happy and smiling.

We had arrived around eleven in the morning. Felipe had asked me to come early as he wanted to talk before lunch and not in front of his kitchen staff. He was a gourmet who went to inordinate lengths to have his chef prepare what he thought his guests would like. Like a true gourmet, he was slim but savoured every morsel that entered his mouth. I'm not a gourmet. Two minutes after I've eaten, I doubt if I could tell you what I just had. I am almost as happy with a hamburger as I am with Beef Wellington.

There was a Victorian provincial race meeting that day. I knew I wouldn't be betting with the Babe on these races; I was in Melbourne for the Cup Carnivals, not a bush meeting at Werribee. If I didn't bet I couldn't get into trouble. I wanted to be at my keenest and best for Saturday, which was why I had come to Melbourne so early. I intended to be completely relaxed and in control when I stepped up at Caulfield.

My mind was made up on this score. Over the years I have been invited out on a Friday evening to homes where every trick known to man has been used to get me to quote a price about a horse racing the next day. I very rarely weakened, as it was too foolish without full information.

After lunch, Felipe soon returned to the subject of racing. He wanted some ground rules for our coming battle. 'How much are you prepared to gamble over this carnival?'

I had never been asked as directly as that, but I replied, 'While I'm hoping not to lose, if necessary I am prepared to risk $250,000 for the three days of the carnival.'

I was shocked at his response.

'Okay,' he said, 'that's fair enough. I'm prepared to gamble $50,000.' This was not in keeping with his Show Day betting, so he was either cutting back or else expected to win.

Felipe, of course, had the television on and it was getting close to post time for the first race at the provincial meeting at Werribee. In 1967 the racing coverage on local television was first-rate. Each race was televised live and you were given a fair indication of the various prices and form of the runners.

'Now, what will you have to drink? Vodka, Tia Maria, Cointreau, Drambuie?'

I didn't really want a drink, but said, 'Drambuie will be fine.'

He brought back a large whisky tumbler with a four-finger nip of Drambuie. I almost burst out laughing – I thought he must be kidding. I gingerly took a sip as I looked at the television screen.

'Let's have a small interest on the races,' he said.

'No, I'd rather not get involved today.'

'Oh, we won't get involved – just an interest to pass the time while we're talking.'

I could see he really wanted to bet. While it was unconventional, there was nothing against the law or rules of racing for two individuals to bet together privately. My only worry was that he could be setting me up. I didn't know the man, but it would be a crude attempt if this were the case.

Not wishing to appear a damp squib, I replied, 'Okay, but I'm limiting my losses today to around $20,000 to $25,000.'

Felipe was excited and pleased. 'Marvellous! We'll just have an interest, no big betting.'

He wanted to know the prices, so I phoned a friend in Melbourne for the local pricing service, which was the lifeblood of the illegal SP bookmakers. In the first race, after getting the prices, Felipe had $9000 to $6000 on the favourite, and $10,000 to $2000 on another horse. His 'saver' bet won, beating the favourite, so he was $4000 in front. Both George and Frank congratulated Felipe on his betting prowess, and I could see he agreed. He had a look of sublime pleasure and I was beginning to see that this was going to be a $25,000 lunch.

Perhaps I could limit it to $20,000. Obviously he had studied the form and I didn't even know a runner. In the second race, Felipe missed the winner and so, instead of being $4000 behind, I was now about $6000 in front.

I vividly remember that I just wanted to thank Felipe for a delightful lunch, good company and excellent conversation, then grab the money and go. But I couldn't.

We were in one of those modern lounge rooms that spilled out into other areas and to the lawn and pool outside. The room itself was very large but Felipe took me over to a corner. After I'd given him the prices for the next race he said, 'I'll have $35,000 to $20,000 on the favourite.'

'Okay, you've got it – but if it wins I'll be $29,000 behind, and that's it for the day as far as I am concerned.'

'Fine, fine – that's all I want'.

He was whispering, and it was obvious that Felipe didn't even want Frank to know that he was betting so much. Fortunately, the horse lost and I was now $26,000 in front.

So it went on all afternoon. It was quite bizarre. Neither my man George nor his man Frank realised what was going on. They'd heard the bets for the first two races, but after that they were completely in the dark. Before each race, I rang for the prices. Felipe and I would nonchalantly find ourselves slipping away from the other two, who not once asked a question.

I had been sipping my way through that wretchedly large Drambuie and decided to put it behind me by drinking it quickly. I polished it off and with that Felipe replenished it, again to a height of four fingers. There is nothing you can do in circumstances like these. Besides, after a vintage wine at lunch, I was feeling quite relaxed – and I was winning.

We went through the afternoon in this surreal fashion. I realised how incredibly suspicious he was of everyone. He knew he was safe in his betting, as I was in his house and obviously couldn't be involved in any trickery. However, as they say, betting is easy – it's winning that is difficult.

The last race eventually came and it was a fairly wide betting race – 7/2 the field. The favourite won and Felipe let out a cry of joy. His face was a picture of wellbeing. Frank and George both congratulated him. I now emptied my second Drambuie. I wondered what the Babe was going to say. He talked about the form and how it looked the winner, and really only required the normal run of luck to be in at the finish.

What he didn't tell them was that he'd had $150,000 on the winner at 7/2, and so had just won a colossal $525,000 on the race!

Nevertheless, he still lost $25,000 on the day. If his last winner had been beaten, he would have been behind $700,000 – I'm sure that even Frank Ford would have been shocked. When you are gambling you don't look at it as money but rather as units, otherwise you could never be a big gambler.

I had never really been behind all day. After the first race it was Felipe who had been chasing. Although he was generous with his liquor, my mind had stayed lucidly clear all afternoon.

I didn't know much about Felipe at this stage – except that he was allegedly wealthy and a good risk – but $690,000 was an absolute fortune, and we were betting on a bush track. Can you imagine me sitting in the lounge room of a man who I expected soon to be my adversary at the racetrack, and taking bets of $150,000? It was absurd.

I had gone to Felipe's place to learn the form of the punter. You obviously can't change the form of the horse, but it is a different matter with the punter, as I later proved with Ysmael.

Driving back to Melbourne, George said, 'How did you go?' He naturally thought that Felipe had been betting in the same amounts as for the first two races.

When I told him the full story, George looked as though he had been beaten over the head with a baseball bat. George had been through the Duval and Hunter battles with me. If cash had to be found in a hurry he was marvellous, but at heart he was a two-dollar punter. He couldn't understand big betting, even though he was surrounded by it. He couldn't conceive of how someone could win $525,000 under his nose without him realising what was happening.

It showed me what a cool customer Felipe was. He had been down $550,000 and had not revealed his feelings. He had not been rattled – I would have seen it even if he'd tried to cover it. George didn't know what to say or advise, and we wondered what to expect from the Babe in the coming carnival.

In fact, George would have been delighted if I had cancelled all business with Felipe: 'Nothing ventured, nothing lost.' To his credit, George respected my thinking: 'Nothing ventured, nothing gained.'

—

Sir Eugene Gorman was at this stage still my confidant. We had dinner on the Thursday before the Caulfield Cup. I had previously mentioned that I had been invited to Felipe Ysmael's house. Sir Eugene couldn't contain himself, wanting to know what had happened in my meeting with Ysmael. I confided in him, wanting his advice to bolster my confidence.

Sir Eugene all but gave me an ultimatum: 'You must dissociate yourself from the Filipino. You'll beat all the others but not this man. He's too wealthy and will wear you down by the sheer weight of his wealth. Cut out while you can. How much do you want to lose in this mad gambling?'

I was taken aback by the force of Sir Eugene's conviction, as it was the last thing I expected. He had been a big gambler in his youth and always mixed with top gamblers. This was the first time his advice had been so discouraging. I could understand him pushing caution because of the danger of not being paid, but this was the reverse. The danger wasn't the shortage of money but the oversupply of it. However, I believed I could keep Ysmael under some control, so I privately disagreed with Sir Eugene.

His attitude confused me because Gorman had nothing but contempt for Pat Cummings, the biggest pro punter in Melbourne and a man for whom I had a healthy respect, born out of experience for which I had dearly paid. 'You'll wear him down,' Sir Eugene had told me. 'Pat's only a punter and he's only got the brains of a punter. Don't be frightened of him.' Yet I had never been keen to take Pat on. The best I could hope for was to win back the money that Pat had already won from me.

I knew there was an element of truth in what Sir Eugene was saying – Ysmael was indeed a man who could break anyone if allowed to, and he did find winners. So I told Sir Eugene that, while I agreed with him, I was the master of my destiny – not Felipe Ysmael. I intended to risk up to $300,000, a lot of money in those days, but I knew I could win a great deal more with a bit of luck. I said that if Ysmael backed three winners to each win $100,000, I would pull out. I knew it would be hard for Ysmael to hit the treble.

Gorman had no answer to my logic. At that stage I had no idea of his bitterness towards the Babe. It must have driven Sir Eugene crazy to hear of the mad betting the Babe was doing with me.

Foolishly, I fed all the details of my encounter with the Babe to Gorman over the following weeks. He was the only man in Melbourne in whom I confided, but he should have been the last person I trusted.

16

The Filipino Fireball

I HAD THE BABE'S business exclusively at the Caulfield Cup Carnival and there was marvellous betting. Ysmael gave me hiccups a few times but that was to be expected. It's a funny thing – punters always remember their big wins, bookies their big losses.

I do remember the final race of the first day: it was the Toorak Handicap, and the favourite was Tobin Bronze. The horse was close to a champion but I'd never had a big opinion of him. I decided to extend the price and laid a full column of bets against him. I was standing the horse for $100,000 and cut the price to evens. Ysmael must have been watching. Ever suspicious, he obviously didn't want to back the horse when I was over the odds, but when I shortened the price Frank Ford came along and took $100,000 at even money about Tobin Bronze. It was a mile race (1600 metres) and Tobin Bronze was a good miler. He walked in and it cost me $200,000 – not the way I wanted to finish the day.

In my column I lamented: 'When will I accept the fact that Tobin Bronze is a champion?' I had laid it not only with Ysmael but also with the crowd. I wrote: 'When I heard the roar of the crowd, I knew I was gone. I was faced with a queue of punters forming the longest line I can remember. They stretched out around the corner of the grandstand. After all had been paid, the only ones on the course apart from me and my staff were the cleaners.' Perhaps a little like Monty Python's Black Knight who never gave up, I then declared: 'If Tobin Bronze starts favourite in the Caulfield, I suggest you give him a miss as I still don't think he is a true stayer.' I would end up with egg on my face again.

Tobin Bronze had won the Victoria Derby a couple of years earlier, in 1965, in the very slow time of 2:34. To me, the time meant he was suspect about running out a solid one and a half miles (2400 metres). In 1966 he had done everything right. He'd firmed all the time until he became a clear-cut favourite for the Caulfield Cup.

As it happened, Jack and a friend of ours owned an outsider in the 1966 Caulfield Cup. It is everyone's dream to have a runner in a major race, and although the horse was quoted at long odds, they wanted him to run full-out; they believed that with his light weight he should lead all the way. So I knew the pace would be 'on', and I believed this would test the mettle of Tobin Bronze.

This had been a couple of weeks before Duval came on the scene. I stood Tobin Bronze in the Cup for well over six figures. The horse opened up at 6/4 and tightened to even money. I wasn't going to let it go into the red (shortening to odds-on), but the weight of public money had more influence than all the big punters. Tobin Bronze finished up at 11/8 on.

I'd watched the race with bated breath. The champion Adelaide jockey Jim Johnson was aboard Tobin Bronze in a forward position, just off the pace. When they entered the straight, Tobin Bronze dashed well clear and the crowd cheered. However, the fast early pace had told on him and Tobin Bronze weakened, finishing well out of a place. It was clear to me the horse wasn't a true stayer. If the pace was on, he had no finish left in him.

Now, at the 1967 Caulfield Cup, Tobin Bronze was the

favourite because of his easy win in the Toorak Handicap. Because of his inglorious run the previous year, he was at a wide quote of 5/1. I again stood the horse at these long odds, and once more at the finish Frank Ford – or rather Felipe Ysmael – took $200,000 to $40,000 about the horse.

It was a disaster of a race. Tobin Bronze was untroubled to win. There had been no pace on and the race took 2:31.1; the previous year, Galilee had taken only 2:27.8 to win the race.

Tobin Bronze was the only discordant feature of the whole carnival. I had Felipe's business. I did not refuse any of his bets and I did not back one horse back. I kept it all, not sharing it with the other bookmakers. I didn't realise at the time that I was living in a fool's paradise. I was looking in the mirror and only seeing myself.

The Melbourne bookies must have hated me. I hadn't taken just any punter from them, but the punter who would turn out to be the biggest we had ever seen. Further, he wasn't a professional and didn't care too much about the prices. It was all too much. To them it seemed I was stealing the goose that laid the golden egg.

There was now also the glare of publicity. Before my betting with the Babe, his money was always scattered among commissioners and there had been no face for the press. Now there was just one man, Frank Ford, and he was highly visible. The press was in full flight. At this stage reporters were fed the tale that it was not the betting of one man but an 'Asian syndicate'. Felipe abhorred publicity and yet wanted a good public image. He loved being photographed at the races with his wife and five children. He wanted to be accepted into Melbourne society, but on his terms. Publicity for his family was acceptable, but not for his gambling.

The press has a job to do, but few people want their private business made public. After each race the betting sheets were collected by an official and taken to the stewards' room. The press seemed to get access to these sheets very quickly, and so Frank Ford's betting became newspaper copy as soon as a race was over. To get around this, we used pseudonyms.

The Babe had tried in the strangest ways to hide his involvement in racing. He put his horses in the names of his chef and his chauffeur, and even invented names such as 'Mr Gibbon', which he thought was a great joke. It was probably one of the nails in his coffin when the authorities came to investigate him. They thought he'd been making monkeys out of them.

George Thorley became a 'big punter' for a short time. He would meet Frank Ford somewhere in the enclosure to be given the bet to pass on to me. The bet was recorded under George's name, which he thought was great fun until he read his name in the paper. People don't realise how embarrassing it can be to suddenly be projected into print. People can drive you crazy with questions, and you can lose friends through envy.

By the time the Melbourne Cup came around, the Babe had been identified by the press, but he was still hiding behind the pretext of an Asian syndicate. The press knew he disliked them.

On one of the provincial race days in the week leading up to the Melbourne Cup, I received a phone call in my hotel room from Felipe; he asked me what I was doing. I told him I was going to a movie and he immediately said he'd come with me. I expected no ulterior motive. I had been to his Dandenong home again, but not on a race day, and he had agreed that nothing like that first afternoon of betting should occur again.

I planned to attend a two o'clock session. I had told Felipe to arrive around one, which would give us time for a quick snack before the cinema. I am punctual and I knew that he wasn't, so I told him that if he was delayed, he could meet me at the cinema. The Babe arrived around a quarter past twelve, just fifteen minutes before the first provincial race of the day was scheduled. When he entered my suite, he turned on the set for the racing coverage. Still the penny didn't drop

– I would have done the same myself while waiting for a friend to get ready.

But then: 'Let's have an interest in the first race.'

'No. Let's not get involved,' I said. 'We only have time for the first and we still have to go and eat.'

'Well, why not have some sandwiches from room service?'

I acquiesced and ordered some sandwiches but told Felipe I wouldn't phone for a pricing service – I didn't want to encourage him. I was getting to know and understand Felipe better. The average person regularly follows the same pattern of behaviour time and time again. Duval had been impossible to follow and Hunter difficult to fathom, but Ysmael was falling into a pattern already. I sensed that Felipe didn't just want an afternoon's fun but was out to teach me a lesson. I realised that for this to happen he must have a sure thing. You can usually read it on a person's face, and the Babe looked contented.

I accepted the situation. If my hunch was correct, I figured I could work out the horse with a little luck. I had given up on the movie but didn't tell him. He wasn't sure if we were just eating in the room and betting on a couple of races before going to the movies, or if we were settling in for the afternoon. I soon found the horse. It was running late in the program and was easy to locate because it was trained at a private track by a trainer I'd picked as being associated with Ysmael. It was a filly with a Spanish-sounding owner, so I knew it must be his horse. The race, being so late in the day, was a godsend.

Acting on my hunch, and still not letting on that I realised the movies were now out, I set out to unnerve him. I suspected Felipe would try to bet martingale, increasing or doubling his stake until he found a winner. If he wanted to bet big on a certain race, it meant he had to increase his stake quickly. It was dangerous for me if he found winners, but then, if I were at all perturbed, I still had the excuse of wanting to cut out to the movies.

My thinking worked out perfectly. By the time the two-year-old fillies' race came around I had him on the ropes. He was several hundred thousand dollars behind in his betting. To his credit, the Babe showed no emotion. He looked at me and simply said, 'I own a filly in this. I would like to have a good bet on her. I would like to have a million dollars on her to win.'

It took my breath away.

I had never heard of anyone putting a million on a horse. I had certainly never heard of anyone taking such a bet. I hated stalling with any bet and didn't want to now. I looked again in the newspaper. The filly was the short-priced favourite at 6/4. I took the bet but put a limit of 6/4 on the SP price. This still meant I could lose up to $1.5 million – by far the largest bet laid anywhere in the world. It was an amazing amount of money – probably enough to buy a streetful of the priciest houses in the best suburb of Sydney.

The Babe willingly accepted my limit on the odds, which gave me insurance against a long-shot price coup. If the filly was a good thing, I knew he would have had a betting commission at the track, which would bring the starting price in. If I was wrong and there was no commission at the track, the limit I had imposed would save me from annihilation.

At least there was no torture in watching the race, as I was put out of all misery very quickly. The filly jumped to the front and was never headed, simply increasing her lead all the way to the post. But all was not lost. Fortunately, there had been a $100,000 plunge on the filly at the track, which caused its price to shrink to 3/1 on. For all his immense betting, Felipe had won only $330,000 on the race from me. After counting up his earlier losses, the Babe was only slightly in front. Just as I had won a little at Dandenong, so he finished just ahead this time.

I'd had a tumultuous ride instead of a quiet afternoon at the movies, and although there was nothing illegal about two men sitting down and having a bet, it would have been frowned upon by racing officials. I also would have much preferred to have all my business done on a racecourse, for the simple reason that it afforded protection as the bets were enforceable at law. When I went to dinner that evening, there was just the normal banter; no one knew of the enormous milestone in betting which had been reached that day behind closed doors.

—

The Babe's betting for each race throughout the Melbourne Cup Carnival, although gigantic, had become the norm. The first meeting of the carnival, Derby Day, was my testing ground, and it was made complicated by a horse called Red Handed – who wasn't even racing that day.

In the previous year, 1966, I had found myself in a shocking position in the Caulfield–Melbourne Cups double with the horse, which was a bolter from Adelaide that initially had ordinary form and was well out of the doubles betting. It was trained by the champion trainer of stayers, Bart Cummings, who also had another bolter in the Caulfield Cup, Galilee. I had a bookmaking policy of reducing the risk on 'stable doubles', which meant that my odds on the double of Galilee and Red Handed were halved.

The only trouble was that as soon as the Galilee–Red Handed double was backed, Red Handed showed quick improvement, and the odds tightened dramatically for both races. This was a blow, as all value in the odds disappeared. Worse was to come. Galilee won the Caulfield Cup, and now the liability of Red Handed winning the Melbourne Cup leg was crushingly real.

Fate intervened. In his last run before the Melbourne Cup, Red Handed ran in the Geelong Cup and fell. He hurt himself and was scratched from the Melbourne Cup. I was saved.

Now, in 1967, I was ready for Red Handed. I realised that Bart, later to be known as the 'Cups King', had set Red Handed for the previous year's Melbourne Cup when it was so unlucky to be injured. I was sure he would target the race again this year with the horse. However I had kept quiet and when the other bookies' early charts came out I saw that Red Handed was again at a long price. Not with me. I deliberately 'forgot' to put him on my doubles charts. There were about 500 horses entered in each of the two cups, so there wasn't room for all the runners, and having one missing was not noticeable – unless you wanted to back it. It was covered, along with the other long-priced runners, by a statement at the bottom: 'Other runners quoted'.

My hunch was right. Red Handed was a heavily backed plonk to take out the second leg of the double. In the Caulfield Cup it had run second to the favourite, Tobin Bronze, and it was then backed in from long odds to Melbourne Cup favouritism. The bookies were in awful trouble, as they had all laid Tobin Bronze in the first leg with every runner in the Melbourne Cup, especially Red Handed. For me, however, it was a skinner – that is, until Felipe invested on the Derby–Melbourne Cup double.

After the Caulfield Cup, Felipe asked for a doubles sheet and selected Young Brandy for the Derby, which was the third-favourite, and coupled it with Red Handed for the Melbourne Cup, backing the double to win $330,000 at 33/1, his outlay being $10,000. I was aghast – the very horse I was saving was now a potential disaster.

There's a break of a fortnight from the Caulfield Cup to the Derby, and in that fortnight Young Brandy won the Derby trial and became the favourite at 6/4. Meanwhile, Felipe had backed up twice more with the double, each time taking a shorter price – all up, I had a $750,000 liability. I was hooked.

I could not refuse the Babe if he wanted a big bet. For a whole year I had been on my guard about Red Handed and yet here I was looking down the barrel on it again. I thought that at least I had laid the horse at the bottom of the market, but instead the price shortened again, so now I had laid it over the odds. My only hope was that Young Brandy might not win the Derby . . .

Indeed, not only did Young Brandy not win the Derby, it did not fill a place. The race went to Savoy. I was completely off the hook. And I knew what Felipe was going to back in the Cup.

On Cup Day, betting on the big race was 4/1 the field. There were actually two equal favourites at that price: Red Handed and General Command, a good stayer from Sydney that had recently won the Metropolitan Handicap in a very fast time. As the Cup approached, I had only one thought on my mind – the Babe. I had to try to think like he was thinking. I was oblivious to any other punter, which can be hazardous, but it was a risk I simply had to take.

Nonchalantly following the passing parade, my eyes were seeking only one person. In the packed crowds, I caught him out of the corner of my eye coming towards my stand. Felipe was ready to make his bet – for Red Handed. I waited till he was a few metres away and then turned and looked straight at him. Our eyes locked and he momentarily paused.

That was all I wanted. Just as he was about to claim me, I reached up to the board and flipped the price against Red Handed to 9/2. Ysmael looked aghast. He knew that I knew he wanted to back Red Handed, and there I was giving him half a point better than any other bookmaker on the course. With his betting units, that could be worth upwards of $50,000. I could see him thinking, reacting. He must have thought I was challenging him.

Without any hesitation, he said, 'General Command, $200,000 to $50,000.' He turned on his heel and left. It was not the bet he had intended – it was too small for him. I knew that I'd rattled him.

I'd come to appreciate Ysmael's extraordinary suspicion. I was gambling – not about the form of the horses but about the form of the punter. I let Felipe know I wanted him to back Red Handed, he assumed I knew something *he* didn't know – and that's what I was gambling on. By trading on his unbelievable suspicion I caused him to bet contrary to his own opinion. It would never have worked with any other big punter. The only question was whether I was right. I had acted purely to unbalance him and put him off the horse I desperately wanted to save.

When your luck's in, your luck's in. Ridden in masterly fashion by the leading jockey Roy Higgins, Red Handed won the race, with General Command finishing only sixth. A lesser man would have been crushed and perhaps never come back from this. Ysmael, a fabulously wealthy man, just kept going – although I knew his confidence must have been jolted. I felt I was now in the ascendancy with him.

Through the bizarre betting experiences at the Babe's home and then in my hotel room, I had unfortunately opened the door to allow Ysmael to bet with me off-track. He then got into the habit of doing most of his business with me by phone in the morning. Although I could save on the turnover tax, I was reluctant – but I was hooked as much as the Babe, and could not back off.

The tragedy was that during all this time I was confiding everything to the Machiavellian Sir Eugene Gorman. He was aware of my every move. As a result, and most unfortunately, this was to be my last Melbourne Cup appearance for 40 years, something I still look back on with great sorrow.

———

With the carnivals over, the Melbourne bookies had the Babe to themselves again. Occasionally he would venture north to Sydney but more often he'd send a commissioner. They say

My father, Charles Hercules Waterhouse, who died suddenly when Charlie, Jack and I were at the races. I was only nineteen and was desolate.

My kind and caring mother, Elizabeth Catherine Waterhouse (née Fox), in about 1930.

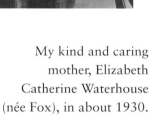

An angel-faced me at the age of four. I was a scallywag.

Pulling a face for fun in about 1928, with my brothers Charlie (left) and Jack (centre).

Our Imperial Hotel in about 1937, several years after the Sydney Harbour Bridge was finished. Note the sign for Richmond Beer, which my father was able to bring in from Victoria as our point of difference because we were not tied to any brewery.

With my siblings, Jack, Betty and Charlie, in about 1940. I am on the right and was the youngest in our close and loving family.

Walking tall with my beloved mother in around 1938.

Off to the University of Sydney, where I made friends for life.

After my father died, I missed out on my University Regiment's deployment to New Guinea. Here, I am farewelling my best friend, Gus Mooney, in January 1942; sadly, Gus was seriously injured soon after.

I graduated with an Arts degree in 1945.

Barry Pheloung with me and our dates in 1945.

At the Trocadero Telegraph Beach Girl Ball with the beautiful
Maide Hahn in 1947.

December 1950, at the East Grinstead Memorial Hospital, after being left for dead in a car crash on an icy English road when my good friend Lionel Murphy was driving.

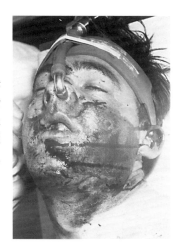

My Jaguar XK120 – there were just three in Sydney at the time, and mine was iridescent blue. Its form was so unique that wherever I took it people would stop and admire it.

On an early date with Suzanne at the exclusive Princes Restaurant and Nightclub. We were engaged in 1952.

By 1958, Suzanne and I had had three children in four years – a handful for Suzanne, as I was now the bookmaker and no longer the barrister, and I was working seven days a week.

With Robbie and Louise in 1960, on the site of our Kirribilli St Charles development of 88 strata title home units. I included the children in my business affairs from a very early age.

Showing David not to be afraid of horses in about 1960.

Robbie and Louise at Jack and Vida Muir's Wallacia property in about 1960. Years later, my grandchildren Tom and Kate also learnt to ride with Vida Muir.

My parents-in-law, Mr and Mrs Dart (Lance and Rewa), with our three children in 1961. They were wonderful grandparents.

By the late 1950s I had finally decided, as I loved bookmaking so much, that I would not be going back to the law.

Suzanne and me in the late 1960s.

Louise, Suzanne and Robbie at Delphi in Greece in January 1966. Unfortunately, I was a late scratching as work back home called.

When my licence was not renewed in 1971, I took the children on an extended holiday through the USA in the Christmas holidays. Here, we are on the trainer Arnold Winick's boat in Florida Keys.

VICTORIA RACING CLUB

OAKS DAY

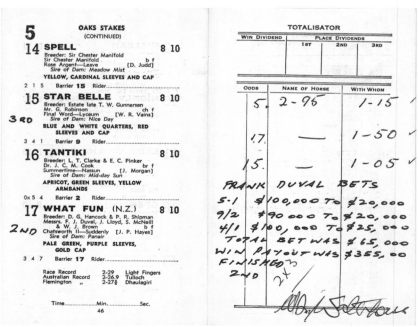

5 OAKS STAKES
(CONTINUED)

14 SPELL   8 10
Breeder: Sir Chester Manifold
Sir Chester Manifold   b f
Rose Argent—Leave   [D. Judd]
   Sire of Dam: Meadow Mist
YELLOW, CARDINAL SLEEVES AND CAP

2 1 5   Barrier **15**   Rider...............

15 STAR BELLE   8 10
Breeder: Estate late T. W. Gunnersen
Mr. G. Robinson   ch f
Final Word—Lyceum   [W. R. Vains]
   Sire of Dam: Nice Day
3RD   BLUE AND WHITE QUARTERS, RED
           SLEEVES AND CAP

3 4 1   Barrier **9**   Rider...............

16 TANTIKI   8 10
Breeder: L. T. Clarke & E. C. Pinker
Dr. J. C. M. Cook   br f
Summertime—Nassun   [J. Morgan]
   Sire of Dam: Mid-day Sun
APRICOT, GREEN SLEEVES, YELLOW
   ARMBANDS

0x 5 4   Barrier **2**   Rider...............

17 WHAT FUN (N.Z.)   8 10
Breeder: D. G. Hancock & P. R. Shipman
Messrs. F. J. Duval, J. Lloyd, S. McNeill
   & W. J. Brown   b f
2ND   Chatsworth II—Suddenly [J. P. Hayes]
   Sire of Dam: Panair
PALE GREEN, PURPLE SLEEVES,
   GOLD CAP

3 4 7   Barrier **17**   Rider...............

Race Record   2-29   Light Fingers
Australian Record   2-26.9 Tulloch
Flemington   ,,   2-27½   Dhaulagiri

Time...............Min..............Sec.
                46

TOTALISATOR

WIN DIVIDEND	PLACE DIVIDENDS		
	1ST	2ND	3RD

ODDS	NAME OF HORSE	WITH WHOM
5.	2-95	1-15
17.	—	1-50
15.	—	1-05

FRANK DUVAL BETS
5-1 $100,000 To $20,000
9/2 $90,000 To $20,000
4/1 $100,000 To $25,000
TOTAL BET WAS $65,000
WIN PAYOUT WAS $355,00
FINISHED
2ND   2X

My racebook from Oaks Day 1966, in which my clerk recorded Frank Duval's record-smashing bets on What Fun in the Oaks. My clerk had me sign the list to verify the extraordinary amounts.

A cartoon by Wells after the colourful 1966 Melbourne Cup Carnival, in which I battled Frank Duval.

A Steve Richardson cartoon in about 1966. Note the cartoonist's joke on my betting bag: 'REG. A.P.C.' – an aspirin powder – rather than the AJC.

Taking on English racing with my English bookmaking partner, Wilfred Sherman, representing the Sydney betting ring at Royal Ascot in 1967. Wilfred was actually standing up on a box on my stand, which shows the large height difference between us!

Two of racing's top professionals, bookmaker Albert Smith and punter Ray Hopkins, during our marvellous ten-day trip through France and Spain in 1967. Hoppy's and my betting was always on credit and fluctuated wildly.

Posing for a *National Times* feature with Aub Wilson and my son Robbie as a young clerk in the early 1970s. *Photo by Rob Walls*

My brother Jack, in front of his interstate Rails stand at Randwick in around 1969. We are with a Ladbrokes man, who had come to check out Australian racing following my stint in England.

At my stand in Melbourne in the early 1970s, pausing briefly from writing the three to four thousand tickets I would write at each meeting.

Neville Wran had remained one of my closest friends since university days, and occasionally he acted on my behalf in the courtroom. Here, we are attending the Huxley bankruptcy hearing in 1971.

Settling was a major task which, in the days of handwritten ledgers, took several hours after each race meeting. This was in the mid-1970s.

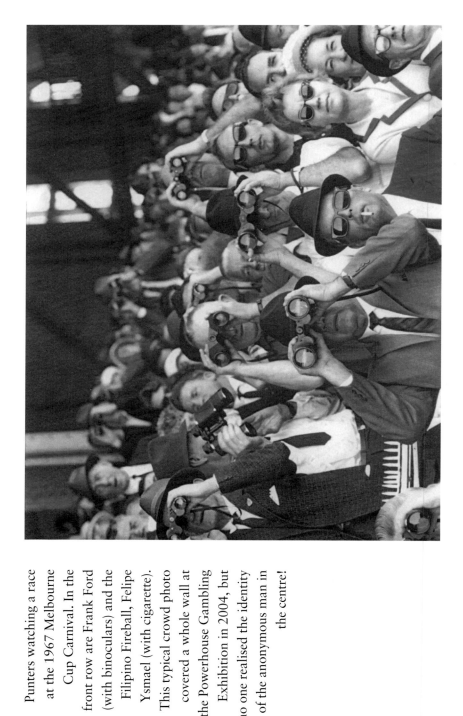

Punters watching a race at the 1967 Melbourne Cup Carnival. In the front row are Frank Ford (with binoculars) and the Filipino Fireball, Felipe Ysmael (with cigarette). This typical crowd photo covered a whole wall at the Powerhouse Gambling Exhibition in 2004, but no one realised the identity of the anonymous man in the centre!

Robbie and Gai's wedding in 1980. My daughter, Louise, and Gai's friend Snowy were her bridesmaids. Rob's cousin Charlie and brother, David, were his groomsmen; sadly, they were both to sue me in later years.

Tom brought a whole new dimension to our lives when he was born in June 1982.
Photo by David Motte/ Newspix

I was happy to pay up on a fun bet with Gai at a family Christmas lunch at our home in about 1982. Coincidentally, the old ten-dollar notes featured Henry Lawson, who used to drink at our Lily of St Leonards hotel – he always sat on the same bench, which we still have to this day.

Father Christmas (me) with Gai, Tommy, Valerie, Rob, and young Kate and Tom, who is pulling a face similar to my own 'photo grimace' from 70 years earlier.

Giving away my daughter, Louise, at her wedding in our garden at Kirribilli in November 1983. I was so proud.

Our family photo at Louise and Guenther's wedding. Gai was pregnant with Kate at the time, and also present was Viktoria Raedler MBE, Guenther's mother. My grandniece Priscilla, John and Jackie's daughter, was Louise's flower girl.

Still living close to Luna Park, I was excited when it reopened in 1995 and went on an impromptu visit after lunch one Sunday with Gai, Rob, Tom, Kate and Louise.

Tommy Smith and me, with my son Robbie and our mutual grandson Tom, inspecting the newly built 'Greencliffe' apartments in Kirribilli in 1996.

Family outings always played a central role. Here, Suzanne and I are with Louise, Tom, Rob, Kate, Gai and Guenther in the mid-1990s.

With His Majesty King Taufa'ahau Tupou IV in Sydney in 2000. The King was the highest-ranking visitor to the Games. Louise, who was the Tongan Olympic Attaché, is wearing the Tongan Olympic uniform, while I am wearing His Majesty's Silver Jubilee medal.

Her Royal Highness Princess Anne attended the official lunch we gave in honour of the King of Tonga at our new Kirribilli home during the Sydney 2000 Olympics.

This John Shakespeare caricature summed up our feelings when Rob was finally allowed back to field at the races in 2001.

In January 2002 Rob was invited to the Te Rapa Carnival, becoming the first bookmaker allowed to operate in New Zealand for around 100 years. He asked for his stand to be located in front of the track – as stands once were in Australia – which added a lot of colour and interest.

The fourth generation of the Waterhouse racing dynasty was cemented with my return to the track at the age of 80 in 2002, so I could train Tom in my style of bookmaking. *Photo by Renee Nowytarger/Newspix*

Suzanne visiting me at my stand at Rosehill in 2002, on my first day back as a bookmaker after seventeen years. Our grandchildren Tom and Kate were my clerks. There were so many cameras around the stand that it was hard to do business at first!

I often travelled with Francis Grant, my partner in Fiji, to pursue my more 'out there' business ideas. Here, we are taking time out to visit the Great Wall of China.

Celebrating becoming an octogenarian with my biographer, Kevin Perkins, his wife, Cynthia, and Guenther.

My 80th birthday celebrations were held at the Watermark restaurant at Balmoral Beach. Here, I'm with Louise, Suzanne and my good old friend Neville Wran. It was wonderful to celebrate with old friends such as Gough Whitlam, Andrew Rogers and Ratu Epeli.

Suzanne and I listen to Guenther's speech, which was followed by a yodel, at my birthday party.

On holiday in Thailand in the mid-1990s with my friend Yuko Fujita, whom I met when Suzanne and I divorced.

At the racetrack in Samoa, with my friend and partner in the Pacific, Peter McCoy, and Major General Rabuka (the coup leader who was later elected Prime Minister of Fiji).

An audience with His Majesty King Taufaʻahau Tupou IV of Tonga at the Palace in about 2002. He was a loyal and lifelong friend.

In Vavaʻu, Tonga, with the special book project *A Little Seahorse in Love*, which I sponsored and produced for the children of Tonga in 2003, to help their education. Tonga has one of the highest rates of literacy in the world – 98.5 per cent.

Receiving the award of Commander of Tonga from His Majesty King George Tupou V, during his coronation celebrations in Tonga in 2008. *Photo by Peter Halmagyi*

The coronation ceremony for the new King of Tonga, George Tupou V, was unforgettable. My whole family, along with Tom's girlfriend Hoda Vakili and Kate's friend Luke Ricketson, travelled to Tonga for the celebrations. Louise was one of His Majesty's official courtiers. *Photo by David Hahn*

With our good friend King George Tupou V, an enlightened man with a vision for Tonga. His Majesty attended the 2008 Victorian Racing Carnival with my family.

With Louise in Tonga for the King's birthday celebrations in 2009. His Majesty awarded me the Grand Cross of Queen Salote, in recognition of my 35 years representing the Kingdom.

Kate stands on her own two feet as a fashion and style ambassador and writer. *Photo by Lisa Maree Williams/ Stringer/Getty*

Three generations of Waterhouse bookmakers: Tom, Rob and me.

Backstage at *Dancing With the Stars*, on which Tom appeared in 2006.
I flew down to Melbourne to go backstage.

Suzanne and me, on the terrace of our lovely apartment in Kirribilli,
which was built on land I had bought with my brothers in the
mid-1940s.

Victoria Derby Day at Flemington in 2008. I was so proud to see Tom standing in my shoes. He held more money over the Melbourne Spring Carnival than all the other local bookmakers put together. He is now the number-one on-course bookmaker in Australia.
Photo by Colleen Petch/Newspix

coming events cast their own shadow, and I knew that if he sent Frank Ford, then it was a big go. Because of his fabulous wealth, the Babe's betting could still hurt me. If he thought he had a winner, he backed it well.

In January 1968 he had an unraced colt. Nothing was known of it. On the Friday morning before its first race it was assessed at 33/1. On the Saturday morning its price was very little different. Newspapers write about the bookies' 'secret information service', but really it is only trackmen, race watchers or form students. They're good – if you know how to utilise their service. One of them had seen the colt and told me to be careful.

Because it was Ysmael, I automatically knew it could be substantial plonk, and when Frank Ford came to Sydney I knew it was on. I opened the horse at 7/4 – a tenth of the price Frank expected – and the other Sydney bookies followed suit. Frank had been told to back the colt at 20/1 or the best price. After getting over his shock, Frank still put $100,000 on with me at 7/4.

Anyone else would have been furious, but the Babe was ecstatic because the horse started odds-on at 1/2 at the track in Melbourne and won easily. His judgement had proved correct and he'd had a substantial win. Frank Ford had gone out on a limb, without knowing the Melbourne on-course prices. As far as he knew, the horse might still have been 20/1 back in Melbourne.

Ysmael continued to bet big but still tried to remain private. However, his pretext that he was betting for an 'Asian syndicate' now started to fade. In May 1968 the Sydney newspaper columnist 'Poitrel' wrote: 'What's going to be the wash-up of the mad betting and buying spree by the *Asian Syndicate*? Recently at Newcastle the group's betting reached an all time high when it had an even $100,000 on Silver Streak from the biggest bookie we have ever seen – Bill Waterhouse . . . I am convinced it is a one man band, with Filipino Mr Filipe Ysmael the major domo of all transactions.'

Then, much to my amazement, the Babe jumped at the chance of doing a television interview with me, in which he spoke frankly and honestly about his betting. He finally admitted publicly that he was the 'syndicate', and thereafter he became known as 'the Filipino Fireball'.

—

I visited the Babe in the Philippines several times. He was a charming host but the visits were unnerving. Each time I was met at the airport with a limousine and a full-time bodyguard, complete with a machine gun. Ysmael's compound in Quezon City, a leading suburb of Manila, was an enormous mansion surrounded by expansive grounds and enclosed by a three-metre-high iron fence, patrolled by guardsmen with ferocious Doberman pinschers. It was like walking onto a movie set – but this was real life.

Felipe ended up owing me Brewster's millions, which I finally had to write off. He was, however, firmly in the sights of Victoria's racing administrators. They mistrusted his power and influence, and his enormous bets made them nervous. Felipe was begrudged by many as an Asian interloper. They were egged on by Sir Eugene Gorman, who was riddled with jealousy about the Babe's clout and had been waiting for the right moment to wipe him out.

Neither Gorman nor anyone in the establishment acknowledged that Ysmael had invested millions and millions into Australian racing and was an extraordinary asset to the sport. He was called in by the stewards on numerous occasions, and finally they alleged that a runner of his, Follow Me, had not tried in its debut race. He had backed the winner with me at the course and so the stewards thought he had pulled his horse up. They threw the book at him and he was disqualified from all racetracks.

However, the Babe was totally innocent of any wrongdoing. As I knew, his nature was always to try to win, and in this case, unknown to anyone else, the Babe had actually backed Follow Me with me in the morning. His bet at the course was a 'saver' – to cover his earlier stake in case Follow Me lost.

It was horrible – I might have saved him, but the bet had been made over the phone and so wasn't in my race books. The Babe had started this 'off the record' betting, and it was to be his ultimate downfall. I was prepared to come forward if he asked me to, but I was relieved that he never did as I would have risked losing my licence. In any case, they might not have believed me. The Babe understood the situation and realised that neither of us could reveal the morning bet. He was an honourable man. It was one of the great regrets of my racing career that I couldn't help him.

The Babe was heartbroken to be disqualified. He sold up in Melbourne and left the industry, moving to Sydney. President Ferdinand Marcos appointed him as a special ambassador to Australia to give him some official status, but he was blackballed by the diplomatic corps because of the racing disqualification. It was a great pity he was not treated better by the Melbourne establishment.

Ysmael finally went back to the Philippines, but the disgrace in Australia followed him and he ultimately fell out with President Marcos. He was a broken man when he died there in 1984.

—

There is always a lot of conjecture about the golden age of any sport, but to my mind the post-war period up to the mid-1960s was the golden age of racing in Australia. In those years, racing flourished in a remarkable fashion. No other racing arena in the world could compare.

The three enclosures (the Flat, St Leger and Paddock) were

always full of bookmakers. My 1966 Oaks Day racebook lists 236, including 32 on the Rails (plus three designated bookies for the 'Ladies Members Area'), over 80 in the main ring, 80 on the hill and 40 in two interstate rings. Crowds were steady, usually around 40,000 and on a big day around 80,000 to 90,000. 'Fashions on the Field' for the women was a major event at the carnivals, with prizes like a new Falcon Deluxe Sedan.

In this stimulating atmosphere, many big punters competed with one another to get set, often trying to outdo each other with the size of their bets. And the racing – because of the even competition between punter and bookie – was fair. The centre of Australian betting until then had always been Sydney. Without any doubt, through my betting with Duval and others in the 1960s, it had now moved to Melbourne.

Melbourne made me and at the same time it was recognised that my gambling made the Melbourne betting ring, enhancing the carnivals and putting the city on the world gambling stage. When the betting reached its peak in 1967, Sir Eugene Gorman publicly stated that never in the world had there been betting of the magnitude now occurring in Melbourne. Then Keith Robbins and other racing journalists described the betting at the 1968 Melbourne Cup Carnival – the first after I had departed – as the weakest they could remember.

17

Heartbreak

WHEN I HEADED back to England to work the Epsom and the Derby in June 1968, Suzanne came with me. I led a tour of about 30 racing enthusiasts, bringing some of my own punters. By now my column was appearing in *The Daily Telegraph* newspaper, and so the trip was sponsored and promoted by the *Daily* and *Sunday Telegraphs* and was a great success.

The tour lasted six weeks and, apart from Royal Ascot and the Derby at Epsom, took in other major sports, such as the Ashes cricket tour. We Aussies made quite a dash. The English *Daily Express* wrote: 'An international syndicate of millionaire punters has invaded Britain. They have brought with them their own bookmaker and a trainer to advise them on form.' And the London *Sun* wrote: 'The most stylish assembly of Australian racing men ever gathered together will form . . . a distinguished Aussie assault on the Epsom Derby . . . The NSW Premier, Mr Bob Askin, will complete the team.'

We had a great time, but English racing was still suffering under a stifling profits tax of five per cent on winnings. They regarded bets of £1000 as large, whereas back in Australia I regularly bet in hundreds of thousands of dollars.

After England I took the group to Las Vegas, where we stayed at the Stardust. Moe Dalitz gave us the royal treatment –

285

he was impressed that a group had wanted to accompany me to the Derby. The group was fascinated, as most of them had never been to a casino – there were none in Australia.

—

Although I didn't know it at the time, my glorious run in Melbourne was already over, and for the first time I saw the furtive hand of Sir Eugene Gorman at work behind the scenes.

Earlier that year, in March, my suite at the Southern Cross Hotel in Melbourne had been raided by the Victorian police. The raid had been precipitated by an unsigned letter to police that alleged illegal betting in my hotel room.

I realised I had been set up by Gorman, who had even arranged for his man Joe Metz to visit me in my suite with a list of bets Metz wished to place. Joe had on previous occasions rung me with his bets and it was highly unusual for him to visit me. He put his list on a table in a far corner of my room and left.

When the police came they went straight to this far corner, obviously looking for Metz's sheets as evidence of illegal betting. But I had tidied the papers away after phoning the bets through to Jack, who then recorded them in his ledgers at the track. When the police found Joe's sheet, I realised they knew what they were looking for, so obviously Joe had shown it to them previously.

The police stayed on a while to answer my phone calls, but anyone who may have wanted to place a commission for me to lay at the track was obviously frightened off by the police wanting to know who they were.

At the time I was in the habit of taking bets in my room and then taking them to the track or phoning them through to Jack to enter in his ledger – and so the tax was being paid. The police had arrived before the scratchings for the meeting were announced, so it was too early for any real betting.

A few days before I was to leave for England, in May 1968, the New South Wales police apologetically arrived at my office with two summonses that alleged I was 'using premises for illegal betting' and 'conducting a common gaming house'. The policeman said, 'Anyone would think you were a murderer – the Victorians have given us a full dossier on your movements to make sure you are served before you leave for England.'

The Daily Mirror ran a page-one headline: 'Waterhouse charged – SP Raid.' It gave me a lot of bad publicity, bursting my 'gentleman bookmaker' aura. The summonses snowballed with other events to wreak havoc for me for years to come. However, taking commissions for bets was not against any rules and the case was thrown out, after a full hearing before a magistrate in Melbourne and despite behind-the-scenes manipulation by Gorman to control certain witnesses.

I was defamed by the *Mirror* because their story implied a criminal offence, and so, for the first time, I sued for defamation. My case was strong, as the 'hotel raid' charges had been thrown out of court. An unsigned letter with a Melbourne postmark was sent to certain English newspapers, along with a clipping about the hotel room betting charges – no doubt designed to stop me working in England. However, none of the British press published the story.

With the Melbourne Autumn Carnival over, I had thought I would be back later in the year for the Spring Carnival. Straight after I was charged in May 1968, however, the VRC brought in a policy banning all interstate bookmakers from operating at Flemington. The rule was obviously aimed at me, as I was the only one. Many of the local bookmakers, who had benefited from the stimulus I had brought to the Melbourne ring, were surprised and disappointed.

A Melbourne journalist with *The Age*, Tony Kennedy, wrote

at the time: 'Neither the Government nor the Police Department inspired the action against Waterhouse . . . [and when the facts come out] Melbourne will get a rude shock . . . The spotlight [being] on Waterhouse all the time created jealousy. It must also be understood that the feelings against Waterhouse were not general amongst Melbourne bookmakers. The majority were on his side.'

Kennedy referred to the 'prime mover' who was 'a man of considerable influence' – which he later privately admitted to me was a reference to Sir Eugene. Gorman vehemently denied any involvement to me, and also to Suzanne, at a dinner arranged by our mutual friend Jacob Ballas, the head of Singapore's stock exchange.

Gorman then wrote to me: 'I've always had high regard for you. Never having wished you anything but well, I confess that I was gravely hurt by hearing rumours that you believed that I had done something detrimental to your interests in connection with what happened in this State. That such an idea should enter your head or be entertained by you completely astounded me . . . you ought to remember I begged you to be careful.'

But later investigations by journalist Kevin Perkins and others showed that all paths led to Gorman. He told Perkins he thought that what I had done in Melbourne – taking away all the Ysmael business from the local bookies – was disgraceful, and that I deserved everything that was coming to me. Perkins, in his book, *The Gambling Man*, published in 1990, made no bones about the fact that Gorman was the man responsible for my downfall in Melbourne.

I well and truly dropped off Sir Eugene, although he should never have known I was onto his treachery; my father had always taught me, 'Never show your colours to the enemy.' Gorman's man Joe Metz had called into my Sydney office to see me soon after the Melbourne court hearing. I was polite but cool.

Unfortunately, George Thorley, who of course knew my thoughts about Gorman, had a hot-headed moment and gave Joe a piece of his mind: 'How dare you come up here when you and your friend Gorman set Bill up!'

My troubles were still not over. I would again be amazed by the lengths taken by Gorman to cause me harm with no gain to himself.

—

My personal life had gone along smoothly. I had consciously kept my racing separate from the family. I chuckled one day when I overheard young Louise telling her friends I made books. It had never occurred to me that my world could fall apart, but I was in for a momentous shock that would knock me right off balance.

In my days as a single man, I'd never had a girl stolen from me, and the thought of such a thing happening never entered my head. A gambler does trade on his nerve a lot and I knew I had my shortcomings. I had spent limited time and money with my family, preferring to work very hard with my brother Jack and to plough the money back into our business enterprises.

I worked six and a half long days a week. I didn't realise it at the time, but I had regularly been away from home for four to six months each year. Apart from England, there were the Melbourne carnivals, and I also went bookmaking to Toowoomba in Queensland and even to Perth.

Whilst I had always hidden my emotions at the track, Suzy would feel my bad days keenly. She said she could tell by my footsteps to the front door whether I had won or lost. Racing is a full-on commitment. It becomes all-consuming and I thrived on it. Yet I had always considered myself a good father and husband. The time I did have with Suzy and the kids was quality time together, and I loved the whole family deeply. After all, they were the reason I was working so hard – I knew I needed to create security for their futures, and for all my extended family.

One Saturday evening in late 1968 I went out to the kitchen to get a cup of coffee and found Suzanne sitting alone. She looked terribly unhappy.

'Are you all right, Suzy?' I asked. 'Is something the matter?'

At that she burst into a flood of tears. I was at a complete loss and immediately felt a real heel. I'd come back from the races that day no more tired than normal, but I thought I must have done something or said something to hurt her feelings, so I apologised at once.

'Darling, I'm very sorry. I don't know what I've done to hurt you, but whatever it is, I'm sorry and I promise you it was unintentional.'

Suzy had a look of sheer misery and hopelessness. Her crying subsided to a soft sobbing, and her face was awash with tears.

She had come from a respectable middle-class family of school inspectors and bank managers. They were straitlaced conservatives and I'd never heard of any trouble of any sort. Now it appeared something was very wrong. I was prepared for anything, but I was stunned when Suzanne said she wanted to leave me, and that she was in love with someone else.

It just didn't sink in. I felt an air of relief that nothing serious was amiss. I may have been a conceited male chauvinist, but to me it was inconceivable that Suzy could really leave me. I thought she was obviously suffering a temporary mental aberration, and I think I gave a nervous laugh.

Suzanne's mood changed and hardened. I suddenly realised that she meant what she said. I'd always been in control but now I was at a complete loss. I tried to sit down with Suzy and

290

understand her feelings, but she had set her mind on it: she intended to leave.

I did something I never thought I would do. Even though it was late, I phoned Suzanne's parents and asked them to come across to the house right away. I didn't tell them why but I left them in no doubt that something serious had happened. I had never been close to my in-laws, having always addressed them as Mr and Mrs Dart. They hadn't approved of their daughter marrying a Catholic, but to have him turn from being a barrister to a bookmaker must have been even harder for them to swallow.

It was right to call them. They immediately wanted to help and told their daughter not to be silly. But Suzy was a strong-willed girl and her mind, if not fully made up, was firm. She had met a doctor when she had taken the children skiing. As usual, I hadn't gone. I always had business – on this occasion, to Fiji to look at the manganese mines. Evidently, a Dr Jim Whelan and his son were placed at their dinner table all week in the hotel dining room. Although Suzy had not been unfaithful, by the end of the week Whelan had professed his love for her and wanted her to leave me and marry him. He'd done his best to charm her when she was on her own.

When Suzanne said she was leaving me, I never actually asked her to stay even though I didn't want her to go. I thought that if she'd decided to go, then I wouldn't stop her. The doctor was an ear, nose and throat specialist whose first wife had committed suicide. In the beginning, he repeatedly told Suzy how wonderful she was and she believed his charm. I guess many marriages that break up because of a third party follow a similar pattern. I told her very strongly that I was sure her new suitor was a fortune-hunter, and that when he found out he'd get nothing from her, he would drop her. I also told her that I loved her.

She told me I was wrong, that the doctor wasn't interested in her money and that I was too obsessed with money. She also told me that she loved me but she felt I didn't really love her.

I suggested to Suzanne that she needed some guidance from a counsellor or psychiatrist. She didn't want to go and I said I would go with her. When we got there on the Monday morning, she was extremely nervous and upset, so I said to the head-shrinker, who happened to be a woman, 'Perhaps it might be better if I did the talking first. Suzanne can hear what I'm saying and, after I leave, you can help her.'

So I talked and talked. It was, however, a settling morning at the Tattersalls Club. I'd had a losing day on the Saturday and most of my debts had to be paid out that morning. In those days, settling on a Monday was a big event; the tables would be stacked with bundle upon bundle of high-denomination notes. The time was getting on, so I said to the psychiatrist, 'Well, it's getting late. I've got to go. I think I've covered everything. I'll leave you to talk now with Suzanne.'

I felt an icy chill with her words in response: 'Yes, we must not keep you Mr Waterhouse. You are far too busy and important to stay.'

I tried to repair the damage. 'I'm sorry. I certainly didn't mean it that way. It's just that I have to go to settling, and besides, Suzanne is the one who needs your counselling.'

Her reply was to the point. 'Don't you think that perhaps you are the one who needs the help and advice that I've got to give?'

I was infuriated by her presumption, but then I looked at Suzanne and saw that she was smiling for the first time in many, many days. I left and recall thinking the visit was worth it.

To see if we could make it work, Suzy agreed to go with me and the children for a two-week Christmas holiday on the Gold Coast. I commuted back to Sydney for the races. In my newspaper column I wrote about how the trip was marred by the misfortune of having my home burgled, but naturally I kept silent about the turmoil in my private life. Suzanne was not impressed by my returning for the races.

By the end of the two weeks Suzy decided she wanted a divorce so that she could start a new life with the doctor. She flew back to Sydney and I drove back with the children over a couple of days, to allow Suzy time to pack and move out without traumatising her or the children.

I agreed to a divorce and helped Suzanne to get it. *The Daily Mirror* wanted to cover our private affairs, and Suzanne was distressed by the impending publicity. So I offered to drop my defamation action against the paper if it did not write about the divorce, which then passed through without much notice.

I insisted to Suzanne that our three children stay with me, saying, 'The man you are marrying will not want our children.' I assured Suzanne she would always be their mother and in no way was she deserting them. We both realised that by staying with me during the week, the children would continue life as normal as possible. It was the reverse of what most families do when they split. Suzanne often had the children on weekends. She and the doctor were living near Wollongong on his Millbrook Farm of about four hectares, where he kept some horses. I encouraged the children to spend as much time as possible with Suzanne and still sent her skiing with the children. Suzanne and I always remained on good terms and there was never any tension or resentment.

Suddenly I had three children on my hands full-time. From seeing them for a few minutes in the morning and a little more each evening, I was now driving Louise to school each day and spending more time with all of them.

Suzanne had literally walked away with just her clothes and her car. She did not make any financial claim, nor did I offer her anything. The new man got the shock of his life when he found out she had no money.

Suzanne later told me the story of how Robbie gave her a briefcase one day and said, 'Oh, Mum, here are your shares.'

The doctor later asked if he could have a look at them and then said, 'Is that all there is?'

18

The Doping of Big Philou

IN 1969 I MADE a significant change to my betting operation. My nephew John had taken out his bookmaker's licence and had the potential to do well. At the invitation of Sir Frank Packer, an AJC committeeman, I decided to transfer to the locals and work only on Sydney races, leaving a gap for John to work on the interstate races.

I had welcomed John into the business like my own son. Born in December 1945, he came to work with Jack and me after he sat his Leaving Certificate. He was a tall, good-looking boy who was eager to please. I put enormous faith in him; he was my brother's son, so I looked upon him as I would my son. We were a very close-knit family at that time.

John went out with various girls, but no one was happier than I when he decided to marry Jackie Fitzpatrick, the daughter of our good friend Ray Fitzpatrick. Jackie had it all: she was beautiful, charming and switched on, and she adored John. Sadly, Ray had passed away a year or so before, but not before confiding in me that it was also his dream to see our two families unite.

John and Jackie married in 1969 and moved in next door to my family, in the Kirribilli property Jack and I had bought ten years earlier to be Jack's home. My children were often next door after school, and when John and I went to the trots or the dogs on Friday and Saturday nights, the children would go over to be with Jackie. Jackie was especially kind with my children and they loved her. She was their cousin by marriage but she took on the role of being an older sister and friend to the three of them.

—

Back at the track, my move from interstate to local races had been a major change. It may sound simple but there was actually a world of difference. Instead of being guided by the 'home' bookmakers interstate, I took the lead with my prices on the local races. Betting on 'locals' is much more precise and risky, as you are on the horses' home turf and are dealing with all the informed connections. I was expected to bet big and I did, yet my clientele was entirely different, as was my racing information network. To hold his own, a bookmaker needs an army of experts around him, and one of these is a student of form. These people are as rare as hen's teeth. Without exception they are brilliant, but they can often be erratic and volatile as Don Scott was. Nevertheless, I was able to adapt and very quickly established myself as the leader of the local ring, maintaining my position as the leading Australian bookmaker.

I don't think I've ever been caught by a con trick. My father had warned me that the confidence trickster had only his victim's greed to work on. Once you control your greed, you need have no fear of being taken by a con.

I was owed as much money as any bookmaker had ever been owed in Australia. I state this not with pride but as a fact. If you bet big and fly high, you have to accept this as a part of life. I did refuse credit to many people whom I regarded as poor risks, but I also gave credit to a host of people whom I didn't know. Nobody likes bad debts, and once a person has taken the knock with me I never forget it. For me, a man's word is his honour, and not to pay a gambling debt shows a lack of integrity.

At Rosehill one Saturday I was approached by a man of about 50, conservatively but expensively attired in a tweed jacket, looking exactly what he said he was – a property owner from the western districts of Victoria. Obviously well educated and with a good appearance and manners, Paddy exuded wealth simply by not displaying it.

My guard dropped when he mentioned my Melbourne solicitor friend Ray Dunn. I would have done anything for Ray and I never doubted that Ray had sent him, because no one knew that Ray and I were mates. Paddy told me he was on his way to the Gold Coast for a holiday and that Ray, who knew he liked a bet, had suggested he call on me at the races. I asked what betting credit he wanted.

'Oh, nothing big – perhaps a couple of thousand,' he said.

I wondered why Ray hadn't phoned me to tell me of Paddy's visit, but I wasn't worried because the amount was small. I then forgot to check with Ray that evening simply because Paddy didn't come back that day.

I next saw Paddy some ten days later at a Wednesday meeting at Randwick. He approached me full of smiles and bonhomie. I had not the slightest doubt about him. After all, he had not taken advantage of the credit granted to him previously. Paddy had a bet on the first race and I immediately felt some misgivings. It wasn't the bet itself, which was small – it was just him. When you spend your lifetime on a racetrack you develop a sort of sixth sense based on experience.

The horse was beaten and Paddy made his second bet. Now he didn't appear to me as a wealthy man having an enjoyable, relaxing day at the races, but as a punter very keen to find a winner. I suspected he was a phoney. If I was right, I knew he would drop off as soon as he found a winner, or else he'd try to martingale me.

The horse lost and, sure enough, Paddy continued to increase his bets. He didn't back a winner all day, but I kept his losses down to about $6000. I had done this by a series of ploys, just in case I was wrong. I phoned Ray Dunn that evening, and of course Paddy was a phoney.

Sir Eugene was the only man who knew Ray and I were friends, and I knew he still met Ray for dinner once a week. Ray laughed and said, 'Do you think our mutual friend Sir Eugene has had a hand in all this?' I guessed why Paddy had not bet on that first Saturday: he knew I would have limited his betting until I'd checked his credentials with Ray. Naturally, Ray, when asked about Paddy, would have been indignant and mentioned it to his old mate Sir Eugene at dinner. In that way Gorman would have been alerted to warn Paddy. So Ray said, 'I certainly won't be saying anything to Gorman.'

I notified the police about Paddy the next day, and on Saturday two plain-clothes police officers approached me at Rosehill and suggested that I send someone down to the on-course police office if Paddy turned up. I felt sure he would come back.

Sure enough, Paddy turned up. I saw him some distance away, watching my stand. He didn't realise I saw him, but he was obviously checking to see if there was any danger. Then he walked to my stand and I welcomed him in a friendly manner.

He looked at me, trying to read my face. 'I had to go back to Melbourne to get some cash,' he said. 'It was an awful day on Wednesday. I suppose I was lucky not to lose more – you know what it's like when you're chasing your losses.'

'Yes,' I replied. 'Well, let's hope your luck improves a little today.'

'I hope so. By the way, you may as well take this cheque. I only want a few thousand from it now to settle some small debts from Wednesday, and I'll get a cheque for the balance from you later in the day.' He handed me a certified bank cheque for $20,000. 'And, of course, I think I owe you around $6000, so please deduct that from the amount also.'

'Sure, Paddy, and thanks very much. There was no need to go to Melbourne just to pay me – you could have done that anytime. You want a couple of thousand now? No worries. My money hasn't been delivered yet from the armoured truck, so come back in around 30 to 45 minutes and we'll fix that up.'

'Thanks, Bill,' he said. 'You've been most kind, and I appreciate it. I'll come back after the first race.'

I had to be very careful now, as I realised that Paddy would be watching my every move from some observation point. He wouldn't be having a nice day at the track and I didn't want to lose sight of him. As he walked away, before he could see what I was doing, I sent a clerk immediately down to the police to ask for only one man to come to my stand.

A senior officer arrived and I gave him the cheque. He looked at it and said, 'You can't act on this – this is a legitimate bank cheque. It's as good as cash.'

'No, I'm sure it's not legitimate,' I replied. 'I want him arrested.'

I had the devil's own job convincing the officer that the cheque was phoney. The officer came back after the first race but Paddy didn't. The policeman said he couldn't just stand around all day and that I should send down for him as soon as Paddy came back.

Paddy didn't reappear. Something had obviously caused him concern, but the money was a big draw. He was suspicious but not certain. If he walked away, he might be walking away from a nice little nest-egg. How he must have agonised. Around the fifth race, when the crowd had come back from watching the running and the mob was at its thickest, I saw him in the distance about a hundred metres away. He was between a liquor bar and a hot-food stall, lost in a small, milling crowd, and he was watching my stand.

Keeping him in view out of the corner of my eye, I told one of my staff to wander off casually and to bring back the officer. When he arrived, Paddy was still there, watching. Nonchalantly, as though I was just talking to a friend, I described how Paddy looked and was dressed and told the detective exactly where he was standing. Paddy moved out of sight into the bar. The detective hadn't seen him but went and found him in the bar, based on my description, and arrested him. He brought Paddy back to the stand and I identified him. Paddy professed his innocence but I saw his look of hopelessness.

The cheque wasn't a forgery, but one of a batch that had been stolen the previous year from a bank in Melbourne. Paddy was given a three-year sentence.

—

In 1969 I was heading for trouble again – but not of my own doing. In doubles, I still followed my long-standing practice never to lay the same horse to win both legs. The logic was simple. Irrespective of the price of the horse in the first leg, it is obviously so much the shorter for the second leg, and hence it becomes too difficult to finance or lay off. I had learnt from my awful trouble back in 1956 and 1957 with Redcraze and then Tulloch. I was no longer working in Melbourne, nor was I working on the Melbourne races in Sydney, but I still had the doubles going for events in both cities, which was a nice little business.

The 1969 Caulfield Cup was won by a horse called Big Philou, trained by Bart Cummings. I was delighted, as we hadn't laid Big Philou to win the second leg, the Melbourne Cup, so it was a skinner for me in the doubles. Indeed, it would be a tremendous result for my doubles if Big Philou were to win the Melbourne Cup, so it would be a distinct disadvantage to me if the horse did not run.

However, Big Philou was a very late scratching, pulled out of the race in sensational circumstances about half an hour before the start. The horse was found to be scouring badly. Big Philou was the equal favourite and had been backed to win almost $1 million from the bookmakers at Flemington. Of course, being a late scratching, the bookmakers had to refund the non-doubles bets on Big Philou. Subsequent tests showed that the horse had been fed laxatives.

The nobbling of Big Philou was a sensation. Not since the 'alleged attempt' to shoot Phar Lap before the 1930 Melbourne Cup – which some said was really just a newspaper beat-up to sell papers – had there been such an endeavour to prevent a favourite from starting in a big race. Drugging horses, whether to win or lose, is as old as racing itself, yet one never expects it. I certainly have never wanted any part of such behaviour.

In Melbourne, no one realised that I had transferred from betting on interstate racing to the Sydney local Rails. However, a malicious rumour started down there that I was behind the Big Philou scandal. I wasn't concerned at first, as I had a clear conscience and obviously I had nothing to gain. I had *wanted* Big Philou to win – it was the dream result for me. It was sheer stupidity for anyone to suggest I could be involved, especially as I wasn't even working on the race. Looking back, I think it was done from jealousy or hatred, or perhaps the real perpetrators were trying to throw investigators off their scent. My problem was that once the rumour started, it was actively fanned by one very powerful man.

One of the offenders was eventually tracked down in New Zealand – but not before I was the subject of a lot of innuendo, unwanted newspaper headlines and implications that I had something to do with the scandal. During the police enquiry and VRC stewards' investigations into the Big Philou case, it turned out that the person extradited from New Zealand was one of Bart Cummings' strappers, Leslie Lewis. He made the wild claim that he had been getting money from Sydney bookmakers to dope horses. To me, that was obviously a furphy. Lewis was subsequently charged with the doping, but strangely he was acquitted.

When he was dying of cancer some 30 years later, Lewis admitted to doping Big Philou and that he had lied. He said, 'Money was speaking all languages . . . And you get a thousand dollars waved in front of you, when you're only working for a dollar an hour . . . It's a lot of money to have put in your hand. A lot, and you're willing to take that risk for it.'

I again sought advice from my Melbourne lawyer friend Ray Dunn. He had been following the case closely and agreed it was disgraceful, but said there was no way I could stop the rumour mill. Ray told me not to worry, adding that if there was the slightest scintilla of evidence, I would be investigated and called to the hearings. He strongly recommended I just allow the storm to pass as there was nothing I could do.

Some Melbourne bookmakers were interviewed, however I was never even approached by police or the Melbourne stewards. The police investigations cleared me as there was simply no connection. And I was pleased when the AJC took copies of my doubles books, proving that a win by Big Philou would have been a windfall result for me. As far as the AJC was concerned, it put paid to any suggestion of participation by me.

Yet I still had my name thrown around! Ray's advice was all very well, but when mud is thrown a little will always stick. I was frustrated not to be able to answer the rumours and publicly clear my name. Still to this day, every now and then someone brings up the subject, or a journalist calls me looking for the 'inside story'. Of course, there is nothing I can add as I knew nothing about it.

—

The facts of the Big Philou case shone through and led to my forming a lifelong friendship with a journalist. In the winter of 1968 I had received a phone call from Kevin Perkins, the news editor and deputy editor of *The Sunday Telegraph*, one of the major Sydney papers. Although I was writing a column for the same paper at the time, I hadn't met Kevin before. I agreed to see him and he arrived one Monday afternoon at the office, saying that he intended writing a biography of me.

I thanked him very much and said that it would normally be a pleasure to cooperate with him, but that it was a bit premature. I was still relatively young, 46, and had many plans for the future. In reality, I was just trying to fob him off.

Kevin laughed and said that he intended doing it now, with or without my help. He said I could stop him talking to my friends but not to my enemies. Naturally, he would prefer to have my cooperation. He said I should think it over and he would call back and see me in a week.

He left me a copy of his latest book, *The Last of the Queen's Men*, a biography of Sir Robert Menzies. I looked forward to reading the book, mainly because Suzanne's uncle, Bill McCall, was the federal member of parliament who had been instrumental in bringing down the Menzies government in 1941. However, the book was a merciless assassination of Menzies in practically every sphere. I realised I was in a bind and had no choice but to go along with him.

When Kevin came to see me again the following Monday, I greeted him with: 'Mr Perkins, it will be my pleasure to work with you and help you in every way I can.'

Our friendship found seed slowly, as we had a healthy respect for each other. One doesn't trust a journalist lightly, and journalists are trained as a rule to trust no one. But once we had each other's confidence, covering many ups and downs, our friendship became firm and remains right up to the present day.

Kevin had written three books. One was about an Australian ballet dancer, Elaine Fifield, another about the Bodyline cricketer Harold Larwood, and the third was the Menzies book. Kevin was a friend of the celebrated author Morris West, who had advised him that he should find a universal subject for his next project. So Kevin came up with gambling and racing. He narrowed his search down to the three names that kept coming up: Tommy Smith, the leading trainer; George Moore, the leading jockey; and me. My name captured his attention, and so I was selected.

One evening a week for about a year, Kevin called at my house to interview me, and he probed and took tape recordings of our sessions. Although sharp and worldly, his knowledge and understanding of gambling was limited, so it was slow going. Then he abruptly disappeared. About three months later he turned up again and I realised I hadn't seen the last of him after all.

'I suppose you've been wondering what had happened to me?' he said.

'Er . . . yes, of course.'

Perkins explained that his absence was due to Big Philou and other rumours. He was doing a thorough study of me and, accordingly, he had taken time off from the newspaper to investigate. If the rumours were true, he would have to cover them faithfully in his book. It would be unethical to be on friendly terms and then to castrate me in print. He had long been an investigative reporter before becoming a news editor and was used to digging for the facts.

I listened politely but without much interest until suddenly he won my undivided attention.

'Bill,' he said, 'I've done a full investigation on Big Philou in Melbourne. I know you didn't do it. Let me tell you, you seem to have a powerful enemy down there. You should be careful.'

I could have kissed him. I had found someone who accepted that I had not doped Big Philou, without my having to argue my innocence to him. Kevin had gone to Melbourne and interviewed countless people, and there was apparently one common strand when it came to the rumours about me – Sir Eugene Gorman. All the sources of rumours against me could be traced back to him. Gorman, trying to distance himself from the rumours, told Kevin that 'many people believe Waterhouse nobbled Big Philou because he stood to lose so much on the race', which Kevin knew was incorrect.

And although I still had to prove myself along the way to Kevin, our friendship had taken root.

A few months later, in early 1970, Perkins phoned me and he was livid. The Peter Huxley case had just broken and Kevin, as news editor, was given the advance tip that Huxley had bet with me. I had not told him about Huxley and he was ropeable.

'You could have made a laughing stock of me. I'm well on the way with the book and if I had published it without reference to Huxley I would have been made to look a bloody idiot. By not mentioning it to me you have been unfair, and you will pick up the tab for this.'

'Now, hold on, Kevin,' I told him. 'You're completely wrong here. I did mention Huxley, but I knew him then as Hunter. If you go back through your records you'll find I said there was a big punter whose name was Hunter, but he was a man who wanted no publicity. And I respected his wishes.'

Kevin listened to me but I didn't think he was convinced, especially as the Huxley case was sensational. To his credit, he went back over his tapes and found that what I'd said was true, and he was mollified to some extent. It meant that his book, then in a first draft, had to include an extra chapter on Huxley.

Kevin was to experience the same frustration a number of times over, as other dramas unexpectedly erupted, meaning each time he thought the book was finished he had to add more. Perkins showed great perseverance to get to the bottom of things, even if it did take him 22 years.

19

Keeping the Home Fires Burning

M Y FIRST HOLIDAY alone with the children was to South Molle Island in the Great Barrier Reef in early 1970. It was just the four of us, and for the first time I put a holiday before the races.

Then after Christmas in 1970 I took them on a two-week driving holiday around New Zealand, which to my surprise I thoroughly enjoyed. In Queenstown I was caught short. I still did not book in advance as I didn't like to be tied down. However, I hadn't counted on Queenstown being such an extraordinarily scenic place, nor had I expected it would be completely booked out for the holidays. The kindly tourist office manager took pity on a father with three children and rang around; he found an elderly man with a house who would take us in – in one of the best locations downtown, overlooking Lake Wakatipu.

The owner of the house told me he wanted to sell and had given an option to Travelodge, but they looked like pulling out. I immediately offered to buy the house – the price was so low, just a few thousand dollars, and the position superb. I saw it was a good opportunity but Travelodge then went ahead without further delay. I was happy, as at least I'd helped the kindly old man complete his sale.

When the AJC didn't renew my licence in August 1971, it

meant I had more time on my hands and was able to go on longer holidays with the children. That Christmas the four of us went to the United States. I bought us each a 'See USA' air pass and we flew from Hawaii to Los Angeles, Las Vegas, New Orleans and Miami, and then from New York back to the west coast. In Hawaii we stayed with my friend Ron Jeffries, who ran the Moana, one of the best hotels in Honolulu. We were given a suite that had my name engraved on a brass plaque on the door. Obviously it was a time before people expected privacy and discretion.

In Vegas I introduced the children to Moe Dalitz and his charming and delightful partner, Barbara Schick, the electric shaver heiress. We stayed at the Stardust Hotel; the children were gobsmacked by the 'movie star suite', which came complete with spa baths and mirrors surrounded by light bulbs.

Robbie was seventeen at the time and when Moe asked him what he would like to see – meaning a stage show – Rob asked instead to see the inside of a casino. Robbie had already asked me but I had refused, because he was underage and casino licensing rules of the Nevada Gaming Commission were strict. Nevertheless, Moe took the three children on a guided tour through a new casino. Although Robbie had never been to a casino before, he amazed both Moe and me with his knowledge as we progressed through the various gaming rooms. He knew the house percentage of every game. I'm sure Moe thought I'd been coaching him.

The kids had a ball in Vegas. It was Christmas and the town was full. They were taken to Circus Circus, a casino-cum-circus show, and they loved the circus action while being close to the gambling atmosphere. Every night we went to a different show and always had the best table right in front of the stage. We saw Sonny and Cher, Dean Martin and other top acts. No matter what we did, I couldn't put my hand in my pocket – Moe had laid everything on for us. We had Christmas dinner at

Moe's home with Barbara, who was a perfect partner and aide to Moe. Moe gave Robbie a golf ball engraved with 'Thanks for the memories – Bob Hope'. It came from a box of twelve balls he'd been given by his friend Bob for Christmas.

We had one funny moment with Moe. David, who was thirteen, had worried us as he was a non-reader, which was affecting his schoolwork. Before we left, however, he had picked up my copy of Mario Puzo's *The Godfather* and couldn't put it down. Suzanne was aghast because of his impressionable age, but I was pleased he was at least reading a book. Without my knowledge, he had bought himself a black shirt and white tie, along with a three-piece suit, and he had brought them overseas with him. One night in Vegas Moe took us for dinner in an exclusive restaurant, and David, wanting to impress, wore his three-piece ensemble; Moe looked decidedly embarrassed to be sitting with someone who looked like he was from the mob – even at the ripe old age of thirteen.

We went on to New Orleans, where a friend of Moe's had insisted on making a reservation for us in the best hotel in town. It was a beautiful suite but with a breathtaking price. We were fascinated by the French quarter, and we went to a live music show in the rear garden of a converted terrace in Bourbon Street.

In Miami we met up with a famous American trainer, Arnold Winick, who entertained us on his boat in Florida Keys. We drove up to Orlando, where Disney World had just opened. The rides were a world away from my Luna Park days.

Still in the deep south, in Atlanta, the children and I were shocked and disgusted when a white cab driver pulled over to pick us up, telling his black passenger to get out. I was furious, but the poor black man insisted we take his taxi. It was a great lesson for the children and me to see the prejudice against black people in the south.

Our last stop was New York, where we were looked after

by a friend of Barbara's, the well-known Polly Harrison. We all went to the 21 Club for Louise's sixteenth birthday. It was one of the most exclusive spots in New York city. When the head waiter heard we were from Australia, he arranged for us to be shown the cellars. The 21 Club had been a bootlegging joint in the days of Prohibition, and the entry to the cellar had a secret spring. Once inside, we saw a mass of bottles all neatly stacked; they were named for patrons of the restaurant, and they read like a who's who of America. I was so impressed by this that on my next visit to New York I deposited a bottle of Buchanan's Royal Household Scotch in the 21 Club cellar. I intended at the time to open it for Louise's twenty-first birthday, but I never did and it's still there – I hope.

On one of my other visits to the 21 Club with Polly, Frank Sinatra was sitting next to us. Later Polly said to me: 'You are the only person I know who could sit beside Sinatra all night without even commenting or turning to look at him.'

—

The children often surprised me after my split with Suzanne. I bought a map-of-the-world jigsaw puzzle, wanting them to learn about the globe. We loved doing it together and so I got into the habit of buying more puzzles. The two boys and I would aggressively attack each new game. We'd then lose interest, but Louise would continue alone. She finished every one. Then, inspired by Jackie's mother, Claire, Louise also learned to make tapestries. After that I always brought her back a jigsaw or tapestry pattern from my trips. She made some beautiful tapestries, which still hang at home today. I guess it was this as much as anything that showed me her tenacity of purpose.

I always took the children to the Royal Easter Show. When I was young I had taken great delight in winning chocolates at the sideshow games. I tried to interest Robbie in winning, and David, only around thirteen, also wanted to play. It was David who won. He came home with boxes and boxes of Cadbury Roses chocolates.

I bought a table tennis table for our newly extended playroom and taught the children how to play. The only trouble was that I wanted to win all the time. David wanted to win too and hated losing. From being the weakest of the four of us, he became the best. Louise also ended up taking out her school table tennis championship.

A major reason I wanted the children to stay with me when Suzanne and I split up was that I didn't want them to have a stepfather. My mother had had the misfortune to be raised by a difficult stepmother, and I swore I would never let that happen to my children. I spent so much more time with them and I learnt about their own little worlds. It was a wonderful time. I decided I needed to teach each of them to fend for themselves, so I taught them how to cook basic foods such as steak or eggs – and that meant everything from boiled to scrambled, fried, poached or omelettes. The children especially loved my French toast. For the first time we became very close.

We were an unusual family. While it was logical to me, it wasn't common then for children to stay with their father after a marriage split. I treated the children as young adults from this time. I included them in my activities wherever possible. I shared everything with them. At thirteen Robbie would help me count the money after the races, and sometimes I would let him sit in on my discussions with businessmen.

I allowed the children to make their own decisions, and if I felt they might be making a mistake, I just pointed out the consequences but still let them make their own choices. It gave them a sense of responsibility and independence. They would often take themselves off to the city by train to see a movie on a Saturday on their own.

We went to lovely restaurants together, which was also quite unusual for children back then. We used to go out two or three times a week. If I won at the races we'd go to the Suehiro, a marvellous but expensive Japanese restaurant in Walker Street, North Sydney. If I lost we usually went to a little Greek café near Shore School. We always went somewhere special if it was one of our birthdays or I had an overseas visitor. We loved the Trianon, the Summit and Pruniers.

Suzanne had gone to a lot of trouble to gain a place for Louise in the highly regarded Ascham School on the other side of the harbour in the Eastern Suburbs. It meant a lot of travelling for Louise at first, but she loved going 'overseas' by ferry to the city and on by bus. After Suzanne and I split I started to drive her to school, and in the car we chatted about her daily life and I tried to guide her for the future.

I trained the children to be tough on themselves. I was driving Louise to school one day when she said she felt ill, so I stopped at the side of the road at the park under the Harbour Bridge. She looked like death warmed up. After she had been sick, I asked if she felt better. She said she was, a little. 'Good,' I said, and I continued to drive her to school. She accepted it and it turned out she had a good day.

A funny thing happened when Louise got her driver's licence. It was against the rules to drive to school, but, living on the other side of the harbour, she had a lot further to travel than most girls and had extra family responsibilities. So she started driving there. Everyone knew she did – it was probably the worst-kept secret at the school. One day I asked her to take my Cadillac for a service at Rushcutters Bay on the way. The next day, *The Sydney Morning Herald*'s 'Column Eight' noted on the front page that a girl was 'seen driving across the Bridge in an Ascham uniform in a black Cadillac'.

Louise was sprung. Nothing happened, but a few weeks later Mrs Danziger, the feared Ascham headmistress, made her point, saying, 'I haven't had my pound of flesh yet.' So a friend of Louise's, Judy Pongrass, loaned her a blonde wig, which she wore with a red jumper to drive, and parked away from the school. She wasn't harming anyone.

I would like to think the children kept their feet on the ground. They were not spoilt, just privileged and lucky. They were taught not to waste a dollar. Sometimes the children felt I was tight with money – but they had not been through the Depression. I never overindulged the children, or gave them the impression we were wealthy, and some days at the races it certainly didn't feel like we were. When a comment about me being a millionaire was made to Louise, she was amazed. It didn't feel to her that we were so wealthy – after all, we were always short of money, and I never wanted to spend anything unless it was absolutely necessary.

I wanted the children to know they never had to prove anything to anybody. I wanted them to stand on their own two feet. Family was very important to me, even if my work kept me busy a lot of the time.

Each night after dinner the children and I would go for a walk under the Harbour Bridge with Fury, our great dane. It was a glorious setting, and a superb place to inspire them about life's opportunities for the future. Louise often jokes that I raised her like a boy, because I discussed business with her just as I did with the boys. Even though it was just the four of us, they were special times.

After our split, Suzanne's mother, Mrs Dart, had come to stay for a month, to cook our meals and take care of the children. She was very good in an emergency. Both grandparents had always played a major role in the children's lives. Saturday was the day for Suzy and the grandparents to take the children on excursions.

We had a number of live-in housekeepers who cooked and cleaned the house. Not all of them were successful. One was 'on the plonk' – I noticed the spirits in the liquor cupboard being slowly emptied. In the early 1970s one housekeeper was a bit of a health fadist. She cooked lentils and other health foods, which might have been good for the children but it was not to their taste. When I was overseas the children decided to let her go. Robbie was only sixteen, but I respected their judgement.

The children then decided to have daytime 'help', and so Mrs Holland came to look after the house and Louise took over the cooking. I supported their decision. Louise shopped on the way home from school, buying the meat and vegetables. Louise loved it and she would go to such trouble; she used to make filet mignon wrapped in bacon and sitting on fried bread, which she had seen at some of the nice restaurants. She would then do her hours of school assignments. Sometimes I'd come home and say, 'Come on, let's go out,' and we'd go to the local self-service restaurant for a quick meal.

The children were in close touch with Suzanne all the time. Louise, for instance, often met her after school for an iced chocolate, and she'd take a train down to Wollongong every second weekend. I was well aware that Suzanne needed the children, and vice versa. There was never any tension between us, which was terrific. I don't think either of us ever spoke badly of the other, and certainly not to the children. I always wanted them to help their mother and understand how life can follow unexpected paths.

I was right about Suzanne's marriage. It didn't last long – about a year.

—

I had wanted the boys to go to public schools but Suzanne was adamant that they should have the benefit of private education. Robbie was an intelligent young fellow. He was never guilty of doing much homework; he knew he could get through school with a minimum of work and that is what he did. A month or so from his HSC exams he had fallen seriously behind in mathematics. Louise organised her maths teacher from school, Mr Komaromi, to tutor Robbie. Years later Mr Komaromi told Louise that he couldn't believe how Robbie picked up almost the whole syllabus in a month, a feat he had not seen before or since.

Louise was a hard worker and did extremely well at school. She was diligent and loved the challenge. She was already showing an interest in the world of business. No doubt our regular chats inspired her. However, business leanings weren't catered for at Ascham, which in those days concentrated on the classics. Louise developed a close rapport with one of her teachers, Elaine Cassidy, the daughter-in-law of the famous barrister Sir Jack Cassidy, who had appeared for me at the AJC a year or so earlier. Mrs Cassidy understood Louise's frustration at not being able to take economics even for the final two years at school, and she took up the case to introduce the subject to the school's HSC syllabus. Louise became the first and only student at the time to take Level One Economics at Ascham.

This all worked well for the first year, as Louise was self-motivated and able to liaise closely with Mrs Cassidy, even without the benefit of a class environment. However, early on in Louise's final year Mrs Cassidy had a falling-out with the headmistress and resigned immediately. This didn't faze Louise, who went on to attain a great pass in her HSC, without having had a teacher for much of the year.

David was probably favoured because he was the youngest and always needed extra care. He was a shy child but always a big boy – two sizes taller than other boys his age. It meant he had an advantage in rugby at school. However, David was denied the one sport where he excelled when an opposing school refused to play if he was in the team. After the divorce, David probably wasn't getting the same attention that he'd received from Suzanne. By the time he was fourteen, David was overweight and lacked self-confidence. Suzanne and I had tried everything, from taking him to nutritionists to in-hospital monitoring of his diet.

Some of David's problems were understandable. That's not to say he was ignored or wasn't loved. I saw more of him than when Suzanne was around, and he was my son. I did everything for him. We had a very special bond. We'd call ourselves 'Dad and Dave', after the popular radio show of yesteryear, and we played a lot of table tennis and backgammon together.

When I look back, David was crying out for attention but nothing I tried seemed to work. Happily, he started to become very friendly with my sister, Betty, and would stay with her some weekends. Other times he would stay with Jack and Gwen. I couldn't really understand why he wanted to stay with the others yet I didn't stop him, knowing he was in good hands.

Life was hard for David at times. He didn't talk properly until quite late. We sent him to special pre-schools and Suzanne took him to speech therapy. School was difficult for David but I knew he was intelligent. At Shore, Robbie acted as David's defender with the masters until he left in 1972. The next year I was called to the school by the headmaster, Jika Travers. David, then fifteen, had been caught making a book on the Melbourne Cup and had a large list of student clients. Fortunately, Jika saw some humour in the incident and took no action.

As it turned out, David had inherited 'the book' from Robbie. Once we knew this, it explained Robbie's actions one day when he had come home unexpectedly in the lunch hour. He had told Suzanne he'd forgotten his money, which Suzanne assumed meant his lunch money. In reality, he was after ready cash. Apparently, his student punters had all but cleaned him out and he had come back to get reserves.

Jika's tolerance of David's attitude towards studying was not to last. Jika gave me an ultimatum – to take David out of the school. I wasn't happy about this. David hadn't done anything really wrong – after all, school isn't for everyone. I knew I could place him in the family businesses of building or racing. I knew he was able, so I took him to Fiji to learn the betting business under Francis Grant.

David had always been street-smart, and in Fiji he used the system to get a driver's licence, even though he was still only fifteen. When he returned to Sydney he expected to drive and was not impressed when I put my foot down in our first serious confrontation and wouldn't let him.

20

Sweet and Sour

AN EXCITING NEW business opportunity had arisen from one of my trips to Las Vegas, where I'd met one of the nicest guys you could ever hope to meet, Charlie Kandel. Charlie was the credit manager for the high-rollers at the Sands casino, owned by Howard Hughes. Kevin Perkins, who came to know Charlie through his attempt to write an authorised biography of Hughes, suggested I look Charlie up. I was very pleased with the introduction as it resulted in not only a good friendship but also a great business.

Charlie had been a soldier with the American forces during World War I. He told me the Americans had been unprepared for battle, and how frightened he was when they reached the front in France. The authorities had thrown in an Australian brigade to help them, and Charlie had been amazed by their bravery and toughness. He never forgot those Australians. Every time he met an Aussie he threw out the hospitality mat. He was unbelievably generous – if he had anything you admired he would insist on giving it to you.

We hit it off immediately. I introduced the Australian chicken kings, Bob and Jack Ingham, to Charlie and they couldn't believe his generosity. He was just that sort of guy. He knew everyone and everyone knew him. He realised most people wanted to meet stars and he would take you straight to them, saying, 'Bill, this is my friend Jack Jones, who is singing here at the Sands. Jack, this is Bill, a real regular guy.'

When I first met Charlie he had some Brut aftershave by Fabergé stacked in a corner of his office. I was fascinated, as whenever I went overseas, I was always asked to bring Brut back with me. It was not only hard to get in Australia but also very expensive. Charlie asked me whether I would like to be the distributor and represent Fabergé in Australia. His good friend George Barrie was the chairman of the company and could arrange the agency for me. I was very excited.

My nephew John, who was 23, had come to work in partnership with Jack and me and needed something extra to complement his racing role. I thought this could be a good project for him to manage and Charlie put me in touch with George Barrie. I met Barrie in New York and was blown away by his sumptuously avant-garde offices – the corridors were all black and dimmed with coloured neon tubing, which led you to the various departments. Up a spiral staircase was George Barrie's huge office, with a large piano – he was a great musician – and also a bar with a robot that served drinks.

George told me how he had supported Cassius Clay when he was a poor young fighter; when Clay became world champion George asked him to launch his new product, Brut 33. Clay was pleased to help and refused to take any money. The television ad was a huge success with Clay saying, 'Float like a butterfly, sting like a bee; I am the greatest and so is Brut 33!'

Fabergé's directors included Elizabeth Taylor, Roger Moore and Cary Grant. On one visit to New York I was invited to stay in Cary Grant's apartment. Although he wasn't there himself, I still loved seeing his personal photos and memorabilia all around.

Jack and I set up Fabergé Australia in the second half of 1970, placing 'young John' in charge. We owned 49 per cent of the business and were one of the only Fabergé operations in the world not wholly owned by the parent company. When we acquired Fabergé, Brut had almost no presence in the Australian market. Aftershave was basically new and was regarded as something for sissies. Old Spice was the leader in our small market.

When we started to sell the product at Christmas, the demand took us all off-guard. We set up a mini production line upstairs in our office, and the children helped our racing staff fill bottles of Brut, glue on the medallions and put them in their boxes so they could go on sale in pharmacies.

In no time Fabergé was the trendy up-market alternative to Old Spice. Under the guidance of John and some clever marketing people, and backed up by our financial resources, we created a whole new market. With classy and provocative television ads, men who had never dreamed of wearing fragrance suddenly thought aftershave was sexy, and it became the favourite gift of girlfriends or wives at Christmas or Father's Day. Brut took the Australian market by storm, achieving a market share of around 60 per cent, the brand's highest anywhere in the world.

We'd rewritten marketing in Australia with our expensive and flamboyant campaigns. We brought Roger Moore, Leslie Howard, Margaux Hemingway and other stars to Australia. We launched other Fabergé products, as well as the more affordable Brut 33. Fabergé was the first cosmetics marketer to take fragrances, traditionally the preserve of department stores, to the masses. When Brut 33 was introduced to supermarkets, sales went through the roof.

At this point my family was on top of the world. We were the largest bookmakers in Australia, and I was billed as the biggest gambler in the world. I had set Melbourne on fire with my betting, and represented Australia twice at Royal Ascot and Epsom. We'd branched into overseas betting in Fiji, and I was a popular racing columnist. We'd built and operated several hotels, including the most successful in Australia, the Chatswood Charles. We'd developed major residential projects and now we were diversifying into toiletries and perfumes – a whole new world that couldn't be more removed from racing.

During this period I applied to the Queensland government for a casino licence and the idea was accepted in principle. Tom Foley, a Las Vegas lawyer, came out for meetings, while my interests were watched over by Neville Wran QC – before he went into politics. The casino proposition eventually foundered when Sir Joh Bjelke-Petersen, the premier of Queensland and a larger-than-life character, changed his mind. Sir Joh had been pressured by the church and at the last moment had reneged.

I was livid, as a lot of money had simply been wasted. I wrote a stinging full-page article for *The Sunday Telegraph* that was very critical of Sir Joh. To his credit, when he was attacked on the floor of parliament by the Queensland opposition, he simply stated, 'There's nothing to reply to. The facts were correct. I changed my mind.'

—

Despite the successes over the last decade and my optimism for the future, a number of unfortunate events over the late 1960s and early 1970s had affected my standing and reputation. They seemed to follow one after the other – the hotel raid, my divorce, the Big Philou rumours and, by association, the troubles of two of my biggest punters: the racing disqualification of Felipe Ysmael and the arrest, trial and jailing of Peter Huxley. When the AJC refused to renew my bookmaking licence in August 1971 I was given no reason, but I had no doubt it was because of Huxley and the adverse publicity, which they considered had harmed racing. I took the 'punishment' on the chin and decided to concentrate on other areas while waiting for my year's banishment to pass.

At the end of the 1971–72 racing season, I reapplied but my application was again rejected. Previously it had been clear the AJC had meant my suspension to last only a year. Now that had changed for some reason, but I didn't know why.

This rejection would ultimately mean another eighteen months on the outer, and it soured racing for me. It was galling to think that the people who controlled racing had such power to affect a person's livelihood and yet were above criticism themselves. If they had made a mistake, who was to know? They were certainly not going to tell anybody. In those days, when a man was denied his livelihood by the racing authorities and not given a reason, he had no right of reply.

The non-renewal of my licence created a family business problem for me. Jack and I had been partners in everything since the early 1940s. We had built up our assets equally. Since 1964, when we had concluded the three-way partnership with Charlie's estate, Jack and I had formed a new partnership between ourselves. We both worked hard, each focusing on different responsibilities for the benefit of both. We had complete trust in each other and I didn't worry when I contributed more through my successful big betting or took on a greater load.

The situation began to change with me not able to work at the races. My nephew John became more assertive and friction developed between us. I was still running all the business affairs and also everything to do with racing off the course. John was working hard for us with Fabergé and as a bookmaker in the interstate Paddock, and he had his own young family. So he demanded a one-third share in all the businesses, including racing, properties, building, breeding and Fabergé. My view was that things were already divided equally between our two families. However, I agreed to John's wishes as I didn't want any trouble with Jack on the issue.

I saw John as a part of our future. Jack had been at the top for a long time but was now cutting back on his betting activity, wishing to concentrate more on stud breeding. We already had a huge string of horses at the farm and about 80 horses in training, and so the whole running costs were a bottomless pit, which of course appalled me. Nevertheless, if that was what my brother wanted, it was okay with me.

I also appreciated there was another star on the horizon: my own son Robbie, who had already started working for me as a clerk and was in his final years at school. He would probably come into the business and be entitled to a share as well.

—

Another year passed in the racing wilderness. After I reapplied again for my licence in June 1973, I received a batch of urgent messages at my office from a C. Pearson to phone a certain number, saying it was in my interest and concerned my bookmaking licence. Pearson was a disreputable jockey and I thought it was some trick, or simply an attempt to extract money for information that would be worthless. Then I got a call from Morgan Ryan, a Sydney solicitor, saying he had a client, Chicka Pearson, and he thought I should listen to what he had to say. This was a different matter.

I had known Morgan for close on 30 years. Although we had never been close friends, we had never had a disagreement of any kind. He was a close friend of my old friend Lionel Murphy and I knew he would be trying to help me, so I phoned Pearson. He told me enough on the phone about the AJC trying to prevent me from getting my licence back to worry me. He wanted to see me, so I arranged for him to come to my house two days later.

I was so concerned that the following morning I went to see Neville Wran. He was flabbergasted and asked if Pearson would give me a statutory declaration. When I said I thought he would, Neville said, 'Well, if you can get that, you have got the AJC on toast.'

I was still hesitant, saying it all seemed too simple, too pat. Although I had never met Pearson, it was obvious he had gone to a lot of trouble to see me, which made me suspicious.

Neville looked at me and said, 'I've known you too long not to respect your sixth sense. If you have any doubts you must be cautious. This is a criminal matter, whether the allegations are true or false. I think we should report this at once to the Criminal Investigation Branch.' He phoned the superintendent of the CIB and briefly told him the problem.

Neville advised me to liaise with the police myself, and to also have an independent person not connected with racing as an intermediary. He said I shouldn't meet Pearson unless in the presence of this person.

I asked Kevin Perkins if he would act as the intermediary, saying I did not want any publicity. He said he would do it only on condition that he could take part officially as a news-paperman, reserving the right to report the affair if it became public, and only if his newspaper approved of the arrangement. I wasn't happy about the newspaper having a role but I had little choice so I accepted the situation. I had known Kevin Perkins for a little over four years at this time. Aside from our growing friendship, he was the one person who was aware of the problems surrounding me.

When Pearson came as arranged, I asked him if he would mind discussing everything in front of my friend Kevin, because the matter was serious and I needed some corroboration. I told him Kevin was a serious-minded and respected member of the community and also the news editor of *The Sunday Telegraph*. He agreed when I said it would be a safeguard for him too.

Pearson told an incredible tale. As a jockey, he'd been told by Frank Lynch, the AJC's senior racecourse detective, that he would not have his licence renewed unless he cooperated with them. Lynch did not want to see my bookmaker's licence re-issued and wanted grounds for the AJC to reject my application. Accordingly, Lynch wanted Pearson to say that he had been approached by me to pull up horses, and that I had also asked him to approach other jockeys to do the same.

Kevin and I were shocked by these preposterous claims. After he left, I rang and spoke to the superintendent at the CIB, who put two Consorting Squad detectives on the matter, including Detective Sergeant Brian Ballard. The detectives said I should ask Pearson to my house again; they would wait in another room and listen to what he told Kevin and me, and hear the allegations themselves. I arranged a second meeting with Pearson.

The police officers came to see me about an hour before Pearson was to arrive. I already had Kevin Perkins with me. There was an instant tension between the two camps. It was obvious that the police thought it was a spurious allegation and that Pearson was just looking to make money. Perkins, however, tended to believe Pearson's story, and I wondered if Perkins' views were perhaps influenced by his wish for a good newspaper story.

Their exchanges were acrimonious and I doubted the wisdom of what I had done. The police intended to listen to the conversation and, as soon as Pearson asked for money, to enter the room and arrest him for fraud. They said it was ludicrous to assume that anything that Pearson had alleged was even remotely true, and it was obviously a try-on for money.

On the other hand, Perkins wanted the chance to draw out Pearson and get details of the alleged conspiracy. Despite Kevin's protestation, the detectives were adamant in their intention to make an arrest as soon as he asked for money.

I wasn't sure what to believe, but I was leaning more towards the police interpretation. I never really thought Sir Brian Crowley or any of the AJC committee members would be involved in such an outlandish scheme. The committee, which included Sir Frank Packer, were the leaders of society, industry and business. All wealthy, they performed an unpaid role and I couldn't see any of them behaving in such a fashion. Although I doubted their understanding of bookmaking and thought some of them were square pegs in round holes, I didn't doubt their integrity.

However, even though I knew Lynch was hostile towards me, at this stage I didn't consider for one minute that there could be lobbying and even manipulation behind the scenes by Sir Eugene Gorman.

Pearson turned up right on time and we went into my study with Kevin. The two detectives waited in the adjoining sunroom. Pearson told the same tale once more, but – with further probing by Kevin – added much more detail about the alleged conspiracy to implicate me in pulling up horses. Pearson described how he had been directed by Frank Lynch to drive from Nowra on the south coast and check into a motel, where Lynch had called around with another AJC officer, Dennis 'Dinny' Ryan, to discuss the plot. Pearson gave explicit details of how he had been bullied by Lynch, who told him that, as a jockey with a cloud over his head already, he would never ride again if he did not help them. Pearson said he realised his only hope was to tell me the truth and expose the officials. He said that he wished he could get them on tape to prove his allegations.

Having reiterated that Perkins was a leading journalist, I thought Pearson would have run a mile if he was a phoney. Instead Pearson said he was grateful to have the opportunity of explaining everything to Kevin, and he asked whether Kevin could get a tape for him to use in his next talk with the AJC officials the following Monday at Randwick Racecourse. Kevin said he would get a recording device for Pearson to wear during the meeting.

This had all taken a couple of hours. All parties were satisfied. Pearson was staying at the Strata Motor Inn (now the Metropole) at Cremorne, about two kilometres away, and Kevin arranged to phone him and have another meeting.

Pearson left and the scenario changed from a spy thriller to a *Keystone Cops* comedy. The police had now changed their whole approach to the matter. They'd realised that perhaps Pearson was telling the truth, as he wasn't asking for any money. If what he was saying was true, they were on to a most sensational case. Before our talk with Pearson was over they had decided to split up. One of the detectives had gone to wait outside, intending to follow Pearson once he left my house.

The only trouble was that Pearson had not come alone. He had a companion waiting in his car. This friend saw a man leave the house and go to a car and get in, but not drive away. He realised he was waiting for someone. Pearson's friend got out of his car and waited in the shadows, watching the detective who was now watching the house. Pearson soon went to his car and, without looking for his friend, drove off. His friend then saw the stranger take off immediately after Pearson.

The detective followed Pearson back to the hotel, where Pearson met a man who turned out to be Cliff Carey, the well-known racing radio personality. Carey later told police that he had been contacted by Pearson, who said he was about to break the story of the century but that it was too early to disclose any details. Pearson's friend later told him of the 'tail', so now Pearson realised he had been followed.

The following Monday, Perkins met Pearson in Centennial Park, not far from Randwick, and introduced the detectives, without saying they were police. The detectives placed two bugs on Pearson, who enthusiastically whipped off his coat and shirt to show his cooperation. They all drove to the track offices in an unmarked police car, and Pearson checked the two bugs again. Both were working as he set off for the meeting, but soon after he entered the building both bugs went dead, although one did record some brief conversation indicating that Lynch was not present.

The police and Kevin waited for about fifteen minutes and Pearson re-emerged. As soon as he had left the offices both bugs started functioning again, as Perkins and the police could suddenly hear footsteps.

After getting into the car, Pearson said, 'Well, did you get all that? Wasn't it exactly as I told you?' When told that they had got nothing on tape, he seemed bitterly disappointed.

Kevin was suspicious and immediately thought a trap had been set for me and now sprung! Whichever way you looked at it, it had been a fiasco and was impossible to work out. The police were doubtful of Pearson too. They decided to approach Sir Brian Crowley at the AJC offices the next day, as serious allegations had been made against officials and, therefore, the AJC itself.

When the police met Sir Brian to tell him what happened he was, naturally, staggered. His first reaction was, 'Thank God you've come, otherwise a terrible injustice would have been done.' Yes, he knew about Pearson but had not met him. Yes, he knew Pearson was assisting his officials, and yes, he knew he had been at the offices recently assisting the club in the Waterhouse matter.

Sir Brian had been told that I had approached Pearson, saying that I wanted his help in getting something on the AJC; then, apparently, I had placed electronic bugs on Pearson, which Pearson had showed to the officials as soon as he entered the building. The officials had reported this to the secretary, who had informed the chairman.

My application for the renewal of my licence for the 1973–74 season was actually due to face the full committee the coming Friday. The chairman told police the officials were to give evidence of my perfidy to the full committee – in my absence. I would not have been told of the allegations against me when I appeared. My licence would have naturally been refused, and I would never have known why! This was a plot that would have done credit to Agatha Christie.

When the police told me the full picture, Kevin and I could see the hand of Sir Eugene Gorman. He had been a VRC committeeman and had the ear of the AJC committee. His right-hand man in Melbourne was Frank Harding, the VRC's racecourse detective and Lynch's counterpart. Lynch and Harding were close friends. Naturally, Lynch would believe whatever Harding told him.

There was evidence that Harding had been in Sydney in the lead-up to the events. Indeed, he had called on Kevin Perkins at *The Sunday Telegraph* to introduce himself and have a friendly chat. He said he was a mate of Frank Lynch and understood that Perkins had known Lynch from Perkins' days as a police cadet at the CIB in Sydney when Lynch was a senior detective there. Harding had denigrated me and criticised my racing career. Perkins knew Harding was close to Sir Eugene and put two and two together.

However, the matter still had a way to go and became even more complicated. Lynch's offsider, Ryan, had observed Pearson returning to the police car and had taken down the number. Lynch had then rung the police department to find out the owner, as that might have been further evidence against me. Imagine his surprise to find it was a police registration.

Sir Brian did not know about the police vehicle when the detectives visited him. Why wasn't he told at once? After the police visit, Sir Brian informed his secretary, who then told Lynch. Two things followed quickly. Pearson disappeared as though he had fallen down a hole, and Lynch and Dinny Ryan denied the police's allegation that they had approached Pearson and claimed the police were working for me and in my pay!

Sir Brian now was in a flap and was forced to go public, and so an official police inquiry began. Now that matters had been taken away from the star-chamber methods of the AJC, there was a chance of getting at the truth. The inquiry centred on the man who started it, Chicka Pearson. He had conveniently disappeared. The AJC officials denied any wrongdoing, blaming Pearson for the allegations.

The question that could not be answered was why Pearson went to so much trouble for no gain. He had spun a web of intricate and delicate planning. Lynch and Ryan were up to their eyeballs in the plot, and I suspected Harding and Gorman were in the background.

It nearly worked and would have permanently sealed my bookmaking fate. I had survived only through luck and caution. I had had the common sense to take the advice of Neville Wran and include a journalist, Kevin Perkins, and to report the matter to the police. All these steps had saved my fate.

I was especially grateful to Perkins, who, with the approval of his paper, went out on a limb to get at the truth of the matter. I realised Perkins was not a typical newspaperman just looking for the story – he was very astute and passionately wanted to see justice done.

A 90-page police report was compiled by two senior detective inspectors, Wal Bailey and Jack Palmer, and was given to Police Commissioner Fred Hanson. The inquiry extended over almost six months, with some 80 people interviewed.

Although they couldn't find Pearson, they took note of the earlier report by Detective-Sergeant Ballard, which had been submitted to the superintendant in charge of the CIB. It read: 'From inquiries made . . . it would appear that a Criminal Conspiracy between Lynch, Ryan and an unnamed member of the AJC Committee might have taken place, to do something wrongful and harmful to . . . the man Waterhouse . . .'

The confidential report completely exonerated me of any suggestion of impropriety. Bob Askin was furious about the conduct of the AJC, called me into his parliamentary office and asked me if I wanted a royal commission. But I wasn't interested in scalps – my only concern was to clear my name and get back my licence.'

The AJC made sure they cleared themselves in their releases and the only one criticised was Pearson. The whole matter had been given extensive coverage in all branches of the media, and questions had been asked in parliament. Opposition leader Pat Hills said, 'We are concerned about these Australian Jockey Club hearings as being "Star Chamber" operations with no appeal against their decisions.' My licence could hardly be refused any longer.

In the end I had the support of some powerful people, including Bob Askin and AJC committeeman Sir Frank Packer. Initially, Sir Frank had been livid about the bad publicity for the AJC until Perkins, a trusted former employee, had given him all the evidence. Then he was 100 per cent on my side. Nevertheless, the AJC took its time in restoring my licence, which was to take effect only from 1 January 1974.

I had wondered if I should be returning to racing at all, as I was so disillusioned. But Sir Frank, a true friend, was shocked: 'What? After all we've done for you?' I realised it would be a gratuitous snub not only to the AJC but to those who had done so much to help it happen. I decided to go back and work for six months till the end of the racing year in July.

I have no doubt I would have been back working after the original twelve months without my licence, except for these powerful machinations behind the scenes. After matters started to unravel in the Pearson affair in mid-1973, Sir Eugene suffered a heart attack and died. I learned from various independent sources, including bookmakers and journalists in Melbourne, and interviews Gorman had given to Perkins, that the man was set against me. The strange thing is I never did anything against him. I still don't understand why he turned. I'll never know – he never left his card!

21

The Comeback

A WAY FROM THE TRACK, we were full-steam-ahead on our building projects and were cashed up from a windfall sale of a little office we had built at Milsons Point. We still had our old-world real-estate agent Bill Halliday scouting for property. He followed our directions, used his enterprise and did the legwork to pull together a few beauties.

Jack and I had moved away from the large-scale projects like the Bronte Charles Hotel and the St Charles home units at Kirribilli and were enjoying success building smaller apartments in suburbs like Artarmon, Wollstonecraft, Cronulla, Lakemba, Campsie and Narrabeen. In most cases we wanted to save the extra cost of a lift, which was so high it was almost as much as the construction cost for the whole building.

I had always loved Balmoral and remember going there by tram with my mother in the 1930s. As a little boy I couldn't keep still for very long and so would inevitably become motion-sick during the journey. One of the special sites Bill Halliday amalgamated was a prime corner block of several properties on the Esplanade at Balmoral. It was a perfect location, halfway along the bay and just across the road from the beach. The design of the building of twelve units was ahead of its time, with luxuries like ensuite bathrooms, apart from the generous proportions and large terraces with lovely views. The cost to construct the building at Balmoral was around $100,000; nowadays the individual apartments sell for more than $2 million.

Jack and I were proud of the small but exclusive project, and when we finished the units in 1970 we told our friend Jock Rorrison he could have the pick of any one of them. Over the years Jock had been such a great friend. With his love of hoarding cash he had more than once unquestioningly helped with liquidity after a bad trot at the races. We gave him a life-occupancy, rent-free in the top-floor apartment, where he lived for over 25 years.

While waiting to swing the satchel again, I moved the children in with me at the Charles Hotel at Bronte. I now had the time to run it myself and to try to make it work. It had never really made money but, with my experience at the Hotel Charles at Chatswood, I thought I could turn it around. Within about twelve months it was doing much better, although it never set the world on fire.

—

Our mining syndicate DAWM had been exercising my mind. After Ben Dickinson's tip-off to Insel in 1969, where we were stuck with a one-sided royalty agreement, I went to New York with Neville Wran and met Paddy Laine, Insel's vice-president, with whom we had done all our negotiations. He admitted they had been wrong in their approach and agreed to create a new royalty agreement in the spirit of our initial discussions.

However, this new proposed agreement was still not as promised, and so I decided to challenge the agreement by taking it to court on the technical grounds that the original agreement was void because Insel had not complied with proper foreign investment requirements. We were granted an injunction and, as it was an international issue, the matter ended up in the High

Court, advised by Sir Maurice Byers QC. Faced with this legal challenge, Insel agreed to a settlement in October 1973 with a new, fairer royalty rate.

I needed to go to Toronto to sign the new agreement on behalf of DAWM. I decided to take two advisers: Ken Watson, our solicitor, and Vince McMahon, who had come to work for me after retiring as the deputy commissioner for taxation. I suggested we all fly economy so that they could bring their wives with them – a first-class fare almost equalled two economy tickets.

Vince was extremely conservative, methodical and tenacious – traits that had obviously held him in good stead at the tax office. Vince's title was 'business manager' but we soon jokingly called him the 'no business manager', as he always found some fault with every idea or venture I would run by him.

However, his thoroughness paid off in spades. I had been delighted with his work, which had saved Jack and me a significant amount when we sold a small building we had put up in Alfred Street, Milsons Point, for a windfall profit.

Soon after we had built this little project we started to receive offers from a party wanting to buy it. Jack and I didn't want to sell as it was fully leased, and we also had our own offices there. We only ever sold an asset if we had a good reason, such as a shortage of cash-flow for the races, or perhaps to pay some tax. Vince politely wrote back declining. The offers kept on increasing, but each time we refused. I then did some research and found that someone had bought up all the land around us. We eventually did sell, but for a figure more than triple the original offer – $450,000. It was a record per square metre for Milsons Point in 1970 and almost equalled the highest price ever paid in North Sydney.

We couldn't believe our luck. It had been the missing piece of a much larger project that eventually became the Milson apartment and retail precinct, with the historic Milson Cottage at Milsons Point. The tax department had their eye on this massive profit, but Vince McMahon believed it shouldn't be taxable. In those days there was no capital gains tax, but if you sold a project to make a profit it was taxable as income – you were regarded as a developer. He and I went to Canberra and successfully argued that it was built as an investment and we hadn't intended to sell, but the offer had become too good to resist. It proved the old saying: 'the truth is not bad'! I wanted to reward Vince and couldn't think of anything nicer than to take him to Canada, where he and his wife could have a holiday.

Also, I decided to take Louise with me. She was in her second-last year at school and I had an idea to send her to a finishing school in Switzerland to learn languages and business. Louise knew she wouldn't be allowed to take the time off, as the Ascham headmistress, Rowena Danziger, had a reputation for not letting anyone miss out on school. I went to see the diminutive but formidable headmistress and explained that Louise would learn more on this two-week trip than at school, so she agreed. Suzanne claimed I must have charmed Rowena, but she had just wanted the best for Louise.

After the talks on the nickel mine agreement were completed, Louise and I spent a day visiting Niagara Falls with Vince and his wife and the sight took our breath away. We then flew to London en route to Switzerland. Louise was seventeen and a pure delight to be with: vivacious, beautiful and intelligent. I must have driven her mad with my continual teasing. I used to tell her when we went out that most people would be thinking I was a dirty old man and she was my girlfriend. Louise light-heartedly made sure she clearly addressed me as 'Dad' everywhere we went. When we arrived in England, walking along Bond Street I spontaneously took her into a fur salon to buy her a fur coat. She laughed and said, 'No, Dad, I don't need an expensive fur.' I realised the gambler was taking over from the Depression boy.

I caught up with my friend Charles St George and told him I intended sending Louise to a school in Switzerland. He was alarmed and said I should speak to his younger brother, Edward, who happened to be in town, before going any further; his two daughters had gone to a finishing school over there.

Edward counselled me at once against sending Louise to Switzerland for any level of education. He said the drug situation was almost out of control there, pushers were supplying anything and everything to the rich young students, and he had removed his daughters. That put the kybosh on Switzerland and I decided to have a few days in London with Louise and then return to Australia via the United States.

Don Scott was also in London with his attractive wife, Judy, and we all met up. Don was a moody and morose but very gentle man; I had only really met him a few weeks earlier in Sydney, when Rob, who had read about Don and the Legal Eagles splitting up, suggested we approach him about helping with the Sydney form for me when I eventually returned as a bookmaker. We agreed that he would give us his market and in return he could do all his betting through us.

I looked after Don and Judy in London, taking them out for dinner and seeing some of the sights. We got to know each other better and further discussed working together. Don was fascinated by my betting exploits, and a year or so later he wrote a play about me called *The Next Greatest Pleasure*, which he read with great passion for my family and me at his home. It also ran at the Playbox Theatre in Melbourne.

Louise enjoyed London very much and really didn't want to leave. She had missed out on the trip to Switzerland, but I only had a certain amount of time and I wanted to see George Barrie from Fabergé in New York. I said, 'Let's take off and we'll have a few days in Las Vegas after we finish in New York.' Louise was disappointed but understood. In New York we met up with George Barrie and then went on to Vegas. We were given a beautiful suite in the new MGM Grand. Louise was spellbound, as the suite was glorious, with a sunken bath. It had been a hectic trip and we had been on the go most of the time. Now I intended to have a few days 'R and R' and take in the shows with Louise.

I knew Al Benedict, the general manager of the MGM Grand, from his days at the Stardust. Al invited Louise and me to dinner and gave us a guided tour of the hotel, which had just opened and was billed as one of the world's biggest. I knew a little about hotels from our building experience, but the huge proportions of the MGM Grand were mindblowing. We went to the MGM spectacular that night and Louise was overjoyed. She planned to spend the next evening at another show.

The next morning, however, I received a call from my secretary, Mary-Jane Pratten, informing me that His Majesty King Taufa'ahau Tupou IV, the King of Tonga, wanted to see me and would like me to call in to Tonga on my way home. His Majesty had completed an arts/law degree at Sydney University while I was there. During the war the law faculty was very small and lectures were often combined, so everyone knew one another. His Majesty had been a brilliant student and also a great sportsman, holding the broad jump record. He loved his boxing and also played football for the university. He was highly respected by both the students and the professors.

I regarded the invitation as a royal command. I looked at Louise and said, 'I'm sorry, but I've got to cut short our stay. We'll have to leave this afternoon.' She looked dismayed but understood the sense in leaving early, as there were only three flights a week into Tonga. I flew to Suva, where Francis Grant joined me to continue to Tonga, and Louise carried on to Sydney.

His Majesty wanted to see me because he had heard of my development ideas for the Pacific and wanted to ensure Tonga wasn't forgotten. Tonga was to become a very special part of my life.

—

I started bookmaking again at Randwick on New Year's Day 1974. I had been invited to the Tattersalls Club early luncheon at the track but felt a little uneasy. I hadn't 'bookmaked' for almost two and a half years and it felt strange. Apart from everything else, *I* had changed. There were new faces and I had a new stand – a bad one. I was at the very end of the Rails, and at Rosehill I was not even on the Rails but right at the far end of the main ring. I had to start all over again, work my way back up and prove myself. More than a few thought I couldn't do it. Any fool can bet big – the trick is whether you can keep it up. Big betting soon separates the men from the boys.

I hadn't gone back to bet big or be the biggest bookie. I went back mainly to clear my name. I believed I had always conducted myself honourably – I may have cut corners, I may have bent the rules, but I was never a crook. In the 1950s and 60s I had been dubbed 'the Gentleman Bookmaker' – then my name had been dragged through the mud.

Waiting by my stand to be my first punter that first day back was Jack 'the Bird' Sparrow. A funny thing happened – I had a crayon from my old stock, which was then several years old, and much to everyone's hilarity it crumbled as I wrote this first bet for $1000.

Even on the bad stands, where the big punters had to walk a long way to find me, I soon got into my stride. As I settled into it, I realised how much I'd missed bookmaking – the adrenaline and the challenge. I loved horse racing because I saw it as the most exciting game in the world. Once again, I was quickly the top money-holder on the course. Big punters appreciated my policy of letting anyone on to win the significant amount of $10,000 at my price on the board, and they came flocking.

Not all the punters were pleased about my return, however. When the newspapers announced I would be returning to bet on Sydney events, professional punter Michael McHugh said to Dave 'the Dasher' Segenfield, 'It's great news that Bill Waterhouse is coming back to bet – it'll make it much easier to get on.'

The Dasher reportedly replied, 'Son, you're dead wrong. Bill Waterhouse is the best informed bookmaker in the country. You won't get any overs from him. He won't let you on anything that has got any real chance of winning. It'll be a disaster. The rest of the sheep will just follow him. Heed my words – you'll find it hard to win once he starts betting on Sydney races.'

I had the benefit of Don Scott's markets, which were calculated to just 85 per cent instead of the normal 100 to 115 per cent. Don had found it hard to get his bets on with the bookies, so I let Don on, based on a notional betting unit of $2500. To make it as attractive as possible, we offered to pay Don the top fluctuation odds reported in the *Herald* the next day. This was probably the first 'top fluc' betting – now one of the most popular bet types. Don won from me but it was worth it, because his opinions and assessments were valuable.

One funny scene I remember was Clive Evatt, also formerly of the Legal Eagles, a man six-foot-six tall and wearing a black pinstripe suit and a homburg, tearing 200 metres through the crowd from the Rails to my stand in the outer, to claim a bet from me before my price went off. When the price shortened on the Rails, he knew he had to run to beat my groundsman, Robbie, who this time was no match for Clive with his long legs. It was like watching a scene from *Chariots of Fire* to see him sprinting right through the ring, hat and all. I remember some poor innocent punter complained that Clive was a danger when he knocked him over for the second time. Barrister Clive quickly retorted, 'You're always complaining about me!'

Rob, who worked as my clerk, was approached by a punter asking to lay a horse through me. Rob enthusiastically said,

'Okay – if you put the money in first. He handed Rob $20,000 but didn't come back to tell him which horse he wanted. It was a bad day and the cash came in handy to pay out on our losses. At the end of the day we waited for the punter to come back for his $20,000 – we knew we would have to write him a cheque and explain why he was not getting his cash back. No one came. Then we expected him to come for his money at settling the following Monday and over the next weeks.

One of the bad results that race day had been a big plunge at racecourses and SP joints all around Australia on a horse called Blockbuster. We heard the plunge was orchestrated by George Freeman, the 'colourful racing identity' who was later exposed as a gangster.

Several weeks later the punter came and apologised profusely about the bad 'mail' on Blockbuster; he said he had been tricked by Freeman. He hoped we hadn't lost too much after laying it for him when it blew to 7/2. He had obviously forgotten he hadn't passed on the name of the horse! Luck had helped me. I had the $20,000, rather than laying Blockbuster.

It turned out that Freeman had set up several bookmakers to try to lay the horse and to blow the price, so that he could back it everywhere. He had cleaned up punting SP when Blockbuster's price blew and he was able to back it at the longer odds of 7/2 instead of 5/4. Freeman later boasted in his autobiography of this tricky practice to manipulate the prices and set up the bookies.

—

Rob had first come to work with me at the age of sixteen. He loved it and took to racing like a duck to water. Rob had never really been to the races before, but as a training exercise when he was a young teenager I had him writing columns of numbers as quickly and clearly as possible. In his spare time, even while watching television, he would always have a pen in his hand and be writing the numbers one to ten. I had also done this as a young boy and it had stood me in good stead. Writing a legible ticket with both the win and place return was a special skill, and Rob learned to do it too.

Suzanne had always thought he would become a stockbroker because of his maths skills. However, after starting for me as a clerk in 1970, his interests changed. He went to Macquarie University to study economics, arranging all his lectures around the races. He found university boring compared to the excitement at the track, and it was not long before he was telling his mother he was deferring for a year. Suzy was a realist and resignedly said, 'You'll never go back.'

When I came back to racing Rob was nineteen and was my weekend clerk. He had already had a provincial and country bookmaker's licence, and he'd been running his cousin John's bookmaking stands at the trots and sometimes the dogs. When Robbie was twenty he started out as a bookie on his own at the trots. A man he knew quite well told him in conversation that a certain horse, the favourite, was not trying and to get whatever he could out of it. I was out there to watch, and when Robbie told me about this I laughed. Thinking back to the lessons of my father on ignoring information on 'dead-uns', I had no doubt the man was not sincere and would only be trying to get Rob into trouble.

Rob dismissed the tipster's advice. The horse won, and when Robbie reproached the man he simply said, '*Timeo Danaos et dona ferentes*,' which they both knew was Latin for 'Beware of Greeks bearing gifts'. The man, known as the 'Swamp Rat', had a Greek background.

By the end of the 1974 year the Waterhouse bookmakers were holding sway again at the track. I was the top holder of the locals ring, Jack was the top of the interstate Rails, my nephew John was the leader of the interstate Paddock ring, and Rob was soon leading at the provincials.

The big punters quickly found me. These included Malcom Rich and Leon Fink, and of course Hoppy was also back in action with me. My top turnover meant I was promoted to a stand on the Rails at the Sydney Turf Club in 1975, but it took several hard years before my position on the Rails at Randwick was improved by the AJC. In those days your turnover didn't automatically give you a better stand, and no officials were going out of their way to help me.

Cash was still king, and nowhere was cash used like at the track. We would all carry large amounts as our tools of trade. From the early 1960s I had employed a trusted settling clerk and client manager, Keith Jones. He had been a wool classer before coming to us and was terrific. We had complete trust in Keith and thought nothing of giving him large sums of cash to transport to settling or the races. Handling cash was not without risks.

One Saturday before the races, as we were working on our prices at the office, Keith as usual left early for the track to set up in advance, taking his briefcase with the cheque books and $40,000 in cash. A few minutes later, a group of four kids wandered up to our office door, holding Keith's unopened briefcase. Keith had inadvertently left it on the footpath when loading the car. These boys had seen Keith drive off and wanted to know if we knew him. Rob immediately grabbed the bag and tried hard to give them a reward, but they wouldn't accept anything. Not knowing the contents, they didn't realise how much they deserved a good present. Nobody was more relieved than Keith when we met him at the racecourse with his bag.

Keith was on friendly terms with all our punters and also had the unenviable task of chasing slow payers. After the races Keith would stay back at night with me at the office to do the laborious manual settling and cross-checking, which usually took well over an hour in the days before computers. Keith took over the weekly settling from me, and with John, and later Rob, would go to town to pay our credit clients by cheque or cash. Hundreds of thousands of dollars would change hands between bookmakers at the Tattersalls Club in the city every Monday. Not only dollars changed hands, however.

One Monday Keith took his swish Samsonite briefcase with $20,000 in cash for our settling. After stopping for a friendly chat with other bookmakers at City Tatts, where he briefly put the case down, he arrived at the Tattersalls Club, opened his case on the desk and saw just four oranges. An identical bag had been switched with his.

With bookmakers settling in so much cash, it was not surprising when in the mid-1970s masked gunmen held up more than 50 members of Melbourne's racing fraternity during settling at the Victorian Club, escaping with several million dollars in untraceable notes. Although police believed they knew the identities of the Great Bookie Robbers, they were never brought to justice. As underworld figures, however, they all came to a grisly end.

—

After a lot of anguish Suzanne pulled her life back together after breaking up with the doctor. She went to live with her parents in Manly and worked as a dental nurse. To get her divorce, Suzy went to a Sydney lawyer, Roy Turner, who was surprised that I was so helpful to Suzanne and later told her he had never seen a more gentlemanly approach by a previous husband.

Suzy moved to an apartment in Vaucluse, and later she came back to the spare bedroom of our home. It seemed like a natural progression. Despite our split, Suzanne was always welcome at home and often came over to cook dinner. I suggested she change her name back to Waterhouse by deed poll. 'You are a Waterhouse,' I told her. I wanted her to still feel part of the family. I don't think Suzanne ever really stopped loving me – or me her – but she had found me difficult and cranky at times, particularly when I'd had a bad day at the races.

I had always enjoyed rude health and despite the early demise of my father and brother, I felt I had a lucky run and was invulnerable. I had a fatalistic attitude to my smoking and had developed into the archetypal chain-smoker. I smoked 80 to 100 cigarettes a day. One journalist wrote of me that 'he would probably make it more except that he's only got two hands and one pair of lungs'. Every time I was interviewed on television the cameras caught my addiction, and people in the media commented that while I was around, there was no need for cigarette advertising.

One day, after I had disciplined our great dane, Fury, with a rolled-up newspaper, I was feeling off-colour. Suzanne noticed me recovering on the bed and, knowing full well I wouldn't go to a doctor, came up with her own strategy. I was on friendly terms with Dr John McNamara and so Suzy invited him around for a drink that night, apparently after wising him up.

Since it was a social visit, John didn't make any comments about my health but still made a crack about my smoking. Making fun, he took my cigarette out of my fingers and stubbed it out in the ashtray. I lit up again and he stubbed that one out too. That happened a third time, and as I lit up a fourth he said, 'Too weak, Bill, to give it up, eh?'

He had got to me. I looked him in the eye, said nothing, took a few puffs and then deliberately put it out. That was the last cigarette I ever smoked. As luck would have it, I had just bought a gross of packets wholesale through the hotel.

22

The King and I

I KNEW A LITTLE of Tonga before I was summoned to the Friendly Isles.

His Majesty King Taufa'ahau Tupou IV had ascended the throne on the death of his mother, Queen Salote, in the mid-1960s. The kingdom has an unbroken bloodline in the royal family going back 1100 years to the Tui Tonga, who were believed to have come from God. It was the last kingdom in the Pacific.

Tonga is the only Pacific nation which has never been colonised or conquered. In the nineteenth century, with the unbridled lust of the major Western powers, the Pacific was about to be appropriated, annexed or swallowed up in the space of a few short years. The Maori people of New Zealand had been integrated, New Guinea was divided between Australia and Germany, Samoa had been split between Germany and the United States, France took New Caledonia and Tahiti, Fiji was taken by England and Hawaii went to the United States. Even the smallest islands lost their independence.

In 1845 King George Tupou I united Tonga and realised he had to secure Tonga's independence. He entered into a series of friendship treaties with various countries, including France in the 1850s and Germany in 1875, and a 'protected state' treaty with Britain in 1900. When World War I broke out, Tonga's treaty with imperial Germany was still in force.

These treaties meant Tonga was never a protectorate but rather a protected independent kingdom, so when the rest of the Pacific was looking to regain independence, Tonga had kept its autonomy all along.

King George Tupou I gave Tonga its own constitution, based on British law, and in this forward-thinking constitution he ensured that every Tongan male, when he reached the age of eighteen, would be entitled to a block of land of four hectares, on which he could grow his own crops, as well as a block of land in the village on which to build his own house. By enshrining these land entitlements in the constitution, the King made sure no Tongan would ever be homeless or starve.

However, for around 50 years after his reign Tonga went into a period of relative isolation. It was not until Queen Salote attended the coronation of Queen Elizabeth II in 1953 that she realised Tonga had allowed the world to pass by.

Watching the coverage of the coronation on movie newsreels not long after we were married, Suzy and I were amazed to see – in the middle of the royal procession – the statuesque Tongan Queen riding in her open carriage despite London's heavy rain. I will never forget how she sat so upright, smiling and waving at onlookers. Sitting beside her in the carriage, the diminutive Sultan of Kalimantan, from Indonesia, looked miserable and wet. By insisting on travelling in an open carriage to Westminster Abbey despite the rain, Queen Salote had won the hearts of all.

People often mention to me the famous impromptu wise-crack made by Noel Coward during his television commentary of the coronation. When his co-commentator asked who the gentleman sitting in the carriage beside Queen Salote was, Coward mischievously quipped, 'Her lunch!'

When Queen Salote returned to Tonga she aggressively set about transforming Tonga and remedying its isolation, but it was hard for much to be accomplished without a great deal of difficulty. Even the tourism boat had passed Tonga by – there was no commercial wharf, and the nearest South Pacific international airport was 700 kilometres north in Nadi, Fiji.

I found Tonga to be a natural paradise full of unspoilt beauty – no poverty, no crime, no lawlessness. Its people enjoyed life and showed love and respect for one another. Tongan society was still based around village life; the cry for 'black power' had never been needed since Tongans bore no resentment to Westerners.

Tonga actually wasn't the hospitable place Captain James Cook thought when he gave it the name 'the Friendly Islands' on his first visit in 1773. At the time the Tongan chief Finau was war-mongering and wanted to attack Cook's ship and kill him for the booty, but his fellow chiefs hadn't agreed on a plan of attack by the time Cook left.

Another ship, the British privateer *Port Au Prince*, wasn't so lucky. In 1807 it called in to the Ha'apai Islands of Tonga for supplies, but after welcoming the boat's captain and crew, King Finau attacked in the middle of the night, killing almost everyone on board. He wanted the guns on the ship to help him conquer all the Tongan islands.

Among the few survivors was the ship's cabin boy, William Mariner. He had been hiding under a table below deck. When the chief found this tall good-looking boy he spared him his life, believing Mariner could show him how to use his new guns. Finau was very taken by Mariner and he adopted him as one of his own princes, and made one of his many wives his 'mother'. Mariner learnt the Tongan language and lived on the islands of Ha'apai and Vava'u with his own princely estate for four years.

Mariner introduced the chief to Western values. The written word amazed Finau. He couldn't believe a word could be repeated from seeing it in the sand. He was unimpressed at the concept of money, which he considered would encourage greed and selfishness. In Tonga, produce from the soil or fish from the sea was always shared before it rotted. Mariner returned to England; his story became an international best-seller and was translated into several languages. People were hungry for information on the pre-Christian culture of the Pacific islands.

To make up for the lack of women at the new colony of Australia, in 1787 Lord Sydney included in Governor Phillip's orders that 'dusky beauties could be recruited from the Friendly Islands and this would be the happiest arrangement to keep the colony pure in deed' – but without 'compulsive measures' or 'false pretences'. Phillip soon realised that 'to send for women from the Tongan Islands, in our present situation, would answer no purpose than that of bringing them to pine away in misery'. Sydney Cove was not suitable for island girls, as had so optimistically been assumed in London!

Nowadays, there is prosperity in Tonga, although not financial wealth as we think of it. Tongans have an abundance of fresh food and a love of traditional family life. Almost anything can be grown in the volcanic soil. They have a good lifestyle, as has been recognised by the United Nations, which recently listed Tonga as 46th in its scale of human development, ahead of Fiji, Samoa and Cuba.

Tonga is one of the last unspoilt paradises of the Pacific. It has the same climate as Hawaii, and crystal-clear waters that abound with tropical fish and corals. It is a safe haven for whales, which mate and give birth to their calves amongst the glorious islands of Vava'u each winter.

—

His Majesty had wanted to see me because he had heard about some of my projects, including a Volkswagen car production line and campmobile concept for Fiji, which I had proposed when visiting VW in Wolfsburg, Germany. The Fijian government rejected the idea, and His Majesty was interested in it for Tonga. However, the kingdom was too small for VW.

His Majesty had maintained strong ties to Australia since attending Newington College and Sydney University. Now, in the 1970s, the King and I got on famously and he asked me if I would be his honorary consul-general in Australia.

My friendship with His Majesty flourished, and we would often sit together and talk about Tonga's future. Then we would turn to our shared passion for history and would go right through the Napoleonic battles on to the World Wars. I used to send him books I thought he might enjoy; after I sent him *Dreadnought: Britain, Germany, and the Coming of the Great War*, by the American historian Robert K. Massie, I received a lovely personal letter from His Majesty to say how much he had enjoyed the book – in fact he had read it three times.

We also shared a love of animals – on one occasion I brought him some geese. His Majesty preferred undomesticated animals, perhaps because they could one day be eaten if the need arose.

I would like to think the King regarded me as his closest personal friend outside the kingdom. Whenever I went to Tonga, he would give me a long audience and always made an effort to include me at the highest level. I usually sat at His Majesty's own table – an honour normally reserved for royalty.

As my position was totally honorary, I have never received payment or reimbursement for my expenses, but I have loved representing the Kingdom for over a third of a century. My daughter Louise helped me through the years, as did Suzanne, who was president of the Consular Women's Club, and also several Tongans living in Australia, including Tony Naufahu, Joe Helu and the Reverend Sione Pinomi. A journalist once asked me why a busy businessman like me would take on an honorary position that cost time and a staff-member's salary.

I told him, 'It's like asking how much it costs to run a boat. If you have to ask, you can't afford to do it.'

—

I spent a lot of time on Tongan matters and attended all the diplomatic events, hoping to interest other countries in helping Tonga. The social calendar was always full, as by this stage the consular corps in Sydney was on the way to becoming the largest in the world.

At one function I met the senior trade commissioner of the USSR, Dr R. 'Sergey' Tikhonov, however it turned out that he was believed to be the head of the KGB in Australia. He was very attentive to my ideas on how Russia could help Tonga.

His Majesty asked me to go to Iran on a new project; he was hoping to get help for Tonga from the Shah's government. It was surprising to see the bustle of Tehran: the wealth and the poverty, the affluence and the squalor. One of my hosts had a brand-new but old-fashioned custom-made Duesenberg car which had cost US$180,000. He was also wearing an ankle-length sable-fur coat. I was sitting in the lounge of the Tehran Hilton, sipping a cold beer, when I saw an attendant serving coffee from a large pot. I then watched him pick up a dirty cup and saucer, empty the coffee dregs into a bowl, wipe the cup 'clean' with his soiled tea towel and pour fresh coffee into the cup for another guest. I stayed with my bottle of beer.

I knew Ronnie Dabscheck from Australia; he had been a big punter and was now building a new racetrack in Tehran. Ronnie flew me up north by a private plane to where he was opening his new racetrack, not far from the Caspian Sea. We were picked up in new American limousines and taken in a twelve-car convoy through numerous mud-hut villages – it was as though we were from another planet. Iranians, who are against gambling, considered racing a leisure activity. Poker machines were also purely for entertainment. In one hotel owned by the Shah, I saw a row of three slot machines surrounded by wildly excited players who screamed loudly as each win was recorded. I said to my host, 'They're poker machines – how can you say you don't allow gambling?'

'No, Bill,' he replied, 'that's not gambling. The sign says, "These machines are for amusement only. No more than ten per cent of your stake will be returned."' I had no answer.

The Shah's political troubles were already starting and soldiers were everywhere, which put paid to the King of Tonga's proposal. After the fall of the Shah no country wanted him. I obtained permission from His Majesty to offer at least temporary sanctuary to the Shah, who still had immense wealth.

I had many ideas for Tonga and over the years I have found potential investors, including fisheries and sea mining experts and hoteliers. I also tried over the years to interest powerful individuals in Tonga, but one turned out to be a conman. John Meier was a former top aide to Howard Hughes in Las Vegas; he duped both me and His Majesty with his promises to help the kingdom by building an international airport. The King had acted in good faith at all times, and when it turned out Meier was wanted in the United States, His Majesty acted quickly to help the authorities.

I formed a warm friendship with His Royal Highness the Crown Prince Tupouto'a, who asked me to call him HRH. On his first visit to see me in Sydney, my mischievous sense of humour got the better of me. I prepared Suzanne for meeting him that evening by describing him as a large islander who would be wearing a lap-lap and have bare feet. I said, 'You will have to be careful as he may take hold of you and say, "Me want woman!"'

Of course, in reality the Prince was highly educated, having attended Oxford University and Sandhurst College in England. He was cultured and sophisticated, a linguist and an historian, with immaculate dress sense – he wore Saville Row suits and a monocle.

When Suzanne was presented to the charming Prince, he stretched out his hand and said in the most perfect English accent, 'How do you do?'

Suzanne was lost for words and didn't forgive me for leading her on, and then – worse still – for chortling over the incident with the Prince, who enjoyed learning about the gag as much as I did pulling it.

The Crown Prince had the last laugh another time. Having dinner with him at Sydney's elegant Abbey restaurant, I tried to be the gracious host by suggesting he choose the wine from the extensive wine list. He obliged – and it turned out to be a Château Latour from the cellar, as I found out when I got the bill.

'That's the last time I let you choose the wine, HRH!' I said.

The Prince often delighted in telling the story of my odd values. He would joke that I was prepared to win or lose $100,000 at the races, but baulked at a $200 bottle of wine.

23

Splintered Family

BACK IN AUSTRALIA in the mid-1970s, we were still on top as bookmakers. Jack, John and I were the leaders in our betting rings, a situation without precedence for one family. The family cohesion was not to last.

My own son Robbie, with all the exuberance of youth, was emerging fast and it was obvious that he would soon be betting as large as anyone. Anyone can bet big, but without the necessary ability they won't last – and Rob had more ability than anyone I'd ever met. Rob had always been fascinated by gambling, and once I realised he didn't want to be a lawyer or a stockbroker I never tried to change his mind. I gave him as good a backing for bookmaking as possible.

I sent Rob to bush meetings to work on local and 'away' events. I also sent him to the provincials, the trots, the provincial trots and the greyhounds. He went to most courses between Newcastle, Wollongong and Canberra – he went everywhere and did it well, becoming the leader of the ring at every one. Rob was never on an ego trip. He had come up through the ranks and was now earning his place in the Sydney ring. I didn't realise it then, but I think John felt threatened by Rob's success.

John and Jack owned two-thirds of our joint businesses. I didn't really mind as they were family. Also, Robbie was well on the way to a great career in bookmaking, and in time would no doubt be entitled to his share – which would bring it back to 50 per cent for each family. Perhaps in the back of John's mind was the fact that Louise and David were coming along as well.

The tension between John and me came to a head during the Easter Racing Carnival in Sydney in 1976. I was betting big and had a great win of over $750,000 on Easter Saturday. Then on Easter Monday I had a bad day, losing about $740,000, mainly to Malcolm Rich, who won almost $500,000. I took it in my stride, as Malcolm still owed me more than that from his past losses.

John blew up, claiming he couldn't stand the ups and downs of the business. One thing led to another and we decided to break our partnership from 30 June that year. Jack would go with John, and naturally Rob would stay with me.

It was the betting loss that had split us. Yet it was not effectively a loss, because I had been playing with my winnings from the Saturday. I suppose John feared I might lose heavily two or three days in a row, but he knew my style was letting people on to try to 'get out' if they wanted to. I would let them play with their money, rather than mine. There was no question of us getting into trouble. However, I wasn't going to argue, because if John didn't want to remain in the partnership, I wasn't about to force him.

It was a terrible wrench agreeing to break with Jack, as we had been partners all our lives. Little needed to be said, as I knew it wasn't him wanting to split. I just said, 'I understand. You have to go with John – he's your son.' Jack looked at me and said nothing. My brother and I would part three months later on the best of terms and without any enmity.

On our separation, Rob and I stayed in our offices on the Pacific Highway in North Sydney. Jack decided to work from home, while John based himself at Fabergé's offices. The split also meant dividing up our staff. I was surprised when my loyal secretary, Mary-Jane, decided to go with John and Jack, while

Keith Jones, who had often suffered under my bad moods after a losing day, elected to stay with Rob and me.

I knew that I'd miss Jack very badly, but I was pleased to have made the break with John. Jack had been the bond that kept us together, and I knew this was never going to be enough to keep our sons in partnership. Rob had brought in a whole new way of bookmaking, and I looked forward to our future together.

—

John had been placed in a position of trust with several of our properties. One of these was the St Charles Farm at Wallacia. Jack was worried about John being called up for national service; aware that you couldn't be conscripted if you were a farmer, Jack wanted to put the St Charles Farm into John's name. I didn't have a problem as I knew it was held on trust for us all.

When we bought Pemberton Park in 1966, the Vietnam War was in full action. Jack again became anxious about conscription, and he asked to put this larger farm into John's name too – so there could be no question he was a farmer. I understood Jack's concern and agreed John could hold it on trust.

Just as I had trusted Jack, I trusted John with my life. I had even said to Suzy, 'If I die, you do whatever John tells you – even if it doesn't sound right, it will be.'

How wrong I was. When we split the partnership, I realised that Jack, John and I needed to get a document signed between us to sort out our affairs. Because I'd had such complete trust in my partners I had never bothered to document these arrangements. Even our shares in Fabergé were all in John's name.

It was a nightmare. As they say, possession is nine-tenths of the law. John obfuscated and continually delayed things. He made it very difficult and it was really only through the tenacious efforts of Vince McMahon, who worked with the accountants, Hartigans, and the lawyers, Moore and Bevins, that we finally had a letter setting out the position. It was signed by all three of us on 30 December 1977.

To get John to sign, I had to make a number of serious concessions, including that he could have a one-third share of Pemberton Park – even though we had bought it well before he became our one-third partner. As well, John got to keep our building company and also our champion Charolais stud, which at the time was extremely valuable. I didn't want to fight because he was my brother's son – I felt I had to go along with what he wanted.

There was a hidden sting in the tail of our split. Jack, John and I had a joint overdraft account, limited to $100,000, with the Commonwealth Bank. The bank had required each of us to sign guarantees for the overdraft. The debt had been paid off within a year or so after our split, and naturally, while we all still banked with the Commonwealth, we assumed the guarantees we had signed had ended with the closing of the overdraft account. Not so! But that was a problem which came up later.

With Suzanne back in the home, our social life also came back on track. When Louise was about 21 and at university, Prince Charles visited Sydney. Suzanne and I were invited to the official reception at Government House but were delighted when Louise was invited too – as one of Sydney's eligible young ladies – to meet this most eligible bachelor. Louise had met Pierre Cardin, the designer, who was also touring Australia, and she wore one of his *haute couture* long white silk gowns and long white gloves. She looked so beautiful and I was a very proud father. Suzanne and I were having an enjoyable evening in the magnificent grounds under the stars, but we were thrilled to see the Prince suddenly twirling Louise around the dance floor, so we went and joined them for a waltz! However, the Prince's charm was lost on Louise when he tried to entertain her with some typical aristocratic toilet humour, and I realised that perhaps I had been too successful in shielding Louise from the rough lifestyle of the racetrack.

Louise was studying for her Bachelor of Commerce, majoring in marketing, at the University of New South Wales, and had a vision of going into Fabergé. She worked most holidays for the company and did a number of her studies on Fabergé products. Louise excelled in her degree and had been awarded the university's Lintas Prize as the top graduating commerce-marketing student.

As Louise had focused her career in this direction and had always got on well with John, I thought it would make sense for me to eventually hand over my one-third share in Fabergé to her. I was still a director and also a guarantor for Fabergé, and I proposed the idea to John but he wouldn't have a bar of it. I should have realised he had other ideas.

—

Following the split, my biggest mistake was taking my late brother Charlie's adult children more closely under my wing. Even though they were of a similar age, there had always been some tension between Charlie junior and John. Although Charlie's children weren't now involved in our new ventures, they still had a one-third interest in the assets we had built up prior to June 1964.

Over the years I had watched over them and they regularly came to me for help and guidance. I had found careers for them. I had helped Charlie junior to start bookmaking, and Billy, his youngest brother, to become a builder. Fatefully, I also encouraged the middle brother, Martin, to study law and become a barrister.

Martin had been a troubled young man and had caused us all no end of anxiety and concern. After his father's death, he'd resented his mother having boyfriends in their home, so Patty had sent him to live with his concerned grandfather, Chicka Schramm, in the Sydney suburb of Frenchs Forest. One day Chicka came to see me as he was very upset with incidents that made front-page newspaper headlines, but I engaged the very best legal counsel for Martin in Neville Wran QC and we had a good outcome.

As a special favour, Brother McCallum arranged for St Patrick's College at Goulburn to accept Martin because of our help and the funds we'd donated for his charity events over the years. Martin showed no gratitude. Although I often drove to Goulburn to visit him, he was always threatening to run away. At one point I said, 'If you run, keep running, because I'll be finished with you.'

After his difficult year in Goulburn, I was able to arrange for him to attend Trinity Grammar in Sydney. I supported him, telling him it was vital he finish his schooling because he wanted to study law. When he failed to get into law at university he was devastated. I advised him he could still get there by starting with another degree and transferring across after a year, which is what he eventually did. It always seemed to me, however, that Martin never appreciated anything I did for him.

When Charlie junior heard that Jack and I had gone our separate ways, he approached me about working out of our office. I happily agreed as I wanted to help Charlie and try to inspire him. Rob and I funded him back into bookmaking a couple of times after he hit bad runs, and we shared our know-how and form knowledge with him. We never saw any repayment – not that it mattered. We were happy to help.

At around the same time, Martin decided to give up being a barrister, even though I had called on favours around the traps from many of my legal friends. As Rob and I had a long debtor's list, I gave Martin an office and employed him as our debt collector. He was a resounding success, tenacious and ruthless. He would send the sheriff around once he had an order from the court, and he did not accept any excuses. Bringing Martin into my office was something I would come to regret bitterly.

—

In about 1974 Rob and David flew with me to Las Vegas to attend a function at the MGM Grand Hotel to honour Moe Dalitz. We were seated with Moe on the main table, along with the MC, Bob Hope, and Johnny Weismuller, of *Tarzan* fame, and other VIPs from Las Vegas and Hollywood. Tarzan entertained us all with his jungle calls, and Bob Hope was the life of the party. David had shot up to be a good-looking boy of over six-foot-six, and he told some young starlets we met at the casino that he was a talent scout. This did nothing to dent his appeal to the impressionable girls, and reminded me of my own baloney when I was a young bachelor, which had landed me in trouble with Gretel back in Davos twenty years earlier.

To train David in racing and bring him under my wing, I had him take out his clerk's licence to work for me at the races. He was my bagman on the first day he worked, and when I corrected him for something small after fifteen minutes, he just put my bag down and walked off. That was the end of his career as my clerk.

Trying another approach, I sent David to my wise old bookmaking friend Albert Smith in Melbourne, to learn racing down there. He stayed with another friend of mine, Jimmy Wallace. But instead of learning bookmaking, David was punting all the time, and I started to hear rumours that he had lost badly. It happens to many children of racing people – they see others winning and are overwhelmed by the opportunity. When he returned to Sydney, I sat him down and asked what he was doing, telling him I'd heard he was losing money and that I could help him. He denied it and I accepted his word. Sadly, the Melbourne incident led to David's decision to leave home. I was devastated and felt so sad.

Mark Read, a young up-and-coming bookmaker, rang me and said, 'You owe me about $17,000 from your son's betting. I only let him on because he's your son. You know you'll get terrible publicity from me if you don't pay his debt.'

This got my back up, because I knew Read's father-in-law was Jack Elliott, the prominent racing editor of the Melbourne *Herald*.

'So you say that because he's my flesh and blood, I'm responsible for his bets?' I asked.

'Absolutely. You've got to pay.'

'You've convinced me,' I replied. 'Now, your mother, Mable, still owes me $58,000. Will you please send me the $41,000 difference?'

Mark was lost for words and didn't appreciate the irony of his position. After a short silence he said unconvincingly, 'Her bets are nothing to do with me.'

As a matter of honour, I was prepared to pay those bookies who did not sue.

A funny thing happened when I took David to Tonga in about 1978. We were sitting in the Dateline Hotel lounge in Nuku'alofa. David was reading a book and I was sipping a cold beer. The people of Tonga are very natural and friendly. I was approached by an attractive young Tongan lady who blurted out, 'Waterhouse, sir, I love your son. He is so handsome!'

I was totally unprepared for this, but David continued reading without even looking up. I couldn't restrain myself. Looking the young lady in the eye and holding back a smile, I replied, 'You do? Very well – you may have him.'

David, unimpressed by my playful banter, closed his book, got up and calmly walked away without a word, leaving the puzzled young lady with me to work things out. Unfortunately, after just a few days in Tonga, David and I argued and, being headstrong, he left early on his own.

Even at the times when he wasn't talking to me, I was happy to guarantee David, as I did for his credit card and also with the Commonwealth Bank. I was also happy for David to live in a house we owned in Kirribilli through his troubled times.

Naturally, Robbie, Louise and Suzanne remained close to David, and I never stopped trying to help him behind the scenes. David regularly came to my office and I was happy for him to use it as a base. He was still part of the family and was best man at Robbie's wedding in 1980, so any tension was one-sided and not serious.

David got into trouble in 1983 for attempting to take $210,000 in cash out of the country instead of simply sending it through the bank. I was the one he called from the airport in his time of need, and it brought us back together. I gladly helped him by arranging legal representation at short notice over the weekend, and we all went with him to support him in court.

I was pleased to be on good terms with David again and hoped it would last.

24

The Betting Goes On

People have asked me, 'What are the odds, Bill?' all through my life. When Neville Wran was facing a cliffhanger state election in May 1976, he was regarded as the underdog. I was really rooting for my old friend and had faith that he could win.

Although the New South Wales election was on a knife edge, I told the journalists that I had him at odds-on – 4/6 – and I thought he was 'a shoe-in'. My odds headlined the front page of *The Daily Telegraph* on the morning of the election, suggesting the 'smart money' was on Wran. After being in opposition for ten years, it made them look like winners.

Neville was thrilled and said, 'Thanks for the support Bill, but I still don't think we will get over the line.'

The last time I had given my opinion to a newspaper about Neville was when I facetiously wrote in *Honi Soit*, the Sydney University student newspaper, that our culture-vulture Neville was 'the playboy of the group'. This time he became premier of New South Wales.

I was delighted for Neville and he came around for dinner that week. In my study he noticed my newly framed *exequatur* for my consular appointment, signed by none other than Sir John Kerr, who had controversially dismissed Neville's federal counterpart, Gough Whitlam, some months earlier.

Making light, I pulled myself up tall, poked out my chest and said, 'I am the consul-general for the Kingdom of Tonga!'

Neville smiled and said, 'And I am the premier of New South Wales!'

—

I once candidly told a writer, P. D. Jack, 'Racing is a really hard, tough business – tougher than any other . . . But there's more money in racing than in any other business. It's bigger than BHP, and that's why I'm involved in it.' Journalists described betting with me as a kind of bloodsport. I kept laying big bets as a new wave of punters emerged. Many of them preferred to take under the odds with me because they wanted a personal duel, but most bet with me because they knew they could get set for a large amount in one hit.

I remained a 'gambling' bookmaker rather than a 'figures' bookmaker. I was prepared to stand horses I didn't like, rather than cutting bets to spread my liability across all the runners. When I fancied a horse I kept its price slightly shorter than the price offered by rival bookies, although that didn't mean I didn't get caught. Even so, laying favourites under the odds for large amounts is good policy over a period, as even a small extra percentage on your board can translate into good profits.

Form assessment is of paramount importance to a gambling bookmaker – you pin your life on it. I set my markets and was prepared to live and die by them. One of my prices men at this time was John 'Darby' Munro, a professional punter and a friend; he was a natural form man who could walk onto any racecourse and frame a market in a few minutes. Derby was incredible in that he could add up pages of figures in pounds, shillings and pence in his head and give the correct amount immediately. He was invaluable to me over many years, although he would not accept any remuneration.

I used the form not to find winners but to find the prices. I knew that if I could get punters to take 3/1 on a horse that should have been 7/2, then I must beat them over time. It was all about value.

My survival depended on my skill in picking the tops and bottoms of price movements. In stockmarket terms, a good bookmaker is almost an instinctive chartist. He carefully watches the price resistance levels, such as when a price tightens from even money to 10/9 on. I knew that if I could ease the price back to even money, I would get a flood of bets.

Challenge, challenge, challenge – it was all a game and I loved it.

Bookmaker Terry Page was a great player of the man. He was single-minded about not letting professionals bet with him. His strategy was to blindly put up a duplicate of my markets. If I was 5/1 about a 20/1 shot, so was Terry. I guess this was the ultimate compliment.

As leader of the ring with an influence on prices, I had the opportunity to bring out the punters. This backfired on me one Wednesday at a lacklustre meeting at Canterbury Park.

Normally, if betting appears stifled, some bookmakers will often extend the price of a horse to see if there's any reaction from punters. If there is, they will purposefully shorten the horse, hoping the general public will see this as a betting lead. However, I would sometimes quickly short-circuit this by cutting a horse's odds as though it had been substantially backed, and most other bookmakers would then automatically drop their prices, giving the impression of a plunge.

If there was a commission to be placed on the horse, this tactic would flush it out quickly as the punter would be frightened that the price would collapse, especially for horses that are 'smokeys'. This strategy can also be used for a favourite that looks a good thing. The favourite's price is the most important price on the board because it affects the price of every other runner.

On this day at Canterbury Park, when one of my punters who was a favourites-backer was $250,000 in front, I dropped the price of the favourite a fraction. There certainly was a reaction from my punter, but it wasn't what I expected. Ross King, Terry Page's groundsman, called out that I'd laid the favourite and had turned it off. This caused my punter to spear into Terry Page and have $100,000 on it with him, not me. The horse was beaten into second place in a photo-finish.

The punter started to chase his losses – the dreaded disease of all punters. He finished up wiping out his winnings through his bets with Terry and me that day. He had trouble settling but I cut the cards and accepted some diamonds – no doubt they were overvalued, but I was happy to get anything. Taking goods in lieu was, unfortunately, commonplace, and over the years I have accommodated cash-strapped clients by accepting property, jewellery and even a new lounge suite for our TV room.

Malcom Rich remained one of the biggest punters through-out the 1970s. His family owned the Beberfalds department store opposite the Town Hall. However, he was a slow payer and Keith Jones was regularly at his home trying to get paid, as Malcolm strung us out as long as he could.

Although we had stopped the labour-intensive doubles mailout business in the early 1970s, our doubles betting continued at the track, and as a bookie you could still get yourself into trouble. I'd put Rob in charge of our doubles. Arthur Browning was running a price war with us and was in the habit of extending his prices to beat ours. Rob enthusiastically decided he could stop that. In a novel approach, he doubled the prices of the first leg, and halved those for the second leg of the double. The end payout was the same for us. Arthur's man followed suit but only in the first leg: he bettered the prices there but didn't lower the price in the second leg. This, in effect, doubled all his potential payouts with dire consequences. Malcolm Rich charged in and took a bet and cleaned up $100,000 when it won. Poor Arthur jumped on his hat once again.

Sir Tristan Antico, the corporate giant, loved his punting but developed a reputation for disputing his settling, so we all had to be careful that our records were always well kept. We knew when his letters of dispute arrived because they were written with a green typewriter ribbon.

My punters included Joe Gazal, the textile supremo, who led the way in importing cheaply made garments from Asia, and Kevin McIntyre, who loved to bet everywhere on everything – he was a true professional who had an amazing memory. Others were Graham Pash (later chairman of the Sydney Turf Club), Nick Columb and Kingsley Shaw, who still today comes to our office to get the form. And of course Kerry Packer.

Sir Robert Sangster blew in and blew out of Australia, punting with me on his visits. Sangster helped put Australian breeding on the map by bringing great broodmares and stallions to Australia.

'Hollywood' George Edser came back to the track in the mid-1970s after a prolonged absence at the pleasure of the AJC committee. He was fair dinkum and, in my view, one of the most colourful characters ever on a Sydney racetrack. He was once quoted saying, 'Money means nothing to me on a racecourse. I forget I have family. If I have money I bet until every penny has gone.' George joked about finally making it into the Randwick members' enclosure in 1983, when 'I walked on a bottle and broke my ankle in three places. They carried me through the members on a stretcher.'

Ray Hopkins continued as one of the best punters to last the distance. No matter where he went in Australia or overseas, he had a knack of finding a winner – even without closely studying the form.

Don Longley was one punter who wanted respect and

recognition above all. At times he could bet as big as anybody, but then he'd run out of funds and disappear from the scene. Anyone can win a bundle betting but few can keep it, but Don always came back – the hallmark of a true gambler. Building up a bank from nothing simply by applying skill and judgement will always get respect – especially if you can do it again and again. Don had this knack.

He revelled in the life of being accepted by the top bookies, who were his gods. Funnily, in his normal life Don never got the respect he deserved because he looked like a loser. Invariably he was in old, well-worn clothes and hardly appeared the successful dashing gambler, yet when he had cash he could give anyone the hiccups.

Leon Fink, whose family owned the Southern Cross and other hotels, probably had the best nerve of the lot. He was a successful businessman and entrepreneur; his hobby was the punt, and while he may not have won at it, he certainly survived.

Mentioning Leon reminds me of a funny incident in London in the mid-1970s. I was munching a small chicken pie at the counter in the lower restaurant at Fortnum & Mason when a young woman sat beside me and began talking to me when she noticed my Australian accent. I immediately recognised her as the feminist Germaine Greer, author of the bestseller *The Female Eunuch*. She was then at the height of her fame. I knew she didn't know me and I couldn't resist pulling her leg. I asked what she did.

'I'm a writer,' she replied.

'What paper do you write for?' I asked.

'I don't work for any paper.'

'Oh, that's bad luck,' I said. 'No matter, you keep going and you'll eventually land a job. Just don't give up.'

'I'm doing very well as it is, thank you – last year I earned £400,000.'

'Yes, yes – but don't give up.'

She looked at me as though I was nuts, and eventually asked what I did. When I said I went to the races she asked if I knew Leon Fink, and with that we had found common ground. Germaine spoke fondly of Leon. Later I learned that she had written of how she'd lost her virginity in the back seat of Leon's white Jaguar.

A year later Leon turned up at my stand at Randwick with Germaine Greer. She gave me a wry smile as an unspoken reminder of our lunch at Fortnum & Mason.

—

When he was only twenty years old, Rob ran my stand at the trots. I hadn't been able to make a go of it but somehow with his fresh approach he was consistently able to win. The day he turned 21 he applied for his own licence and got his own stand in the Leger, before being promoted to the Paddock.

Rob, like me when I was young, was the only one who worked on all three codes – gallops, trots and dogs. He found himself working six days and nights a week – his record was thirteen meetings in one week. By 1980 he was the top gambler at the provincial tracks, where he built up the surprising annual turnover of $25 million. At the time he was quoted in *The Sunday Telegraph*: 'Bookmaking is my whole life. It's more a way of life than a business to me.'

Losing your shirt by heavily laying a winning horse can still be a great result. This was the case with Rangi Bill, a trotter on which Robbie had repeatedly won when 'standing it'. One night at Harold Park, after Rob laid Rangi Bill one more time, it got up and won – the payout line was so huge that Rob and I were almost the last people to leave the track. We'd heard some loud bangs from the street, but hadn't paid much attention. As we walked to our car we saw a crowd around it, including some policemen. We'd been in the habit of giving $10 to a knockabout to 'look after' the car. On this evening he had more than earned it, spoiling the plans of some would-be robbers who were intending to hold us at gunpoint. When our man challenged the bandits they fired shots at him and escaped. Thanks to Rangi Bill, we had been saved from a dangerous hold-up. This time, the heavily backed winner was also a great result for the bookie.

In 1980 Rob was promoted to the local Sydney Rails with me; in effect, we became competitors. Our styles were very different. Often after the races, although I also used Rob's form, we would find that Rob had won and I had lost, or vice versa. He was one of the first 'opinion' bookmakers. He didn't play the man as much as I did, but rather relied on his expert assessment of form. He became skilful at reading markets during betting, seeing the betting trends and capitalising on them.

Rob and I would work in the same office, listen to the same people, talk together, work on the same markets and go to the racetrack together – yet often we would make exactly the reverse book to each other. Whereas I was content to stand the favourites, Rob developed his own style, laying more runners and standing the ones he didn't like. It wasn't long before Rob was holding more money than me. By the age of 25, Rob had astounded me with his success. He coped very well with the new breed of 'informed' punting syndicates, since he had his own edge.

The latter part of the 1970s were marked by a number of successful betting syndicates. With the advent of the first computers, people could computerise form data. Jim Mason had a large team doing this, among them John McSweeny, Kevin Young and Dave 'the Dasher' Segenfield. Michael McHugh had formed a new 'Legal Eagles' syndicate with Clive Evatt, Lindsay Turnbull and Peter Wake, and they were formidable. Bob Charley and Ken Langbien both operated on their own.

Dominic Beirne, whose father was a well-known and skilful bookmaker, started out as a clerk for Terry Page, and when Terry retired, Dominic – aided by Terry's clients and his own skills – quickly built up a strong bookmaking business. Although he was only a bookie for eight years, at his peak Dominic was a top holder in the Sydney ring. He also bet each-way, which did not appeal to Rob and me as it was a 'loss leader'. Dominic was one of the biggest punters at the races and his form was excellent.

His brother Greg was ahead of his time. He first bet on the exotics (quinellas and trifectas), then he owned his own tote, but eventually he turned his skills to the stockmarket and he was lost to racing.

Bookmaker Mark Read was also proving to be a large punter and was behind a number of successful carefully planned betting coups, which, although they were not illegal, would cause havoc in the bookies' ring in the years to come.

—

Still wanting to expand internationally after ten years operating our bookmaking franchise in Fiji, I started one in Papua New Guinea following its independence in 1975. The new government under Prime Minister Michael Somare wanted to legalise bookmaking operations in PNG, which was then regarded as the last wilderness. My name was mentioned in parliament as an expert in betting, and I was approached to open betting shops in partnership with a local, Agnes Taureka.

I had a big reputation in PNG, which was further enhanced when a young Australian judge there, Warwick Andrew, asked me for a tip for the 1980 Melbourne Cup. He told me Michael Somare wanted some 'inside knowledge'. I tipped him Robert Sangster's horse, Beldale Ball, at 15/1. Warwick passed this to Somare as a 'dead-set certainty', and Somare put $5000 on the nose, as did his secretary, who borrowed the money for her bet after she had taken the message. That was probably as much as she earned in a year. As luck would have it, Beldale Ball won and they both cleaned up $75,000 – an absolute fortune. Later, when Warwick was made a CBE for his services to Papua New Guinea, he couldn't help feeling Somare might have been particularly well disposed towards him because of his tip!

Our first shop began with a small turnover of about 15,000 kina a week – not a big deal and not really worth worrying about, but causing no harm. I sent a school friend of Robbie's, Teddy Speirs, up to run the business in Boroko, a suburb of Port Moresby. It operated on Saturdays and Wednesdays. Teddy would phone down to get our prices, and he knew enough about bookmaking not to make any stupid mistakes.

After about six months I had a free racing Wednesday and flew up to Port Moresby to see the operation for a few days. Teddy wasn't planning to run a book on the Wednesday as it was just a small provincial meeting at Wyong outside Sydney. I told him to open the shop anyway, and even I was impressed at the result. The shop was busy with expats from Australia.

However, I was surprised that no locals were betting. I was told that if the locals were allowed into the shop to bet, we'd lose our expats' business, because they wouldn't mix with the nationals.

'If we think like that,' I said, 'we should leave the country and forget about Papua New Guinea. Let the locals bet.'

The response was even greater than I could imagine. It was amazing. The locals loved it and the shop was jam-packed. The business really prospered under a new manager and junior partner, Luke Messer, a young distant relative of mine who had already worked for me as a clerk. We opened betting shops around the country, operating six days a week, and the turnover shot up to around 50,000 kina per week at each shop.

New Guinea crystallised my thinking. I had always believed Australians led the world in horse betting, and that was true, but it was not because they were Australian. Rather, it was because the Australian facilities for betting allowed or encouraged it. People often ask me why bookies have been so big in Australia. I am sure it's because Australia was the first country to make rules for bookmakers and supervise them, which was done because of the trouble the authorities had early on. Australian bookmakers flourished under the regulations and became an essential part of racing.

The bookmaker excites the public, taking only a small margin of just a few per cent from the pool of money, and this gives the punter a fair chance. In Papua New Guinea I realised that people in the developing world were no different to us – they shared the same pleasures. Contrary to what the 'holy Joes' were preaching, this was not crazy addictive gambling but an easy relaxed search for a winner with a small outlay – inexpensive entertainment. Luke Messer was the ideal man for the job. He worked hard, followed my instructions to the letter and was honest.

There were some problems, however. One shop in Rabaul went bust under a sub-manager. In a robbery one evening, so-called 'rascals' broke in and tied up the sub-manager and his wife, escaping with a fairly large sum of money. Luckily they were not hurt. But unbeknown to the sub-manager, the rascals had moved the clock in the betting office back by a few minutes. It was a remote area that didn't have a race broadcast, so the next day – with a time break – the rascals knew the results 'ahead' of the race time and used the stolen money to back the winners, cleaning out our funds. Harry Solomons of the 'phantom broadcast' from the 1940s would have been proud!

Typically, the government did not understand the business of betting and treated it as an easy source of revenue. Taxation rates mushroomed and, as a result, our business was decimated. My top right-hand man, Luke Messer, lost interest and came back to Sydney.

25

Bad Payers – and Bad Eggs

WHEN I WAS in Johannesburg one time, the leading bookmaker there expressed some interesting views on punters. He'd read about my betting saga with Frank Duval and wanted to talk about it.

His view was that big bettors were a menace to the game, as they didn't pay when they got into trouble. Like the straw that broke the camel's back, after they had lost or passed a certain point which would 'embarrass their resources', they usually welshed on the whole debt.

I had to agree that, in many cases, he was right, but that is one of the natural hazards for any big gambler. In general, however, his attitude was too simplistic. It is an accepted fact of life in bookmaking that some big punters can't settle at times, but they still might bet with cash and not on credit. Indeed, sometimes they may still be afforded credit by other bookmakers, even by the bookmaker to whom they owe money. It all depends on who the punter is and their circumstances.

I recall talking to Sir Eugene Gorman once about large bets I had laid to a big punter; I was concerned whether or not he would settle if he lost.

Sir Eugene exploded at me: 'It has always bewildered me why people like you give credit to those whom you know have taken the knock before, and will do so again when it suits them!'

In some ways he was right in this appraisal, but he was also wrong.

Bookies do still do business with defaulting punters, and Gorman conceded that all the big bookies had done the same thing over the years. He had been friends with Sol Green, an old-time leader of the Victorian betting ring who had achieved an annual turnover of £1 million. Sir Eugene wanted Green to post slow-paying punters at the Victoria Racing Club so they would be publicly outed and no longer able to go to the races. Sol would have nothing of it.

No one likes to lose at the best of times, and they certainly don't like to have their noses rubbed in the ground when they do. Sol wasn't the only bookie who wanted to preserve his customers' privacy. Big-betting bookies such as Bob Jansen, Wallace Mitchell and Albert Smith carried a coterie of slow payers, or alternatively gave them fresh lines of credit. It was not uncommon for some punters to be on their second or even third credit account.

To me the answer on slow payers is quite simple. A bookmaker has to pay his debts, and wants to be paid in return, but unlike a punter, he has to stand up and work on every race at every meeting. A punter can go and have a beer and miss as many races or as many meetings as he wants. To keep working, a bookmaker must have clients. You may say that a client who is a non-payer is no client at all – but the point is that eventually they *do* pay, even if slowly or only sometimes.

It's a bigger worry if they win too much when they are on a second account – punters have to understand that the larger portion of their new winnings will be applied to their old debt.

—

The perils of accepting bets from a client who wasn't paying took on new meaning for me when I encountered the adult son of a recently deceased leading businessman. Like most big punters before him, he sought recognition but did not want publicity. He wanted to see the force of his betting cause the prices of his horses to shorten in the market.

This was rather like the Marquis of Hastings, who last century probably lost more money in today's value than any man before or after him by backing any horse he fancied into favouritism. This isn't a great idea unless you are a great judge.

My punter wasn't a regular racegoer, preferring to direct his attention to illegal SP bookies. One day at Randwick he bet with both Jack and me and had a bad day. On the Monday when he settled, he asked if I had a phone number he could use the next Saturday to have a chance to get square.

The year was 1976. I was 54 years of age and a big boy. Jack and I, along with John, were still partners and we'd given up our city SP offices way back around 1964. And we'd kept out of it since then, except for Felipe Ysmael and Peter Huxley – both disasters. I well knew it was virtually impossible for an SP bookmaker to beat a wealthy client one-out because you can't balance your book. Further, the off-track bookie has no legal protection as wagers are unenforceable in a court of law. But this punter was wealthy, powerful and not one you would expect to 'take the knock'.

So against my better judgement I agreed. When I look back at some of the stupid things I've done in my life, this is right up there. Here I was again breaking every rule I'd laid down. The reason I agreed, though, was simple – his wealth meant that all worries of payment were conveniently pushed to the back of my mind.

I didn't want him to bet big and he agreed that he wouldn't, as he only wanted a chance to win his money back. My main concern was to encourage him back to bet with us at the track, where Jack and I had all his business. I had no clerk to leave on a phone for him, so I asked my trustworthy secretary Mary-Jane and another to stay behind and accept his bets.

On the Saturday the punter tried the martingale. He bet in thousands in three states – in Sydney, Melbourne and Brisbane – starting off small and gradually increasing his betting. He only backed one winner, having $25,000 on Arctic Flash at 11/4, and one other place bet – $10,000 each way on Rathdowney at 8/1. From an outlay of $1,131,000 he had a return of only $123,750, giving him a loss of $1,007,250 on the day!

The punter was Kerry Packer, and I've still got the sheet of his betting that Mary-Jane wrote that day.

I was simply flabbergasted at the size of our win. I'd thought I might win or lose $100,000 or so. Although pleased to have won so much, I was furious at what Kerry had done. He knew I'd left two inexperienced people to handle his business and he'd taken advantage of them. The fact that he had lost did not excuse his conduct. Also, the amount lost was so enormous that my bookie's instinct told me I could have difficulty in being paid.

I phoned Kerry on the Monday. He was sore at himself for losing so badly but acknowledged the bets and the amount owed. He asked for a short time to settle as he was in a temporary bind, and he said he was finished with betting. As you would expect, a short time became a long time.

I tried hard to find a way out of the impasse, suggesting we settle for an asset he could nominate, but he wanted nothing of it. He said he couldn't give us a post-dated cheque for a multitude of reasons, and he could not acknowledge the debt publicly. If it came out, it would wreck his reputation and his standing as the new head of the Packer media empire – at the time he was buying control from his brother, Clyde.

It was a ticklish situation for us. The bets were unenforceable at law. Worse, if the AJC became aware of how the bets were laid, Jack, John and I were liable to have our licences cancelled. We could do nothing but sit it out.

It would have been better to call Kerry and say, 'Let's forget all that nonsense and start again,' so we could still have him as a client, but I could never bring myself to do that.

The tragedy was that despite all our best efforts, not only did we not get paid, but we also lost Kerry's business. When I look back, I realise Kerry could have won a million bucks from us that day and we would have paid him. Instead, he lost a little over that and didn't pay us a penny. I suppose you could say we were lucky he didn't win.

The years slipped by and Kerry had not only taken control of the family empire but had significantly grown it with his successful World Series Cricket and other ventures. One night in 1980 I saw him at the trots, where Rob was working. Although I wanted nothing to do with him, Rob wanted Kerry to bet with him as he was now Australia's biggest punter. He was an imposing person, always well-dressed – often in a black mohair suit – and would arrive in a chauffeur-driven limousine. I knew Kerry was embarrassed about the debt, but I also knew that unless I did something he would continue to ignore it.

I decided to broach the subject with him. 'Robbie's working out here tonight if you'd like to have a bet,' I said. 'I know we have an outstanding amount between us at the moment but this may help you reduce it.'

'What are you thinking of?'

'Well, I don't want you to bet big – Robbie's young, and this is the trots, after all. But if you're agreeable, you can bet from a second account, which you will need to pay each week if you lose. You can still collect if you win, unless they are big wins – in that case some will be deducted from our outstanding debt.'

Kerry agreed, saying he only wanted to bet small at the trots. The first evening he won about $20,000 and was promptly paid. We knew he was following punter George Freeman's tips. The next week at the Inter Dominion final, he broke his promise and took $100,000 to $10,000 each way about the winner, Koala King at 10/1.

Keith Jones, my faithful settling clerk, phoned Kerry on the next Monday, expecting him to agree to an adjustment to credit part of the $125,000 owing to his old debt. Keith came to me shattered and red-faced. 'Kerry wants the lot and won't deduct anything,' he said.

I phoned Kerry and held myself in check, merely asking how much could I take off his outstanding debt. He was indignant. Of course his previous account would be settled in due course but, he claimed, the trots betting was nothing to do with that. He demanded payment of the $125,000 forthwith. I talked without losing my temper, as I had everything to lose and nothing to gain, but there was no way I was going to pay him anything like $125,000 when he hadn't had the decency to pay off a brass nickel of his massive debt.

Eventually Kerry could see that the position wasn't going to change and, very coldly and deliberately, he said, 'Anyhow, you've been talking to people about our debt. You can go and get fucked and whistle for it. You'll get nothing from me.' With that he slammed down the phone.

In fact, I had not spoken to anyone other than my business partners about Kerry's debt, but it would have been an exercise in futility to phone him back and tell him so. He was only looking for an excuse to 'brass' me and welsh on the bet. I never spoke to him again.

Kerry's settling man never asked us for the money, but we had now well and truly lost him as a client forever. Kerry avoided me at the races by skirting around the fringes of the betting ring. Later, Kerry's betting in millions with other bookmakers, such as Bruce McHugh, would make headlines.

Kerry was a larger-than-life character who will go down as one of the great Aussie larrikins. I could never forgive him for not honouring his betting with us – even if he might have been short at the time, it was not long before he became a billionaire and was spending crazily, tipping lavishly and betting everywhere. Kerry became Australia's richest man but he still owed us more than a million dollars.

I had to acknowledge that through my poor judgement we had allowed ourselves to face untold risk for no real gain, and had allowed a punter to take advantage of the situation. Kerry was my biggest ever defaulter, but the most galling thing was that I had lost him as a future marvellous punter.

—

Reg Kennedy was the biggest bookmaker operating in the provincial areas of Victoria, and I knew him during my ten years in Melbourne. I was once caught in a double-play that had very bad repercussions for Reg.

New punters are always coming into the racing game – often out of nowhere – and then disappearing just as mysteriously. I was approached by a man just down from Brisbane. He wanted to bet over the Sydney Spring Carnival before going south for the Melbourne Cup Carnival – perfectly logical and understandable. He didn't want credit and would put in cash to cover his betting. He wanted to settle after each day if he won, with losses deducted from his bank if he lost. He gave me $100,000 in Treasury bearer bonds. These are like bank notes but can be carried in large denominations, so they are not bulky.

My new punter was called Wal Smith and looked more like a country bumpkin than a punter. I was proved wrong as he won consistently over the carnival. He had borrowed some money, about $15,000 against the bonds and I had paid his net winnings of $14,500. He won over the next meetings and I paid him a further $42,000 and then $65,000. He said he was heading down to the Melbourne Carnival, leaving the bonds with me and to collect on his return. I didn't think anything of it as it was common for punters to use bookmakers as their 'bank'. Wal returned quicker than that. He came to the races in Sydney despondent and said he had lost all his winnings at Caulfield. Having run out of ready cash, he had to return because he had left his bonds there with me. He started to bet.

As is always the case when your luck is out, he couldn't find a winner. At the end of the day he said he'd had enough and was going back to Brisbane to lick his wounds. He lost $75,000. He asked if he could collect the balance of his bank on Monday morning. On this one day he had whittled his money down to about $20,000, which I paid him by cheque. He asked for it to be 'opened' (made negotiable) and immediately went to the Commonwealth Bank and had it cashed. With this money paid, plus his previous winnings, he was well in front of me. I handed over the bonds to my bank to be cashed.

A few days later I was working at Randwick when I received a message to wait after the last race as some detectives wanted to see me. After the last race, two senior detectives arrived and we went to a quiet section of the ring to talk.

'How did you go today, Bill?'

'No good at all. I lost.'

'Well, it's worse than you think. You have lost an extra $100,000.'

'What do you mean?'

'That $100,000 in bonds that you banked were stolen property and will have to be returned to the rightful owner.'

There is nothing like news like this on a losing day to cheer you up. I had no way of tracking down the punter, as all I knew was his assumed 'name'. Naturally, I opposed the return of the bonds, which it turned out had been stolen from Reg Kennedy's home. Being bonds, they were identifiable by their serial numbers.

I believe bookmakers should stand firm with their debtors

on amounts they are owed. It is essential to be firm but also reasonable – assessing each situation on its merits. Therefore, soon after the matter surfaced, I spoke with Reg on the phone to suggest a compromise, as only one of us could win and it would save the costly expense of litigation. Unfortunately, Reg was bombastically and aggressively wanting an independent verdict from the court. It is so easy to be wise after the event, but Reg didn't handle himself to his best advantage.

I engaged Andrew Rodgers QC to represent me, and the case was heard by Justice Kearney, who was later to sit on our long-running family equity matter. It was decided in my favour: I had taken the bonds not knowing they were stolen and so I didn't have to refund the money. Reg lost in every way. Sitting in the court and taking note of the proceedings were officers from the taxation department. Reg had given evidence of having the bonds in another name to be 'discreet' and so, as he had not declared the bonds, he now had to face the department's wrath. The subsequent penalties inflicted on him broke him as a big bookie. He later told me he was flat-out earning a living and paying off the tax debt.

He surely must have known of the peril he faced in regard to the undeclared bonds, but he chose to ignore it and picked up the tab for his emotional decision-making.

It was a bittersweet victory. I received no pleasure from his predicament and felt sorry for him. Although I won an order for $8000 in costs, I didn't pursue Reg as I felt he had been through enough.

—

Bob Trimbole was also a client of mine in the early 1970s. He also bet later with Robbie. Although he always paid his debts as soon as they were due, I felt there was something not quite right with him and I could never work him out.

He was a big gambler, and big gamblers are not usually mugs. He either had ability or was getting good information, because he often won. He usually had bets of $20,000 but eventually he moved his betting to another bookmaker, who I knew was closely associated with George Freeman. I then suspected Trimbole could be working in conjunction with Freeman.

Trimbole became one of the faces of the darker side of racing in the late 1970s. Previously we all knew there would occasionally be skulduggery; for instance, trainers would often give their first-up performers an easy run. Now corruption was organised and endemic in racing.

Trimbole was described as a 'marijuana salesman' by Bill Fisher QC in the New South Wales Royal Commission into Drugs in mid-1978. Mr Fisher referred to 'examples of timely race wins' and how Trimbole had frequently taken his winnings by cheque from bookmakers such as Terry Page and myself, along with my brother Jack, Bruce McHugh and Arthur Browning, and also from numerous TABs and the tote.

Racing was rocked by the sensational revelations in *The Age* newspaper of police phone taps, where we all learnt Trimbole was race-fixing to launder his drug profits. He had an extraordinary number of jockeys and trainers – and also police – on his payroll. These tapes also revealed Trimbole's other criminal activities, including marijuana and heroin trafficking. It turned out he was closely linked with Terry Clarke, the international heroin dealer who headed the Mr Asia drug syndicate.

Before police could act, Trimbole hurriedly fled Australia in 1981 after being tipped off that he was about to be arrested for the 1977 murder of Griffith anti-drugs campaigner Donald Mackay. This tip-off was also recorded on the phone taps. Trimbole died in Spain in 1985 while still on the run.

—

The 1970s also saw a more sinister and all-powerful influence come into racing.

Rob was eighteen and running my stand one Saturday at Rosehill. He became aware of a new punter, Joe Hourigan, who had been betting with Terry Page. Observing him, Rob noticed he was well dressed in a fawn cashmere overcoat and was always standing with another man with a shock of white hair who was wearing a navy cashmere overcoat.

Rob offered Hourigan credit and he began betting with Rob and me every week and was up and down like a yo-yo. And either we or the punter seemed to be always paying the other $100,000. It turned out the man always standing beside Hourigan and calling the shots was George Freeman.

The word around the track was that Freeman would always pay his gambling debts to show how honourable he was – even if he had to rob a bank to get the money. However, one week he asked for a week or so to pay us the $80,000 he owed. We were quite relieved, as it meant he wouldn't be betting for that time. Six weeks went by, so I rang him and asked him how he was going.

Freeman was cocky and said, 'I could have paid you any time, but Terry Page owes me $80,000 so I've let him owe it to you.'

I realised then that Freeman was a strange man with a strange set of values. He was hard to beat and won often. It would turn out that he was pulling horses and fixing races. It got pretty serious.

Freeman came into betting on the horses through Melbourne Mick Bartley, after Mick had been robbed at gunpoint in his SP business. Joe Taylor had recommended that Mick hire Freeman as a gun-toting bodyguard and assistant. With that, Freeman saw the money that Mick was making in racing through his mathematical ability and organisational skills, and he became heavily involved with illegal betting.

Freeman was also a standover man who ran protection rackets. Having started out as a petty criminal, Freeman was eventually regarded as one of three or four main crime figures in New South Wales. Allegedly, he had friends in the highest places – on race committees, in the police force and in government.

Kevin Perkins got hold of a photo of Freeman sitting in the Randwick grandstand with the chief magistrate of New South Wales, Murray Farquhar, and Dr Nick Paltos and published it in *The Sunday Telegraph*, which caused a public outcry.

I could smell that George Freeman was a menace to racing. He bribed contacts with cash gifts and tipped winners to those of influence. He built up an influential support network around him.

Freeman became Sydney's biggest SP operator – in partnership with a registered bookmaker. He was also probably the largest SP punter at the time. He owned and raced horses under other peoples' names and was connected with casino ownership. Freeman changed everything. He ruined the Sydney trots and then moved on to the gallops, where he was also rigging races, corrupting jockeys and manipulating prices.

Due to Freeman's corruption, the 'computer' syndicates which had flourished in the late 1970s, could no longer survive. Freeman made a mockery of their form analysis.

Freeman wanted an on-track bookmaker to help him push out the prices for his SP betting coups. He linked up with another bookie but hated me because I wouldn't play his game. I could sense the corrupting influence of his operation. Both Robbie and I made him take short prices. When Freeman was fixing races and trying to land SP coups, I usually suspected what he was doing and cut the artificially elevated prices at the track. This cost him a lot of money, which was spoiling his game.

Really, I just wanted to keep my distance.

In my experience, Freeman was ruthless. He was out to win at all costs and had no concern for what damage he did to you or the racing industry. In fact, I would say he was merciless. Freeman rang me one day at home and we had a heated discussion. Suzanne overheard me shouting crudely, 'As long as my arse points to the ground, I don't want anything to do with you!' And I hung up.

In a veiled reference to Freeman, I told journalist Colin Mackay of *The Sunday Telegraph* in 1980: 'I don't want to be part of any cartels or deals. There is a lot of corruption in the racing game . . . human nature dictates that there will always be the smarties around who try to beat the system with illegal methods. My job is to see they don't beat me.'

One day Robbie ruined Freeman's SP 'go' on a horse called Pure Magic by collapsing the price under the weight of his off-course betting. Freeman was furious and later rang Rob at the office and threatened him: 'You will be lying in the gutter looking up at the stars but your eyes will see nothing . . .'

Kevin Perkins told me at around this time that he had been tipped off by an underworld contact that I was being targeted in a criminal plot. He said Freeman was behind it. I bought cartridges for my licensed .38 Smith & Wesson, and Rob, also licensed, armed himself too. I never did find out how close they came to carrying out their threat.

Freeman and others had a ripple effect in the late 1970s. Many professional punters complained about losing 'for the first time', with the doping of horses ruining their markets. But professional punter's days of getting 8/1 on a 5/2 chance week after week were gone. From about 1976, professionals bemoaned that it was nearly a miracle if you got 4/1 for a 5/2 chance.

Matters were made worse for professionals with the publication of Don Scott's books, which gave rise to a new generation of punters who concentrated on value and were able to frame fairly reliable markets. Computers and, later, the internet also led to ratings services, which made reasonably dependable prices available to a host of on-course and off-course punters. 'Mug money' began to disappear from the track. These changes heralded the end of the golden era of punting and bookmaking.

—

One Saturday morning in early February 1979, we were working away at our North Sydney office preparing for the races and phoning our prices to our betting shops in Papua New Guinea and Fiji. Suddenly the police turned up and raided us. They arrested and fingerprinted me, Rob and a licensed clerk – as though we were carrying out some criminal operation.

We were angry, flabbergasted and disbelieving. I sensed at once that some person against us was responsible and we'd been set up. We were charged under a long-forgotten and obsolete part of the Gaming and Betting Act dealing with licensed betting shops that not even the lawyers knew about. Yet as minor as the charge was, it could have led to the loss of my bookmaker's licence. I was fined $100 in the District Court, which was a disaster. I was represented by Michael McHugh QC and the matter was thrown out on appeal, just as it should have been, but not before we had suffered very bad publicity.

Police later told me that the criminal George Freeman was behind it. Freeman had his own trouble with racing inquiries. In the early 1980s there was an inquiry into the running of his horse Mr Digby, which had won by eight lengths just two days after being badly beaten – the charge was that it had run 'dead'. Freeman had won handsomely on it: he boasted that his winnings paid for his lavish wedding in the following days. His best man was a future chairman of the Sydney Turf Club; another Sydney Turf Club director also attended, as did several registered bookmakers. Many normally honest people were influenced by Freeman's flamboyant lifestyle. People were addicted to his tips, and even if his tips didn't win, he would still throw money around.

A stewards' report and then a special inquiry on Mr Digby was held after allegations were aired in parliament about the suspicious form reversal of the horse, but they failed to nail Freeman. Then, in late 1981, the AJC reopened its inquiry, and the horse's trainer, Harry Clarke, and jockey, Keith Banks, were disqualified for twelve months. Freeman was given notice to 'show cause' why he should not be warned off, but with the threat of an appeal to the Privy Council in England, the AJC dropped the notice.

A few years later I felt the need to be more outspoken about Freeman and was more direct. In a fateful interview with *Penthouse* magazine in 1984, I said: 'George . . . hates me. Well, what do you think? I'm the leader – I set the prices. He can't get me. I'm too big . . . But these pricks, they're just a tiny, tiny part of the game. An ugly part, but infinitesimal.' I would pay a very high price for my lack of discretion in publicly exposing Freeman. When the Fine Cotton scandal broke a few months later, Freeman seized his chance to manipulate behind the scenes and ruin Rob and me – the two racing people who had stood up to him.

As the years went on, Freeman continued to manipulate racing and laugh at authority. When he launched his autobiography in 1988, he scornfully had an ice statue of Mr Digby as the centrepiece of the event.

Although there were threats on his life, and even one attempt to murder him, Freeman died of a heart attack following a bout of asthma in 1990. Some might have missed his corrupting generosity, but racing as an industry didn't.

—

Raids, phone bugging and even threats of murder have been the occasional serious hazards of being a Waterhouse – or Australia's most successful bookmaker. Some of those who bet large sums with me sometimes wanted to blame me for their losses.

I am well aware there was rampant phone tapping – many of us in racing were subject to it. At times it was clear that some people could not have known certain details without having listened in to my private conversations. One time I was told I had been bugged and was given a full written transcript of a conversation I'd had with another bookmaker. Another time a person I was talking to in Melbourne asked me to turn the music down on my radio. 'I haven't got a radio on,' I said, and then the music abruptly stopped – someone had been listening in.

We employed an anti-bugging technician to check our place and, sure enough, he found a bug in the ceiling – although you wouldn't know if it really came from the technician's pocket.

I knew that in those days people at telephone exchanges bugged the calls of well-known jockeys, trainers and, of course, bookmakers. One group of eight technicians allocated two or three lines to one another and then swapped the tips. I couldn't believe it one day when I was reading out prices on the phone and a woman listening in from the postmaster-general's department interrupted and corrected me – I had given the wrong number of a horse. Obtaining racing tips was a perk of the job.

Bugging was not restricted to amateurs; the police also did their share. The police told me they had once spent several weeks based in premises across the road from our North Sydney office so they could use high-powered listening devices. They were also watching to see who visited us. They concluded that all we were involved in was racing and betting and nothing else. I could have told them that.

I heard stories of threats against me, although in most cases I was never told of the danger until after the event. I'm not even sure how many were genuine. I rarely felt threatened and wasn't frightened. You might consider me naive, but mostly I took no extra precautions. I didn't think anyone would do something so rash as bump me off. I did, however, have firearms lessons at the police academy, and I practised out on the farm.

One thing that did shock me was police evidence of criminal intentions towards us by prison escapologist Darcy Dugan. He was almost a folk hero in the late 1960s because of his several daring escapes from custody. He was, nevertheless, a hardened criminal – he was arrested in a dawn raid by the famous Detective-Sergeant Ray Kelly, after Dugan and his accomplice, William Mears, had shot and attempted to kill a bank manager during a bungled hold-up in 1950. After being paroled in the late 1960s, Dugan was arrested again and police found he had been planning to kidnap my nephew John for ransom.

Dugan had rented a flat opposite Jack's family home in Upper Pitt Street in Kirribilli and had kept a diary on John's movements. Dugan targeted John because he was the young heir to Jack's fortune. John was the flamboyant young man about town, and quite obviously Dugan was waiting for the right time to kidnap him. The police treated it very seriously.

—

No matter how careful you are, you can become the victim of non-payers and fraudsters in the bookmaking world.

In the early 1980s a punter known as Andrew Stathis began betting with Rob. We didn't know much about him, except that he was a commodities broker and high-profile businessman who in early 1982 had bought the Bishopsgate insurance company, a respected but unexciting general insurer. Stathis was a big gambler on and off the racetrack, and he traded heavily on the gold and silver futures markets in Australia and the United States.

Stathis started to bet big with Rob. There had been a run of wet tracks in Sydney and Stathis hit a purple patch by following certain jockeys; one Saturday he notched up the huge win of around half a million dollars.

Stathis demanded not only to be paid immediately but to be paid in cash. He refused to take a cheque and was belligerent. To obtain the cash we had to make special arrangements with the Commonwealth Bank in Martin Place. I remember it was a Friday in early August 1982. Rob was taken to the bowels of the bank, where the cash was stashed into a worn army kitbag by a teller.

Rob had arranged to meet Stathis at a certain time on the corner of Pitt and Hunter Streets in Sydney. Stathis turned up on the street corner and took his money. He then bet with us again the next day, the Saturday. However, this time he lost around $250,000 and we were relieved to think we were going to get some of our money back.

Stathis could not be found for settlement on the Monday. He had skipped town and taken a plane to Paris, no doubt with our $500,000 cash safely on board. We didn't see the kitbag again either!

We were to find out that Stathis was also known as Andrew Stathopolous. He came to Australia from Greece with his parents when he was two. He went to the exclusive Cranbrook School, after which he studied law. When he bought Bishopsgate from the recently floated P&O Australia, he only paid a downpayment on the purchase price of $4.75 million. It was later shown that he started misappropriating money a few weeks after he took over the company; in total, he stole $19 million in insurance premiums and left Bishopsgate insolvent.

In 1979 he was committed to stand trial over some $60-million worth of marijuana trading. That case was somehow overlooked within the office of the Director of Public Prosecutions, and it never proceeded beyond a 1983 court mention – which was after Stathopolous had fled Australia. It was said he also lost more than $1 million on gold futures in Australia, although I don't know if he paid those debts either.

Stathopolous has never returned to Australia. He was arrested in 1987 in Pireaus in Greece with 23 kilograms of heroin in a suitcase and was sentenced to life imprisonment. The Australian charges against him still stand.

26

The Good, the Bad and the Ugly

THE GLARE OF PUBLICITY always seemed to find its way to my family's door. I didn't seek it but nor did I fight it, regarding it as intrusive but also good promotion for our business.

I allowed the popular ABC series *A Big Country* to film a program about me and my operation in the mid-1970s, and it made a big impact. Looking back, it was really a window onto the times – many people said it showed the aura and standing I had in racing. However, I made an unfortunate choice of words when trying to emphasise how I needed to concentrate on big punters; I referred to small bettors as 'roughage', simply meaning they filled the book. It was taken the wrong way and I copped a bit of flak from some of my punters and in the media.

I was interviewed by the international television host David Frost when he came to Australia for a prime-time show. There were often cover stories and features on me in newspapers and magazines, including *The National Times*, *The Bulletin*, *The Woman's Weekly* and *The Good Weekend*. One newspaper series called 'King of the Bookies', by Roy Miller, ran for a week in *The Daily Mirror*.

I was on good terms with all the newspaper racing writers: Keith Robbins, Bill Whittaker, Bert Lillye, Max Presnell, John Holloway, Bill Casey and Mike Gibson, Craig Young and Ray

Thomas. I was also friendly with earlier racing writers such as Ossie and Fred Imber, and Des Corless in Sydney, and Jack Elliott, Bill Condon and Tony Kennedy in Melbourne. 'Sitting' Pat Farrell of *The Daily Mirror* always said everything I told him was 'confidential' but it never was – he would write it all.

Another media approach was to bring my family one of our happiest outcomes. In 1978 I received a phone call from T. J. 'Tommy' Smith's daughter, Gai, asking me to go on television for some corny racing variety show she was doing with John Singleton called *Racing's New Faces*. Gai wanted me to sing a song. Now, even when I was in primary school, when singing lessons were on I was sent out to do the gardening. I didn't tell Gai this; instead, as a fob-off, I said I'd love to come on the show but that unfortunately I would be away from Sydney that evening. However, I mentioned that I had a son called Robert who had a 'tremendous voice' and that no doubt if she phoned him he would oblige.

I don't think Gai was very impressed by this. She wanted a big name and doubted Rob was all that well known. I'd never heard Rob sing and I strongly suspect that he hadn't either, but that didn't deter him. When Gai phoned him he tentatively agreed to go on the show, but he suggested they talk about it over dinner.

Rob didn't go on the show but he knew from that first date that Gai was the one for him. An eligible bachelor and a popular man about town, he broke away from other dalliances and courted Gai for the next year until they were engaged. Rob struck a racing chord with Gai's famous father, and her mother, Valerie, also took to him, seeing him as a kind soul with 'lovely eyes' and 'different' to some of the rougher racing people she had met.

At that stage Gai was firmly focused on her acting career and not interested in following in her father's footsteps. Tommy didn't see any sense in his daughter being on the stage and found an ally in Rob; together, they encouraged Gai to go into racing.

Rob and Gai's marriage, in December 1980, was the wedding of the year in the racing world. Both Tommy and I had received a flood of publicity in our time, and the wedding, held at the historic Swifts Chapel at Darling Point, was the talk of the town. Robbie chose his brother, David, as his best man, and his cousin Charlie was a groomsman. Louise was Gai's bridesmaid. Gai looked radiant in an embroidered dress designed by Mel Clifford. My cup overflowed with joy and happiness and I was on top of the world.

With all the euphoria, Suzanne and I decided to remarry. It was a simple family service in our lounge room at our Kirribilli home. The marriage celebrant was Franca Arena, later a member of the New South Wales parliament. Not too many people marry each other for a second time, but we were in good company with the likes of Richard Burton and Elizabeth Taylor.

When we took this decision, I explained to Suzy that I would maintain my friendship with Yuko Fujita, whom I had been close to over the previous decade. I'd met her when she was an attractive young hostess on a Qantas plane; I chatted her up and gave her my phone number. She rang me and we developed a strong friendship. I spoke to a friend, Jack Egerton, the larger-than-life Qantas director, who arranged for Yuko to be the first hostess Qantas sponsored to migrate to Australia.

Yuko has done very well. She has worked hard and saved wisely and was astute with her real-estate buying. She's always been financially independent and certainly has never been a kept woman. Proud and private, Yuko comes from a noble Japanese family; her grandfather was a leading surgeon. There was never any question of marriage with Yuko, although she is a wonderful person and I usually catch up with her twice a week. My relationship with Yuko was never a secret from

Suzanne, and I talk well of each of them to the other. Although they have never met, I am sure they have tried to spy on each other a couple of times.

One can never underestimate the importance of the fairer sex, and I've been blessed with the women in my life. Yuko has been a very loyal and kind friend to me. In some ways she would provide a sanctuary through all the trials and tribulations of the terrible years that would follow.

—

Louise was undeterred by John's refusal to allow me to pass my Fabergé interest to her. Although she had established a successful marketing career with American Express, she felt her rightful place was with our Fabergé business. Louise approached John directly for a marketing position at Fabergé, and I guess he felt he couldn't turn her down. She was in her element as a product manager, working with the bright young marketing guru Toby Brown. Louise was responsible for relaunching the original Brut and Fabergé's classic fragrances, as well as developing and launching new cosmetic ranges, including Fiducia deodorants and Ceramic Glaze nail-care products.

However, Louise also saw a different side to John. With his staff he was always referring to 'his' farms and 'his' properties and 'his' Fabergé business, conveniently omitting any reference to me. Aided by clever marketing, Fabergé went from strength to strength in the 1970s and 80s. It grew to be a $110-million group, controlling Fabergé Australia, Elizabeth Arden, Max Factor Australia and Yves Rocher.

However, in the late 1970s, when things became tense between us, John stopped showing me the accounts. When I asked for them he refused, so I told him he couldn't expect me to be the guarantor unless I had access to them. John had also refused to put in writing that Fabergé was one-third mine, and so I declined to increase my guarantee, when the bank asked for more, until my shares were transferred into my name. John was furious and removed me as a director.

John was now reluctant to sign anything more to say that he and I actually were in a partnership with Fabergé. He decided that he'd done all the hard work. I was concerned when, in 1988, an article appeared in a business magazine claiming he was the sole founder and owner of Fabergé, but it came to a head a year later when the family was all in court and John, under oath, suddenly denied that I had any interest.

—

Louise met her future husband soon after Gai and Rob's eldest child, Tom, was born in 1982. We were all so excited about young Tom, who was named after both sides of the family – Gai's father, Tommy Smith, and my two early Australian ancestors called Thomas Waterhouse. Louise snapped some photos of baby Tom in hospital and took the film to a newly-established quick photo lab in Kings Cross. Its owner, Andrew Strauss, recognised Louise. He knew she was a keen skier and told her he had a friend coming to town who had been a German national team skier. Would she show him around Sydney? Louise agreed, jokingly saying she was one of Sydney's best tour guides.

Nothing was arranged, but three weeks later Louise called in to collect some other photos. Watching the passing parade from behind the counter was a handsome European man. Louise asked him if he was by chance Andrew's friend from Germany.

'Yes,' he said. 'Are you Louise?'

Louise said, 'Yes – can I at least take you for a coffee?

Guenther Raedler was from Oberjoch, Germany's highest

village in the Bavarian Alps. An engineer with a Masters degree in chemistry, Guenther was also a natural sportsman interested in the business side of skiing. He invited Louise to the beautiful Queenstown ski area, on New Zealand's south island.

Needing a break a couple of months later, Louise flew over to Queenstown. Just as I had been a confirmed bachelor, I didn't think Louise intended to marry either. It took her just three hours talking and driving around Queenstown to decide that Guenther was the one for her. She later told me she shocked herself and Guenther by proposing to him on that first day.

Louise didn't know that Guenther was one of the most sought-after bachelors in Queenstown, or that his friend Andrew had told him she was a champion skier. Although Louise was a gun skier on hard Australian slopes, she had never skied in knee-deep powder before. Guenther had won many ski races in Queenstown and also the international 'Powder 8s' skiing competition, for which the prize was a week's heli-skiing. He offered to take Louise and she thought, 'Why not?'

When Louise told me how the helicopter dropped them on a narrow ledge at the top of the steepest and most remote areas of the southern alps, and how her heart raced at its limit, I was reminded of my own experience at the top of the Parsenn in Davos, Switzerland, with Gretel 30 years earlier.

She didn't want to show her fear to Guenther or anyone else in the small group, but she soon crashed badly in the deep snow on the sharp incline, her impractical white poles disappearing deep into the powdery snow. Poor Guenther, who had just skied a hundred perfect turns through the powder to the bottom of the slope, had to climb back up to rescue her. Unlike my angry companion on the Parsenn, Guenther guided Louise down the mountain in good spirit.

They were engaged within a few months and in late 1983 had a delightful wedding in our garden in Kirribilli, with the

Opera House and the Harbour Bridge as a backdrop. Six tall and impressive athlete friends of Guenther's dropped in from Europe and were a hit with Louise's girlfriends, several of whom fell for the handsome men.

The day before the wedding I had a bad losing day at the races, but that Sunday, as I walked Louise down the garden path, she took my breath away in her stunning wedding dress. The clouds parted to reveal the blue sky and no one was prouder than me. The moment they took their wedding vows, Suzanne completed the magic by releasing a thousand pink and white balloons.

Guenther's mother, Viktoria, had been the first Bavarian woman to be awarded an MBE by Her Majesty Queen Elizabeth II. Guenther has often teased his mother, suggesting she must have been a spy for Britain in the war, but actually she was honoured for her sterling efforts in post-war Anglo–German relations; she built up the British army's ski championships and helped to develop the 'Snow Queen' ski exercises in her mountain village, and they gradually extended the training to the whole Bavarian Alps.

Being an MBE, Viktoria could invite Guenther and Louise to have a European blessing of their marriage at St Paul's Cathedral in London, in the Crypt for the Most Excellent Order of the British Empire, where they knelt on the same stool as Charles and Diana. My good friends Charles and Christine St George hosted a reception for the couple in their stylish Mayfair home. In mid-1984 Suzanne, Rob, Gai, Valerie and Tommy, with the young toddler Tom, attended the blessing, along with an array of European guests. Unfortunately, I had to stay back to 'mind the shop' in Sydney.

I couldn't have asked for a better son-in-law. Guenther has been as solid and loyal as you could possibly imagine. Like Robbie, Louise has been blessed with the right partner she chose in life. I've often teased him about making my daughter a tough businesswoman and perfectionist! And in reality he has been her great supporter and sound adviser.

Guenther is a successful businessman in his own right, making astute property investments in Europe and New Zealand, while always remaining financially independent. I was so proud when in 1997 the mayor of Queenstown and a former government minister, Warren Cooper, wanting to recognise Guenther's passion, help and promotion for the area, made him the Honorary Ambassador for Queenstown. Local businessmen John Martin and Fraser Skinner held a surprise bash for 300 well-wishers, where they recreated a Bavarian snow-capped forest indoors. That same year he became a New Zealand citizen.

From blissful family weddings we would run into a tangled mess of family brawling, perfidy and distrust. This would be the worst kind of crisis – the disloyalty and hurtfulness coming from within our own family.

—

Jack and I had supported Charlie's children while they were educated in private schools, and also Martin when he went to university. They wanted for nothing, and I had given them money whenever they needed it. In later years, as they grew up, advances from joint accounts or the sale of joint assets allowed them to buy their own homes, cars and other necessities. They also invested their money in properties or factories.

In the late 1970s I reluctantly agreed to sell the Bronte Charles Hotel for $1.35 million when Charlie junior wanted it sold. I knew that was cheap, but still I was amazed when a decade later, after it had been converted to residential apartments, it was sold for around $100 million.

Charlie, Martin and Billy all worked with me in various roles. However, I never felt any gratitude from them. Perhaps

I should have foreseen it, but in fact Charlie's children bore a deep-seated resentment at having been left out of our new ventures since the middle 1960s. I had the shock of my life in March 1982 when animosity suddenly raised its head. This occurred after our accountants, Pannell Kerr Forster, needed some documents signed by all the children of the three families.

In the early 1960s, with the best legal and accounting advice, we had set up a series of trusts for the benefit of all the children. We all usually just signed the trust accounts automatically, but in 1982, out of the blue, Charlie's children refused to sign.

Then my sister, Betty, rang and told me Julie had said to her, 'We'll put that bastard in jail,' referring to me. I called a meeting with Charlie's four offspring for the next Sunday to ask them what the trouble was and why they were not signing the accounts. I also invited along Rob and Louise. Charlie, Martin, Billy and Julie all said they wouldn't sign any document as they were going to sue Jack and me as trustees of their father's estate.

Neville Wran's prophecy – that Charlie's children were too young to realise what was being done for them, and when they grew up there would be no gratitude but instead they would expect more and finish up suing us – rang in my ears.

I told them everything that happened with the estate was a matter of record and that, as always, they were entitled to go to the accountants for any explanation. I told them how when their father had died the money from his estate would not have lasted them very long, and how Jack and I had gifted them, out of our own pockets, one-third of our income for a decade. This had meant their unfinished home was completed, they had been sent to the best schools and provided with food, clothing, cars and help to buy their own homes for almost 30 years. They now had investments and all were wealthy and established for life.

I then hit a nerve when I said to Martin, 'Even when you got into your trouble, I paid out of my own pocket to help you.'

Martin jumped up and screamed, 'And you hated me for it!'

I retorted in a strong voice, 'I most certainly didn't like what you did but I didn't hate you for it.'

Louise then said, 'I am in the same position as all of you, in that I'll get the same return from the sale of various assets. Yet I can only feel gratitude to my father and Uncle Jack for the tremendous start in life, and the support they have given me over the years. All through my life I have been taught the importance of family, and to regard your family – my late Uncle Charlie's – as my family.'

Despite the extraordinary allegations, I knew I had done nothing wrong. At Martin's request, I allowed him to stay in my office for a month until he could find new premises. After stalling for the month, he simply moved his office to his home. I didn't know until later (when Martin admitted it in cross-examination) that he had stayed back in my office at night, copying documents relating to my business and the family companies. Several months before Martin left, I had been told by Vince McMahon, who was working in my office two days a week, that 'Martin's going through my files; you need to be very wary of him'.

I didn't have a guilty conscience. I had gone above and beyond for my late brother's children. It was no secret that I had never liked their mother, Patty. Nevertheless, I had tried hard to help her and the family. Charlie had asked me to look after Patty but only left her a small allowance in his will. Jack and I gave her so much more, yet our support was continually abused. We had given Patty charge cards – once she went on a shopping spree and bought 36 dresses.

My two brothers and I had been partners in everything. We were inseparable and had complete trust in one another. When my brother Charlie went bust as a bookmaker in the late 1930s, I had gone to him with all my savings and we had started up again together. Later we included Jack. We acquired all our assets together and were equal partners. However, it turned out that Patty had told her children that the business was actually owned by Charlie and that Jack and I worked for him! This was the basis on which the children alleged we had stolen their father's assets. In fact, Jack and I had given them one-third of our assets for a decade and had made them all millionaires in their own right.

Sure enough, my nephews and niece took us to court in August 1982, eventually claiming 100 per cent of everything Jack and I owned. It would have been ridiculous except it was serious.

Our lives were certainly thrown around by the court case. Martin, running the case for his siblings, immediately froze all our company accounts and then put a caveat on every piece of property. I was annoyed but not too worried when our legal counsel advised we just agree to the injunctions, on the basis that we would have our day in court later. After all, I had never lived on the money from our properties, as my income came from racing. The idea was always to earn money bookmaking and then put it into property.

It took over three years for them to actually lodge a statement of claim, which ran for hundreds of pages and was bristling with outlandish allegations. Martin was not only suing Jack and me for 100 per cent of our assets but he also claimed the Commonwealth Bank had been a party to our alleged breaches of trust, so he instigated wide-ranging proceedings against it too.

I couldn't imagine that the set of circumstances surrounding my father's epic testate battle would ever repeat itself – but here it was, happening before my eyes.

27

Fine Cotton

SOME NEW HEAVYWEIGHT BOOKIES were jostling for supremacy by the early 1980s.

I was still holding sway, although in my mind I was scaling back. A big gambler can only stay at the top for so long. I transferred to the interstate ring in mid-1984 at the age of 62. I had gone full circle, having started in interstate betting almost exactly 30 years earlier. Whereas in those days interstate meant only Melbourne, now it included Brisbane and occasionally Adelaide and Perth. Journalist Keith Robbins wrote for *The Sunday Telegraph* that 'with Big Bill back on the interstate scene, it does give Sydney the strongest line up of bookmakers in the world'.

Rob, although under 30, had now made it in his own right. He was bigger and, I think, better than me with his modern skills – he was beating the professional punters. He was regarded as the young giant of the Sydney Rails. Following in my footsteps, Rob also went to field at Epsom and Royal Ascot in England. Whereas in 1966 I had trouble finding any big punters over in England, now the Sydney Turf Club put on a trip of 250 members, which meant Rob had his clientele ready-made. In 1984 Rob had his lovely and glamorous wife, Gai, and – with the birth of a daughter, Kate, that year – two adorable young children. He was on top of the world.

Terry Page had now retired but his protégé, Dominic Beirne,

was a real force. Mark Read had previously moved up from Melbourne to the Sydney interstate ring, and we were sizing each other up. Max Presnell humorously called it the 'Battle of the Bookies'; he had me in front on points, noting my edge by putting up the prices 'before the television quotes came from interstate', which Read promptly copied. I let Read on with his punting, but on the rare occasion I wanted to bet with him, he didn't let me on.

The characters of the ring inspired Harry Robinson to write *The Bookie Book*. In a light-hearted way, Robinson called me the Emperor, Rob the Prince, Dominic the Duke and Read the future King.

Rob told Robinson then, 'Racing is like driving a fast car. Don't let the car go too fast or you'll lose control. With the least amount of effort I could hold four times as much as I do by blowing the odds, but the result would be a disaster. You've got to go at the right speed. I would be terrified to go to a race meeting and bet the way I bet without doing my own set of prices. I am looking to lay horses, and the only way you can do that is to have an opinion.'

Also in Robinson's book, Dominic summed up the evolution of the new breed of punter, saying the punter of the early 1980s was far tougher than his counterpart of fifteen years earlier. He worked harder, knew more and had more to help him; through race films he could watch provincial races without attending, and also he could buy computerised form. This kind of punter was now prepared to treat it as a big job. He still had to pick a winner.

Robbie referred to another category of smaller bookmakers who did no work, simply copying prices and betting only with the public. To a big bet they would say, 'No, thank you. I make a good living betting little fish.'

Beirne later told Max Presnell there were bookmakers such as Bruce McHugh, Terry Page and Bob Blann who played the man without knowing much about the odds. He recognised that Rob and I tilted on either side, saying 'Bill tended much more to play the man but went to the track with an opinion'.

A series of successful organised betting plunges rocked betting rings in the late 1970s and early 1980s and netted the principals huge amounts of money. One of these plunges led to remarkable scenes in January 1982. A meticulously planned coup on the unknown Melbourne horse Getting Closer stripped at least $1 million from Sydney bookies, apart from other interstate courses and even on country tracks. It was regarded as the biggest coup on a Sydney race for over twenty years. The colt, part-owned by Mark Read, was quoted at 200/1 in early betting. It had failed at its only two previous starts in Victoria, finishing eleventh in a maiden race at Ballarat.

This coup made front page headlines in *The Sun-Herald*, with racing journalist Ian Manning saying it was professionally organised, taking even the most experienced bookmakers at the Canterbury track unawares. It didn't really touch me, although I was still on the locals then, but Robbie was among the many hit, laying the colt at odds of 50/1 and losing $70,000 on the plunge.

The press said 'the secrecy and execution of the plunge was straight out of a Banjo Paterson poem'. Of course, Mark Read was non-committal about the coup, refusing to tell reporters whether or not he had backed Getting Closer.

Another time Rob and I spoiled a Mark Read plunge in Canberra. We were going down to work on the Canberra Cup. Rob did his form and noticed that an unraced three-year-old colt, Maniwreck, was entered with 'good company' (well-performed horses) rather than in a 'maiden' class race. When Rob checked the Australian statistical record books, he saw it had been bought at the sales for $100,000 by one Mark Read. He then noticed the horse was racing in the name of a

Mrs Elliott – who happened to be the wife of Read's father-in-law, Jack Elliott.

Normally we used to take our own money to the provincials. This time, however, Armaguard offered us their service. We declined, but were surprised when we got to the track to see the Armaguard van with an army of Mark Read's clerks swarmed around it. Yet Mark Read wasn't fielding as a bookmaker at the track . . .

Awake to an impending plunge, Rob sent our clerks around the ring, backing the horse right in from 33/1. By the time Read came to back it with Rob, it was odds-on at 4/5 and he was livid, screaming, 'What are you doing to me!' It was a good result – even if Mark didn't think so.

The betting coups continued and bookies had to be on the lookout for signs of the next one. No one, least of all me, expected that the next headlines would be about a farcical ring-in surrounding a picnic performer called Fine Cotton.

—

The Fine Cotton story has been told many times before but not by me.

This is the first time I have given my take on the betting scandal, and I do so with some reluctance. You could write what I knew about it before the event on the back of a postage stamp. The background I've included here comes from what I've been told, heard and read.

Fine Cotton was a blot on racing, but the subsequent inquiry by New South Wales racing authorities was an even greater stain on the sport's integrity. Their actions demonstrated their inability to deal with the incident without showing prejudice and partiality.

The AJC took away seventeen years of my livelihood and destroyed my career on the most obscure charge – 'prior knowledge' – which they created to cover the situation. I have always categorically stated that I had no prior knowledge of the Fine Cotton scam, and there was never one skerrick of evidence that I was guilty of any wrongdoing whatsoever. I denied it then and will till the day I die.

The ill-fated incident occurred on Saturday 18 August 1984, when a moderately performed horse called Bold Personality was rung-in for the poorly performed Fine Cotton in a scam organised by a shonky horse dealer, John Gillespie, at Eagle Farm Racecourse in Brisbane. There was a sensational betting plunge in Brisbane on the horse racing as Fine Cotton, which firmed from being a long-priced outsider at 33/1 to start as a 7/2 favourite everywhere around Australia, including Warwick Farm Racecourse in Sydney, where I was working on the interstate races, and on the TABs in all states.

Now, rank outsiders are rarely sensationally backed in to start as favourites, and certainly not on metropolitan tracks. The peculiar thing was that the switched horse, Bold Personality, only just won in a close photo-finish.

The facts of the case would have made a good script for the Marx Brothers. As racegoers know, each horse has its own unique characteristics, by which they are identifiable by keen racegoers and administrators. The two horses concerned had actually been racing in the same area and so must have been known not only to the local trainers, jockeys and strappers but also to the punters. Indeed, the stewards and other authorities should have easily been able to distinguish the two horses, especially as they were of distinctly different colours. Bold Personality was a bay, while Fine Cotton was dark-brown with white hind legs.

This is one reason a ring-in is always going to be a crazy thing to do. It is almost impossible to get away with.

Apparently, the perpetrators of the Fine Cotton scam had initially selected a horse called Dashing Soltaire for the ring-in. It supposedly looked a little like Fine Cotton and had reasonable form. However, two weeks before the attempted sting, Dashing Soltaire injured itself on a barbed-wire fence. Instead of calling off the scam, Gillespie went looking for a substitute and – showing just how bumbling and stupid people can be – decided on Bold Personality, which was so different in colour and markings that he and trainer Hayden Haitana resorted to dying its coat and painting its hind legs.

To this day, I still wonder how anyone in their right mind could ever think that Rob and I would have been mixed up with such fools.

The scam was obviously a poorly kept secret, as no sooner had the horse passed the post than a group near the finishing line started yelling, 'Ring-in, ring-in!' As the horse pulled up hot and sweaty, reports said the paint was even running off its hind legs.

Sure enough, an official promptly produced the registration cards not only of Fine Cotton but also of Bold Personality. The winning horse was immediately disqualified, which meant that all money bet on Fine Cotton was gone – the tote and bookmakers were entitled to keep it.

Racing in Queensland was conducted under the rules of the Queensland Turf Club, which began an immediate inquiry. The Queensland police stepped in because there was fraud and it became a criminal matter, with the police inquiry naturally taking precedence. A year or so later, Fine Cotton's trainer, Hayden Haitana, the mastermind, Gillespie, and another Brisbane man, Robert North, were convicted of the ring-in and jailed.

The Queensland Turf Club then recommenced its inquiry and those who had been convicted in the criminal court were disqualified and warned off. As well, a commission agent, Mort Green, who had bet on Fine Cotton was warned off – for just a year.

In my view, the Queensland racing authorities handled the situation very well. Appropriately, they let the police investigation proceed, delaying their own inquiry until the criminal charges had run their course, after which they acted decisively and firmly.

However, the AJC, which controlled racing in New South Wales, also opened an inquiry. Contrary to the protocol where criminal investigations should take precedence, as it did in Queensland, the AJC did not defer to either the Queensland or New South Wales police inquiries. It chose to ignore the Queensland Turf Club investigations, in whose jurisdiction the scam took place.

It still amazes me that the AJC believed it should act ahead of the Queensland Turf Club, and especially ahead of police in both states. I believed, and so did many others at the time, that it would have been proper for the AJC to adjourn its inquiry, as the Queenslanders had done, to allow the full facts to come out. Instead, the AJC rushed ahead and looked for scalps or scapegoats.

The result was that the AJC charged eight people, including Rob and me, with having 'prior knowledge' of the Fine Cotton affair. They found us guilty and warned us off all racecourses, for a period at the committee's pleasure. Seven of us appealed to the newly-established Racing Appeals Tribunal, which confirmed the finding of the AJC in six cases.

By definition, charging the eight people in Sydney only with 'prior knowledge' meant that the AJC accepted that none of us took part in the actual ring-in. However, a charge of 'prior knowledge' implied that the perpetrators, having planned their amateurish masquerade, had actually phoned one or more of those in Sydney who were accused of prior knowledge and told them of the planned ring-in, so they would place the bets. This is an unbelievable presumption.

Now, I've been in racing all my life, and I can assure you

that nobody tells his commissioner very much. Why would he? It's in his interest to keep everything very close to his chest. In 1984 I hadn't worked commissions on a racetrack for almost twenty years, but I had seen dozens upon dozens of commissions go on. There is nothing untoward in getting someone else to put your money on – it is a normal business practice at the track. But as a bookie, you'd never ask how much the total commission was or why they were backing it.

Now, if the eight of us who were 'warned off' weren't directly involved in the Fine Cotton ring-in, then how could anyone who understands racing assume we had 'prior knowledge' of anything improper?

—

The real trouble lay in the events that emerged after the ring-in was exposed. It was indeed a sensational event. A ring-in on a metropolitan track! The newspapers played it up, closely followed by all other sections of the media. A few weeks passed before the AJC directed its stewards to hold an inquiry. A large amount of money had been placed on the horse in Sydney. The press, through a young sportswriter, seemed to have detailed information about the scam before anyone else, indicating to me there was media manipulation from behind the scenes.

Unknown to me, however, in the lead-up to the race Rob had been approached to place a commission of $40,000 on a horse, which at the last minute he was told was Fine Cotton. Rob asked Ian Murray, a large and well-known punter, to put on a commission of $50,000, which included an extra $10,000 from Rob. Murray, naturally thinking it must have been a good thing, also placed some bets of his own. Apart from Murray, Rob had given some small amounts to a few others to be placed on Fine Cotton at two or three provincial tracks. None of these people knew anything more than that Rob had asked them to place a commission. And there was absolutely nothing wrong with placing commissions.

However, when the AJC stewards' inquiry began Murray was the first to be interviewed, and he denied that he had put money on for anyone. He said that with his bets he was simply 'following the money' and truthfully denied any prior knowledge of a ring-in. Murray was no doubt concerned about the intense publicity and a possible police action that might follow, and wanted to distance himself from the affair.

Of course, he was not alone in taking this stance. Fine Cotton's race was only a small interstate event, but the horse had been supported sensationally by a multitude of punters in Sydney and all over Australia. The stewards called several dozen witnesses who had backed the horse. Some had placed bets as high as $20,000. All this money on a horse with no form! Yet every witness had denied he had known anything about the plunge, although the tip was everywhere. Despite that, all denied that anyone had 'tipped' them the horse. Each and every one claimed to be 'following the money', meaning that having seen someone else backing the horse, they were impressed by the amount of money being placed and simply followed suit.

Now, nobody places large sums of money on a horse unless, at the very least, someone has given them some advice. Yet all these witnesses were believed by the stewards – all except the ones who were somehow connected to my son, Robbie.

Rob had told me on the way to the races that there was a strong tip for a horse in Brisbane and to be careful. He didn't tell me the name but said he would send someone to my stand to let me know before the race. I didn't take much notice, but once betting had opened for the fourth race, Robbie sent a runner to tell me the horse to watch in Brisbane was Fine Cotton.

Nevertheless, I was still prepared to lay it, even if I was being cautious. When Murray came up wanting to back Fine Cotton to win $40,000, I cut his bet to $14,000 to $1000.

After I took the bet, Murray said to me, 'Be careful of this one, Bill.' It would only be much later that I found out Murray's betting included a commission arranged through Rob.

I thanked Murray and, as there was suddenly so much intense interest in the horse, the price collapsed. I 'blinked' – turned the horse's price off the board – for a short time to ensure I wouldn't get caught any more until the price had settled. I had nothing to hide. Logically, anyone knowing of 'skulduggery afoot' would certainly not have drawn attention to the horse or himself by turning the price off his board.

The AJC stewards' inquiry failed to come up with any evidence against me, but they were totally selective in what they would believe, even ruling that the bet I'd taken from Murray on Fine Cotton was fictitious. Even so, the stewards could not find any charges to lay against me.

The committee, in an unprecedented move, was persuaded to take control of the matter out of the hands of the stewards. This had never been done before, as it had always been the case that stewards made their findings and then any appeal went to the committee. Further, because the AJC couldn't find any offence under the rules of racing, it came up with the puerile charge of 'prior knowledge', which had never been laid before. This raised an obvious question: prior knowledge of what?

Tom Hughes QC, acting for me in the case before the AJC committee, wanted to be sure that he wasn't going to be surprised by something I hadn't told him. I assured him there were no hidden surprises. Tom was simply astonished by the lack of evidence against me. He told me I didn't really need him, because as far as he was concerned, there was no case against me. 'You'll walk it in,' he said.

The committee, however, was determined to take my scalp, despite its own legal counsel, Murray Gleeson QC, summing up that there was no evidence against me. It had decided Robbie was guilty of knowing 'something', and that, because I was Robbie's father and partner, I must also be guilty.

They saw Rob as having some mysterious connection with some of the Fine Cotton betting and obviously wanted to show the world they had done the 'right thing' by racing. I have no doubt that if we had not been so high-profile, they would not have gone to such trouble to sink us. And they were acting well ahead of the Queensland Turf Club and the official police inquiry.

The AJC's premature and incorrect findings would have devastating ramifications for me and also my family. I was 'warned off' – banned from all racetracks around the world – purely because Rob was my son.

Rob's mistake was in lying about arranging the commission with Murray and the others. Rob, a young man of 30, was in a difficult position. Murray had said to him, 'Whatever you do, don't say I put the money on for you.'

When Rob went before the stewards, Murray had already told them he was just 'following the money'. Rob no doubt felt beholden to Murray and took the 'easy way out' by distancing himself as well. This was Rob's fatal mistake as, through his lies, he left himself wide open.

Rob later said he shouldn't have been so stupid to agree to put money on Fine Cotton – he should have realised something was afoot. Of course, hindsight is a wonderful thing. If you think about it, most punters on a racecourse bet because they think they have some edge or know something no one else does. The commission Rob agreed to arrange was a mere fraction of the amount put on Fine Cotton by punters around Australia, but only those associated with Rob got into trouble.

I later learnt that Gary Clarke, who was working for Rob as a clerk, had asked Rob to put a commission on for an unknown party and Rob had added a bit of his own. Rob arranged to send a clerk up to Gosford to put some money on, and on the spur of the moment gave some money and a tip to poor Father O'Dwyer who, looking to make some money for his holidays, backed it himself. I am sure no one would pass on a tip like that if they thought there was something hot afoot. Most of the poor unfortunates who were warned off were guilty of nothing more than putting on a commission or, in my case, innocently accepting bets.

I am certain that if Rob had known it was hot, he wouldn't have taken the commission or bet on the horse. When Gary Clarke came along and wanted Rob to handle the commission, he agreed. I've often said that if Rob had been a girl, he'd always be pregnant because he couldn't say no. Sometimes you have to be cruel to be kind, and in this case Rob learnt the hard way.

His real offence was not in putting the money on but in protecting Ian Murray. Foolishly, Rob lied to shield Murray – and of course himself – which then led to a series of lies. Rob became embroiled in the situation. If he'd just come forward in the first place and admitted to putting the commission on Fine Cotton, he would not have been in any real trouble.

Robbie's problems deepened when Murray agreed to change his testimony at the newly convened Racing Appeals Tribunal, presided over by the retired District Court Judge Goran, who was appointed with the AJC's blessing. After being 'warned off', Murray had evidently been to see the AJC's legal counsel to see if he could cut a deal. They were not in a position to agree, but Murray reportedly told them where he was going fishing in Tasmania. The chief steward, John Schreck, followed him and persuaded him to come back to Sydney. Murray was to give a number of different versions about his betting on Fine Cotton. Now, at the appeal, he reversed his earlier testimony and told the tribunal that he had in fact put $50,000 on Fine Cotton on behalf of a friend of Robbie's.

Murray also confirmed that his bet with me was genuine and that he didn't believe I was connected to the betting at all. This was the truth, but the tribunal nevertheless did not reverse my warning-off.

Alf Goran really shocked me with his decision. He was quite irrational and unfair. I had been at law school with him and we were young barristers together. He was a nice fellow then and we had got along well. The lack of logic in his judgement showed he was prepared to do anything to justify his position, even to the point where he didn't accept Murray's evidence about his bet with me.

I felt betrayed by the system. Alf knew something like this was totally out of character for me, and his judgement inexplicably sidestepped the facts in my case. I couldn't believe that Alf had ignored the fact there was no evidence against me, and further that Murray had corroborated that the bet I took from him on Fine Cotton was genuine.

Goran was particularly unfair towards Rob, who had done the wrong thing by lying but would pay an enormous price and suffer great and prolonged degradation for not telling the truth straight away.

Rob wrote to the AJC after the tribunal's findings and said he wanted to come clean, but the committee refused to see him. The AJC was obviously livid that racing had been put through the Fine Cotton disgrace and blamed Rob for the wide media coverage. It made him its fall guy.

After the Racing Appeals Tribunal, we were all heartbroken. Our lives were in tatters and our much-loved racing was denied us. We had suffered the ultimate racing disgrace of being warned off – for 'prior knowledge' of something of which we'd had *no* knowledge. Even though no charge was ever laid against me, my disqualification stood for fourteen years, and my bookmaker's licence wasn't returned for seventeen years.

Yet they had nothing on me – not a thing. How anyone could have thought I might have been remotely involved, I don't know. There was nothing the AJC could point to that would justify what it did to me and my career.

28

The Aftermath

THE EFFECT of my warning-off was calamitous.

No one will ever understand the extreme financial strain my family was under in the 1980s. We had now lost our main source of income, racing. All our assets were frozen because of the family court case, including the inter-family bank accounts. On top of that we had a large overdraft, partly because of the hundreds of thousands of dollars of legal fees in the Fine Cotton case.

We were *personae non gratae*, in that we were warned off all racetracks around the world. The damage to my reputation everywhere was catastrophic. The old guard of the AJC gratuitously sent 'mug shots' of Rob and me to various clubs including the racing clubs of Tattersalls and City Tattersalls, advising them to inform their members we were warned off, and we were stripped of our memberships.

We couldn't keep on our loyal and long-serving staff – it was hard to have to let them all go after so many years. My right-hand man, Keith Jones, was immediately snaffled by Roger Manning. With the benefit of all my clients, Roger went on to become the leading bookie for a while before getting into financial trouble and giving the game away. Keith still stayed in contact with me over the years, and I was saddened by his passing in mid-2009.

In Papua New Guinea, local regulations required that I have an indigenous partner in each betting shop. These local partners took advantage of my warning-off and seized control of the businesses, quickly going bust on their own. However, the Fijian business, owned by Jack, Francis Grant and me, was able to keep going through the strength of Francis's loyalty. It was to prove a saviour for me. With our income all but dried up, we took over the Sydney responsibilities of supplying the racing information to Fiji and were able to cover some of our office expenses. Rob turned his focus to the form and the punt.

There was one bright spot at this time. The only Australian racing body which gave me a fair go was the Harness Racing Authority, under the chairmanship of Michael Cummings. In an unusual move, the AJC wrote to the HRA, asking it to recognise our warning-off. The HRA wrote to me, asking me to show cause why I shouldn't be warned off at the trots also.

It gave me a fair hearing, listening to my evidence for over an hour. The panel was surprised at what I told them and accepted I'd done nothing wrong. On that basis the HRA refused to warn me off trotting tracks. I was very grateful that it stood up to the AJC and the negative headlines from sections of the media.

In doing so, the HRA also defied the wishes of the state minister for sport, Michael Cleary, who told parliament he had expressed his disappointment to the HRA and told them their action was imprudent. The courage of the HRA board members in standing up to the political pressure was admirable – especially as they were threatened with funding cuts or even legislative changes.

It was a small victory but very sweet, and a great tonic for my self-esteem.

—

Before the Queensland police had concluded its investigations into the Fine Cotton affair, in mid-1985 the New South Wales police charged Rob and five of the others who were warned off with conspiracy and numerous other charges, which we knew were unsustainable. I was not charged, however, which was finally some sort of acknowledgement that I had in no way been involved in any organised betting on Fine Cotton.

All the charges except the conspiracy charge were thrown out by the magistrate, and when that charge came before Judge Smythe, the prosecutors were clear to point out there was no suggestion that Rob was in any way involved in the ring-in itself. After hearing the Crown case, Judge Smythe threw it out, ruling that the Crown could not point to any offence. The judge said that just about every bet ever placed is because one thinks one has some special information or knowledge about it.

The barrister who won the case for Rob was Frank McAlary QC. He was such a skilful cross-examiner that people used to say he could slice off his opponent's head without them even being aware he was drawing blood. This was the case with Arthur Harris, whom the investigating officer, Detective Sergeant McKnight, said had harassed him to lay charges against Rob. McAlary's cross-examination caused the normally straitlaced court to break out laughing.

Now that Judge Smythe's ruling had made it clear that Robbie was not connected to the ring-in, we felt the way was clear for him to get his licence back. The warning-off had no timeframe, and Rob kept hearing encouraging reports that the AJC wanted to let him back. It seemed logical, as the betting ring had been weakened by his and my absence.

The AJC committee didn't see it that way. Rob made applications in 1986 and 1987 to no avail. It wouldn't even see him. After that, Jack told me he had heard from an AJC committeeman that if Rob kept bothering them with more applications, they would have him charged with lying. Dismissing this as scuttlebutt, Rob – ever the optimist – applied again in 1989. Sure enough, soon after applying, he was charged and pleaded guilty to lying to the tribunal six years earlier.

Rob had been treated severely, but through it all he maintained his dignity and never complained about his lot. Incredibly, he still kept the ship afloat and was able to continue to earn a living through racing. He just kept working and working.

To his enormous credit, Rob didn't take his problems home. To this day, Rob and Gai's children, Tom and Kate, say how they were totally oblivious to all the trials and tribulations of the time. And of course, Gai supported Rob 100 per cent, knowing that what he had done by betting on Fine Cotton and then lying to the authorities was stupid but not the cardinal sin it had been made out to be.

—

I was still on the outer and treated as a leper. The phone stopped ringing and Suzanne and I were dropped from the social scene like hot potatoes. People we thought were friends avoided us, especially in the beginning.

I was left with nothing to do for long periods, and at times I wondered how I was going to make ends meet. On some Saturdays I would just get in the car and drive around.

The one thing that did continue as normal was my position as honorary consul-general of the Kingdom of Tonga. The role had been very dear to me for over a decade. The media was so vicious toward me after Fine Cotton that they even wrote to the King, trying to cause trouble. His Majesty dismissed any misgivings and stuck by me. I learnt exactly who my true friends were, and probably the best of them was His Majesty. He treated me exactly as he always had done.

Some in the consular corps in Sydney were amazed that I didn't lose my post, and a couple even snubbed me for a while. However, I was still treated by governments with the normal dignity afforded to a diplomat in my role and was invited to official events, including those at Government House in Sydney. I was determined not to hide away and didn't miss one function, which helped me through this difficult time.

Later, when I had a medical check-up, the doctor told me I'd had a mild heart attack in this period. I had always thrived on pressure, but with Fine Cotton on top of the unfortunate family litigation, there was extreme financial strain. I still had no access to any of my assets. Actually, I think I found the AJC's warning-off even more stressful than the family court case.

—

Have you ever noticed the sick rooster in the yard? As soon as the other roosters see his weakness, every bird wants to peck him, even down to the lowest hen.

As if I didn't have enough dramas to contend with, the ABC produced a *Four Corners* 'exposé' on our family. This was November 1986, two years after the Fine Cotton affair. The program was scandalous. It seemed to me it was an hour-long attempt to destroy me and my family.

Four Corners claimed that Jack and I had cheated my nephews and niece and took all their money: we were the 'greedy' uncles who had 'stolen everything'. They didn't balance the program with the fact our nephews and niece had started with little and had overwhelmingly benefited from our generosity and hard work on their behalf.

It was all so one-sided and biased – a disgraceful piece of journalism. They even had actors playing roles and recreating scenes as though it was some kind of melodrama. It was awful. *Four Corners*, a program that relied on a reputation for presenting the facts, had been decidedly misled by some bitter and twisted enemies.

I was overseas at the time, but Rob and David unwisely tried to get an injunction to prevent the program from going to air. Of course, all the injunction did was to create amazing free publicity for the show. Instead of being low-key, we had, in effect, elevated the program to must-see viewing status when it went to air.

Eventually ordering that it could be broadcast, the judge said he couldn't stop *Four Corners* on legal grounds but told the ABC that it could expect a huge defamation claim against it. We wrote to the ABC board, including its new chairman David Hill, asking it not to run the untrue allegations and risk defamation, but our request fell on deaf ears.

The ABC had as its sources the self-confessed liar Arthur Harris and other unstable racing riff-raff, including my former friend Jack Muir. The program had also been used by our opponents in the equity case as a means of promoting their claims against us.

Rob had relied on Arthur Harris for his very good form analysis and had tried hard to get him to use a computerised form system – one of the first in racing at that time – but Arthur refused to use it. I think he resented the fact that Rob and I would win bookmaking while 'using his tips' to help our own form, yet he himself lost when punting with us. His form was just one of the factors we used, and Arthur had totally ignored our own gambling ability.

Something turned Harris against Robbie. Perhaps it was because he had lost money to me. It was hard for Rob to understand why Harris had become so embittered, particularly since Rob had always paid him well and treated him with respect – far more than I ever could. After Fine Cotton, when we could no longer employ Harris, he became quite extreme towards us, fabricating and spreading the story that Rob had organised the Fine Cotton scam.

After the ABC aired *Four Corners*, to high ratings, Rob and I brought a landmark criminal defamation suit against the program's executive producer, Peter Manning, and presenter, Tony Jones. You could tell they had thought they were on to a 'good story'. They believed what they had been told by blatantly unreliable sources pushing their own agendas. The journalists didn't know the truth. Clearly, they should have investigated it much more thoroughly before setting out to destroy reputations.

Normally defamation is a civil matter, but our barrister, Clive Evatt, told us it was one of the worst defamation matters he had ever seen, and that, in his opinion, we had been targeted maliciously by the ABC. He advised that it was a rare case where we had grounds for a ruling of criminal defamation against the producer and presenter – a serious offence which provided for a jail sentence, not just damages.

A chamber magistrate agreed with the argument put by our solicitor, Philip Pollack, that there were grounds for criminal defamation. He issued a summons to both the reporter and producer to answer criminal defamation charges in the Magistrate's Court at the Downing Centre.

Following Clive Evatt's powerful opening address, which outlined all the scandalous untruths and inaccuracies resulting in the alleged criminal defamation, it soon became apparent that the defendants were very uncomfortable. The magistrate gave them both the opportunity to defend themselves but they appeared to be rattled. The magistrate formally committed them to stand trial for criminal defamation in the District Court. The next day the papers reported they could face a penalty of up to seven years' jail.

Behind the scenes, the ABC vigorously lobbied the new Liberal state government. Eventually, the court action was stymied when John Dowd, the new Attorney-General, no-billed the criminal defamation charges. So much for the openness so often called for by the media.

It was disappointing, but nevertheless it had been a significant victory to have the journalists committed for trial. It was a triumph we savoured, as we hoped it would make them and others think twice before producing outrageous stories without first verifying the truth and accuracy of their information.

In 2001, with the benefit of hindsight, Peter Manning had a more objective view when he said: 'My memory of the Waterhouse programme was that it basically profiled the split in the Waterhouse family about the heirs to the estate. It was a very difficult programme to make . . . a very complex family internal matter, but on the other hand the Waterhouse family are part of the royalty of Sydney . . . Yes, criminal defamation is no joke. I've got to say I was a bit shocked to be charged with criminal defamation by anybody, let alone the Waterhouses . . . it certainly was a big stress that I carried during that time as executive producer.' I found this a most interesting acknowledgement; clearly, Manning didn't like it when the heat went on him.

Four Corners had been so very damaging to me. I felt like screaming, 'It's not true! It's just the opposite – I gave those children just about everything they had!' Of course, there was no point.

29

That Sinking Feeling

ROB AND I HAD DECIDED that a good investment for the future would be on the land, growing crops. We had acquired two beautiful soil-rich crop properties of 10,000 hectares, or about 35 square miles, in the Murrumbidgee Irrigation Area with a fifteen-mile frontage on the river. This was in 1983 and our partner was Peter McCoy, a leading Canberra bookmaking friend of Rob's.

The properties, Rudds Point and Burrabogie, were laser-levelled to have a perfect even fall for irrigation purposes, and with their abundant supply of water, drought would never be a problem. The land was thought the equal of any sheep country in Australia. Burrabogie had been one of the top merino studs in New South Wales – the ram on the back of the ten-cent coin was from Burrabogie's adjoining sister property, Uardrey.

We took eagerly to farming. Australia competed well inter-nationally with farm produce, holding its own both on price and quality, without paying subsidies to its farmers. Australia could do this mainly because the land was good, cheap and there was plenty of it. Peter McCoy was the farmer and the driving force behind this venture, but Rob also was keen. Although 700 kilo-metres from Sydney was a long way, I drove there often.

I was struck by the natural beauty of the vast countryside, with its endless plains and fields of waving crops, while the gently flowing Murrumbidgee River meandered through the land. The property was so flat you could see the earth's curvature on the horizon. Tall, stately gum trees lined the river banks as though a colonial artist had placed them there. I couldn't believe the wildlife. After Pete and Rob built a 50-hectare irrigation dam, thousands of wild ducks, white cockatoos, galahs and sparrow hawks flocked to it. The cockies brought back memories of the ones I trained to talk at the Imperial Hotel. The property also had plenty of kangaroos, foxes, wild boar and emus. Guenther brought a special rifle back from Europe for Rob, and we went shooting to cull pigs, rabbits and foxes.

The first thing Pete and Rob did was plant a couple of thousand hectares of corn, but they soon had a setback: a plague of locusts wiped out the entire crop. They then planted a summer crop, only to suffer one of the most awesome infestations I have ever seen – a mouse plague.

You can't comprehend the havoc that a mouse plague causes until you see it first-hand. The ground moves with millions and millions of these tiny creatures. One mouse might be cute, but to see this endless swarm is quite scary. In their search for food, they soon lose their fear of humans and, by sheer weight of numbers, they seem insurmountable. They flooded the fields of maize, even eating the stalks.

Fortunately, the plague ran its course and disappeared as quickly as it had arrived, and we started off again, focusing on our wheat. However, now there was a world oversupply, and governments began subsidising their wheat farmers more heavily. A price war emerged between Europe and the United States; even Saudi Arabia, which produced the most expensive wheat in the world, was underbidding Australia. We realised wheat was no longer viable.

With so much grazing land and water at our disposal, we decided to cut our losses and bring in some sheep. So we introduced about 25,000 merinos, but even here we struck trouble, losing 1500 head of lambs because of an unseasonal cold snap. The lot of a farmer is certainly not an easy one, but it's a great life and brings a tremendous sense of achievement. I wasn't a farmer – I was always a city slicker – yet I never failed to enjoy the country life.

I took Louise and Guenther down to the property after convincing them to have a few days away from the pressures of business. Gai, ever the organiser, recognised Guenther's handyman skills and had him working for the whole of his stay, replacing flyscreens and doing small repairs. Rob had bought a large cubby-house kit for Tom and Kate to play with, thinking he could assemble it quickly. Guenther watched Rob and me hopelessly messing around for most of the day before he moved in, saying, 'Leave this to me.' It took him into the night to build it but it stood for many years.

Not being able to go to the races after our warning-off, Rob focused on the farm, and he and Gai even toyed with the idea of moving there permanently. However, the properties were a bottomless pit, always requiring more funds, which we couldn't provide as our assets were still frozen in the family litigation and our income had stopped.

Peter eventually took over our half of the farm properties, with the agreement that he would pay us out later. However, the debt stood; times were tough on the farm and he wasn't able to afford it, having troubles of his own. Peter eventually sold the properties.

I had very excitedly gone into a major housing project near Lake Macquarie in New South Wales in the early 1980s. Punter Ben Westbury and I acquired a wonderful tract of land, and we gained approval to build 300 houses and townhouses on it. The sites all had glorious views to the lake, but the project hit a few hurdles because of the economic downturn. Nevertheless, it turned out to be a very nice subdivision, even if we didn't do as well as we hoped financially.

—

No sooner had I absorbed the horror of Fine Cotton when I was hit a bodyblow by Lloyd's of London, which I had joined as an underwriter nearly twenty years earlier. I had been warned off by the AJC in late 1984 and went to London the following June to get my Lloyd's results.

I had built myself up to the highest level of Lloyd's underwriting by this stage, and I had included many of the family – Jack, John, Rob, Louise, Suzy and David. I had also recommended many friends, such as Francis Grant and Peter McCoy, for membership. I was looking forward to a substantial result, especially as this was the one income stream not frozen in the family litigation. Substantial it was, but not the way I expected.

Through Charles St George, I was on some of the best underwriting syndicates at Lloyd's. Apart from the most sought-after Peter Cameron-Webb syndicates, I was also a foundation member of Ian Posgate's syndicate, which became one of the hardest to join as it was a resounding success. I had also joined Charles's own Oakley Vaughan syndicates.

Cameron-Webb, however, turned out to be a crook. He thought his syndicate members were profiting too much and began siphoning off monies. The wheels eventually fell off, Cameron-Webb was exposed and, although £41 million was paid back to the syndicate members, and the committee of Lloyd's set aside over £200 million to cover these losses, it still left an enormous deficiency.

Further, Posgate, the most successful of all the new Lloyd's underwriters, and a man who had been given the soubriquet of 'Goldfinger', had also now foundered and was suspended by the Lloyd's committee. The Oakley Vaughan syndicates ran aground too.

It appeared that I was involved with every losing syndicate

of the time, associated with either asbestos claims, poor business practices or even fraud. Incredible as it may seem, I was completely unaware of these financial disasters at Lloyd's before my visit in 1985, as the formal results had not yet been sent.

The losses were horrendous. I had gone there expecting a profit of around £100,000 but was met with a deficit of £460,000. This had been further aggravated by the fall in the Australian dollar. The previous year when I was in London the Aussie dollar was worth 66 pence. Now it had dropped to 41 pence, meaning my losses for the year exceeded $1 million.

Lloyd's accounts were always delivered three years in arrears. It had to be this way to enable all claims to be lodged, examined and assessed, adjudicated upon where necessary, and then settled. With a sinking feeling, I realised that these results, which represented the 1982 accounts, were in all probability going to become much worse in the following two years. The nest-egg I had built up over twenty years now was in jeopardy.

I also realised that, as a member of Lloyd's, I had unlimited liability. Further, with all my assets frozen back in Australia, I was now facing a situation where I would be unable to meet the claims likely to be made against me in the short term. Just as I feared, the 1986 year compounded the losses of the previous years and wiped out all the profits and reserves that I had built up over two decades.

It is a sad fact of life that once you're on a losing trot, it's awfully hard to turn it around. After two glorious decades, I had been unfortunate enough to follow a friend whose underwriting syndicates had sailed into unmarked waters, and at the same time be on the syndicate of an unscrupulous cheat. My Lloyd's of London experience cost me well over £1 million. Further, I felt sorry for introducing so many others who also suffered through these unprecedented Lloyd's losses.

But there's no point in dwelling on the dark side.

—

After Fine Cotton, my daily routine was dramatically changed, as you might imagine, just by the mere fact I wasn't allowed on to a racetrack. Going to the races was the one thing I had done all my life. To while away the time, I played backgammon, read the papers and books, and didn't stop doing crosswords.

Rob turned to punting and was the only one able to provide regular income to keep the family going. I have always regarded Rob as a mathematical genius. The intellectuals of form analysis appreciated him because he looked at the form of horses differently – totally differently to how I did. I was a gambler, but Rob was a calculated risk-taker.

Our situation was hopeless – I had no income and the family litigation continued. I had built up assets worth tens of millions of dollars – I had even unwillingly been listed in the Rich List in 1983 – but now I couldn't even borrow to buy a pub or any other business to keep us going. Nevertheless, my Depression background stood me in good stead; we lived on what could only be described as the smell of an oily rag.

The inimitable character of Mrs Witt, a former punter, was to assist me in no small way. A number of punters who owed money did not settle and there were some we had to sue. The one person who was reliable all along was Mrs Witt. She was a real character, aged about 80, who owned a timber yard. She loved to bet and she used to come out to the races every week. She always paid in post-dated cheques of $1000.

In earlier times I had regarded her method of paying as a bit of a nuisance, but after Fine Cotton she gave our clerk Keith Jones a whole stack of post-dated cheques, each for $1000 a month, for years in advance to cover her debt. These cheques became pretty important, and I blessed Mrs Witt each time a cheque would fall due for helping keep me afloat. The supply lasted years, and I still have six cheques bearing dates in 1993 and 1994, which I didn't worry about after she passed away.

Even though Rob and I weren't even allowed to set foot on a racecourse, racing was still our lives. You could take us out of racing but not the racing out of us. Rob had a good friend with whom he formed a punting partnership. This friend was also a mathematical genius. Together they used computer programs to do the form, and Rob adapted easily, changing from bookmaker to punter, as they played the trifectas and other exotic forms of betting.

Rob started sending a girl (later two) to the races; she would take a computer with a special betting program that calculated hundreds of small bets, which would have to be frantically called to the tote operator within the last minutes before each race jumped. We were nervous they wouldn't allow Robbie's girls onto the tracks, so in those early days the girls had to be discreet about who their principals were. Nevertheless, it eventually became known, and soon tote officials were courting the girls because of their high turnover. The totes even indulged them with nice lunches and flew them in chartered planes to the various provincial meetings!

Rob was extraordinary. He kept his children in private schools and, sharing costs with Gai, was even able to afford the occasional holiday.

—

David was now back in the family fold. It felt a little like the return of the prodigal son. David had made his own way in the world. What he felt he had missed out on at school he picked up travelling.

David had developed a flamboyant lifestyle and always had beautiful girlfriends. With his champagne tastes, he bought a mansion with harbour views in Vaucluse, and he needed me to guarantee his finance for the purchase. I had all my assets tied up but I was still able to give him another personal guarantee. Although it was against my lifetime policy, I just wanted to help my son.

With his new house, David had become interested in the art world, as he realised it was better to spend money on artworks rather than renovations. David had a friend in London scouting for him; incredibly, he found a long-lost painting by the famous Australian artist of the Heidelberg school, Frederick McCubbin. This huge painting, *Bush Idyll*, was a masterpiece, a beautiful painting of a young girl lying in the grass being serenaded by a boy, with gum trees all around – it was considered by many to be one of the finest works of Australian art. David bought it in 1984 for about £150,000 – they said it was a bargain – and sold it at auction fourteen years later for $2.3 million.

The Australian art world was so excited by this discovery that they organised a major exhibition called 'Golden Summers' with *Bush Idyll* on the wrap-around cover of the catalogue.

David started going to auctions himself. He had a great eye for art. He paid the record price for an Arthur Streeton, *Bathers, Killarney,* using an old yearling sales auction trick of jumping in at the beginning with a high bid to shock and knock out the other bidders. Then in 1985 David bought *The Bath of Diana* by John Glover for $580,000. Glover was one of our earliest colonial artists and regarded as the father of Australian landscape painting. It turned out to be one of Australia's most significant artworks, being the first depiction of an Aboriginal in a mythological European setting.

By this time David had a series of loans where he'd asked me to go guarantor for him, as I did around ten times over the decade. However, in March 1986 I woke up to see I had landed on the front page of *The Sunday Telegraph* through one of these guarantees; along with my picture, the article read: 'Former bookmaker Bill Waterhouse, warned off all Australian racecourses following the Fine Cotton ring-in scandal, is listed to appear in the NSW Bankruptcy Court.'

This was sorted out, but by 1989, and before putting one of his paintings to auction, David needed to refinance his loan. David again offered my guarantee but the Westpac bank manager wanted something more substantial. Banks liked bricks and mortar, not paintings. So David, desperate not to lose his painting to the finance company before the auction, came to Rob and me and asked what we could do for extra security. Looking straight at Robbie, David said, 'What about your home? It's not frozen.'

I think Rob wanted to disappear under the desk. The home, which Rob had bought himself, was the only property not covered by injunctions and caveats.

'You should help your brother,' I told Rob.

The bank manager assured Rob that David's painting was still his first security and that the house was only to be a back-up for the short-term loan. So Robbie, without even mentioning it to Gai, allowed his family home to be used as security for David's loan for the 'few weeks' until the auction. This would later cause Rob intense anxiety.

David's art deals also led him to a Melbourne art dealer and gallery owner, Brian Pearce, but these deals led to a lawsuit. Our assets were still frozen when David's case came to court in mid-1989, and in these hard times we were 'eating the paint off the walls'. I had recently settled a defamation action I had against a Sydney newspaper for $25,000, knowing the money would be hugely welcome. But when David needed money to pay his legal team, I gave it to him.

I drove down to Melbourne for each of the five weeks of the hearing to support David. His barrister, Peter Searle, a junior, was a tax expert, but on the first day the judge was scathing towards him. Searle quit, totally demoralised, but I persuaded him to stay on and not ruin David's case. He fought on strongly against a senior and a junior counsel. Justice Ormiston dismissed each side's case.

In his 137-page judgement, the judge was especially scathing towards David, saying he was a 'devious and unreliable witness' whose 'weaknesses were displayed when he was asked matters of detail', and whose 'most frequent defence was prevarication'. Justice Ormiston summed up: 'He [David] is also, I regret to conclude, a person whose commercial morality was of the lowest order.'

30

Family Blood Spills

THE FAMILY DISPUTE with Martin and his siblings took seven years to finally reach court.

The publicity surrounding the claims made for sensational reading. They alleged that all Jack's and my money belonged to them. In effect, they claimed we had stolen their money! They won the initial media support because, early on, our barristers had told us, 'Look, you just have to accept this bad publicity; there's no point fighting it now – wait till we get to court.' And so there was nothing in the media to show how extraordinarily generous we had in fact been to our nephews and niece.

When the court case began, on 4 September 1989, it immediately attracted headlines. Ian Barker QC, famous from prosecuting the Lindy Chamberlain case, was acting for Patty, Martin and the others. He took three days just for his opening statement.

My brother and I got the shock of our lives, Barker presented their case as though we were like Jack the Ripper. I was just stunned and taken completely off-guard. I thought the issues were clear-cut and would be quickly resolved in our favour once the full matter was presented in court. I knew I'd done the right thing and believed the court would see that straight away.

I couldn't believe what I was hearing as I sat there listening to all the wild allegations Patty had made about us, including the preposterous fabrication that Jack and I had stolen a 'new luxury' Cadillac from her. The publicity was ghastly. The next day in *The Sydney Morning Herald* the front-page headline read: 'Where is the Cadillac?'

It was no new Cadillac but a pre-war bombed-out old LaSalle, which Charlie, Jack and I had owned for many years and used to tramp around concrete, liquor and livestock. When the *Herald* ran our side of the story, it was not on the front page – no headline for us.

The case was set down for three months but in fact ran continuously for a year. Preparing for the case, we couldn't pay our legal bills, so we were always behind. We had to go through laborious, costly and humiliating applications to the court to release our money from the injunctions by my nephews and niece, and even then it was never enough for the lawyers.

We were inundated by the other side's demands for sworn answers to thousands of questions, or interrogatories going back over minutiae for 35 years. It was totally unreasonable. Just trying to answer them all took months, eating up time and funds that we should have been using to prepare our defence.

I had explained to our legal team that after the funds ran out they would have to wait until the case was over to be paid. Without warning, the solicitor went before the judge the next morning and told him he had sent all the barristers and counsel home because we had no money. I was far from impressed; so much for loyalty. Martin couldn't have looked happier.

We were now left unrepresented in court, so I went and sat at the bar table with the other side's barristers to face the judge until we could find a new solicitor, Michael Delaney, and funds to pay the legal team. It had been 35 years since I had last sat at the bar table as a barrister.

The court allowed us to borrow on the security of one of our properties in Kirribilli, which had been frozen since the early 1980s. This was about the only property in our entire portfolio which was not in dispute. With no income to service the interest, and at a time when interest rates were going through the roof, we had to accept the extortionate rate of 22 per cent, capitalising on the $1.5 million loan. The other side also needed money and so was allowed to borrow on the same property as second mortgagee. It was hard for me to cope with the sheer madness of both sides borrowing millions, on the same property, just to fight each other in court. It felt like we were on a runaway train, spending hundreds of thousands of dollars in legal fees each month and sitting for mind-numbing days in Court 8C in the Supreme Court. It was like putting a match to money.

On the promise of more funds being released by the court, our very able barrister, James Allsop (later Justice Allsop and president of the New South Wales Court of Appeal), agreed to come back – as long as we also hired a QC to lead the case. More expense again. Allsop recommended a young QC called Francis Douglas. When I met him, Douglas told me, 'I think you and your brother have done an extraordinary thing for these children and I believe I can get your family a good result.' It might now sound glib, but in my vulnerable state I think I was happy to hear anything encouraging.

Jack and I needed to establish clearly and effectively how we had looked after our brother's family. Throughout the case I was the strategist, keeping the lawyers on their toes but I couldn't be on top of all the detail. Before the proceedings, Louise and Guenther had spent much of their time in Germany and also New Zealand; Guenther owned a ski school in Europe and was the director of the ski school in Queenstown. They had a lovely carefree life, and Louise also gained her ski instructor qualifications. Now I asked her to come home and help with the case. It was a steep learning curve, but Louise rolled up her sleeves and worked extremely hard. She started out in the 'maiden class', photocopying and finding documents, but by the end was virtually running the whole show.

In the witness box, Patty was caught out on many of her claims – including one that she had never held a gun in her life. In cross-examination Douglas showed her old photos Jack's wife, Gwen, had found of Patty holding a rifle and standing in front of the old Cadillac bomb! At another point Patty slipped up when she volunteered, 'This is the one thing I haven't made up!' I had no hesitation in believing *that* statement.

Patty alleged that all our money and most of our assets had belonged to Charlie before he died, and that after his death Jack and I 'took' two-thirds of everything for ourselves. She made the malicious claim that there had been no partnership between my two brothers and me. Hearing her make these claims helped me understand how my nephews and niece could have become so bitter towards Jack and me. They had obviously been fed these lies from a young age.

I wanted to destroy them in cross-examination because I felt my wonderful relationship with my late brother had been tarnished. Also, Martin had admitted to stealing our documents while acting as our in-house solicitor. But we were still behind the eight-ball.

Louise pointed out to our legal team that the affidavits by my nephews and niece, which alleged certain conversations 30 years before, were uncannily similar. She took them home that night and compared them word for word. It became obvious that they had been cut and pasted using a computer, sometimes changing the order but using almost identical words for each one.

Martin was forced to concede in court that he had drafted these sworn affidavits for his brothers himself. As well, inconsistent statements in Martin's own affidavits, sworn several years apart, were not to help his credibility. Our barristers were delighted but I was disappointed not to see blood on the floor.

Yet it was extraordinarily hard to find documentary evidence to show that Charlie, Jack and I had been equal partners 35 years before. Bloody hell! We were brothers. We had never had a written partnership agreement and many other records were no longer around; not even the tax office had files going back so many years.

Firsthand witnesses of our partnership were also hard to come by. We did track down a few, however. Bookmaker Owen Durham was able to give strong evidence in our favour, but sadly he died just before he could appear in court. Jimmy Plunkett, who had been a clerk with us at the races, struck a chord in court when he said his memory from so many years back about the partnership was vivid because he said he was young and impressionable and had 'never seen so much cash in all my life'.

Barry Pheloung, my life-long friend, had suffered a stroke and was dying, but he insisted on giving evidence of our partnership arrangements from his sickbed. We also found our old draftsman, who gave evidence about joint instructions on our early building projects. My sister, Betty, and Jock Rorrison were also able to come forward with recollections of partnership discussions. Although their testimony was strong about us being partners with Charlie rather than his employees, we still feared it was perhaps not 100 per cent conclusive.

Believe it or not, it was the AJC that proved our point. One of our solicitors, Clive Jeffreys, was going through all documents subpoenaed by Charlie's wife and children and for some reason looked in the boxes from the AJC. Clive found Charlie's bookmaking licence application for 1947. On the back was a list of our assets, which showed that we each had a one-third share in everything, including those in Charlie's name.

The discovery was an enormous relief and a vindication. This old licence application, which was in my handwriting and was signed by Charlie, proved a saviour. How ironic that the AJC records, subpoenaed by our opponents, were to prove the truth of what Jack and I had said all along.

During the hearing Martin was forever running up to the bar table and giving instructions, sending notes or complaining to his counsel – it must have driven them mad. On one occasion, Ian Barker QC snapped to him, 'If you don't shut up, I'm going to put that Louise Waterhouse back in the box.' She had refuted Martin's claims very strongly when she testified. I chuckled and took that as a big compliment to Louise, coming from the opposing QC.

Despite the heavy nature of the hearing, I was quite bemused by Martin. He was the client but wore the same traditional barrister's 'stroller' – old-fashioned striped pants with a black coat – every day of the year that we were in court. Only on one day of the whole case did we see him not wearing that same attire – he wore a brown suit instead. I could only surmise that perhaps he had sent the pants to the dry-cleaners.

I had tried to settle the matter a few times. Barry O'Keefe, our QC early on, had done a lengthy calculation in October 1983 and made an offer based on his worst-case scenario. I wasn't happy to offer them more than I thought they deserved but agreed O'Keefe could do it. Ironically, the amount was comparable to what Charlie's four children would ultimately receive at the end of the case. Of course, back then they had rejected our offer out of hand.

Now, in the middle of the hearing – it was October 1989 – Justice John Kearney implored both sides to settle, pointedly looking straight at me. They wanted nothing of our offers, including one of $15 million plus a third of our Fabergé shares and payment of their substantial costs. We thought that amounted to around a third of all the assets, including those built up after 1964. But Martin wanted 100 per cent of everything, plus millions more in compensation.

Justice Kearney was a very fair man. None of the judges in the Equity Court had wanted to sit on the mammoth case, but he had taken it on less than three years out from his retirement. It turned out to be his swansong.

Having run the business for all those years, I bore the brunt of the accusations against Jack and me. I was in the box for five weeks, going back over minute details of the last 40 years. Ian Barker cross-examined me aggressively over and over, time and time again. It was so intense that the judge ordered that we should have Fridays off. At 67, I found the pressure relentless and tiring but I just had to put up with it. My barrister asked the judge if I could suck mints to help me while giving evidence, and he kindly agreed. I was grateful for this small mercy.

I believe such extended cross-examination is virtually unheard of; under modern court rules, such long interrogation is no longer allowed. I've never been a whinger and I've taken most things in my stride, but I'm not sure how much more I could have taken.

—

Charlie's wife and children not only claimed 100 per cent of the real estate that Charlie, Jack and I had built up, but also Fabergé. John had still not transferred my shares or formally confirmed that he held them on trust for me, even though he had signed acknowledgments in 1977. Under cross-examination by their counsel in court, John now refused under oath to acknowledge that I owned one-third of our Fabergé interest at all.

My nephews and niece were after Fabergé too, so I felt attacked from both sides. It was dreadful. I just wanted my rightful one-third share of the business I had acquired and financed.

Because John now suddenly denied my part-ownership, he could no longer be represented by our barristers, as they said it was a conflict of interest. At the last minute John had to get his own legal team to defend himself against the claims by my nephews and niece – a whole new team of solicitors, plus senior and junior counsel. I wanted to put my own Fabergé claim for my one-third on the backburner, so as not to compromise the main case. My hand was forced, though, when I was told by John's counsel that if I wished to assert my one-third interest in the Fabergé shares, I had to speak now or 'forever hold my peace'.

So, incredibly, I was now forced to engage an entire additional legal team, since our existing counsel – who were acting for both Jack and me – also had a conflict of interest on Fabergé.

Poor Jack, embarrassed and under pressure, now turned around and retracted his sworn interrogatories about my share of Fabergé and the farm, which had been put in John's name because of the Vietnam War, and gave contradictory evidence to suit John. Greg Burton, Jack's and my junior counsel, looked to be furious.

It was our worst nightmare. We were imploding. No longer did we have a united front to defend Charlie's children's wild allegations, but were forced by John to deal with the Fabergé situation then and there.

It's amazing what you find in subpoenaed files. File notes from our former solicitors, Moore & Bevins, recorded John as telling them, after my Fine Cotton drama, that I was about to skip the country and go to live in Tonga! You had to see the funny side of it.

With all the parties fighting one another, the bar table was crowded too. We suddenly had four QCs and six juniors, plus four firms of solicitors, all arguing over the same pot of money. The lawyers were feasting.

As it turned out, Martin helped win the Fabergé case for me, but his work wouldn't prove his own claim. Through his doggedness, he discovered all the letters and agreements John had signed with me regarding Fabergé. And through the brilliant work of Clive Jeffreys, who – along with Michael Adams QC (now Justice Adams) and a young barrister, Dr Kevin Conner – proved that I did own my one-third share.

By now it was a one-third share of an empty box. The Fabergé business finished up as a disaster, disintegrating in front of my eyes while the case was running. In 1989 Unilever acquired Fabergé Inc for US$1.55 billion, taking over all of Fabergé worldwide, except our half of Fabergé Australia. We were a separate entity because of our franchise, and we all thought we were in for a huge payout.

But John overplayed his hand. Denying my part-ownership, he attempted to sell the Australian franchise to Unilever. However, Unilever wasn't prepared to pay anything like the Australian proportion of the international deal, since our licence was nearing the end of its second ten-year term. John wouldn't allow anyone else into the negotiations, nor did he keep me informed. He reached an agreement with Unilever but then tried to improve the deal as it went along, using a 'salami-slice' strategy. This was his mistake. Unilever pulled out completely, and although John tried to sue the company to complete the transaction, it was able to show that the deal wasn't done because John had tried to change the terms. John lost the case and also the appeal. He had let a fortune slip through his hands.

Unilever was eventually able to take over our half of Fabergé Australia for virtually nothing. Unbelievably, the iconic Fabergé Australia company, which had taken twenty years to build up, was no more, and its products like Brut and Brut 33 became just a few more brands in the Unilever lineup. And we got nothing. Unilever sold all its trademarks in the Fabergé name in 2007 to an upmarket luxury goods company, and Toby Brown, our earlier marketing manager and now owner of Pharmacare, eventually bought the Australian rights to Brut.

When John lost the case, Unilever harshly bankrupted him to claim its legal fees. Although these were not large and they had effectively obtained our half of Fabergé Australia without paying us, they were obviously bitter about the experience. I guess there are two sides to every story.

John wanted me to support a Part X settlement, where, in special circumstances, creditors can agree to accept a part-payment and forgo the remainder of the debt if a majority agree to the terms.

The court had decided that John owed me plenty – over $4 million. However, his proposal was to pay some creditors in full through his father, and then walk away scot-free from the rest, including me. We had massive legal fees as a result of John forcing us to fight the case at that time, and he still had some assets in trust, so I felt I couldn't possibly support him, even though he was Jack's son. John bitterly resented me for not bailing him out.

—

In the middle of the equity case, Louise found some extra-ordinary Commonwealth Bank documents, which Martin, in leaving no stone unturned, had subpoenaed from the bank.

I already had a problem at the bank because the interest on my racing overdraft had been capitalised while I had not been earning income for the last five years. Jack and John also had liabilities because they had not been travelling well at the races ever since our split. Jack later told me he couldn't seem to make a go of racing after we separated. Apart from anything else, I was no longer doing their prices and holding everything together. But at that stage I knew nothing about the enormity of their debts.

The bank's internal memos showed it was planning to assert that the old guarantee I had signed in about 1974 – for a joint overdraft of $100,000 in favour of the old partnership between Jack, John and me – was not only still in place but was for an unlimited amount, for each of us individually.

When I had signed the overdraft forms in 1974 the bank had told me a guarantee was needed to cover the $100,000 partnership overdraft limit. Fifteen years later, it was claiming that this guarantee document was an unlimited and open-ended personal guarantee for both my ex-partners' future liabilities. This meant, in effect, that no matter what debts John and Jack amassed at any time later in their lifetime, the Commonwealth Bank considered that I was liable for them all.

This was in spite of the fact the bank knew that we had split up our partnership, that we had paid back the $100,000 overdraft in full, that we had closed the account and had no further liabilities, and that the partnership was dissolved. The bank also knew there was tension between John and me but at no time did it advise me that it believed the guarantee was still in force.

I had banked with the Commonwealth since I was twelve years of age, and had regarded them as having a responsibility towards me as a client – in those early days your bank manager was there to help and advise you. The last thing I expected was sharp or dishonest practice.

To my astonishment on reading the bank's internal memos, they wanted to rely on me to cover Jack's and John's debts, which now – so many years later – were over $20 million! To rub salt into the wound, the memos clearly instructed the bank manager not to inform me about these contingent liabilities. I was astounded that the bank would hide its intention to allege such contingent liabilities from me. In my view, the bank should have cancelled the guarantee when the $100,000 limit was repaid and the partnership dissolved. At the very least it should have informed me that it considered the guarantee was still active so I could have taken any necessary steps.

The bank's conduct and the alleged liability would not have been discovered in time for us to challenge it, had Louise not found the damning documents. When we asked the bank for clarification, it refused to give us details of the claimed liabilities on the grounds of client confidentiality, but its formal letters of demand soon followed.

This was a new fight for my family and me. Our expensive equity case lawyers claimed a conflict of interest, but eventually we found the most senior solicitor from Clayton Utz, Geoff Kirby. He was astute, thorough and meticulous, and had a reputation for credibility.

We had little money but somehow Rob and I funded the fees, and Kirby – with Louise assisting him – put our case forcefully to the bank. Two years later we finally reached a settlement to pay the bank a compromised amount, based on the value of the security. I was glad that the deal helped Jack as much as me.

At the end of it all, the unassuming Mr Kirby was full of praise for Louise. I am proud to say that at his retirement dinner, in front of a who's who of the legal world, he made special mention of her, saying she had an ability to grasp extraordinarily complex problems, which he likened to playing 'three-dimensional chess'.

Our troubles certainly had come from all sides, but still had not played their full course.

31

The Gambling Man

*T*HE GAMBLING MAN was published in late November, 1990. The next time I saw the author, Kevin Perkins, I angrily said to him, 'I am seriously thinking of suing you.'

'Why would that be, Bill?' he asked.

'You have described me as mean, you have exposed my off-the-record betting, and you have deeply embarrassed me about the women in my private life,' I replied.

Perkins rejected my concerns with a laugh. 'All true,' he said.

To my surprise, he didn't take my feelings seriously at all. Perkins was a tough man with a reputation for hard-hitting journalism. I knew this from the first time he came to see me in 1968, when I told him I did not want a book written about me. 'I'm doing it whether you like it or not,' he had replied.

Back then, I felt I had to cooperate but at first I only paid him lip-service. However, Perkins pressed me through the coming years, while doing his own investigations along the way. As things developed and I found myself in trouble with the Chicka Pearson matter, I came to trust Perkins. I respected his integrity and ability as an investigative journalist. I was told that three of his newspaper publisher bosses over the years, Ezra Norton, Sir Frank Packer and Rupert Murdoch, had nothing but respect for him.

Perkins was not a person you could tell what to do. He was his own man. I have no doubt that Perkins would have crucified me if he thought I was a crook.

When I heard he was releasing his long-worked-on biography of me, I had very mixed feelings. It had been 22 years in the making. No doubt Perkins wanted to take advantage of the intense publicity arising from my family's equity battle; he had gone ahead without telling me.

I believed it was inappropriate for Perkins to release his book while we were still waiting for our judgement, but by the time I knew of the impending publication Perkins said, 'Too late – I've waited long enough.'

When the book came out Kevin came to my office and presented me with an autographed copy. I liked the title but was surprised he had not put a photo of me on the front. I sat down and read it from cover to cover.

I cringed at some of the things I read. I was very embarrassed about some of Kevin's assertions about my love life – he took liberties and said things I certainly wouldn't have said. It upset my wife, Suzanne, and also my dear friend Yuko, who was very private and embarrassed to be included. He also caused me to lose an old-time friend, Justice Adrian Roden.

Kevin held nothing back in his book, finding skeletons in various people's closets that even I wasn't aware of. He concentrated on the trials and tribulations of my life but from his perspective, having lived through so many of them himself. He was merciless in exposing the activities of many people, relying on the sources he had built up through his days as a leading newspaper editor. From my own experience I knew Perkins to be a thorough investigative reporter who was a stickler for checking and double-checking his facts.

The book produced mixed emotions in me. Apart from the fact that I was annoyed and would not have written much of what Perkins wrote, I admired him for his courage in producing such a powerful book. Although I knew he would have stuck to the facts from his investigations, I was concerned for him as I read through the exposé, as it was an explosive book and I expected he could be sued for defamation.

The Gambling Man exploded on the scene and was the talk of the town. Without any advertising or promotion, it received extraordinary publicity, being featured on television, talk-back radio and in newspaper spreads. Perkins' tell-all revelations about the AJC and other racing matters created a storm.

For me, the most enthralling aspect of *The Gambling Man* was the revelations from Perkins' painstaking investigations into the Fine Cotton ring-in. For the first time, the whole incredible story came out. People started coming up to me and asking to shake my hand. They said things like, 'It's hard to believe that racing officials can get it so wrong and be so unjust – I admire how you have handled your problems with dignity.'

Among the most amazing disclosures by Perkins was that the gangster George Freeman had caused serious trouble to Robbie and me over Fine Cotton by influencing or manipulating people of authority in the background. These included Freeman's contacts in the media, the police, politics and even at the AJC. Perkins revealed that Freeman, with his hatred for us, took advantage of the situation to make sure Robbie and I were the fall guys.

However, the defamation writs soon flew at Perkins. The book was taken off the shelves under the threat of litigation, and some booksellers were even threatened with bricks through their windows unless they removed it.

—

Francis Douglas QC made a passionate address in submissions, focusing on all the extraordinarily generous and overwhelmingly beneficial deeds we had done for Charlie's children. He likened the family dispute to an 'Icelandic saga or blood feud'. In a very rare show of emotion for any barrister, at one stage his voice broke and he shed tears, overcome by the depth of his feeling about the unfairness of our overwhelmingly magnanimous deeds being used to portray us as greedy and even fraudulent.

It took fifteen months for Justice Kearney to plough through the transcripts and submissions before handing down his 450-page judgement in November 1991. I was in Bulgaria, looking to set up a business in the newly opened Eastern bloc. When I was told with a day's notice that the judgement was finally to be handed down, I jumped on a plane but couldn't make it back in time.

Patty lost her case, and Francis Douglas and our defence team had effectively knocked over most of the extreme claims against us, but the judgement still came as a disappointment. We were ordered to give Charlie's children one-third of all our assets, including the assets that Jack and I had created after ending the old partnership in 1964. This was because we had allowed the bank to take security for our racing overdraft on the Charles Hotel at Bronte. To add insult to injury, the judge found four instances of 'equitable fraud', as we were a bit slap-happy and had not crossed the t's or dotted the i's.

However, to put the case in a proper perspective, Justice Kearney summed up: 'I conclude that the very substantial efforts of the trustees over many years have been the mainspring for the acquisition of the many assets comprising the trust property, the subject of these proceedings. In particular, the striking success of their bookmaking activities, involving intense and dedicated personal skills and labours of the trustees, provided the source for much of the success of the investments made by them. It is also relevant that the trustees contributed two-thirds of the capital and income of the overall enterprise and were co-owners in that proportion with the estate in its assets. Accordingly, I conclude that it is just and proper to make allowances to the trustees. Such allowances are indicated in my findings.'

In that statement the judge did, however, overlook the fact that the estate's one-third of the capital had actually come as a gift from Jack and me, after taking into account the value of Charlie's will.

Justice Kearney found that Patty's evidence was 'without regard to the truth . . . essentially unreliable and simply unacceptable'. He also said, 'She gave me the impression of having learnt her lines. When diverted from them, she appeared to have no genuine recollection . . . What purported recollection she did express was quite selective.'

Justice Kearney also said, 'I regard this explanation [by Martin] not only as deficient, but also as demonstrating the contrived nature of his evidence before me . . . Further his manner of responding to this change in his evidence did not impress me.'

Recognising that we had won on many issues, and that most of the extreme claims by my nephews and niece were unsubstantiated, the judge ruled that we should pay less than half of the overall costs.

The judge also ruled in our favour regarding our ownership of one-third of the family's shares in Fabergé, including Yves Rocher and the proceeds of the Max Factor sale, and also the farm that we had put in John's name. However, Charlie's children missed out on their claim to those assets. It didn't surprise me when Martin told the media he was unhappy with the judgement, as he had expected much more.

As Justice Kearney was to retire at the end of February 1992, we needed to have the court orders finalised and the amounts of compensation finally agreed before that time. Louise and Greg Burton (now SC), our junior barrister, worked intensively for weeks, even through the nights, to try to finish.

We knew the compensation figures proposed by the other

side's legal team weren't right. Our solicitor, Michael Delaney, asked, 'Why are we rushing when we're not happy with the numbers?' Suddenly the penny dropped and I realised we shouldn't accept anything we disagreed with. It could be fairly decided later by the Master in Equity. This changed the whole momentum of the case and was our turning point. By not having agreed figures, they couldn't move on the full judgement and would have to talk with us.

Louise began the conversation with Martin, after having not exchanged one word with him during the year of sitting in the same courtroom. It was cathartic. Having been 'mortal enemies' since the action began a decade earlier, here we were trying to agree on how to split up our hard-earned assets, the fight over which had torn our family apart.

They finally agreed to a deal which I could also accept. We all wanted to separate ourselves totally, and so we agreed to give them two properties, rather than giving them a one-third share of everything. We granted them the whole of the Chatswood Charles Hotel, which had become hopelessly run-down through our decade of fighting. Its real value lay in its fabulous siting in the metropolis of Chatswood. We also gave up 300 prime acres of one of the farm properties at Wallacia and took over their outstanding litigation debt.

I resented giving my nephews and niece more than what I believed they deserved. However, they took far less than what they had wanted. It was also less than our earlier offer of settlement. With the crashing of property values in the 1992 recession, our $15-million offer, made three years earlier, now looked overly generous.

After ten years it felt like throwing off a financial straitjacket. I was happy to cut the cards put the nightmare behind me, and think of it as a bad trot at the races.

—

David ended his relationship with me in 1992. He simply left the family, even though I was the guarantor for his debts, and he later sued me for an inheritance. 'An inheritance?' Rob had asked. 'I thought you had to die first!' I had tried to help David wherever I could, which made his conduct even more hurtful.

David would not sell his extremely valuable paintings. The bank wouldn't wait any longer for him to repay his loan, and so you can imagine Gai's horror when she opened the mail at three o'clock one morning before trackwork to find a letter from the bank notifying that it intended to sell her home – the home Rob had put on the line to help David.

David served a statement of claim on Jack and me two days before Christmas in 1993, based on the trusts Jack and I had set up in the 1960s for the benefit of all our children.

—

The distributors of *The Gambling Man* decided to name Rob and me as 'indirect' cross-defendants in their defamation suits, on the basis that the book was allegedly 'semi-authorised' and that we had supposedly told Perkins defamatory information which went into the book. The basis for joining us was feeble, as most of the offending claims were ones I wasn't even aware of before reading them in the book.

However, in January 1995, we were suddenly included as full defendants when one matter came to court for hearing. This was on the strength of an unidentified affidavit, which alleged that I had largely written and financed *The Gambling Man* to 'get square' with people like my former friend Jack Muir. Incredibly, I was not allowed to be shown the affidavit in court, nor was I even told of the actual allegations. It left Rob and me nonplussed. We couldn't believe that anyone could possibly assert such an outrageous scenario.

What we didn't know then was that these allegations were actually made by David. It was bad enough to be facing court claims again, but when I learnt it was David I was dumbstruck and profoundly hurt.

In April 1994 David had written an affidavit alleging I had told him I had written the *Gambling Man* book. I did not write the book or any part of it, and neither did Robert. Even more annoyed than me was Perkins, who valued his reputation as a journalist of integrity. He was irate at the allegation that someone else had written his book, which was the culmination of so many years of difficult research. Perkins had written his book well before the time alleged, and he had his drafts going back years.

In fact, in the mid-1980s, at the insistence of Suzy and Louise to keep me busy after the warning-off, I had actually sat down and written my own memoirs, writing everything in longhand. Our office assistant, Lee Wigmore, had painstakingly typed it up on an old-style golfball typewriter. That manuscript was later dusted off and has formed the basis of this autobiography. Being totally different in style and substance, my manuscript focused on my own experiences.

Now, in court and having been forced into being full-blown defendants, but without even knowing the nature of the allegations, we had to think on our feet. Rob and I went and sat at the bar table. We took advantage of our rights with regard to jury selection, but because there had been so many parties who had been exercising their rights to object, the court ran out of candidates, causing the matter to be adjourned to the next day. Then, at short notice, our barrister Clive Evatt was able to represent us.

By making Rob and me joint defendants with Perkins and the publisher, the plaintiff had made a poor decision. This meant their long-awaited hearing date was abandoned and they had to wait for another date months later.

There were several other defamation matters against Perkins, but the one by Arthur Harris was the only case that went to a full hearing. As 'minor' cross-defendants, and not wanting to waste money, Rob and I acted for ourselves. The trial saw one of the most extraordinary court scenes ever. At one stage, under cross-examination by Tim Hale (now SC), who was instructed by Philip Beazley, Harris completely turned away from the judge, jury and the court to face the corner, sulking like a naughty child. Harris had brought the defamation matter, but it was soon clear that he was the one on trial. The jury found that Harris was 'a cheat', 'a self-confessed liar', 'a slanderer and a scandal monger'. It also found Harris 'supplied the Australian Jockey Club . . . with false information harmful to the Waterhouses, knowing the information to be false'. This was the man who had contributed to the *Four Corners* program that defamed us; who had caused dramas with racing authorities by making up stories about Fine Cotton; and who had conspired with others to cause us harm over a period of fifteen years. However, we were all amused at the end of the hearing when the jury members asked if they could keep their copies of *The Gambling Man*.

All along, Perkins stood by his book, only agreeing to sign settlement papers to dismiss some defamation cases at the request of the other defendants, and he never paid compensation or damages to anyone. He fought the claims against him for over a decade, and without funds he represented himself most of the time, successfully keeping teams of lawyers at bay.

As radio man Frank Crook summed up on the local ABC radio, 'Kevin Perkins has devoted much of his life to putting this book together. He has certainly put his career and reputation on the line in the writing.'

Despite my earlier misgivings, I am glad the book was written.

—

David brought the trust claim to court. He tried to hire Steven Finch SC, the barrister who had acted against us in the family case, but Steven later told me he couldn't possibly take the brief because he felt Jack and I had been through more than enough. David did hire Martin's solicitor, who, after the case was over, sheepishly contacted me for help in pursuing David. I was not about to assist a third party against my son.

Justice Windeyer found in Jack's and my favour, but it was a hollow victory which gave me no pleasure. David subsequently asked for a settlement and agreed never to make any more legal claims.

David made many allegations without foundation and told the world I had cut him off, but he divorced himself from me and hurt me irrevocably. Recently, he stated, 'I was born into that family but I am not a member of it.' I have lost not only my son but also two grandchildren, a boy – I was pleased to see that David still felt enough of a Waterhouse to call him Henry – and a girl, Olivia, whom David sent to Ascham, following Louise and Kate.

I wish David no harm. He has chosen his own troubled path, but I just don't want him in my life any more.

—

Despite all the litigation, I had always thought that the one child of my brother Charles who was fair dinkum was Charlie junior. The poor fellow was always taking pills for indigestion, and it turned out he had stomach cancer. He had been badly affected by the litigation he and his siblings had brought against Jack and me.

Sadly, like his father, he was to die young. Two days after Charlie's death, his brother-in-law nervously came to see me. Charlie's family wanted him to be buried with his father, in the family plot I had bought for Charles, Jack, Betty and myself – so that all four of us could be buried together. Despite my long-held plan, I happily gave away my plot. I was pleased that Charlie was buried with his father. And after all, I didn't need it – at least not yet.

I also told Charlie's brother-in-law that my family would attend the funeral, which was to be held at St Mary's Catholic Church on Miller Street, North Sydney. I received a message back that we *could* come – but we were not to talk to anyone.

32

Gai Days

NOT LONG AFTER meeting Rob in 1978, Gai joined her father, T. J. Smith, at his famous Tulloch Lodge training stables at Randwick, giving away her acting career, which had been strong when she was in London; she had starred opposite Patrick Cargill and Trevor Howard. Back in Sydney Gai had found it hard to land good parts; everyone knew her as TJ's daughter.

Gai had first gone to the stables as a little girl, keeping her pony there. As a teenager she rode trackwork, but now she joined the stables as her father's clocker, and she also worked in the office in administration and client liaison. It wasn't easy in the early days, when Tommy's brother Ernie was the foreman. At one point, out of frustration, Gai toyed with the idea of 'crossing the line' and becoming a bookmaker. Although not really a whiz at figures, she obtained her licence as a bookmaker's clerk and ran my bookie's stand at Gosford in my absence in the early 1980s. She eventually fought her way through to become licensed as the stable foreman at Tulloch Lodge, managing all the early-morning trackwork and organising the stables.

When Rob and I were leaving the AJC in shock after being warned off in late 1984, Rob's concern was for Gai and whether his troubles might affect her in her work, now or in the future. As we walked through the car park, Rob asked his barrister, Doug Staff QC, if the warning-off might create any problems for Gai. He advised it would not, in view of the new Anti-Discrimination Act, which prevented discrimination against spouses.

However, being married to a warned-off person had an immediate and discriminatory effect on Gai's rights. Under the Australian Racing Rules, the ban on a disqualified person also applied to that person's spouse. Rob's warning-off prevented Gai from racing a horse on any track in Australia until it was lifted or expired.

Despite a public plea from her father, who argued that the rule was 'introduced in Captain Cook's day' and should be changed, the AJC refused and ordered that Gai would have to relinquish her ownership of racehorses before it would allow them to race, affecting two runners that were to race within a few days of Rob's warning-off. Gai had to quickly sell all her shares in thirteen horses.

Gai was so angry about the warning-off, which had taken away Robbie's livelihood, that she told the newspapers it was 'like cutting off your arms and legs and telling you to swim'. In defending the 'gentle man she had married', she said on television with Kerrie-Anne Kennerly, 'Robbie is only 30 years old and absolutely the leading, most brilliant bookmaker in Australia, and to think his livelihood is being whisked away . . . it just seems there's a farce going on.'

Gai bravely continued on with her career as her father's stable foreman, attending the races and having to deal and mix with the very people who had warned her husband off. Many racegoers snubbed her or talked behind her back, but some others were supportive and said the AJC had been over-zealous in making a scapegoat of Robert for the embarrassment caused to racing by the Fine Cotton affair.

Despite the turmoil in their lives, Gai and Rob were terrific partners and loving parents to their two young children, Tom and Kate. They had the children participating in everything to give them a broad education. Rob became an even more attentive father. For many years, every Saturday afternoon Rob devoted his time to the children, taking them swimming or riding or on other activities. He was doing what I had missed out on with my own children.

Family occasions were always given high priority, and every Christmas, perhaps thinking I had a natural likeness with my big stomach, Gai would have me dress up as Father Christmas and arrive 'ho-hoing' with all the presents. My cover was blown when Tom, just four years old, asked why Father Christmas was wearing 'Grandpa Bill's shoes'.

One time Rob and Gai organised a 1920s-themed 'Murder Dinner Party' in Bowral. Fortunately, the actress Bunny Gibson, who also ran North Shore Costume Hire and was a long-standing tenant in our little office building in North Sydney, had just the gear we needed. Kate came to the office and organised flapper costumes for her and Suzy; at just ten, Kate already had very definite ideas about fashion, and she made a perfect 1920s glamour girl. She also helped choose outfits for the rest of us, deciding to dress me as 'the gangster'. The clues to work out the whodunit were lots of fun, and a family friend, barrister Tim Hale, turned out to be on the wrong side of the law as 'the murderer'.

The Smith and Waterhouse families became close, and our grandchildren brought a lot of joy to all our lives. Tom and Kate would stay with us overnight every week, and when Gai and Rob travelled they usually came to stay with us. The children loved coming over and we loved having them.

It was a special time. Tom was always so much fun and Kate was a delight to have around. Sometimes, without letting Suzy know, Kate, Tom and I would watch movies and eat chocolates all night. I was in my element with them, playing games and buying the latest toys, like any grandfather would. I did incur

Gai's wrath when I bought them water pistols with backpack water reservoirs! We all wreaked havoc together but we had a hell of a lot of fun. I loved going back to the Royal Easter Show with my young grandchildren. Little Kate said, 'We can never get lost – we just look for Grandpa Bill as he's so much bigger than everyone else.'

There was a funny moment when I took Tom to the cricket one day. Bob Hawke came by and said hello, as he usually did. Tom, recognising the prime minister, said to me excitedly, 'Do you know who that is?' I played dumb and said, 'No . . . who?' But Tom realised he was being had and, playing up one of our jokes, held up his little fist and said, 'Do you want this?'

Another time, when Suzy and I took the children to a movie, we were a little uncomfortable about some kissing scenes on the screen. Afterwards, Tom – aged nine – mentioned the scenes and innocently commented, 'Once or twice is okay, but any more is simply boring!' Suzy and I laughed and wondered how long that sentiment would last.

When Kate was just thirteen, Rob and Gai, full of enthusiasm, decided to take up Guenther's mother's invitation for her to visit Germany for a few weeks. Louise was well and truly fluent in German, having spent a lot of time with Guenther in Europe, and wanted to give Kate a head start in her language studies. Kate took the long flight to Europe all alone, and as I was in London I flew over to meet her at the airport. We spent the day together before catching up with Viktoria and her colourful mountain-climbing Austrian friend, Hofrat Dr Ernst Jeitler, for her crash-course in German in the charming Bavarian Alps.

Tom followed Rob in attending Mosman Prep and then Shore, where he thrived in the sporty environment. Suzanne took on the role of the Saturday-morning driver, taking him to tennis or football. She loved her one-on-one time with him. Tom did well at football, despite his trim build. He also loved his tennis and was captain of the tennis team. Tom became a prefect and house captain, and applied himself well at school to achieve an excellent HSC result. Kate followed Louise's footsteps and attended Ascham, where she excelled in artistic pursuits and developed the great skills that serve her in her present career as a newspaper columnist.

—

Soon after the phenomenally successful float of Tulloch Lodge, Tommy had his own worries. Spedley Securities misappropriated Tulloch Lodge's money and left a shortfall in the funds for yearlings the company had bought, causing Tulloch Lodge to collapse. Gai and her father knew they needed to find someone to step in as the white knight and bail Tulloch Lodge out. Gai managed to find the American billionaire John Kluge, and he was persuaded to invest, saving Tulloch Lodge from going under. After this coup, Gai was virtually running the stables and Tommy, the champion trainer, was winding down.

Gai always wanted to be her own person and make her own mark. She loved her father but didn't want to be known as TJ's daughter for the rest of her life. She had learnt so much from her father but also had ideas of her own on the training of racehorses, and she was encouraged by Rob to take out a trainer's licence. But her father was lukewarm – he was worried that racing was a man's world. He knew better than anyone how hard it was to make a training business a success. No doubt Tommy didn't want to see his daughter fail.

Before taking any steps, Gai was told by family friend and AJC committee chairman Jim Bell, 'You go for it. There isn't a problem.' The committeeman responsible for licensing, Jim Comans also said it was a great idea. So it was to her utter shock and amazement that the licensing committee knocked back her application without giving any reason. Their mistake was in leading Gai to believe she would be licensed and then in publicly disgracing her by knocking her back. Gai felt the injustice and was determined to fight back.

The year was 1990 and drama still surrounded us, so it wasn't an ideal time for Gai to pursue her ambition, but Rob and Gai sought advice from Bruce Stracey, a close friend who was also the solicitor who had acted for me in the Fine Cotton hearings. Rob went along to all the conferences and helped Gai decide the best steps to take. Bruce believed the AJC had breached the Anti-Discrimination Act, arguing that the fact Rob was a warned-off person, in itself, should have no bearing on Gai's career. She took her case to the Equal Opportunity Tribunal in November 1990, and Louise went along to support and advise her. The case made headline news and Gai was surrounded by a throng of journalists, photographers and television cameras.

Gai's greatest concern was the free kick the AJC was taking at Robbie's expense. Bruce Stracey, now thinking professionally as Gai's solicitor, along with the bright young Bret Walker, paid no regard to Robbie's position, focusing purely on their client and her case. The AJC committeemen unfairly and unjustifiably referred to him in negative terms under the protection of the tribunal, which hurt Gai so much that she seriously considered aborting her attempt. Although the AJC played into Gai's lawyer's hands by showing it was discriminating against her because of her husband, the negative publicity about Robbie spoiled any chance of him winning public support in his own attempt to get back to the track.

Alan Cameron of the Anti-Discrimination Tribunal had his hands tied by precedent, leaving the way open for Gai to go to the Court of Appeal, where she won. In January 1992 the AJC called Gai in and made her a 'take it or leave it' offer. It would give her a Number One trainer's licence on the grounds that it wouldn't pay her costs and she would have to give up her popular weekly newspaper column. The committee obviously didn't like Gai having a public voice about racing. Gai didn't care – all she wanted was to finally have her own licence. It had taken two and a half years, but the beauty had beaten the beast!

Gai's case led to an amendment to the Anti Discrimination Act known as the 'Waterhouse Amendment', which ensured that married women were treated in their own right. Gai's standing in the community was enhanced throughout this process, and in some ways she became a national celebrity. She was a woman who had brought into focus the denial of her rights, and women everywhere – and also men – admired her for her strength. Gai showed that, like the rest of us, she had real backbone. Gai is a most admirable person and I love her as my own daughter. This victory was also a tribute to the strength of her and Rob's marriage.

Now Gai had to set out from scratch and make her own name as a trainer. Louise used her marketing skills to create a new concept to promote Gai – developing her 'brand' – based on the theme of the 'thrill of owning a winner with Gai'. Rob was also thinking of ideas for Gai. Through his exceptional research into bloodstock and form he was able to advise Gai on great horses to buy, which she trained up to become Group One winners early in her career. He introduced her to concepts like speed maps – so she could position her horses in their races – before that became common practice.

Gai showed she had an extraordinary talent, and it was not long before she established herself as one of Australia's leading trainers and businesswomen. Tommy was so proud of her; one of the last things he said to me was, 'She's better than me!'

Gai equalled her father's record of training 156 metropolitan winners in the 2002–03 season. In 2009 she won her seventh Sydney trainers' premiership, and she's poised to post 100 Group One wins in record time. Gai is simply magic.

—

Even though the protracted and stressful equity case was over, we now had to extricate ourselves from the financial tangle. Just when we needed to sell some of our real estate, the property market was at its most depressed and we were in no situation to develop a project ourselves. But sometimes you strike gold. We were contacted by a man who would later become a world-renowned property developer.

Dr Stanley Quek, quite a young medical doctor, had dabbled in property development in Singapore. Dr Quek came to Sydney over Christmas 1992, looking for opportunities. And with the harmonious Chinese principles of *feng shui* in mind, he thought Kirribilli was the perfect location, with its water foreground and the dramatic Harbour Bridge connecting it to the prosperity of the city lights. Dr Quek would put the tired suburb of Kirribilli back on the map. He noticed the 'For Sale' sign at 'Greencliffe', 51 Kirribilli Avenue, and agreed with me that it was the best site in Sydney.

I had always looked for ways to improve Kirribilli. Over the years Jack and I developed many building projects, including the then luxury St Charles block of 88 home units in Upper Pitt Street. We had then had plans for further high-rise buildings for five other trophy Kirribilli sites. With my vision for Kirribilli, even Sydney Electricity had sought my thoughts on the future capacity needs for the area, but now under planning laws such high-rise development was out of the question. Indeed, Jack told me the council planners had said we could only put a few townhouses on this beautiful site, with each blocking each other's views. Louise and I found a way – through 'existing-use' rights – that entitled us to build apartments.

I retained an interest in the project with Dr Quek, and Sydney architect Bruce Swalwell designed a classically styled building of twenty luxury apartments. Although the design was in keeping with the area, the council was divided, as was the community. The bulding's opponents wanted a park but, not surprisingly, no one wanted to pay for it.

I agreed that a park would be great and offered to donate 200 square metres of prime land at the front of the site if council approved our application. It could be united with the land that had been compulsarily resumed earlier, which now – through lack of maintenance – was almost washed away in the harbour. Brian Smith, council's enterprising parks and landscape officer, couldn't believe his luck to be offered this million-dollar opportunity. Council agreed and we were granted approval, without wasting time and money in the Land and Environment Court, and the community received a marvellous park for free.

Being at the end – or actually at the new beginning – of Kirribilli Avenue, council sensibly allowed us to change the street number of our 'Greencliffe' development to 1 Kirribilli Avenue.

I was happy with Dr Quek's style and also got him to develop the site directly behind. Like Jack and I had done 30 years earlier, he completely restored our historic 'Craiglea' house and built apartments with great views and expansive grounds. We also retained a share in this development. The only problem was that the street number in Upper Pitt St was 49 – which in Chinese apparently sounds like 'death forever'. Council needed to allocate a number on Kirribilli Avenue for the apartments with that street frontage and kindly agreed to the number 88, which sounds like 'lucky lucky'. Dr Quek was overjoyed.

These were the first new luxury apartment buildings in the area for a long time and suddenly enlivened the quiet suburb of Kirribilli. After buying these trophy properties around 40 years earlier and doing our own building throughout Sydney but focusing on Kirribilli and Milsons Point, I didn't mind someone else taking the running and could appreciate the significance of these special developments.

I was delighted that a nice park would eventuate on the foreshore land we had donated. I also thought it would be fitting to name the park after my ancestor, Captain Henry Waterhouse, who, in my mind, was a forgotten founding father of the colony of Sydney. Not everyone was convinced, but apart from highlighting Henry's many worthwhile deeds for the colony, we found the original chart Henry had drawn in February 1788, which showed that he, as a young midshipman and budding cartographer, had helped to do the very first survey of the land we were donating.

And so, with the support of the North Shore Historical Society, including historian and councillor Brian Evesson, the Geographical Names Board named this Kirribilli foreshore park 'Captain Henry Waterhouse Reserve' in 1994. We were then to add further foreshore land to extend this park, but this time we were paid handsomely. Louise and I had discovered that the waterfront land in front of my home at 63 Kirribilli Avenue had been zoned for resumption, which now meant we had the legal power to force government acquisition at market value. Now, instead of a lifetime of fearing and fighting resumptions, we could for the first time be properly compensated for land resumed by government at the stroke of a pen. The multi-million-dollar payment for around 300 square metres of harbour-front land was a sweet end to the long series of inequitable resumptions we had suffered over the years.

Succeeding with the prestigious and state-of-the-art 'Green-cliffe' and the Craiglea residential apartments in Kirribilli was the making of Dr Quek. He went on to become an international developer, controlling projects worth over $1 billion in London, Sydney and Perth. Doing a deal with Dr Quek was also timely for us, enabling us to pay out most of our debts.

I decided to move into the fabulous new 'Greencliffe', with its spacious terrace and gardens, and sold my waterfront Kirribilli home to the Macau billionaire Stanley Ho. I had loved the house; it was the last privately owned single home on the main Kirribilli Harbour waterfront. I had lived there with my family for 30 years and enjoyed every minute. Most of all, it had been a marvellous investment. I had bought it for £9000 in 1958. Now, in 1996, I would receive over $10 million for 1000 square metres of land.

When Diana, Princess of Wales, came to Sydney in 1996, I was not that fussed but Suzanne took me along to one of her charity events. Diana looked absolutely gorgeous and every bit a princess. When we met I couldn't help saying, 'Golly, you *are* tall – certainly taller than your ex-husband!'

I think Suzanne was about to kill me, but Princess Di gave a very natural laugh and said, 'Yes, I know!' and stayed on chatting with me. I was from that moment totally smitten by her.

Our earlier difficulties with the Commonwealth Bank also had a silver lining around this time. The 222-hectare farm at Wallacia had been at risk, as the bank had wanted to sell it to cover John's large debt; the farm was in his name, owing to the 'Vietnam War arrangement'. The equity case had proved my one-third share in the farm, and now we also proved, through correspondence, that the bank had known of my interest all along.

The bank had no other commercial choice but to sell the remaining two-thirds back to me. It was good value and a wonderful asset for the future inside the Sydney basin. I was glad to be in acquisition mode once again. I was still not back at the races, but financially we were back on our feet.

The Wallacia acquisition led to us forming a long-lasting relationship with a very able solicitor, John Miller, but there was also a funny side. The transaction had been set up by Louise before she headed back to Germany. After she'd gone, the solicitor acting for us went on holiday and passed the matter to John, his colleague. When Louise returned to Australia she rang with some further instructions; John was taken aback, as he'd only dealt with Rob or me. He didn't really know what her authority was and so spoke with one of our accountants, who said, 'Don't you know? The Waterhouse property empire is ruled by a skirt!'

—

Rob and I were approached in mid-1997 to breathe new life into a business which had gone bust. Looking back, it was one of the riskiest ventures we would undertake, putting up a large amount of our own cash on a very different business from racing.

Network Entertainment Limited was a high-flying Sydney company floated on the stock exchange in 1996, with prominent directors including Dr John Hewson. The company specialised in video distribution and film rights but suffered a liquidity crisis just months after floating and suddenly dived into the hands of administrators. The shareholders looked like they had done their money cold, although there was intrinsic value in stock, receivables and film rights.

The shareholders were relieved when Rob and I agreed to bail this public company out with a $2-million cash injection in return for a majority of the shares, paying just one cent a share. I became the chairman and Robert a director. To salvage the business, we had to slash the staff from 127 to just seven, cut the remaining salaries and take no pay ourselves.

We tried to reinvent the company with new entertainment options. We changed its name to Cinimagic Ltd, and then ultimately to eTech Ltd. However, no matter what we did, this public company seemed to need more and more money and we had to make a series of further cash injections. With further capital raisings, we increased shareholder numbers from 600 to 4800.

The writing was on the wall that the company's traditional forms of entertainment were rapidly becoming outdated and so we knew we had to transform the whole enterprise. We decided to take it into the world of international gambling – a business we understood. Funnily enough, the company benefited from the high profile we gave it, with every new step given extensive coverage in the media, including one cheeky newspaper poster for the *Herald* in May 1999, which read: 'Bet On Net. Return of Robbie Waterhouse'. The company relisted in August 1998 and, with new public confidence, the share price shot up to around twelve to fifteen cents.

Rob knew the Canbet boys, who ran an internet and phone betting operation in Canberra – he had helped them set up in Australia and they soon had the world's largest internet bookmaking business betting on American sports. They were looking to grow, so we offered them a chance to go public with a 'backdoor listing' on the stock exchange. Once the Canbet deal was set up, we were bought out of the three-year project at a lovely profit.

33

Changing the Odds

MY OLD FRIEND His Majesty King Taufaʻahau Tupou IV had his 80th birthday in July 1998, and I took my family to Tonga to celebrate the week's festivities. In my group was Suzanne, Louise (who since 1994 had been a vice-consul), Guenther, Robbie, Gai, Tom and Kate. The celebrations consisted of feasting, Polynesian dancing, cultural displays and royal audiences.

While in Tonga, I had a strange experience that I could only describe as spiritual. Lying awake in my bed in the middle of the night, I suddenly felt a large hand pressing down on my chest. It wasn't just pressure – I could feel the imprint of fingers on my chest. I really didn't understand the sensation but I knew something important had happened. When I awoke the next morning, Louise told me she had a received a call from our office in Sydney during the night to say that Jack had passed away.

I realised then that Jack had come to me during the night to say goodbye and let me know everything was all right. Jack's last gesture was so important to me.

I had rarely seen Jack after the equity court case ended in 1992. I wrote to him several times, suggesting we should have lunch, along with our sister, Betty, but I suspect the letters were not passed on to him. I was pleased to run into him at the shops in Kirribilli a few times. He sadly told me how miserable he had been after our partnership broke up, and how he felt he'd never kicked a goal after that. My brotherly love for Jack never waned and I am sure his for me didn't either.

Suzanne and I returned home to Sydney at once. One Sydney newspaper ran a story saying I wasn't welcome at the funeral of my beloved brother – gratuitous advice that I ignored. I went, and I felt welcomed by everyone. The service was held at St Thomas's Anglican Church in West Street, North Sydney – the family church of our ancestor, great-grandfather Thomas Waterhouse. Father O'Dwyer, who had stayed close to Jack over the years, conducted the moving service.

Just two months later we also lost Tommy Smith, who died on Gai's birthday. Tommy's funeral was one of the biggest ever seen at St Mary's Cathedral in Sydney, with more than 1500 people from all walks of life, paying their respects to the man who had set so many racing records. Kate and Robbie both gave moving and emotional tributes, and broadcaster Alan Jones recalled Tommy's life of great struggle and even greater rewards.

From a humble start Tommy rewrote the record books to dominate Australian racing – he won 33 consecutive training premierships. He was the first racehorse trainer in the world to win $3 million in a year, he was the first to train 100 winners in a season, and he had 282 Group One winners in his career.

It was so hard for Gai. Not only had she lost a loving father, but TJ was also her mentor. Gai felt his presence the next day, when she won three races in the program.

Although I had always admired his great racing feats, I had only come to know Tommy well after Gai and Robbie married. Trainers and bookmakers rarely mix at the racetrack, and I wasn't one for socialising with racing people anyway. I was pleased to call him a friend and grateful he always stood by

Rob. He was one of a kind and, in my opinion, the best trainer of all time.

—

In 1995 Robbie had applied again to the AJC to have his racetrack ban lifted – simply to be allowed to walk onto a racetrack again. He had been told by some committeemen, including the chairman, Bob Charley, that the AJC was finally prepared, after eleven years, to put the Fine Cotton matter behind it. But Robbie was denied a return to the track yet again. He wasn't even trying to obtain a bookmaker's licence. Gai, too, was disappointed, as after over a decade her husband was still not able to set foot on a racetrack with her – anywhere in the world.

Racing administration was in turmoil and the AJC's role as principal club was taken away. A new body was formed, the Thoroughbred Racing Board (now Racing NSW). And good news was around the corner. In October 1998, after fourteen years in the wilderness, Robbie's warning-off was lifted. He was finally allowed to go back to the racetrack.

Rob's barrister for his application was the brilliant junior counsel Paul Brereton (now a justice of the Supreme Court), who had a great understanding of the law and its interpretation by tribunals. It still wasn't an easy run, with attempts by the old anti-Waterhouse brigade – especially Arthur Harris, who was described by Max Presnell in *The Sydney Morning Herald* as a 'Groucho Marx' – to derail the application.

Unfortunately, having just lost her father, Gai had to undergo cross-examination to angrily reject suggestions that her training business could be influenced by Rob, and that she wasn't her own boss.

As part of Rob's application it was shown that his betting through the tote, despite being warned-off, was $1.1 million over just the previous three months, meaning racing had earned millions of dollars in commission on Rob's punting turnover over the years. This point was not lost on newspaper commentator Murray Bell, who wrote in *The Sunday Telegraph*: 'It does serve to remind us of the hypocrisy of the racing establishment in recent years . . . "we don't want you, but we do want your money".'

However, in lifting the warning-off, the TRB imposed the condition that Rob couldn't apply for a bookmaker's licence and couldn't own a racehorse. Former AJC chief steward John Schreck was quoted as describing this as a 'Clayton's decision . . . Mr Waterhouse is a bookmaker by profession – it's his job. How can he be prevented from doing it?'

My own warning-off was lifted in December 1998, three months after Robbie's. This time it was a low-key affair – without even any lawyers. The chairman of the new Thoroughbred Racing Board, Bill Rutledge, asked me if there was anything further I wanted to add to my written submission. I said no, which prompted Rutledge to say, 'There was no actual admission of guilt, or any contrition . . . You must bear in mind that that is one of the principles we have to take into account when considering your application.'

I replied, 'All I can say in regards to that is that I have always maintained I had no involvement with the Fine Cotton matter, which is justified by the fact that in the police inquiry I was the only one who was not charged.'

I spent all of five minutes before the TRB panel. In lifting the warning-off, the board did not impose conditions. It was almost an anti-climax after fourteen years served for a crime I didn't commit. I didn't bother attending the track. To me, without a bookmaker's licence there was no point.

—

472

I had always been fascinated by my ancestor Henry Waterhouse, and was proud that the Kirribilli foreshore park was now named after him. However, I still felt he was largely forgotten by history. I had learnt of a collection of Henry's letters held by an English family named Pownall, who were my distant relatives. I had fruitlessly tried to track them down over the years, even to the extent of knocking on the door of their earlier home in London – but the door was opened by someone who had never heard of them. I was thrilled to read an historical article in March 1998 saying the elusive Pownall family was now auctioning its historic collection through Christie's.

Rob jumped on a plane to attend the auction, where bidding was hot and Rob was quickly knocked out. I was amazed when the Waterhouse Papers were sold to the Mitchell Library in Sydney for an Australian record price of around £390,000. I felt Henry had finally made it as a colonial father. Rob, however, did acquire Henry's very own first-edition copy of Governor Phillip's book, *The Voyage of Governor Phillip to Botany Bay*, with Henry's own handwritten notes in the text.

After the auction Rob was able to meet the charming Pownall family, who were delighted to know of their distant relatives in Australia. Among other things, they gave Rob a large photograph of a portrait of William Waterhouse, Henry's father, which today hangs above my desk in my office.

When Henry's papers arrived in Australia, I was invited for a private viewing of the collection by Paul Brunton, curator of manuscripts at the Mitchell Library. As I held the historic documents, wearing white gloves, I felt an emotional tug to be looking back in time at my family's history.

Then a previously unknown letter was discovered written by Henry to his supporter, the retired colonial secretary Lord Sydney. Henry's letter reported on his hazardous voyage back from Cape Town after he purchased the first merino sheep and the first thoroughbred horse for the colony. He also referred to some exotic Australian animals, which, as an amateur taxidermist, he had stuffed to give to Lord Sydney's wife. Henry also took back to England preserved animal specimens for Sir Joseph Banks in 1800. Henry obviously knew how to court those of influence.

The letter was going for auction at Christie's, so Louise and Guenther flew across to London from Germany. I was delighted when they successfully bid for the letter, paying £23,000.

A few years later we also tracked down and acquired Henry's journal, featuring his description of Captain Phillip's spearing, along with the original spearhead, which turned out to be a simple penknife blade. We happily loaned these historic papers and artefacts for a special exhibition that toured the country.

—

Suzanne and I have made firm friendships through the consular corps over the years, both with career consuls and the honoraries. I have always loved to travel, but most of the time I have been looking for a business reason to justify my time – a holiday wasn't usually part of my thinking. However, the Egyptian consulate general organised a diplomatic trip to Egypt and Suzanne and I couldn't resist. As a lover of ancient history, it was absorbing to go to one of the cradles of civilisation. We went up the Nile and had VIP treatment, courtesy of the Egyptian government.

Climbing inside one of the Luxor pyramids, I got more than an overweight 75-year-old had bargained for. It was hundreds and hundreds of steps through a narrow dark passageway, and as the group had politely let me go first, I had no way but to go up and up and up. Breathing very hard, I thought that it would be the death of me, but I finally made it.

Back home in Australia, there were still one or two glitches to overcome in the late 1990s before I could look forward to life as plain sailing. The Fiji betting operation was in trouble. Francis Grant had moved to Australia for health reasons and had left the business in the hands of a manager. There was evidence of stealing and a receiver was appointed. Having started the business in Fiji 35 years earlier, I felt a special attachment to the country, and I bought out the full business from Jack's estate and Francis.

Over the years, Francis and I had travelled the world together, pursuing some of my more 'out there' business ideas. One of the most memorable was our trip to China at the invitation of the influential media baron Wu Wei and other high-level Chinese businessmen. Once he retired, Francis was always still keen to lend a hand. He still visited our Sydney office regularly to help with the racing service, right up to the day before he sadly died in March 2009. He had been a long and loyal friend.

I saw owning the Fiji business outright as an opportunity for Robbie's friend Peter McCoy, who had been down on his luck but was experienced in racing, having been a bookmaker and also run his own businesses. Within two months of his arrival in Fiji, however, there was a violent military coup. This didn't throw Peter, who was a decorated Vietnam War hero. Despite the riots and widespread burning and looting in Suva, Peter sent his staff safely home in his own vehicle and stayed on to defend the business against the unruly mob. Later, when the business was secure, he bravely made his way home through the devastation.

Despite a series of dramas along the way, I have been amazed at Peter's initiative and strength of character to keep the business going. Peter is a terrific businessman who inspires his staff and never stops working. Without him, I have no doubt the business would have failed in those difficult circumstances. Under Peter's management the business grew, and

Peter eventually became our partner, earning himself respect in the Fijian community.

—

The year 2000 was a momentous one, with so many things happening around us. Apart from sealing the Canbet deal and buying back the Fijian business, I went on another fabulous consular trip – this time to Italy for a world meeting of honorary consuls. Suzanne and I were taken around Tuscany and also had an audience with Pope John Paul II. We travelled around Italy and then cruised the Mediterranean.

However, in the middle of our last night in our hotel room in Rome, on 19 May, I tripped and fell on the bathroom step, hitting my head heavily on the bidet. My forehead and cheek-bone were smashed, and my eye dropped about two centimetres. I couldn't see out of the eye, but I was determined not to let that stop me from flying home. The doctor had a different plan – he put me in hospital for an emergency operation. It was just as well, as he said I would have gone blind if I had travelled. The Italian doctor couldn't believe it was my first time in hospital for 50 years – after my badly broken jaw in England. But I did have one piece of good luck – I bought our tickets on a credit card that, unbeknown to me, gave us top travel insurance!

I had broken my face so badly I had to have five titanium plates inserted. I had to remain in Rome for four extra weeks and come home in a wheelchair – which cramped my style when I ran into my lifelong idol Sophia Loren in the airport lounge in Rome.

The acclaimed Sydney-born artist Ralph Heimans had done a large portrait of me standing under the Sydney Harbour Bridge, where I had spent so much of my boyhood and teenage years. With Ralph living in Paris, the Australian Ambassador to France, John Spender, launched the portrait at the embassy there in late May 2000. As I was laid up in a Roman hospital, the launch went on without me; Louise and Guenther flew over from Germany to wave the flag.

—

Tonga was one of the very few countries in the late 1990s that still recognised Taiwan as the ruler of China. Gai was training horses for prominent Chinese businessman, Tony Huang from Shanghai. Tony approached me on behalf of the Chinese Ambassador in Canberra and said China wanted a formal relationship with Tonga. This was an awkward proposition because of Tonga's allegiance to Taiwan. China was already helping Tonga launch its communications satellites through Her Royal Highness Princess Piloevu – Tonga had astutely applied for and received eight satellite slots, leaving other countries in its wake. Australia was given only two and New Zealand none.

I spoke to the King and others in Tonga about China's wish, and the wheels began turning to institute formal ties between the countries, which began in 2000. Today the relationship between China and Tonga is strong.

I invited the King of Tonga to the Sydney Olympics, where he was the top-ranking world dignitary. Hosting a lunch for him at my home, I included Her Royal Highness Princess Anne, former prime ministers Gough Whitlam and Bob Hawke, as well as a number of Australian and international Olympic figures. His Majesty surprised me at the lunch, presenting me with his Silver Jubilee Award. I was not quite at my fighting-fit best, because when I had gone to collect the official invitations, which had been sent from Tonga, someone drove into me, breaking my shoulder and writing off my car. Again, though, I was lucky – normally I didn't insure my cars but, as it was a consular vehicle, this one had to be fully covered.

All the dignitaries from around the world travelled to the games by special buses, but I was able to arrange for the King to have his own car and two security personnel. I was even given a royal guernsey to accompany His Majesty to the opening ceremony, and I watched with pride as Louise, who became a full honorary consul that year, and Guenther marched as Tonga's Olympic Attaché and Team Manager.

The Olympic Games was such a special time for Sydney, and the city was sparkling at its best. I loved seeing so many people I knew at the various events. After all the drama of Fine Cotton, it was so nice when the premier of New South Wales, Bob Carr, and also the prime minister, John Howard, crossed a room to publicly shake my hand and say hello.

I felt I was back.

—

At last Rob was allowed back to work as a bookmaker in August 2001, three years after he was allowed back on the racecourse. It wasn't an easy road, with both the CEO of the TRB, Jim Murphy, and Rob taking legal advice. Finally, with a groundswell of public support, the TRB relented and granted approval in June 2001. I thought it was ludicrous to have delayed him for so long.

However, there was still a hurdle that no one had anticipated. The Bookies Co-operative (one of whose committeemen was Martin Waterhouse, then a bookmaker) was required to provide any TRB-approved bookmaker with membership and a guarantee before any licence could be issued. The Co-op suddenly refused to allow Rob (and later me) to become a member. It effectively blocked him, a move never done before. The TRB was not amused. I couldn't fathom the Co-op's behaviour.

The press trenchantly criticised the decision, describing it as 'strangely suicidal' and pointing out that its role was to provide guarantees to protect punters, not to sit in judgement or stop competition from new bookies. Newspaper columnist Richard Zachariah wrote in *The Sunday Telegraph* that at a time when racing was in desperate need of personalities, Robbie and Gai were 'an embarrassment of riches'. He wrote: 'It is ironic that Robbie and Gai are entertained by the Queen at Royal Ascot but have to defend their reputations at home.'

Rob circumvented the spiteful Co-op by providing his own bank guarantee, and the TRB changed the rules and issued his licence without him being a member of the Co-op. Rob made his comeback at Rosehill because the Sydney Turf Club had supported his return. I stood by and watched the swarm of photographers and well-wishers, who helped bring a carnival atmosphere to his comeback. I proudly stood near Rob and Tom, who was making his debut as a clerk. I was soaking up the atmosphere after seventeen years away, but my bubble was quickly burst when a steward ordered me to move away from the stand. Welcome back, Bill.

Word came to the track that, sadly, Melbourne Mick Bartley had died that morning. One of the great characters of the turf, he was specially remembered for telling a stewards' inquiry in 1976, 'You're asking me about a $6000 bet. Do you know what a $6000 bet is? That's toilet paper.' I thought back on how pleased I was to have given Mick his start by taking his prices service in the 1940s, and then having him run our SP business in the 1950s, until he started his own SP business in the 1960s. He became one of Australia's biggest punters. Mick was a knockabout with a good mathematical brain.

Punters loved Rob's return. He transformed the ring by having strong opinions, reflected in his aggressive prices on his board. Legendary big punter Sean Bartholomew told me, 'Things changed quite a bit when Rob got back. He was first up with prices and devastatingly accurate. As a result, the other bookmakers' board prices also became much more precise. For me, however, the opening markets were harder to manipulate. I could no longer shorten one horse and lengthen another with my early bets, as now Rob would stick to his opinion, and the prices wouldn't change.'

After seventeen years Rob immediately adapted to the new style of bookmaking, with electronic betting boards and computer-written tickets and the odds now being expressed as dividends – 2/1 had now become \$3 on the board; just like at the tote, the stake was now expressed in the payout.

However, I felt the new system had unwittingly destroyed the bookies' unique product. The odds, which previously required an arithmetical leaning to calculate a market, were now just computer dividends. Just as calculators have ruined the young generation's arithmetical skills, the modern-day bookmaker doesn't need to understand the odds. With modernised methods, I couldn't help thinking the bookies had lost some flair and the individuality of a handwritten ticket. Not only that, but the machine was so much slower than I could write. Also, we lost our right to offer special odds of up to 4000/1 – years earlier, my punters loved claiming a bet at such long odds.

Rob was a drawcard for punters. Country race clubs began inviting him to field as their celebrity bookmaker at their annual cup meetings. No other city bookie could be bothered, and he was chuffed to be treated like a superstar.

—

I turned 80 in January 2002 and the family threw a party for me at the Watermark Restaurant at Balmoral, where I announced I was taking up my bookmaking licence again because I wanted to teach my grandson the finer points of bookmaking. It was a great night, with Tongan dancers and singers and a cake in the form of the Harbour Bridge. I was delighted when Ratu

Epeli Nailatikau, senior chief and deputy prime minister of Fiji, flew in, and we especially enjoyed the company of Gough and Margaret Whitlam, who had gone through university with me, Neville Wran, Justice Andrew Rogers and his wife, Senator Helen Coonan, many friends from the consular corps, and many others important in my life, along with two young Tongan princes. I appreciated a very fine impromptu speech by Neville, and then Guenther made everyone laugh before giving one of his renowned Bavarian yodels. I was surprised when 'Tina Turner' suddenly appeared and sat on my lap, singing 'Simply the Best'! It was a great performance by Viliami Mafi, a Tongan singer who had once heard me say, 'Tina can put her shoes under my bed anytime!'

After one of my annual trips to Tonga and Fiji, Louise took me to Queenstown to join Guenther. I was blown away to be reminded of what an extraordinary part of the world it is. Guenther flew me all around the area in a helicopter, and we even landed on the west coast to visit a seal colony. I couldn't believe how the seals all came up to me on the rocks as the waves broke around us – they just wanted to play. I could have stayed with them for hours.

Five months after Rob's comeback, I returned as a bookie. I wanted to clear my name but also mentor young Tom, who had been Rob's clerk for the past few months during university and had found betting exciting. It seems the TRB didn't really take my application seriously, writing to me that my licence was granted only on the basis that it would be reviewed to see whether I was actually attending and working the meetings. A few months into my fresh start, the Sydney Turf Club awarded me a prize for being the 'most improved' bookmaker – hooray!

On my first day back in the outer of the interstate ring, the cameramen and reporters turned up for my return as well – at times making it hard for the punters to reach my stand. Tom and Kate were my clerks. As of old, I was first up with the prices and found I loved it all over again.

It was Blue Diamond day and I stood the favourite for a fortune, defying the punters. Unfortunately it got up in a photo-finish. Big punter Sean Bartholomew later told me how he couldn't believe how on my first day back I completely disregarded the price call coming from interstate, putting up my own set of prices. His chosen horse was seven dollars with the bookies and the tote – Sean was stunned when I put up 20/1. He thought I'd made a mistake until he checked the rest of my prices. He took his bet with me and said he was glad I was back. I was glad too, when his horse was beaten.

Trained to be careful, Tom set limits for the professional punters but I was reluctant to cut anyone back. The pros knew this; one day Sean Batholomew waited for Tom to go to the bathroom and asked me for a bet to take out $100,000. I said sure and gave him his ticket.

Tom was horrified and immediately found Sean and swapped over the ticket to win just $3000. Sean accepted it with a smile and said, 'Just testing!' He knew I was dying to get stuck in.

Times changed, and in 2009 at the call of the card for the Golden Slipper, Tom and I let Sean on to win $250,000 on Feeling Ready, which won at 40/1.

—

The family was getting back on an even keel. Robbie was invited to field in New Zealand as a special promotion for racing there. David Ellis, the chairman of the Te Rapa Racing Club, persuaded the government to allow Rob to operate as a bookmaker in an all-tote country – it was the first time a bookie was allowed to work there in a century. A decade earlier

David had given Gai her first Group One winner to train, Te Akau Nick.

I went over to share the historic moment, as did country bookmaker David Baxter, who swung Rob's bookie bag on the day. *The Sunday Telegraph* sent its racing columnist, Richard Zachariah, and *The Sydney Morning Herald* sent John Schell.

I loved being there and it was extraordinary to see the excitement Rob generated in the media, and a record crowd was drawn to the track. Rob put up accurate prices for every race; and although he laid a winner at $12,500 to $5000 – Distinctly Secret – to his host David Ellis, he still had a really good day. No one could believe how Rob had nailed it – on unfamiliar New Zealand horses.

At Rob's request, his stand was placed not behind the grandstand, as in Australia, but out in front beside the track, like in England. There was a throng around Rob's stand all day and he was flat-out taking bets. The club was ecstatic. Australia is the only place where bookmakers are 'hidden away' from the crowd and the action. Once, you could sit in the stand and have a passing parade of every facet of racing: the runners from the paddock, the bookies calling the odds, the punters scurrying about – real colour, real entertainment. When the tote came in, the clubs killed this by putting the bookmakers round the back. There is no doubt in my mind that if Australian bookmakers were relocated out in front beside the track, the betting and colour of racing would increase dramatically.

Just days after our return from New Zealand, and a week before I officially started back at the track, it was Rob's licence under threat rather than mine, in what would become known as the 'Extravagant Odds affair'. It resulted in a series of legal battles and appeals lasting eighteen months.

34

In My Shoes

TOM HAD NEVER PLANNED to go into racing. He had been looking at a career in finance – the stock market – which was one reason he did a commerce/liberal studies degree at Sydney University. When Rob returned as a bookmaker, he casually asked Tom if he would like to work part-time as a clerk. Tom thought it would be fun while he was studying. And he really loved it.

There's no training course to be a clerk or a bookmaker – you just learn as you go. Tom started to rearrange his lectures to allow him to work more at the track, just as Robbie and I had done in our early years.

After Tom had worked just six months with his father, Rob gave him the chance to run his stand on his own at the locals when he went bookmaking in New Zealand. No one could believe the daring move in giving a young clerk the responsibility, but Rob remembered me giving him the same chance when he started with me. After all, my father had put me in charge when I was just a teenager.

When I came back in February 2002, Tom worked with me at the metropolitan races on Wednesdays and Saturdays, and then travelled with Robbie to the provincial meetings through the rest of the week. When Tom turned twenty he applied for his own licence at the dogs.

A lot of other kids from racing families have big egos and think they can take on everyone. Not Tom – he just wanted to learn. After he had had a solid grounding in bookmaking skills from Rob, I was able to teach him how to develop a gambler's nerve. Robbie instilled into Tom that he should start with small steps and grow from there, encouraging him to settle into the role without pushing him.

Rob and I drummed into Tom the importance of *value*. Whilst form is important, it is vital that value is married to it. Indeed, I believe I beat the punters who tackled me because, in the end, they took 'unders' too often. I told Tom that, with experience, you can see how to win more by taking a calculated risk and *then* gambling, provided you don't make mistakes. I taught Tom my philosophy of 'playing up your winnings'. Naturally, you'll have some bad losses along the way, but you'll also have some good wins. You must believe it will happen.

Tom was wonderfully enthusiastic. He wanted to work on all the country meetings he could and learn as much as possible. In 2003, at the age of 21, Tom was granted his own bookmaking licence at the gallops, but he still stayed on with me, working under my licence on my stand. It was a special time for both of us – two generations 60 years apart.

With my guidance and the benefit of Rob's form, our turnover grew significantly, and so when a vacancy appeared on the interstate Rails, although I was 83 I applied for the spot based on my high turnover. I had no joy. Normally stands are determined by turnover, yet Tom and I were ignored and the vacancy went to a younger bookmaker with lower turnover. It took a year of lobbying and writing to politicians, including Premier Bob Carr and the minister for sport, to get a fair deal against what was a clear case of age discrimination.

As I had done throughout my life, I stood up for what was right. I wasn't sitting at home with a blanket over my knees,

I was actively out there doing it. I wasn't given any credit for my 30 years as a bookmaker, when I had once been billed as the world's biggest bookie. Finally, they made room for me on the Rails in 2006.

Tom was starting to make his mark. Rob and I had a lot of confidence in him. In some ways it was like watching a young football player gaining experience through playing with the big boys. I loved teaching my grandson the profession that I had excelled in – few grandfathers get that opportunity. People talk about the generation gap and how hard that can be on a relationship, but Tom and I worked well together. At the track I more or less let him call the shots, and I used our drive in the car to and from the races to lecture Tom on gambling philosophy to inspire him to become a successful gambler.

In the beginning Tom might have thought I was foolhardy and destined to lose badly, but after a while I began to see him develop a true gambler's instinct.

—

In 2006 Tom performed on *Dancing With the Stars* with his partner, Alana Patience, wowing all the girls with his groovy style. He trained every moment he could when away from the track. Suzy and I went down to Melbourne to be in the live audience and see him perform for the cameras. I realised I could learn from him, as he is a far better dancer than I ever was.

He was not the only emerging young star in the Waterhouse clan. While Kate studied she worked for me as a clerk at the track and also at her mother's stables, as a stablehand and then as an office assistant, which gave her a good grounding in racing.

In the meantime, she was blossoming stylishly. Grant Vandenberg, a journalist and PR man, mentioned her potential to the Sydney newspaper columnist Ros Reines, who ran a story and a lovely photo of Kate. That was a springboard which launched Kate into the media, as an identity in her own right in the world of racing and fashion.

Almost at once Kate was selected to become the face of the 2003 Victorian Spring Racing Carnival – an extraordinary role for a Sydney teenager. Coming with a full racing pedigree behind her – not many ambassadors have been a stablehand *and* a bookie's clerk – Kate had the knowledge and experience to carry off the role with aplomb. As Kate was so glamorous, the media couldn't get enough of her; she was the most successful ambassador the VRC had ever had.

Racing commentators said Sydney had missed out on an opportunity. *The Daily Telegraph* moved quickly, securing Kate to write a regular column on the social side of racing in its 'Sydney Confidential' pages. Kate was now in demand and constantly in the media. I loved seeing her not only looking beautiful but also doing so well in other fields, not just racing.

I was more than a little annoyed when a strange comment about Kate 'lapping the room' was made in one of the Sydney dailies in late 2003. Without telling anyone, I wrote asking the newspaper to 'please explain', as Kate was in fact away with the family. When they returned from holiday, they all laughed at my letter and thought I was 'a grandfather being a little precious about his granddaughter'!

David Jones landed a coup in 2004 by obtaining both Kate and Gai as their Racewear ambassadors, covering fashion across the ages. Wherever the mother and daughter pair went they added a touch of glamour and were widely photographed. I envied Kate being a celebrity BMW driver with a week's racing car training for the Victorian Grand Prix in 2006 – I couldn't help thinking back to the days of my Jaguar XK120, which I admit to driving like a racing car.

Kate caught the attention of *The Sunday Telegraph*'s editor by writing a feature on Royal Ascot and her experiences as a 'racing insider'. Young readers loved her enterprise in covertly snapping Her Majesty the Queen at close range. She was then offered the role of social commentator, reporting on the best parties in Sydney in a weekly double-page column. Kate then wrote about her passion for fashion, with her own double page spread called 'Style with Kate Waterhouse'. The new King of Tonga was enchanted by Kate and granted her the exclusive coronation interview, and her story appeared in international media, including *Vanity Fair*. Her role in racing continued as the face and columnist for Racing New South Wales' Punters' Club, and in 2009 she became fashion editor of *The Sun-Herald*. Kate stands well and truly on her own two feet.

I have been blessed to have been so close to my grandchildren and to live so long to see them both develop into special people.

—

Rather than stepping aside for Tom, he and I formed a bookmaking company under new racing legislation and we officially became partners in 2007. Now on the Rails, we were quickly the top holders on interstate racing, and I was chuffed to have made it back to the number one stand, having left it over twenty years earlier.

Tom's introduction to big gambling was not without its drama. The first time John Singleton bet with Tom and me, he won $100,000 on his champion filly Belle Du Jour. That was Tom's first big loss. On a high, Singo said, 'Bring the cash to my office on Monday, mate.' Tom went to great trouble to get the bank to put the cash together and arrived with his bundle at Singo's office. Singo said he'd only been joking and he just wanted a cheque. Tom took the joke in good spirit but didn't make that mistake again.

Another punter of ours was well known in racing circles, having been at the cutting edge of corporate betting before moving into other fields. He was a shrewd bettor who loved the punt. When we first started to take his bets, a steward came over to the stand and warned us that he owed money everywhere and we would be best to leave him alone. Tom still dealt with him in good faith and started to bet big with him. He was winning and Tom had plenty of respect for his bets.

One day in early 2007 the punter lost $1.2 million in a day; but it was a disaster because Tom had laid off many of his bets and we owed the other bookies $800,000. Of course the punter couldn't pay. Tom learnt the hard way that when you lay off a bet, you must be sure the punter will pay you if the bet loses. Plenty of good bookies have gone down the tube this way.

Nevertheless, after six months and good legal work from solicitor Jonathan Bowers-Taylor, Tom and I were paid. The solicitor couldn't believe it when we let the punter on again. Tom still offloads some of this punter's bets but is far more selective in choosing which bets he backs back. He is now fully aware that the risk is not only in the bet but also whether we will get paid if it loses. But I've taught Tom that if you are too fussy about your punters, you won't have any left to bet with.

Another well-known Sydney businessman came to us wanting to bet. He kept winning and tallied up a credit of $1.5 million. Tom thought he would have to give him away as he was just too smart, but Rob and I told him to look closely at his bets. Tom realised he was continually taking under the odds and so, in our view, he couldn't win in the long run. As I have always said, you need value when you bet and you can't succeed in the long run if you keep taking under the odds. Sure enough, over time we not only won our money back but we are now in front.

I knew Tom had hit the big time when in 2008 I left the Rosehill track ten minutes before the last race, leaving him to work alone. The headlines declared that, in those ten minutes, Tom had lost $1.175 million. What they didn't realise was that, after a big day, Tom was playing up his winnings and was still ahead on the day. He would soon be referred to as the 'fearless bookie'. It made me think of the phrase 'he was standing in my shoes'.

———

Under the restrictive rules for on-course bookmakers in New South Wales, Tom recognised that our business could not grow. Tom and Rob lobbied for two years for modernisation of the system, to allow bookies to obtain vital access to the internet. They also wanted to simply offer tote odds, as allowed in other states around Australia.

However, instead of the much-needed reforms we wanted, we were landed with a 50 per cent increase in turnover taxes. Tom and I took the authorities to court to argue that the new taxes were invalid, and in the meantime Tom moved to Melbourne with his telephone clients so he would not risk breaching the new tax laws. I chose the inimitable Tom Hughes QC, another octogenarian and also a racing expert, to run the case, along with our longtime legal crusader Clive Jeffreys, and they did a great job. Even though we proved the new tax did not apply to us, the government simply amended the law to beat the court result.

Now the world of betting is changed. The track is no longer the epicentre and focus of horse betting. The advent of corporate bookmakers, licensed in more favourable jurisdictions, has brought about an enormous shift in betting, as money has flowed away from the track. Punters now prefer the betting service they can access at home or in their office, simply by using the phone or the internet.

On-track betting in Sydney has been restricted by archaic rules and limitations, which makes the modern bookie feel as if he is operating blindfolded with his hands tied behind his back. Incredibly, bookies at New South Wales tracks are still not allowed to match the local tote odds, as is done just about everywhere else in Australia. Nor are they allowed to see what the corporate bookies are offering, or what is happening on Betfair via the internet or phone. Obviously, bookies in New South Wales can't offer a competitive service.

I have always said that on-course bookies should have better conditions than their off-track competitors. This could be easily achieved by reducing the turnover tax on-course, which would in turn allow bookies to offer a more competitive product with better odds, and so attract punters back to the track.

It is sad for me to see that in my lifetime the racetrack has gone from being a bustling, entertaining day out for having a punt, to being an occasional party venue, where the races are only secondary and punters' needs are disregarded.

In reality, it's the punters who make the racing world go around. The sport of racing is funded by the punters through the take-outs and taxes on their betting. Racing is becoming more expensive to operate and administrators are seeking to fund it with extra charges on the punter, which can only result in fewer punters.

—

I was immensely saddened by the death of my great friend King Taufa'ahau Tupou IV, in 2006. He was 88. All Tongans went into mourning for the love of their King, and the funeral, attended by dignitaries from many parts of the world, was a deeply moving expression of Tongan culture and history.

We had known each other over 60 years and I treasured our friendship. At His Majesty's request, I had gone over to Auckland with Louise to see him a few weeks before he died. The last joyous memory I have of him is when I took a group of our old university pals to Tonga in 2005 for a reunion to celebrate the King's 87th birthday.

It was quite a task to track down our elderly student colleagues through my old network of friends. The group included 30 octogenarians, with eminent ex-judges, barristers, solicitors, prosecutors and businessmen, including Justice Jack Lee, Chester Porter QC, Robert Minter, Evan Bowen-Thomas, Keith Draper, David Thurlow, Robert Packam, Bob Westphal and Mavis and Lloyd Sommerland.

The reunion was actually the Crown Prince's inspiration, after the King told him he felt alone as his friends were passing on. The old uni boys were all delighted to be with His Majesty again. The King was the happiest I had seen him for many years. As a special gesture for one of Sydney University law school's most renowned old boys, the university sent its dean, Professor Ron McCallum.

The old boys were feted amid all the celebrations and feasts. The Crown Prince then flew us up to Vava'u, where we enjoyed the islands, feasted again and tried the local drop, kava.

One of His Majesty's greatest achievements was the 98.5 per cent standard of literacy in Tonga – one of the highest in the world. A project that gave the King pleasure was a children's book Louise and I produced and co-sponsored, *A Little Seahorse in Love*, by the German author Michael Schirmer. It was the first dual-language children's book in Tongan and English.

Tonga celebrated the coronation of its new King, George Tupou V, on 1 August 2008. I thought my days of morning suit and top hat were long over, but not so. As a traditionalist, the King followed the style of the European coronations adopted by his legendary Tongan ancestor, King George Tupou I. He wore his remodelled coronation robes, still with their original ermine, and the 24-carat gold crown, reconditioned in London by the royal jewellers, Garrard & Co., who had crafted the crown 150 years earlier.

His Majesty's courtiers, including Louise, wore a uniform made by Gieves & Hawkes of London, based on their design for the first Tongan coronation in the mid-nineteenth century. Louise looked resplendent in her navy tailcoat with gold buttons and braid, white silk breeches, white stockings, black patent leather shoes and buckles, a diplomatic cocked hat with an ostrich feather and a diamante-encrusted sword. It made me think it might have been something similar to the midshipman's uniform my ancestor Henry Waterhouse might have worn. All the female guests were glamorous in full-length gowns with tiaras and long gloves.

First there was a traditional kava ceremony, in which His Majesty accepted his role by drinking kava. The coronation the next day was a splendid Christian service with European pageantry. As the new King was anointed with oil, I found it breathtaking to hear the choral rendition – by 300 glorious Tongan voices – of 'Zadok the Priest', written by Handel for George II's coronation in 1727. As the royal procession moved back down the cathedral aisle in slow-step time at the end of the ceremony, the proud, newly crowned King gave me a broad smile. I was so happy for him.

The coronation was attended by royalty from all over the world, including His Imperial Highness Crown Prince Naruhito of Japan, Princess Sirindhorn of Thailand, the beautiful Princess Ashi of Bhutan, and the Duke and Duchess of Gloucester. His Majesty's close friend from his days at Sandhurst, Lord Glenarthur, the coronation artist Charles Billich, German fashion baron Willy Bogner, Sydney University's dean of medicine, Professor Bruce Robinson, plus longtime royal family friends Mark Johnson and the famous jeweller Michael Hill, who both brought their super-yachts to Tonga for the occasion.

I was thrilled that my family could be there to enjoy such a grand time of celebration for the kingdom. His Majesty bestowed on both Louise and me his newly created Royal Order of Valour, and I was honoured with the Order of Commander of the Crown of Tonga.

The coronation united Tonga. During the coronation week, the new King announced future democratic reforms. One only had to look at the banners all around the capital, Nuku'alofa, to see the love and regard the Tongans had for their new King, such as 'To Your Majesty with Love from Your Humble People', and even 'Democracy Celebrates Your Majesty's Coronation'.

The new King has a vision to improve Tonga. He is well regarded as a scholar, is open-minded and has the interests of his people at heart. His Majesty is also concerned about the deteriorating health of his people, and to mark his coronation the King founded a charity for diabetes, the Royal Endocrinology Society; unfortunately, diabetes is prevalent in the Pacific.

As our gift to celebrate the coronation, we sponsored and produced another storybook about Tonga by Michael Schirmer, *A Dream of the South Seas*, which interweaves Tonga's culture and heritage to inspire Tongan children. All proceeds from the book went to His Majesty's diabetes charity.

As Tonga's consulate, we look after the interests of the kingdom and of Tongans living in Australia. When I started in 1974, there were just a few hundred Tongans in Australia; now we have about 30,000. Louise takes her honorary consular responsibilities very seriously, and His Majesty invited her to accompany him on a state visit to China in 2008. There, they met the Chinese president and premier, and stayed in the government gardens in Beijing. Louise and Guenther have enjoyed holidays with the King in Queenstown, Munich and Lugano.

His Majesty further honoured my 35 years of service to the Kingdom in August 2009, when he awarded me the Tongan equivalent of a knighthood – the Grand Cross of the Queen Salote Order. I am now the longest serving honorary consul-general in Australia.

—

My sister, Betty, sadly passed away in 2006. She and I were always very close, and I gladly gave her financial help throughout the years, sending her children to private schools and helping with everyday expenses. In her latter years I would drive several hours to visit her every week or so in her home, or later at the nursing home. I was very sad to lose her.

In 2008 I lost an old friend in Jock Rorrison. The old-time bookie was 101. Jock and his wife, Billie, used to babysit Tom when Rob and Gai also lived in our block of units at Balmoral. When Rob and Gai moved to their own house in Clifton Gardens, Jock and Billie missed the children, who then would stay overnight with them every Thursday. When Billie died, Jock was 85 and very lonely, so Gai and Robbie invited him to move in with them. I have no doubt that this kindness extended Jock's life, and he would remain with them for fifteen years, becoming part of the family.

There was an amusing incident after Jock took a turn one day. On being revived in the North Shore Hospital, he was asked by the nurses to tell them his name.

'Jock,' he said.

'Who do you live with?' they asked.

'Gai Waterhouse,' Jock replied.

And the staff wrote 'dementia' on his form.

Later that night, when Rob and Gai went to collect Jock, the embarrassed nurses saw Gai and came forward, saying, 'Oh, my goodness, we owe Jock an apology!'

Gai suffered heartbreak later that year with the death of her mother. After 1998, when Valerie had lost Tommy – the focus of her life – Valerie had blossomed as 'the merry widow'. For the first time, her life revolved around herself. She mixed more often with her friends, went on holiday cruises and went to live with Robbie, Gai and the children. Valerie told me one day that these were the happiest years of her life.

Valerie was a stickler for manners and etiquette with her grandchildren and was always immaculately groomed with a silk blouse, elegant pants, high-heeled shoes and jewellery when I would call around at Gai and Rob's home. Valerie loved her racing, owning many racehorses and taking care of Gai's clients at the track.

She kept her *joie de vivre* until the very end, arranging both a holiday cruise and a birthday lunch for fourteen friends on the very day she passed away in December 2008, aged 91. Her birthday celebration became her wake. At the funeral, which was attended by over 500 mourners, she would have enjoyed the operatic singers and Kate's reading of Valerie's best-known poem, which she had written and recited for Tommy.

—

In recent years I have been involved in a number of documentaries, historical features and exhibitions. Memorabilia which I donated from my old-time bookmaking days formed the core of an exhibition at the Powerhouse Museum in 2004, 'Gambling in Australia: thrills, spills and social ills'. It highlighted how gambling is one of the most distinctive aspects of Australian life and was taken all around Australia.

The museum had recreated my old bookie's stand and even had a mannequin wearing one of my old three-piece pinstripe suits and hat. A television show about my gambling, which had been filmed by *A Big Country* in the 1970s, ran in the background and gave us all a trip down memory lane. There was a terrific race-crowd photo blown up to the size of a wall, but – incredibly – no one recognised that the central figure was none other than Felipe Ysmael, the Filipino Fireball.

Tom and I were guests at the Surfers Paradise Carbine Club lunch in January 2009, where we were interviewed by Wayne Wilson. It was terrific to be up on stage with Tom, and the crowd gave us a warm reception. They seemed to love hearing my stories as much as I enjoyed telling them.

I was also part of a DVD that was given to the million readers of *The Sydney Morning Herald* to celebrate its 150th anniversary. Stanton Library recorded an oral history with me on North Sydney, and my boyhood recollections of the bridge being built formed part of two documentaries for the 75th anniversary of the Sydney Harbour Bridge. I was also in a film on my old playground, Luna Park.

I chuckled as I recalled an incident 70 years earlier, when I worked in Luna Park's Crazy House. I was the wizard's assistant, pulling levers in the dark so ghosts popped up in front of their small open carriages, and then tickling them with feathers from behind as they travelled through on the rail tracks. One day there was a malfunction and the lights suddenly came on, exposing me out of the darkness. I heard a patron say, 'That poor little bugger – what chance has he got in life?'

The odds turned out to be not so bad.

35

Dynasty

A FTER BEING SO LONG at the top, and then as an octogenarian making it back to the Rails on the number-one stand, it might be said I should have hung up my bookie's bag. But not so.

The usual time at the top for any big-time bookmaker is five years or so. They are like top fighters – there comes a time when they lose their edge. What has taken me beyond the average span is simply the thrill of winning and the desire to keep going. Keeping the family tradition alive is also of great importance to me. I've been lucky to work with my family, starting with my father in the late 1930s and right through to training Rob and then Tom. I am proud of our 110 years as Waterhouse bookmakers.

Rob's skills as a form analyst are second to none, and it is his brilliant work in predicting market moves that gives me the confidence, in these changed times of well-informed punters, to continue to take them on. As a locals bookmaker in Sydney, Rob's betting markets always lead the ring. Normally the racetrack is not the place for a Mr Nice Guy. There is an old saying at the track: 'If you don't know who the mug in a bet is, then it's probably you.' You always have to be on your guard.

After all his ups and downs, Rob still retains his genial nature and holds no grudges. I can think of numerous people who have been rotten to him, yet his door remains open to them all. He looks for the best in others. Like me, he is an eternal optimist. Rob's positive attitude often reminds me of that line from the Monty Python song: 'Always look on the bright side of life.'

Tom, although so young, has essentially taken over my mantle. He is the fourth generation of my family to make it as a bookie. In the Waterhouse tradition of Jack, me and Robbie, Tom has now become Australia's largest on-course bookmaker. I regard Tom as a consummate gambler. He has benefitted from his father's and my different philosophies. Rob, being a form genius, is very respectful of punters' opinions, because he knows full well that they can win. On the other hand, I have always thought of the big picture, believing that I could take on all-comers and wear them down with big betting.

Tom has developed his own technique by combining the best of both our styles. He says he feels I am right in the overall sense, but on a day-to-day basis he also believes Rob is correct.

Tom still sticks to the 'rules' that Rob and I developed for our bookmaking over the years. When Tom is behind in his betting he becomes more cautious, but when he's winning he opens his shoulders – the hallmark of a professional gambler. By limiting your losses you can stop yourself from going broke when you're wrong, but by playing up your winnings you can win big when you're right. In this sense, Tom is an unlimited gambler. Like his father and me – and like his mother and other grandfather, TJ – Tom is not afraid of hard work. He usually works six or even seven days a week. Racing is like that – it demands your full attention.

I have taught Tom to think differently about money on and off the track, and to think about betting in 'units' at the races, thus removing any emotional attachment to money. I have also taught him to treat money with respect away from the track, as an 'easy come, easy go' mentality has been the downfall of many gamblers. It is not just winning at the races but also what you do with your money afterwards that determines your success in life.

Down in Melbourne, Tom found the forward-thinking regulatory setting so much more favourable for bookmakers and clients that he decided to stay there, leaving me to run the Sydney licence on the interstate Rails with my right-hand man, Bruce Wiley. Loyal and honest, Bruce is a perfect gentleman. Tom has gone through the roof in Melbourne, enjoying the more modern betting environment. He and his clerks often handle a thousand phone bets a day.

Life's circle was completed for me when in 2008 I took out a Victorian clerk's licence to be able to help Tom at the Melbourne Cup Carnival. I was proud to be at his stand on Derby Day. Everyone was amazed when Tom held around $20 million over the four days – more than all the other bookies combined. I felt it was history repeating itself.

Tom is one of very few younger people to take up the bookie bag, transforming a traditional business with his fresh eyes. Unconstrained by the old methods, Tom has developed a new technique, modernising his business by becoming a 'bookmaker trader'.

In contrast to my own style of standing back without showing emotion and letting the punters come to me, Tom is passionate and quick-moving. He darts about his stand, checking his bank of computers, adjusting his board prices and betting on the phones – more like a busy trader on the stock exchange floor. In contrast, I now rely on my 'turn of phrase' more than my 'turn of foot'.

Tom is looking to the wider world. He has launched his betting business on the internet and wants to take on everyone – from the smallest punter just wanting an interest through to the biggest gamblers. His ambition is to offer a unique service based on the Waterhouse experience.

—

My philosophy on property – that location, timing and vision are all-important – has rewarded me many times through the years. Without having poured all our profits into property, I know we would have been finished when we hit our troubles.

I always believe you have to buy the best – I never worried about the return as I know a good location will reward you many times over. I have seen this with my properties in Kirribilli, Balmoral, Wallacia and Chatswood – they all went up many times more than other properties in lesser locations.

I also know that timing is everything. With our cash-flow from racing, we were often able to buy well in difficult times. The market always comes good in the end. That was the case with 65 Kirribilli Avenue – when I saw the signboard totally overgrown with vines, I realised that now, with the passage of time, the asking price would probably seem fair. I remember an old investment guru once telling me, 'Buy the best, even if the price is ten per cent too high, because very soon, with market rises, it won't seem expensive.' This was very much the case with our development at Balmoral.

I still have a vision for several of our properties, especially the 222-hectare farmland at Wallacia. With its great location and its picturesque undulating land, I know it will lend itself to a marvellous lifestyle development one day.

I'll never stop thinking big. I have toyed with the idea of getting into tote betting in Australia and the United States. Over the years, I have put up my hand for the Canberra and the New York totes. More recently, Rob went to New York with Tasmanian tote officials to look into a joint deal.

I still see great opportunities in world racing, especially in the United States. Back in the late 1960s, Moe Dalitz invited me to take over one of his casino's horse betting operations. I was offered *carte blanche* to introduce Australian-style betting, which Moe hoped would give the casino a boost. However, I was too committed with family affairs in Australia at the time. Nevertheless, I have always liked the idea of opening up this potentially massive market.

America leads the world in so many areas, and although it was once the biggest betting nation in the world, its racing and gambling industry today is, to my mind, backward. It must be remembered that the United States put a lid on gambling with the banning of bookmakers back in 1936 in the Prohibition era, only allowing parimutuel (tote) monopolies. America still has outdated rules which mean they are well behind the world's best practice in horse racing.

Just as they do in Australia, the little horse punters get a raw deal in the United States. Big punters enjoy a 'favoured status' through large punter rebates on winning or losing bets or on turnover. These large punters ruin the return for the little guy, because he doesn't receive such bonuses. This means the big punters receive a disproportionate amount of the winners' pool – leaving the little guys as much as ten per cent worse off. Because of these out-dated laws, many American punters bet illegally with offshore businesses, mainly in the Bahamas, where they can enjoy the rebates.

My idea is to bring this betting back onshore, and I can show the American government how to do it. No punter wants to bet illegally and run the risk of not being paid when they can bet legally and be certain of collecting their winnings. My idea would put more gambling money into government coffers and back into the struggling racing industry. This would put a stop to the illegal drain of gambling money.

I am proud of our Fijian business, which has now been operating for 45 years; under the talented management of our partner Peter McCoy, it must be one of the most cost-effective betting outfits in the world. Peter and I have high hopes for the future of international betting, and my idea would not only benefit the United States but also the Pacific.

—

Regrets? Not really. I have loved life and still do.

Looking back from my ninth decade to when things were a lot tougher, I have seen such amazing changes – from the horse and cart through the jet age to space travel, and from telegrams to the internet. Things just get better and better and better. I think I am so very lucky to live in the most magnificent city and the best country in the world.

Medical science is astounding. I have seen modern medicine dramatically improve quality of life, and life expectancy extend well beyond the classic 'three score years and ten'. I never dreamt I would be upright, fit and active at my senior age – and still plying my trade at the track. My father was taken from us with peritonitis at the age of 63, but when I had peritonitis at the age of 84, a few days in hospital and good medical care put me back on my feet.

Since my ancestors came to Australia, the Waterhouses have had our share of ups and downs, but in spite of a few problems along the way, I would do it all again.

I would still treat my brother Charlie's children with the same generosity, although I would do it differently. I know I did the right thing by helping Charlie's children because I did it for my brother. Although David left the family and is out of my life, I still wish him and his young family well.

I admit to having a *laissez-faire* or 'live and let live' approach to life. Rather than dictating to family and friends what I think they should or shouldn't do, I have said, 'I wouldn't do it that way if I were you, but you make up your own mind.' I have been free with my ideas to help others, and I've felt rewarded when people have told me they have been inspired by my advice to go on to bigger and better things.

The law has played a major role in my life. It has brought me lifelong friendships with some of the leaders of Australian society. The irony is that, having thrown away my barrister's wig and gown for a bookie's satchel, I was compelled to go to court a number of times. Like any man, I needed to protect myself and my interests. The experience of being 'on my feet' as a barrister arguing a case gave me the confidence never to shy away from a legal fight. I also knew each time that 'right was on my side'.

Although I have never courted the media, the events in my roller-coaster life have been recorded publicly through my successes, achievements and misfortunes. Looking back through the clippings we've collected, I see that I've been portrayed diversely as 'the Gentleman Bookmaker', 'Big Bill' and 'the Greedy Uncle'. I'm philosophical about that; what I see through that ongoing media story is an immensely colourful and fortunate life.

Racing has been extraordinarily good to me. Even though I have borne the brunt of racing's sometimes roughshod justice, I have always loved the industry and the many characters I have come across in my life at the track. The racetrack is a great place to discover the character of a man. Many times I have had the richest people welsh on me, and I've seen those who can't really afford to pay a big losing bet struggle to meet their commitments honourably.

I still believe in the honour of a handshake. It has cost me money over the years, not only with disreputable punters but also with business deals, where, even though not bound by the written word, I have ignored the temptation for a quick profit by sticking to my word.

Property has been my backbone, and I have been fortunate to have owned my share of our ever-evolving city, which

I have seen transform itself and burst onto the world stage. Through my developments, I have seen enormous progress in construction standards, as well as other improvements such as strata title ownership.

My life has been all about taking the odds, the chase to win and the motivation to make money. In the end, possessing money doesn't really bother me. I have never been fussed by the trappings of success. That doesn't mean I don't like to live in a nice place or drive a nice car, but I don't need them to enjoy life. I thrived on the entrepreneurial challenge of dreaming up 'big ideas', even if at first they seemed impossible. I have kicked a few goals and beaten the odds.

I have been lucky to meet so many fascinating people in Australia and around the world, and nothing has given me more pleasure than hosting many of them at dinner and chatting over a bottle of wine. I have enjoyed loyalty and friendship from a few people in my life, none more so than the King of Tonga, Neville Wran, Kevin Perkins and dear Yuko.

There is one thing I have learned above all. Nothing is more important than family. Everything I have done has been for them. Suzanne has been a loyal and loving wife and has given me my children. I am so proud of Rob and Louise and also Gai, and now Tom and Kate, who have all brought me so much joy. Tom and Kate are the future, and I see them continuing my family's legacy.

Life has been good to me. Every gambling man knows that Lady Luck can be unreliable. She can appear and disappear. But I have made my own luck, and I feel everything has happened for the best. I still feel 'on top of the world'!

Afterword

Big Grandpa Bill

by Tom Waterhouse

ALTHOUGH I AM 27, I still call my grandfather 'Grandpa Bill'. To the punter, he's 'Big Bill'.

Growing up, I remember thinking of Grandpa Bill as the grandparent I had the most fun with. Our time together was spent eating pizza or at McDonald's, playing table tennis or shooting at pigeons with a toy machine gun he bought me. I used to stay with my grandparents most Saturday nights, and Grandpa Bill would wake me up with warm toasted muffins, chocolate and ice cream – a little boy's dream.

All this changed when I went to work with Big Bill at the races. He was different to my warm and fuzzy grandfather. This man was a serious force to be reckoned with.

I started working at the races with my dad, Robbie, when I was nineteen and at university. The track was a new world for me, and unbelievably exciting. I loved working with Dad and learning about the world of racing and how to 'make a book'. I quickly came to think that my father was a form genius – his analysis was pretty much spot-on. He often picked the card for the day.

When my grandfather saw I had a passion for the game, he decided to come back to bookmaking at 80 to train me. Dad was in two minds. While he knew that the lessons Grandpa Bill would pass on would be invaluable, he also knew that the game had changed a lot since Big Bill last reigned supreme at the track.

I was given strict instructions by Dad to start out very slowly and not to let Grandpa Bill bet too big. Big Bill, on the other hand, opened his shoulders on his first day and took on all-comers as though he had never left the track. It was Blue Diamond Day and we had the worst stand, but this was no problem. Big Bill was first up with the prices, betting a few rolls over the favourite and letting anyone and everyone on.

He stood the favourite of the Blue Diamond for what I thought was an astronomical amount – far more than I had seen my dad stand any horse for since I had first started. We lost about $50,000 on the day and I was devastated. I thought my grandfather had lost his marbles. His way of thinking was completely different to Dad's, and it seemed to contradict every-thing I had learnt about bookmaking in my short career. I had become accustomed to Dad's method of working, which was to lay the horses based on form. Big Bill, however, concentrated on the horses the punters wanted to back.

From day two onwards I tried to take the reins of the operation. Whereas Big Bill wanted to stand horses 'out the gate', I would only stand a horse to lose $1500 – and even then I would only lay the horses we didn't like on form.

Big Bill continually changed the prices on our board and I changed them back through my computer. He lectured me every afternoon after the races the entire way home in the car.

One day we arrived at the races and Big Bill told me to drop him off at the gate as he needed to go to the gents. He was very quick and immediately went to our stand and put up prices for the first race at the Gold Coast, even though we didn't normally bet on Gold Coast races. He offered $2 about a horse that was coming in at over $1.50 on the teleprinter. By the time I had parked the car, Big Bill had got $15,000 out of the horse. I arrived at the stand and was distraught. I hadn't wanted to take any risks, and Big Bill was twenty rolls over the teleprinter and laying this horse for whatever he could.

'What are you doing?' I yelled.

He said, 'If it loses then we win the $15,000, and if it wins it will be great publicity that we offered $2 on a $1.50 chance.'

A day at the races with Grandpa Bill is always fun. Despite Suzy's strict control of his diet, every Saturday he sneaks away from the stand to grab a pie, a hotdog, a bag of chips and a Fanta.

Grandpa Bill constantly has older people coming over to speak to him, saying things like, 'You were the biggest bookie we have ever seen. Good on you, Bill.' He even often has 'old flames' come up to the stand to say hello, but he never seems to remember them. On the other hand, he constantly says to the young girls who work for us, 'All right, I give in – come and sit on my knee!'

It was hard in the beginning to see things from Big Bill's point of view. He hated me 'betting back', but as I began to appreciate his methods, I started to hold more money. He taught me a thousand little tricks, such as 'First starter if odds-on – will win; if odds-against – lay it'. Over our six years working together, he and I have gone from holding $10,000 to holding $4 million every Saturday.

I can see that he was right in everything he said. Bookmaking has changed a lot since his halcyon days, but the fundamentals of playing the man and betting big are the same.

I used to be a kid who thought his grandfather was 'past it', but I've learnt so much from him. His experience is still hugely relevant to me today. Since going to work in Melbourne in 2008, what I miss most are the car trips to and from the races and the constant feedback.

Big Bill Waterhouse taught me to gamble, to bet big and to look at the big picture. It is a privilege to work with the living legend, who just happens to be my beloved grandfather.

Index

Index

Index

I wish to thank Catherine Hale (MA), Tim Hale (SC) and Len Loveday for their valuable proofreading comments, and Brian Evesson for his assistance with historical matters.

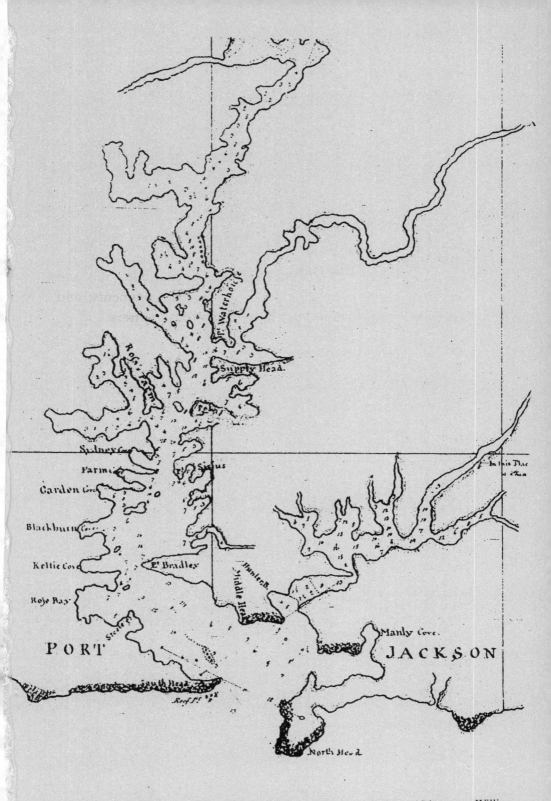

The first map of Port Jackson, chartered by Midshipman Henry Waterhouse and Lieutenant William Bradley in 1788. The headland marked as Point Waterhouse is now the Sydney suburb of Woolwich.

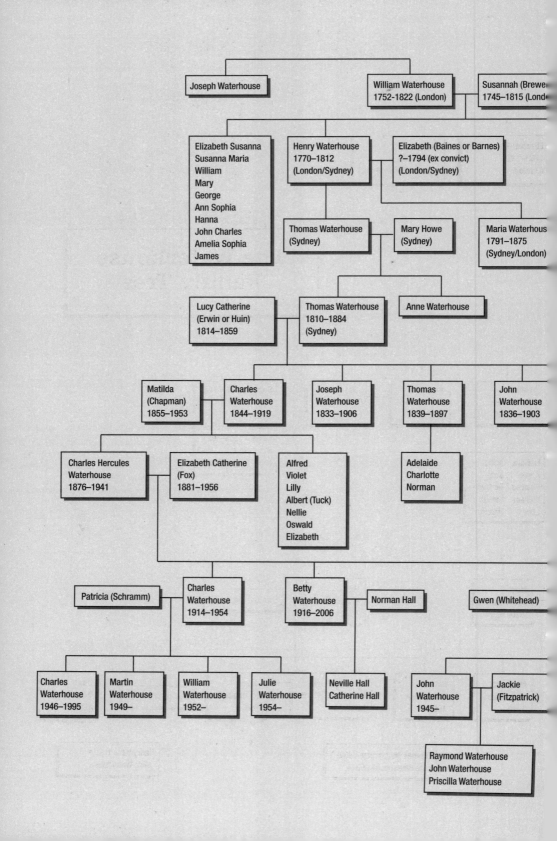